Study Guide

Volume II: Since 1865

A People and a Nation

A History of the United States

SEVENTH EDITION

Study Guide

Volume II: Since 1865

A People and a Nation

A History of the United States

SEVENTH EDITION

George C. Warren
Central Piedmont Community College

Mary Beth Norton
Cornell University

David M. Katzman
University of Kansas

David W. Blight
Yale University

Howard P. Chudacoff
Brown University

Fredrik Logevall
University of California, Santa Barbara

Beth Bailey
University of New Mexico

Thomas G. Paterson
University of Connecticut

William M. Tuttle, Jr.
University of Kansas

HOUGHTON MIFFLIN COMPANY   BOSTON   NEW YORK

Senior Sponsoring Editor: Sally Constable
Editorial Assistant: Kisha Mitchell
Editorial Assistant: Trinity Peacock-Broyles
Senior Manufacturing Coordinator: Marie Barnes
Senior Marketing Manager: Sandra McGuire

Printed in the U.S.A.

ISBN: 0-618-42136X

1 2 3 4 5 6 7 8 9-CRS-08 07 06 05 04

Contents

Introduction

TO THE INSTRUCTOR

The study guide you have before you is meant to be useful to you as well as to your students—no matter what you intend to emphasize or downplay in your classes using *A People and a Nation*. The comprehensiveness of the features makes that possible. Beginning with the list of learning objectives, you and your students can choose items suited to the focus of the course as you will be teaching it and eliminate the rest.

You can do the same kind of picking and choosing to tailor the guide to your own purposes with its other features—except for each chapter's Thematic Guide, which the authors firmly believe every student should read. Because students usually read chapters in segments over several days, they really need help in recognizing major themes, the kind of help each Thematic Guide's overview in easy-to-follow essay form provides. Each chapter's other nine features give you and your students plenty of choices. The Ideas and Details segment provides fifteen multiple-choice questions for students to use as a final check of just how effective their studying has been—along with answers at the back of the book that not only indicate which are the right answers but also explain why the right answers are right and the wrong answers are wrong. The result is a kind of demonstration of question-answer analysis.

Of course, users of previous editions already realize that no student could possibly do all of the exercises this study guide provides or even all the items within some of its features. There are far more Identification and Significance items than any student will need, for instance. They will determine from their reading and what you say in class which ones to work on. Both instructors and students quickly realize that they can get all they need without tackling everything in the book just as dictionary owners realize that they can get all they need without looking up the meaning of every word the dictionary defines.

The multiple-choice questions and most of the other exercises are either all new or somewhat revised to reflect changes in the textbook, but instructors whose students used the sixth edition should be right at home with most features of the seventh edition. They will find some surprising changes, though. One is placement of instructions, especially the instructions for the Organizing, Reviewing, and Using Information feature. By giving the instructions only once per volume and placing them in the opening chapters, we make the instructions simpler to understand and free up room for other things, such as lots more charts and larger blanks in most charts. The instructions also suggest that the charts may be used in ways other than just planning for essays. (The authors hope that you will discover how useful they can be in class on the days you devote to reviewing for tests.)

Probably the most surprising change is the design and contents of the introduction (now called "Instructions and Explanations"). In addition to explaining how to use the features, the introduction provides samples of completed exercises—even a practice essay growing out of an Organizing, Reviewing, and Using Information activity. This new introduction has reduced the theoretical in favor of the practical.

The authors thank you for deciding to give this study guide a try. They hope that you will find it every bit as useful as they have tried to make it. For you and your students they wish success and the joy that comes with it.

INSTRUCTIONS AND EXPLANATIONS

Or, How to Get Your Money's Worth Out of This Study Guide

You have your copy of *A People and a Nation* and this study guide, so now what?

It's mighty tempting to jump in and start highlighting anything and everything in the textbook's first chapter that looks remotely important, but Whoa! Slow down. Don't you think it would be a good idea to get the lay of the land first?

Obviously it would be a good idea to preview the textbook by looking over its title, table of contents, and extras—the appendices and index—before you attend class for the first time and certainly before you and your highlighter plunge into the first chapter.

Previewing your study guide is important, too. A fairly quick look at Chapter 1 (or Chapter 17 in Volume 2) and the introduction should be enough to give you the idea of what it's all about. Don't let your first quick look frighten you, though. Yes, you'll find that each chapter has eight to ten features, each of which has up to eighty items for students to work on. But nobody expects any student to complete every item in every feature or even to use every single feature in every chapter. You are being given lots of choices, but that's exactly what they are: choices. In fact, this Instructions and Explanations section is here to help you see where and when to skip or skimp on items—and where and when not to.

Let's start, then, by examining each feature one by one to find out what each is and when it should be tackled and to look at some examples of completed exercises and study techniques. In the process, we'll begin discovering how to decide which items you can safely omit.

LEARNING OBJECTIVES

The list of Learning Objectives that begins each chapter is an informational feature comprised of a numbered list of learning objectives indicating what you are expected to learn and how you are going to be expected to show that you have in fact done the learning. One of the guide's two must-do features, this list should be especially helpful at two points in the studying process, the very beginning and the very end in conjunction with the Essay Questions.

If you'll turn to any chapter of your study guide for a minute, you'll see that the objectives are specifically linked to two other study guide features: the Ideas and Details (multiple-choice) section and the Essay Questions. The linking of an objective to a specific multiple-choice or essay question is a reminder that those questions are the kind that might appear on a test to find out whether you have accomplished the objective.

You should not be dismayed if your instructor subtracts, modifies, or, possibly, adds objectives. Simply compare your instructor's list with our list and make any necessary changes. Your final set of objectives should include all of those your own instructor has set for your class.

The Learning Objectives feature is likely to enhance the effectiveness of your reading, listening, and note-taking, but it is most likely to do so if you restate the objectives as questions. Having those questions in mind will make you do your reading and listen to your instructor in class more purposefully and with greater focus than you otherwise would.

At this point, even though you still have not read one word in the chapter you are to study in *A People and a Nation*, you are ready to start your work on some of the exercises in the study guide. The exercises you need to begin with are in the Identification and Significance section and the Building Vocabulary section.

THEMATIC GUIDE

The Thematic Guide, the second of two informational features, summarizes a chapter in the textbook by identifying major ideas—or themes—that run through all or large parts of the chapter. These guides are designed to help you grasp the whole thrust of a chapter before the mass of details overwhelms you. You should read the Thematic Guide before you do any of the reading assignments for a chapter or go to the first class at which you expect your instructor to talk about that chapter. The Thematic Guide is one of two must-do features of the study guide.

Since you are likely to be reading each chapter in segments assigned by your instructor over the course of a week or more, it's possible to read it all without noticing that some key ideas run through all or large parts of the chapter. In the very first chapter of *A People and a Nation*, for instance, you could get so involved in all the names of the American Indian cultures and the listings of their accomplishments and religious, economic, social, and political characteristics that you fail to notice the emphasis on geography as a major cause of the variation in these characteristics.

By identifying major themes for you ahead of time, the Thematic Guide gives you a series of coat hooks on which to hang the chapter's details; it helps you to look for details in the chapter that contribute to each of those themes, pick out those that are most important, and understand what makes them important. It also helps you to follow what your instructor has to say and take better class notes. Your job is to read the Thematic Guide carefully ahead of time to get all the themes fixed in your mind, perhaps by underlining them the first time they are mentioned.

BUILDING VOCABULARY

The Building Vocabulary section is a list of words—usually general vocabulary words rather than words that are peculiar to the study of history—whose newness to some students could cause them to misunderstand passages in *A People and a Nation*. In this section you will find one area reserved for writing out definitions of some of the words and, following the list of vocabulary words, a second section for listing difficult-to-spell words and names (spelled correctly, of course) that students are likely to need to use on their next test.

It's true: The authors of your textbook occasionally do use words that are going to be unfamiliar to some of your classmates or even to you. When they use such words, perhaps repeatedly, in contexts that suggest and clarify their meanings, there is no problem. In fact, such use of unfamiliar words not only does not really interfere with readers' understanding but actually contributes to the expansion of their vocabularies. Sometimes, however, the context is not enough to suggest a word's meaning, and not knowing the meaning may prevent you, the reader, from fully understanding the textbook passage you're studying. It is words of this second type that you should be most concerned with.

At this point you should underline all those words in the Building Vocabulary list with which you are totally unfamiliar, put a question mark beside all those with which you have at least some familiarity but are unsure of, and leave the rest alone. As you do this, you will notice that the words are not listed in alphabetical order but in the order in which they occur in the chapter.

Don't bother looking up the meaning of words you have underlined and put question marks beside until you come across them as you read the chapter in your textbook. All you need to do now is to make yourself so conscious of their existence that they will jump out at you when you do come across them in your reading.

When you're reading Chapter 1 and come to any of the words you've put question marks beside or underlined, slow your reading, focus on the word and on its context in the sentence you're reading. If it's one with a question mark beside it, go on with your reading. But if it's one of the words on the Building Vocabulary list that you underlined, you should look it up in a dictionary.

When you do look up a word, you may find that it has only one meaning, as is the case with the word *cartographer*, or that it has several different meanings, as would be the case with words like *fix*, *take,* or *intelligence.* If the word you underlined has multiple meanings, you have to choose the one meaning the dictionary offers that best fits its context in the textbook. (Students whose native language is not English need to use an English-to-English dictionary for this.)

Once you have found the word in the dictionary and settled on a definition for it, write the word and its meaning in the column reserved for definitions. An entry in the definition column for the word *cartographer* should look something like this:

A cartographer is a person who makes maps.

It's also helpful to compose an illustrative sentence in your mind, a sentence whose use of the word reflects the word's meaning. A sentence that would illustrate the meaning of *cartographer,* for instance, would be something along these lines: "When I visited the geography department, I actually saw a cartographer drawing and putting labels on a map of Charlotte as the city existed in 1910." You are probably going to start seeing the words you put question marks beside or underlined all over the place in the next few weeks—or at least start noticing them for the first time. Whenever you do encounter one, reread the sentence in which it appears and think briefly about its context. Before you know it, you'll come not only to know what it means but to feel comfortable using it yourself.

Immediately following the Building Vocabulary section is a section labeled "Difficult-to-Spell Names and Terms from Reading and Lecture." This section gives you a convenient place to maintain a list of all the "hard" names and terms you should be ready to spell correctly on the next test. Writing difficult-to-spell words correctly several times is usually enough to learn to spell them correctly.

One section of your study guide that you need to begin and complete before starting your first reading assignment for Chapter 1 is the Finding the Main Idea section. The Finding the Main Idea section is a study guide feature that appears only in Chapters 1 and 17, chapters that appear in different volumes of the textbook and that, in most of the colleges using *A People and a Nation,* begin separate history courses.

FINDING THE MAIN IDEA

The Finding the Main Idea section of Chapter 1 (Volume 1) and Chapter 17 (Volume 2) in your study guide contains practice and testing exercises designed to teach you to analyze passages in the textbook, pick out the important information from those passages, and determine whether that important information is the main idea of the passage or supporting information (evidence or illustration).

You should do the Finding the Main Idea exercises in the chapter before you read your first reading assignment. By comparing your responses to the responses found in the Answers section at the back of the book, you will find out whether you need help and additional practice in distinguishing main ideas from details that support them.

You are usually going to be reading each chapter in segments; that is, in assigned sections of the chapter. That means that what you are going to be dealing with is a collection of paragraph series—groups of paragraphs that function like small essays within the chapter.

Recognizing the point of a paragraph or paragraph series—its main idea—doesn't have to be difficult. When you finish a passage, simply answer the question, "What does all this add up to?" or, even better,

"What does all this mean?" If the passage includes a statement that answers the question, the passage has an explicit statement of its main idea: the author has given you your answer. If not, the author is merely implying a main idea, which means that you have to determine what the main idea is by analyzing the passage.

Since ideas grow out of pieces of evidence, it is the pieces of evidence that point to or imply the idea. Therefore, to discover what the implied main idea of a passage is, you have to identify the pieces of supporting evidence within the passage. Support for ideas—evidence and clarifying details—comes in two forms: facts and inferences. A fact is a concrete bit of information that can be perceived by one or more of the five senses. An inference is an idea supported by facts or other inferences. Together, the facts and inferences used to support a single idea are often referred to as that idea's support or supporting details.

You are not likely to confuse a supporting idea with a main idea as long as you don't jump into a decision too quickly. Such confusion is likely only if you try to guess what the main idea is before you finish reading the whole passage.

An examination of the following very short passage taken from the first chapter of *A People and a Nation* will clarify the point and show what can happen when a reader assumes he knows the main idea before he has read the entire passage.

> **Sample Passage**
>
> Americans' religious beliefs varied even more than did their political systems, but <u>all</u> the peoples were polytheistic, worshiping a multitude of gods. Each group's most important beliefs and rituals were closely tied to its means of subsistence. The major deities of agricultural peoples like Pueblos and Muskogeans were associated with cultivation, and their chief festivals centered on planting and harvest. The most important gods of hunters were associated with animals, and their major festivals were related to hunting. A band's economy and women's roles in it helped to determine women's potential as religious leaders. Women held the most prominent positions in those agricultural societies (like the Iroquois) in which they were also the chief food producers, whereas in hunting societies men took the lead in religious as well as political affairs.

If you pick out the first sentence that "looks important" in the sample passage before you have read the whole thing, you will be tempted to say that the main point is that there was a lot of variety in the mainly polytheistic Native American religions, right?

On the other hand, if you wait until after you have read the whole passage, you are going to dismiss the variety idea in the first clause as a transitional device and the polytheism idea in the second clause as simply one of the paragraph's details. After all, the only support for the claim about how varied Native American religious systems were is the suggestion that there were two broad categories. As for the polytheism idea, it goes nowhere in the body of the paragraph. The author provides no lists of gods or of tribes and their gods and no information about the average number of gods per tribe.

What a preliminary reading of the whole passage uncovers is these two equally emphasized points in the body of the paragraph:

1. The kind of religious beliefs and practices a tribe had depended on the tribe's economic system, and

2. Whether women could be religious leaders depended on the tribe's economic system.

The equal emphasis suggests that neither is *the* main point. But clearly both points are important. Perhaps the two points add up to some larger point.

Studying the two points makes the function of the word *religious* in the paragraph's opening sentence clear. Religion is part of both of these points. If these two points are the most important points stated in the paragraph, then religion must be the topic of the paragraph. If religion is the topic of the paragraph, then the paragraph's main point has to be about religion.

A closer look shows that both points link religion to economic systems. To figure out the main point of the paragraph, then, all we have to do is add those two points together. Once we do, it turns out that the main point is that both the particular form of religion a Native American tribe adopted and a woman's chances of being a religious leader depended on the tribe's means of subsistence—its economy, in other words.

Of course, there can be other points besides the main idea in even one short paragraph. It's just that other ideas and pieces of clarifying information are subordinate. Once you find the whole point of the passage—the main idea, it's easy to see that the other ideas are subordinate. They contribute to or illustrate the main idea.

If the sample passage we just analyzed were a paragraph you read as part of an exercise in the Finding the Main Idea section of your study guide's first chapter, your answer to the exercise should look like this:

1.   What is the topic of this paragraph?

Religion among the Americans.

2.   What is its main idea?

Both the particular form of religion an American tribe adopted and women's chances of being religious leaders depended on the tribe's economy.

3.   What details support the main idea?

- *Religious beliefs and practices of agricultural tribes focused on the foods they cultivated.*

- *Religious beliefs and practices of tribes with hunting economies centered on animals.*

- *Tribes in which women played important economic roles (cultivation) were the ones most likely to allow women to serve as religious leaders (example: the Iroquois).*

At some point early in your work on a particular chapter in your textbook, you are going to need to begin working out and making sense of complex relationships among ideas and concepts that are dealt with over large and sometimes widely separated segments of the chapter. In addition to the Thematic Guide, the study guide's Organizing, Reviewing, and Using Information section, explained later in this introduction, offers the kind of help needed.

IDENTIFICATION AND SIGNIFICANCE

Identification and Significance sections are exercises calling for students to identify or define persons, places, events, concepts, etc., and indicate how they fit in and are important to the historical time period under study. For the most part, the items are details that you are going to be expected to recognize, remember, and explain.

The Identification and Significance section is one of those sections that you return to time and again as you do the reading assignments for the chapter. The first time is actually before you even begin your first reading assignment. At that time you don't need to write out anything; you simply want to get the items firmly in your mind. Familiarity with the list before you read the chapter or listen to what your instructor has to say about it prepares you to mark key terms in the chapter and recognize them and their importance if and when your instructor brings them up in class.

Only after you complete the reading assignment and your instructor has gone over it in class is it time to compose your Identification/Significance items. Trying to compose while you're reading the assignment is a sure way to lose your concentration on the reading assignment. On the other hand, having your study guide open to the Identification and Significance section and jotting down the page numbers beside items when they are mentioned is a good start that costs nothing in lost concentration. Later, when your instructor goes over the assignment in class, all you have to do is mark each item he or she mentions—a simple asterisk or checkmark will do. After class, you're all set to compose an identification for each item you've marked. Admittedly, you should compose identifications for a few additional items, perhaps—those that you think the coverage in the textbook suggests are most important. You certainly are not expected to write out an identification for every item we have listed though.

Each of your responses to Identification and Significance items should have two parts. The first part (the identification) should be a statement of what or who the item is/was and when he, she, or it existed or took place. The statement may include a description or specific examples. The second part (the significance) should be an explanation of why the item is historically important by indicating the item's historical context and his, her, or its causes, effects, or influence (political, social, economic, etc.)

If, for example, an Identification and Significance item for Chapter 1 were The Lady of Cofitachequi, your response could be something like this:

> The Lady of Cofitachequi was a Native American ruler who in May
> 1540, near present-day Camden, S.C., appeased Hernando De Soto
> and his men and directed their interest away from her village
> (Cofitachequi). Soto had come into the woman's village after having
> wreaked havoc on one Native American village after another on his
> northwestward march from near present-day Tampa, Fla., through the
> Carolinas. Soto took the bait (more riches farther on) but also took the
> young woman captive. On the march northward, she escaped. Her
> trickery in suggesting that the riches Soto wanted could be found
> farther north possibly saved her village and may be seen as an example
> of Native American resistance to the Spanish.

ORGANIZING, REVIEWING, AND USING INFORMATION

Each Organizing, Reviewing, and Using Information section is made up of one or more charts. In these charts, each column and row is given a label indicating specific kinds of information from reading assignments and class lectures that should be reflected in the blanks in the chart. The student is expected to enter terse phrases in the blanks to suggest important information. Because the instructions and assignments based on these charts are standard for all chapters, they are given only in the first chapter of each volume of the guide.

The charts vary too much to provide you with a typical example, but an example of the kind of chart you might see in Chapter 1 appears on the next page. Some, such as the one dealing with the U.S. Constitution in Chapter 7 (Chart B), resemble combinations of several charts covering various aspects of the same topic.

The three most obvious uses for such charts are to (1) plan responses for essay questions one anticipates will be asked on a test, (2) serve as notes for use in giving in-class oral reports and participating in class or panel discussions, and (3) guide practice recitations of information in preparing for tests—almost like flash cards. One essay question or oral report topic might be based on the information in a single column or row, but most are based on information appearing in two or more columns or rows or maybe even two or more charts. The charts in some chapters are clearly linked to the charts in other chapters, an obvious example being the charts for Chapters 32 and 33. In those two charts, the labels above the columns differ—they concern different presidential administrations—but labels at the beginning of the rows are all the same.

Work on the Organizing, Reviewing, and Using Information exercises is ongoing. You should look over the chart before doing even the first reading assignment just to get an idea of the kind of information you're going to be asked to put in the blanks. Then, after reading each assignment and attending each class, fill in or add to as many blanks as possible. The kind of information that ought to be entered in the blanks should get a bit clearer to you as you complete reading assignments and attend classes to hear what your instructor has to say.

On the next page you will find a sample chart dealing with material covered in Chapter 1. Then on the following page you'll find the same chart after somebody has filled in most of the blanks. Since the student filling out the chart had not yet had the advantage of hearing what his or her instructor had to say, the entries you see in the completed chart are based solely on what's in the chapter. (As you work on Chapter 1 of your textbook, it would be a good idea for you to finish this version of the chart, using information you get in class from your own instructor to fill in as many of the gaps as you can.)

Among other things, charts serve to suggest possible test questions and to help you in organizing responses to those questions. That explains one of the three standard Organizing, Reviewing, and Using Information exercises, an exercise that calls for students to compose mock essays—called "mock" essays simply because they are written as answers to pretend essay questions, questions the student merely guesses may show up on the next test. The charts help students make educated guesses about potential questions. Once they have a question in mind, they may have to gather additional details, but the chart itself provides the plan.

One question suggested by the entries in the first column of the following chart is: "Compare or contrast the settlements of Mesoamerica and the settlements of the cultures that emerged in the territory of the present-day United States." Following the chart, you will find an example of a mock essay written by a student in response to that question. In that response you can see the use of information from the almost-finished chart as well as additional details the chart suggests will be needed in the mock essay.

The Pre-1492 Development and Evolution of American Societies						
Ancestors/Predecessors (Name, Time of Highpoint, Cause of Disappearance)	Form or Degree of Settlement	Religion	Social Structure	Economy	Technology	Other
Paleo-Indians						
Olmecs						
Teotihuacán						
Mayas						
Anasazi						
Mississippians						
Aztec						

The Pre-1492 Development and Evolution of American Societies						
Ancestors/Predecessors (Name, Time of Highpoint, Cause of Disappearance)	**Form or Degree of Settlement**	**Religion**	**Social Structure**	**Economy**	**Technology**	**Other**
Paleo-Indians --15000–7000 BCE --throughout North and South America --NA	*nomadic*		*econ. indep. bands of ext'd families*	*hunter-gatherers & Later, Agric w/trade in non-essentials*	*stone-pnt'd spears; cult. food crops; controlled burning for cultivation*	
Olmecs --1000 BCE --eastern Mesoamerica (parts of today's Mexico and Guatemala) - no sugg cause of demise in txt	*urban-- cities w/ temple pyramids*			*agricul-ture*	*architect & building skills for temple -blding*	
Teotihuacán ---300 BCE–600+ CE -- Mesoamerica (central part of today's Mexico) -- no sugg cause of demise in txt	*urban (up to 100,000 people)*	*polytheis-tic mst impt god— Quetzalco atl (fth'd srpent)*		*trade, esp obsidian objs- huge comm. Networks; agricul-ture*	*stonework-ing, building, archt skills for temple -blding and working obsidian*	
Mayas --600 CE–900 CE -- Mesoamerica (eastern part of today's Mexico – Yucatan) -- demise: warfare, inad. food resources	*urban: connected city-states always at war w/each other*		*warriors had impt role*	*agricul-ture*	*Architect & building skills for temple -blding writing syst—first in Americas*	*studied astronomy*

A

The Pre-1492 Development and Evolution of American Societies

Ancestors/Predecessors (Name, Time of Highpoint, Cause of Disappearance)	Form or Degree of Settlement	Religion	Social Structure	Economy	Technology	Other
Anasazi --1000 CE -- North America (Southwest—now Ariz & N. Mex.) -- cause of demise unknown, poss drought	*villages incl. Chaco Canyon w/its 200-room great houses*			*hunting-gathering w/agriculture; also, turquoise trade*	*architecture (Great houses of Chaco Canyon); irrigation; road building*	
Mississippians --1050 CE–1250 CE -- North America (Southeast and Midwest of today's U.S.) -- demise: ovrpop, clim chnge, defor	*settlements ranging frm villages to City of Sun - Cahokia (popul. 20,000)*	*sun worshippers; City of Sun (Cahokia) = rel ctr*		*agriculture (corn, nuts, squash, etc.) and hunting (venison)*		
Aztec --1300 CE – 1521 CE -- Mesoamerican (Valley of Mex—central Mexico) -- defeated by Spanish (Cortés)	*urban with Tenochtitlán as its center*	*poly-theistic—war god primary; relig. involved human sacrif*	*hierarchical city-state built on hereditary classes*	*supported by conq of agric. neighbors and tribute demanded of them*		*Montezuma or Motecuhzomo II king when Spanish arrived*

Sample Mock Essay

QUESTION: "Compare or contrast the settlements of Mesoamerica and the settlements of the cultures that emerged in the territory of the present-day United States."

ANSWER:

Largely because of differences in climate, settlements of North American cultures other than those of Mesoamerica were far less tied to a specific locale or fixed than were those of Mesoamerica itself.

Evidence of the Olmecs' possession of the stone-working and architectural skills needed to construct temple pyramids suggests that, with their ascendancy, Mesoamericans began abandoning their nomadic, hunter-gatherer lifestyle as they learned to rely on cultivation of crops and to build permanent

Copyright © Houghton Mifflin Company. All rights reserved.

settlements. No longer needing to forage for food resources once they found they could count on agricultural production to sustain them, the Mesoamericans all came to live in fixed locales with impressive permanent buildings. The reliability of agricultural production freed the people in Teotihuacán's population center of as many as 100,000 people to develop vast commercial networks specializing in the manufacture and trade of obsidian objects, as well as tremendous military power. Later, the Mayans' commercial and military demands perhaps created or contributed to the need for better communication and time measurement, needs that would explain the great Mayan intellectual advances, including development of America's first system of writing and the study of astronomy (associated with calendars). The Aztecs, like the Mayas before them, likewise were concentrated in fixed cities dominated by a hierarchy headed by a king and dominated by priests and warriors. These civilizations could remain in place until their populations outstripped their food resources—or until they (the Aztecs, at any rate) were defeated by Cortés in 1521.

The development of major population centers of the Anasazi and Mississippian cultures that flourished farther north and east—in the midwestern and southeastern regions of what's now known as the United States—came later, and the locations of their territories meant their settlements tended to be less permanent or fixed than those of the Mesoamericans.

The Anasazi who lived in what's now Arizona and New Mexico indeed settled in villages, some quite substantial, such as Chaco Canyon with its fourteen two-hundred-room great houses. However, climatic conditions lessened the possibility that these settlements could be permanent. The unreliability of agricultural output in their hot and dry territory led to their using agriculture in addition to hunting and gathering rather than as their replacement. The arid conditions in which they lived meant that they had to force cultivation, which they developed great skill in irrigation to accomplish. It also meant their villages usually had to be smaller than the great city-states that dominated Mesoamerica and more dispersed as well, which explains why they learned to build roads to connect their widely separated and relatively autonomous population centers. The availability of turquoise and the degree to which their success in agriculture freed them from having to constantly hunt and gather allowed some of the Anasazi to become artisans with non-essential goods they could trade with others, but in time it also meant that sometimes they had to pick up everything and leave the area in which they had settled.

Climate also affected the contrast between Mississippian and Mesoamerican settlements. The settlements of the Mississippian culture that arose much farther north and east at about the same time as those of the Anasazi (about 1000 C. E.) ranged from simple villages to the great City of the Sun (Cahokia) with a population of some 200,000. Other than the City of the Sun, which was primarily a religious center, the villages in the Mississippians' extensive territory were only semi-permanent at best. Through each year, whole villages moved around as necessary to sustain themselves through hunting in all seasons and through both agriculture and hunting in the warmer months. That means the Mississippian settlements for the most part were unfixed; that is, even less permanent than those of the Anasazi.

In composing your mock essays, feel free to refer to your Organizing, Reviewing, and Using Information charts, Identification and Significance exercises, spelling list, and class notes as much as you like. You are not testing your recall but planning a response. Likewise, feel free to scratch out and revise as much as you want just as long as you remember that you are not trying to write the kind of polished essay you would be expected to produce in an English class.

Any mock essays you write will probably be somewhat longer than what is expected of you on a test. However, when you are writing in an actual test situation, what you recall from a mock essay is likely to be the information that is most important. These mock essays are not meant to be memorized. Remembering the information is a natural consequence of the act of writing them and the concentration that writing requires.

IDEAS AND DETAILS

Each item in the Ideas and Details sections is a multiple-choice question designed to test recall of a specific, important piece of historical information or the ability to a draw logical inference from one or more bits of historical information that have been presented. As a whole, the Ideas and Details feature tests how closely and carefully the student has read the material covered by the questions.

You will find the correct answers at the back of the book. Notice, though, that in addition to being told which answer is correct, you are told why each of the other options is incorrect. Among other things, the analysis of what makes one answer right and other answers wrong serves as a reminder that you and your classmates are expected to interpret information rather than simply memorize it and illustrates effective interpretation in action.

You should not look at the Ideas and Details section until after you have finished all the rest of your studying of the chapter. Then answer all of the questions. Use your results as an indication of what if anything you need to do some more work on.

ESSAY QUESTIONS

The Essay Questions feature is a collection of sample essay questions based on the contents of the chapter of the textbook being studied. As is true of most essay questions on tests, these are expressed as instructive statements rather than as questions ("Compare or contrast ___ and ___" rather than "What's the difference between ___ and ___?"). Each question is linked to one or more of the learning objectives listed at the beginning of the study guide chapter.

Because the essay questions are expressed as statements themselves, they actually sound very much like the statements in the list of objectives. Sometimes it is difficult to grasp what one is supposed to do when a question merely says to discuss or to analyze or to do some such thing. The solution is to recast any such "question" in the form of a real question—with a question mark and everything. Recasting objective statements as questions also helps. You'll find that working with questions rather than statements makes it easier to compose suitable thesis statements to use in the essays (answers) and makes it easier to figure out the kind of information you should include.

If you recast all the essay questions and objectives in interrogative form and then try to write out full answers to all of them, you probably are not going be finished in time to go take the chapter test on the appointed day. That means you must first choose the questions that you think your own instructor is most likely to ask and/or questions that force you to use as much of the information as possible that is likely to be needed anywhere on the test. Next, write out mock essays in response to those questions. You can then answer some of the other questions mentally.

MAP EXERCISE

The map exercise is one or more activities designed to help students locate the people and events they are reading about in the textbook chapter they are studying and understand the relationship between geography and the historical events. They supplement maps and drawings presented in the textbook itself.

Not all of the chapters in your study guide include map exercises, and at exactly what point in the studying process you do those exercises is up to you. Probably it is best to do a particular map exercise when it seems to go with the reading assignment you have just completed. The exercises are important because they help you locate the places referred to in your reading assignments and understand how environment affects historical events as well as what geographical terms mean. Maps used as illustrations in the textbook are extremely helpful as well.

*   *   *

Well, that's it—your guide to how to use your guide. Here's hoping you enjoy the upcoming term, do well in your history course, and turn out to be happy with the help you derive from the following pages.

CHAPTER 16

Reconstruction: An Unfinished Revolution, 1865–1877

LEARNING OBJECTIVES

After you have studied Chapter 16 in your textbook and worked through this study guide chapter, you should be able to:

1. Examine the clash between the executive and legislative branches of government over the issue of Reconstruction, and discuss the events and forces that affected the development of the congressional Reconstruction plans.

2. Examine and evaluate the Reconstruction experience for freed men and women.

3. Explain the divergence between the provisions of President Johnson's Reconstruction plan and its actual operation.

4. Cite the major provisions of the Fourteenth and Fifteenth Amendments; indicate the reasons for their passage by Congress; and explain the compromises embodied in each.

5. Cite the major provisions of the First Reconstruction Act of 1867; indicate the reasons for its enactment by Congress; and explain how and why it diverged from the proposals of the Radical Republicans.

6. Discuss the political, social, and economic impact of the Reconstruction governments on southern society.

7. Examine and evaluate the means by which white southern Conservatives attempted to regain control in the South, and indicate the outcome of their efforts.

8. Examine the events and forces that brought a weakening of the northern commitment to Reconstruction and an end to the Reconstruction era.

THEMATIC GUIDE

Reconstruction refers to the process by which the nation was rebuilt after the destruction caused by the Civil War. This rebuilding was social, political, and economic. Since there were no guidelines as to how it would be accomplished, questions and disagreements arose. Given such disagreements, as well as the emotional aftermath of four years of war and the force of individual personalities, Reconstruction proceeded by trial and error.

As early as 1863, some two years before the end of the war, a debate began between the President and Congress over key questions relating to Reconstruction. In this debate, and in the Reconstruction proposals put forward by President Lincoln and Congress, it was apparent that the two disagreed over the scope and objectives of the Reconstruction process. Despite these disagreements, in early 1865 Congress and the President were able to work together to secure passage of the Thirteenth Amendment and to create the Freedmen's Bureau.

At war's end and as the power struggle between the executive and legislative branches over control of the Reconstruction process became more pronounced, freed men and women renewed their determination to struggle for survival and true equality within American society. On one level they placed faith in education and participation in the political process as means of attaining equality, but they also turned to family and religion for strength and support. Denied the possibility of owning land, they sought economic independence through new economic arrangements such as sharecropping. However, sharecropping ultimately proved to be a disaster for all concerned.

When Congress reconvened in December 1865, it was faced with a Reconstruction policy advanced by President Johnson that not only allowed former Confederate leaders to regain power at the state and national levels but obviously abandoned the freedmen to hostile southern whites. Northern congressmen and the constituents they represented were unwilling to accept this outcome of the long, bitter struggle against a rebellious South. Believing that it had a constitutional right to play a role in the Reconstruction process, Congress acted. This action led to clashes with an intransigent President Johnson and to the passage of two congressional Reconstruction plans.

The first of these plans, the Fourteenth Amendment, evolved when the wrangling between President Johnson and Congress produced compromises among the conservative, moderate, and radical factions of the Republican party. Although Congress passed the Freedmen's Bureau bill and the Civil Rights Act of 1866 over the president's veto, there was concern that the Supreme Court would declare the basic provisions of the Civil Rights Act unconstitutional. Therefore, those provisions were incorporated into a constitutional amendment that was presented to the states for ratification in April 1866. The Fourteenth Amendment demonstrated that Congress wanted to guarantee equality under the law to the freedmen, but its provisions make it clear that the moderate and conservative Republicans who controlled Congress were not willing to accept the more progressive concept of equality advanced by the Radical Republicans.

When, at the urging of the president, every former Confederate state except Tennessee refused to ratify the Fourteenth Amendment, Congress passed its second Reconstruction plan—the Reconstruction Acts of 1867–1868. Although these acts demonstrated some movement in the Radical direction by extending to blacks the right to vote in state elections, congressmen were still limited by the prejudices of the age. They labeled as extremist the suggestion that southern land be redistributed and so rejected the idea of giving blacks economic independence. They naively assumed that blacks would need only the ballot in their fight for a better life.

The same kinds of limitations worked within Reconstruction governments, preventing fundamental reform of southern society. Concurrently, southern Republicans adopted a policy that returned voting rights to former Confederates. These former Confederates, or Conservatives, ultimately led a campaign designed to return political and economic power to their hands by discrediting the Reconstruction governments. Adopting tactics ranging from racist charges and intimidation to organized violence, the Conservatives were able to achieve their objectives, as events in Alamance and Caswell counties in North Carolina demonstrated.

These setbacks indicated that northern commitment to equality had never been total. The federal government even began to retreat from partial commitment—a retreat made obvious by the policies of President Grant, the gradual erosion of congressional resolve on Reconstruction issues, the conservative decisions of the Supreme Court, and the emergence of other issues that captured the minds of white Americans. Finally, with the resolution of the disputed Hayes-Tilden election in 1876, Reconstruction ended. The promise of equality for African Americans remained unfulfilled.

BUILDING VOCABULARY

Listed below are important words and terms that you need to know to get the most out of Chapter 16. They are listed in the order in which they occur in the chapter. After carefully looking through the list, (1) underline the words with which you are totally unfamiliar, (2) put a question mark by those words of which you are unsure, and (3) leave the rest alone.

As you begin to read the chapter, when you come to any of the words you've put question marks beside or underlined (1) slow your reading; (2) focus on the word and on its context in the sentence you're reading; (3) if you can understand the meaning of the word from its context in the sentence or passage in which it is used, go on with your reading; (4) if it's a word that you've underlined or a word that you can't understand from its context in the sentence or passage, look it up in a dictionary and write down the definition that best applies to the context in which the word is used.

Definitions

aggrieved _____

fratricidal _____

enfranchise _____

suffrage _____

adroit _____

usurpation _____

circumspection _____

exultant _____

odyssey _____

philanthropy _____

autonomous _____

staunch _____

vehemently _____

blatant _____

haughty _____

resilient _____

succumb _____

repudiate _____

grudgingly _____

curfew _____

sabotage _____

intransigence _____

reimburse _____

humane _____

irony _____

infuse _____

magnanimity _____

mandate _____

impasse _____

confiscation _____

belligerent _____

conscientious _____

vacillate _____

curry _____

demobilization _____

apprentice _____

adamant _____

exhort _____

contingent _____

vindictive _____

futile _____

ostracism _____

subjection _____

entrench _____

ominous _____

disparate _____

harbinger _____

purport _____

pander _____

emasculate _____

acquiesce _____

Difficult-to-Spell Names and Terms from Reading and Lecture

IDENTIFICATION AND SIGNIFICANCE

After studying Chapter 16 of *A People and a Nation,* you should be able to identify fully *and* explain the historical significance of each item listed below.

- Identify each item in the space provided. Give an explanation or description of the item. Answer the questions *who, what, where,* and *when.*

- Explain the historical significance of each item in the space provided. Establish the historical context in which the item exists. Establish the item as the result of or as the cause of other factors existing in the society under study. Answer this question: *What were the political, social, economic, and/or cultural consequences of this item?*

1. "Decoration Day"

   a. Identification

   b. Significance

2. Lincoln's "10 percent" plan

   a. Identification

   b. Significance

3. Thaddeus Stevens and Charles Sumner

   a. Identification

   b. Significance

4.   the Wade-Davis Bill

    a.   Identification

    b.   Significance

5.   the Wade-Davis Manifesto

    a.   Identification

    b.   Significance

6.   the Thirteenth Amendment

    a.   Identification

    b.   Significance

7.   the Freedmen's Bureau

    a.   Identification

    b.   Significance

8.   reunification of African American families

    a.   Identification

    b.   Significance

9.   special Field Order Number 15

    a.   Identification

    b.   Significance

10.   Freedmen's Bureau schools

    a.   Identification

    b.   Significance

11.   the founding of African American colleges

    a.   Identification

    b.   Significance

12.   Francis Cardozo, P.B.S. Pinchback, Blanche K. Bruce, and Hiram Revels

    a.   Identification

    b.   Significance

13.   the growth of African American churches

    a.   Identification

    b.   Significance

14. the sharecropping system

    a. Identification

    b. Significance

15. cotton and the southern economy

    a. Identification

    b. Significance

16. Johnson's Reconstruction plan

    a. Identification

    b. Significance

17. the black codes

    a. Identification

    b. Significance

18. Radical Republicans

    a. Identification

    b. Significance

19.   the civil rights bill of 1866

    a.   Identification

    b.   Significance

20.   the Memphis and New Orleans riots

    a.   Identification

    b.   Significance

21.   the Fourteenth Amendment

    a.   Identification

    b.   Significance

22.   Johnson's "swing around the circle"

    a.   Identification

    b.   Significance

23.   the congressional elections of 1866

    a.   Identification

    b.   Significance

24. the First Reconstruction Act

    a. Identification

    b. Significance

25. Thaddeus Stevens's plan for land redistribution in the South

    a. Identification

    b. Significance

26. the Tenure of Office Act

    a. Identification

    b. Significance

27. Johnson's impeachment trial

    a. Identification

    b. Significance

28. the presidential election of 1868

    a. Identification

    b. Significance

29. Ulysses S. Grant
    a. Identification

    b. Significance

30. the Fifteenth Amendment
    a. Identification

    b. Significance

31. the southern Republican party
    a. Identification

    b. Significance

32. the constitutional conventions in the former Confederate states
    a. Identification

    b. Significance

33. Republican governments in the former Confederate states
    a. Identification

    b. Significance

34. industrialization in the former Confederate states

a. Identification

b. Significance

35. public schools in the former Confederate states

a. Identification

b. Significance

36. the southern Conservatives

a. Identification

b. Significance

37. the charge of "Negro rule"

a. Identification

b. Significance

38. carpetbagger

a. Identification

b. Significance

39. scalawag
   a. Identification

   b. Significance

40. Republican tax policies in the former Confederate states
   a. Identification

   b. Significance

41. the Ku Klux Klan
   a. Identification

   b. Significance

42. Klan violence in Alamance and Caswell counties of North Carolina
   a. Identification

   b. Significance

43. the Enforcement Acts and the anti-Klan law
   a. Identification

   b. Significance

44. the Liberal Republican revolt

    a.   Identification

    b.   Significance

45. the Amnesty Act of 1872

    a.   Identification

    b.   Significance

46. the Civil Rights Act of 1875

    a.   Identification

    b.   Significance

47. the Panic of 1873

    a.   Identification

    b.   Significance

48. race relations in the American West

    a.   Identification

    b.   Significance

49. William H. Seward
    a. Identification

    b. Significance

50. *Ex parte Milligan*
    a. Identification

    b. Significance

51. the *Slaughter-House* cases
    a. Identification

    b. Significance

52. *Bradwell v. Illinois*
    a. Identification

    b. Significance

53. *United States v. Cruikshank*
    a. Identification

    b. Significance

54. the presidential election of 1876

     a. Identification

     b. Significance

55. the Exodusters

     a. Identification

     b. Significance

ORGANIZING, REVIEWING, AND USING INFORMATION

Look over the following chart or charts and select the one whose subject best fits in with the learning objectives your instructor is emphasizing in your own class. Then, after you complete each reading assignment and attend each class covering Chapter 16, enter appropriate notes on relevant information you derive from the chapter and what your instructor says about the chart's subject in the blanks in that chart. Of course if this chapter provides more than one chart you may complete more than one. Please note that these instructions apply to every Organizing, Reviewing, and Using Information segment in every chapter in your study guide. *(For further explanation and additional help on completing and using charts, see "Organizing, Reviewing, and Using Information" in the Instructions and Explanations section of this Study Guide.)*

ASSIGNMENT 1 Prepare for your next test by reviewing the information in the rows and columns in your Chapter 16 Organizing Information chart(s) that relate most closely to the learning objectives your instructor has adopted for your class.

ASSIGNMENT 2 Get a topic for an oral presentation from your instructor. Using relevant information that you have entered in rows, columns, or a combination of rows or columns in your Chapter 16 Organizing Information chart(s) as a guide, practice giving your presentation.

ASSIGNMENT 3 Once you have completed the Chapter 16 Organizing Information charts, determine whether information you have entered in any of their rows or columns is the information needed to answer questions implied by any of the learning objectives at the beginning of this chapter or essay questions at the end of the chapter.

Write out the questions in interrogative (question) form and choose the one your instructor is most likely to confront you with on a chapter test. Write a mock essay in direct response to that question. *(For a sample of a mock essay created from a completed chart, see "Organizing, Reviewing, and Using Information" in the Instructions and Explanations section of this Study Guide.)*

Chart A

Evolution of Civil Rights and Legal Empowerment, 1865–1878					
Legislative, Constitutional, or Court Action	**Relevance to Blacks** (males, females, any special sub-groups)	**Relevance to Whites** (males, females, any special sub-groups)	**Implications for State, Federal Governments' Roles in Guaranteeing Civil Rights**	**Decisions and Other Factors Influencing Its Impact**	**Fate and/or Impact**
Civil Rights Bill of 1866					
Reconstruction Act of 1867					
Anti-Klan Law (1870)					
Enforcement Acts (1870–1871)					
Amnesty Act of 1872					
Civil Rights Act of 1875					
Supreme Court Decisions:					
Slaughter-House Cases					
U.S. v. Cruikshank					

Evolution of Civil Rights and Legal Empowerment, 1865–1878					
Legislative, Constitutional, or Court Action	**Relevance to Blacks** (males, females, any special sub-groups)	**Relevance to Whites** (males, females, any special sub-groups)	**Implications for State, Federal Governments' Roles in Guaranteeing Civil Rights**	**Decisions and Other Factors Influencing Its Impact**	**Fate and/or Impact**
Bradwell v. Illinois					
Constitutional Amendments:					
13ᵗʰ					
14ᵗʰ					
15ᵗʰ					

IDEAS AND DETAILS

Objectives 1 and 3

1. Many northerners questioned President Johnson's Reconstruction plan because

    a. it promised federal aid to help the South rebuild.
    b. in actual operation, it returned power to the prewar southern elite.
    c. the plan required repudiation of the Confederate war debt.
    d. it did not extend the vote to the yeoman class.

Objectives 1 and 2

2. Which of the following is true of the black codes?

    a. They required the freedmen to pay "freedom dues" to their former masters.
    b. They extended the right to vote to property-owning blacks.
    c. They were an attempt to relegate blacks to a position of servitude.
    d. They extended to the freedmen equal protection under the law.

Objective 1

3. Congress believed that it had a right to a voice in the Reconstruction process because the Constitution

    a. grants treaty-making powers to Congress.
    b. grants Congress the power to declare war.
    c. assigns Congress the duty of guaranteeing republican governments in the states.
    d. assigns Congress the responsibility of "providing for the general welfare."

Objective 1

4. In order to develop a new Reconstruction program, conservative and moderate Republicans began to work with the Radical Republicans because

    a. events in the South convinced them that blacks should be given full political rights.
    b. the Radicals convinced them that black freedom depended on a redistribution of land in the South.
    c. President Johnson and the congressional Democrats refused to cooperate with them.
    d. the northern electorate clearly favored the goals of the Radical Republicans.

Objectives 1, 3, 4, and 5

5. The northern public became convinced that Johnson's Reconstruction policies were too lenient due to

    a. the election of Jefferson Davis to the Senate.
    b. the President's appointment of Alexander Stephens to his cabinet.
    c. the President's insistence that the federal government assume the Confederate debt in full.
    d. accounts of antiblack violence in the South.

Objective 4

6.   The Fourteenth Amendment

   a.   guaranteed blacks the right to vote.
   b.   was strongly supported by President Johnson.
   c.   extended civil and political rights to women.
   d.   was the product of a compromise among the Republican factions in Congress.

Objective 5

7.   The First Reconstruction Act

   a.   required the southern states to ratify the Fourteenth Amendment.
   b.   called for a redistribution of land in the South.
   c.   guaranteed blacks the right to vote in federal elections.
   d.   stipulated that the southern states would be "adjusted" back into the Union over a ten-year period.

Objective 1

8.   The Senate's failure to convict President Johnson of the charges brought against him

   a.   enhanced Johnson's prestige and power.
   b.   established that impeachment was not a political tool.
   c.   is evidence that northern opinion toward Johnson and the South was softening.
   d.   caused a serious rift between the House and Senate.

Objective 6

9.   The new state constitutions of the former Confederate states

   a.   eliminated property qualifications for voting.
   b.   extended the right to vote to women.
   c.   made public school attendance compulsory.
   d.   made yearly reapportionment of legislative districts mandatory.

Objective 6

10.   The decision of the Republican-controlled governments in the southern states not to disfranchise many ex-Confederates

   a.   ultimately put southern Republicans in the position of having to gain white support or face defeat.
   b.   led to the formation of a broad-based Republican party in the South.
   c.   caused the freedmen to support the more liberal southern Democrats.
   d.   was politically embarrassing to congressional Republicans.

Objectives 2 and 7

11.   Blacks participating in Reconstruction governments

   a.   had little interest in the political process.
   b.   were subjected to a racist propaganda campaign against them undertaken by the white Conservatives.
   c.   insisted on social equality for blacks.
   d.   displayed a vindictive attitude toward their former masters.

Objective 7

12. Activities of the Ku Klux Klan in Alamance and Caswell counties in North Carolina

    e.   were disorganized and sporadic.
    f.   were organized by the impoverished classes in North Carolina society.
    g.   were undertaken by the former elite for the purpose of regaining political power.
    h.   had little success in areas where blacks and yeoman farmers allied.

Objectives 2 and 6

13. In the final analysis, the Reconstruction governments of the South

    a.   were able to alter the social structure of the South.
    b.   effected a lasting alliance between blacks and whites of the yeoman class.
    c.   gave blacks the means to achieve equality by giving them the right to vote.
    d.   left blacks economically dependent on hostile whites.

Objective 8

14. In the *Slaughter-House* cases, the Supreme Court

    a.   ruled that the Fourteenth Amendment did not protect the civil rights of individuals from state interference.
    b.   protected a citizen of the United States against discrimination by an individual or a group.
    c.   ruled that corporations were legal persons and were protected under the Fourteenth Amendment.
    d.   ruled that national citizenship was more important than state citizenship.

Objective 8

15. From the outcome of the 1876 presidential election, it is evident that the electorate

    a.   supported an inflationary monetary policy.
    b.   feared that the expansionist policies of Secretary of State Seward would lead to war.
    c.   had lost interest in Reconstruction.
    d.   rejected government aid to business interests.

ESSAY QUESTIONS

Objectives 1 and 3

1. Discuss Johnson's Reconstruction plan, and explain its actual operation. How did Congress respond to the plan? Why?

Objectives 1, 4, and 5

2. Discuss the political, social, and economic views of the Radical Republicans, and examine the role they played in the development of Congress's plans for Reconstruction.

Objective 1

3. Examine the attitudes and events that led to the impeachment of President Andrew Johnson, and assess the outcome of his trial by the Senate.

Objective 6

4.   Discuss the successes and failures of the Reconstruction governments in the South.

Objective 7

5.   Discuss the goals of the white southern Conservatives and the means they used to achieve those goals.

MAP EXERCISE

1.   Refer to the map in Chapter 16 of the text entitled "The Reconstruction." In the table below, list the eleven Confederate states, the date each was readmitted to the Union, the date Conservative rule was reestablished in each, and the length of time the Reconstruction governments were in power in each.

Former Confederate State	Date Readmitted to Union	Date Conservative Rule Reestablished	No. of Years Reconstruction Governments in Power

2.   Why was Tennessee readmitted to the Union before passage of the Reconstruction Act of 1867?

3.   What states were still under Reconstruction governments in 1876? What bearing did this have on the election of 1876? How was the problem resolved?

ANSWERS

Multiple-Choice Questions

1.   b.   Correct. At first it appeared that Johnson's Reconstruction plan would prevent the prewar southern elite from returning to power. However, in practice Johnson did not adhere to his own plan. After southerners defiantly elected prominent ex-Confederates such as Alexander Stephens, vice-president of the Confederacy, to Congress, Johnson began freely to hand out pardons to planters and to former Confederate leaders. This was done despite the fact that some southern state conventions were slow to repudiate secession and some state legislatures in the South were enacting black codes to keep African Americans in an inferior and servile position. Therefore, northerners were angry because it seemed that no one was being held responsible for the terrible war and that the South, despite having lost that war, was still defiant. See page 429.

a.   No. Although Johnson demonstrated a considerable amount of sympathy toward the South, he did not go so far as to promise federal aid to rebuild the region. See page 429.

c.   No. Congress supported the requirement in Johnson's plan that the Confederate war debt be repudiated. Congress was angered when two southern states defiantly refused to abide by this requirement. See page 429.

d.   No. The Johnson plan stipulated that most white southern males, including yeoman farmers, could gain the right to vote by swearing an oath of loyalty to the United States government. See page 429.

2.   c.   Correct. The black codes, adopted by most southern state legislatures immediately after the war, were in large measure restatements of the old slave codes. Those responsible for enacting the codes intended permanently to relegate blacks to a subservient position in southern society. See page 429.

a.   No. Although some of the southern states were reluctant to admit that slavery was a thing of the past, the black codes did not require that freedmen pay "freedom dues" to their former masters. See page 429.

b.   No. The black codes did not extend political rights to any freedmen. See page 429.

d.   No. The black codes did not indicate acceptance of the Thirteenth Amendment and did not protect the civil rights of the freedmen. See page 429.

3.   c.   Correct. Article IV, Section 4, of the Constitution states: "The United States shall guarantee to every State in this Union a republican form of government." It was on the basis of this statement that Congress claimed its right to have a voice in Reconstruction. See page 429.

a.   No. The Constitution stipulates that treaties must be ratified by the Senate, but Congress (the Senate and the House) did not base its claim that it had a right to have a voice in the Reconstruction process on this constitutional grant of power to the Senate. See page 429.

b.   No. The Constitution does grant Congress the power to declare war, but this was not the basis for Congress's claim that it had a right to a voice in the Reconstruction process. See page 429.

d.   No. The Preamble to the Constitution states that one of the purposes of the government is to "promote the general welfare," but this was not the section of the Constitution on which Congress based its claim to a voice in the Reconstruction process. See page 429.

4.   c.   Correct. All those who questioned Johnson's program, even conservatives and moderates, were labeled as "radical" by Johnson and the Democrats. Therefore, to make changes they thought necessary, conservative and moderate Republicans were forced into an alliance with the Radicals. See pages 430–431.

   a.   No. Most conservative and moderate Republicans believed that voting was a privilege, not a right. They did not ally with the Radical Republicans out of the belief that full political rights should be extended to blacks. See pages 430–431.

   b.   No. Most conservative and moderate Republicans viewed property rights as sacred. They rejected the contention by the Radical Republicans that a redistribution of southern land was necessary. See pages 430–431.

   d.   No. The Radical Republicans held views that most northerners rejected. For example, some Radicals went beyond advocating equality under the law for freedmen by advocating political, social, and economic equality as well. See pages 430–431.

5.   d.   Correct. In 1866, northerners began to read daily newspaper accounts of violence against blacks in the South. Especially disturbing were reports of antiblack riots in Memphis and New Orleans in which the police aided mobs in their attacks. Such revelations convinced the northern public and Republicans in Congress that Johnson's Reconstruction plan was too lenient. See page 431.

   a.   No. After the Civil War, Jefferson Davis, former president of the Confederacy, was arrested in Georgia and imprisoned from 1865 to 1867. Although he was indicted for treason in 1866, a trial was never held. He was released on bail from prison in 1867. Therefore, Jefferson Davis was not elected to the Senate after the Civil War. See page 431.

   b.   No. President Johnson did not appoint Alexander Stephens, former vice-president of the Confederacy, to his cabinet. However, Stephens was elected to the Senate under Johnson's Reconstruction plan, and this convinced many northerners that President Johnson's Reconstruction plan was too lenient. See page 431.

   c.   No. President Johnson's Reconstruction plan called for the repudiation of the Confederate war debt. Northerners did, however, become convinced that Johnson's Reconstruction plan was too lenient when two former Confederate states refused to repudiate the Confederate war debt and some refused to repudiate secession. See page 431.

6.   d.   Correct. Conservative and moderate Republicans disagreed with Radical Republicans over extension of voting rights to freedmen. The second section of the Fourteenth Amendment clearly indicates a compromise favoring the conservative/moderate view on this question. See page 431.

   a.   No. The Fourteenth Amendment allowed the southern states to decide whether or not to extend voting rights to freedmen. If a state denied voting privileges to its black citizens, the state's delegation to the House of Representatives would be reduced proportionately. This provision was never enforced. See page 431.

   b.   No. Johnson condemned the Fourteenth Amendment. He actively worked against the amendment by urging northerners to reject it and southern state legislatures to vote against ratification. See page 431.

   c.   No. The Fourteenth Amendment ignored women. See page 431.

7.   a.   Correct. Only one southern state (Tennessee) had initially accepted and been reconstructed under the Fourteenth Amendment. However, under the Reconstruction Act of 1867, the southern states were required to ratify the amendment before returning to the Union. See page 433.

b.   No. Although most Radical Republicans called for redistribution of southern land, most people rejected the idea as being beyond the power of the federal government and as unwarranted interference in private property. See page 433.

c.   No. The act stipulated that the ten southern states to which it applied had to guarantee freedmen the right to vote in elections for state constitutional conventions and in subsequent state elections, but it did not guarantee freedmen the right to vote in federal elections. See page 433.

d.   No. The Reconstruction Act of 1867 did not stipulate a definite time period during which the Reconstruction process would take place. See page 433.

8.   b.   Correct. The Radical Republicans who led the prosecution of Johnson in his Senate trial advanced the belief that impeachment was political in nature. The Senate's acquittal of Johnson was a rejection of that idea. See page 435.

a.   No. Johnson's impeachment by the House and subsequent trial in the Senate rendered him almost totally powerless as president. See page 435.

c.   No. The Senate fell only one vote shy of the two-thirds majority necessary to convict Johnson of the charges brought against him. This is not an indication that northern opinion toward Johnson and the South had softened. See page 435.

d.   No. The Senate's failure to convict Johnson did not cause a rift between the House and the Senate. See page 435.

9.   a.   Correct. By eliminating property qualifications for voting, the new state constitutions made the South more democratic and brought the South in line with the rest of the nation. See page 437.

b.   No. Although these state constitutions extended more rights to women, women's suffrage, advocated by some black delegates, was considered radical and was not adopted. See page 437.

c.   No. The new constitutions did provide for public schools, but attendance at these schools was not compulsory. See page 437.

d.   No. Yearly reapportionment of legislative districts was not made mandatory by the new state constitutions. See page 437.

10.   a.   Correct. Southern Republicans quickly restored the voting rights of former Confederates. This meant that the Republican party would face defeat if it could not gain white support. In courting the white vote, the Republican party abandoned its most loyal supporters—blacks. See pages 437–438.

b.   No. Although the southern Republicans appealed for support from a broad range of groups in the South, they were never able to build a broad popular base for the party. See pages 437–438.

c.   No. In the first place, southern Democrats were not more "liberal" than the southern Republicans. Furthermore, freedmen themselves supported restoration of the voting rights of former Confederates. See pages 437–438.

d.   No. The evidence does not indicate that congressional Republicans were embarrassed by the decision of southern Republicans to restore the voting rights of former Confederates. See pages 437–438.

11. b.   Correct. Charges of "black domination" and "Negro rule" are examples of the racist propaganda used by white conservatives to discredit the Reconstruction governments. See page 439.

a.   No. The evidence indicates that freedmen throughout the South, and especially those participating in Reconstruction governments, were very interested in participating in the political process and did so with great dignity and distinction. See page 439.

c.   No. Those blacks who participated in Reconstruction governments were practical and realistic in their approach to power. They extended the right to vote to former Confederates, did not insist on an integrated school system, and did not insist on social equality. See page 439.

d.   No. The evidence indicates that those blacks participating in Reconstruction governments were not vindictive toward their former masters. Their actions demonstrate their belief in "the Christian goal of reconciliation." See page 439.

12. c.   Correct. Terrorist campaigns by the Klan were organized and purposeful after 1867. This was clearly the case in these North Carolina counties where the wealthy and powerful organized the campaign of terror for the purpose of regaining political control. See page 440.

a.   No. The evidence indicates that after 1867 the terrorist activities against blacks became more organized and purposeful, and the campaign of terror in Alamance and Caswell counties clearly fits this characterization. See page 440.

b.   No. The campaign of terror in the North Carolina counties of Caswell and Alamance was organized by the wealthy and the powerful. See page 440.

d.   No. Blacks and whites of the yeoman class were allies in Alamance and Caswell counties, and the Klan successfully used racism to destroy this coalition. See page 440.

13. d.   Correct. The Reconstruction governments did not demand and Congress did not bring about a redistribution of land in the South. As a result, blacks were denied economic independence and remained economically dependent on hostile whites. See page 441.

a.   No. Although the Reconstruction governments were able to effect some reform in the South, they chose not to demand redistribution of land. This decision is one of the main reasons that these governments were not able to alter the social structure of the region. See page 441.

b.   No. The success of the Klan's terrorist campaign in Alamance and Caswell counties in North Carolina is evidence that there was not a lasting alliance between blacks and whites of the yeoman class. See page 441.

c.   No. Blacks were given the right to vote, but it was naive to believe that the ballot was an adequate weapon in the struggle by African Americans for a better life. See page 441.

14.   a.   Correct. John Campbell argued that the Fourteenth Amendment brought individual rights under federal protection by making the Bill of Rights applicable to the states. The Court disagreed and said that state citizenship and national citizenship were separate, with the former being more important. The due process clause of the Fourteenth Amendment, said the Court, protected only the narrowly defined rights that accompanied national citizenship. See page 445.

b.   No. The Court ruled that the Fourteenth Amendment protected only those rights that went along with national citizenship, and the Court narrowly defined those rights. See page 445.

c.   No. Although the Court later ruled that corporations were legal persons protected under the Fourteenth Amendment (the 1886 Santa Clara case), this was not its ruling in the Slaughter-House cases. See page 445.

d.   No. The Court ruled that, of the two, state citizenship was more important than national citizenship. See page 445.

15.   c.   Correct. The fact that both candidates in this disputed election favored removal of federal troops from the South and an end to Reconstruction indicates that the electorate had lost interest in Reconstruction. This is especially important in relation to the northern electorate. See pages 445–446.

a.   No. The monetary issue aroused a great deal of interest during the 1870s, especially among farmers, who tended to favor an inflationary policy. However, by the 1876 election a "sound money" policy had basically won out. See pages 445–446.

b.   No. William H. Seward was secretary of state from 1861 to 1869. His policies had no direct bearing on the outcome of the disputed presidential election of 1876. See pages 445–446.

d.   No. Since the end of the Civil War, the government had been injecting money into the economy and extending indirect aid to business interests. Most people favored a continuation of this practice, which had spurred industrial growth, especially in the North. See pages 445–446.

CHAPTER 17

The Development of the West, 1877–1900

LEARNING OBJECTIVES

After you have studied Chapter 17 in your textbook and worked through this study guide chapter, you should be able to:

1. Examine the factors that affected the life, culture, and economies of western Indian tribes in the late nineteenth century, and discuss the varying responses of the Indians to the pressures they experienced.

2. Examine the rationale behind, the specifics of, and the consequences of the United States government's policies toward the western Indian tribes from the Treaty of Greenville through the Dawes Severalty Act; and discuss the reactions of Indians to these policies.

3. Discuss the characteristics of each of the frontier societies listed below, and explain the contributions of each to the economic, social, and cultural transformation of the West.

   a. The mineral, timber, and oil frontiers

   b. The farming frontier

   c. The ranching frontier

4. Discuss the role of women and nonwhites in frontier society, and examine the prejudices these groups experienced.

5. Discuss the early conservation movement in the United States, and indicate its successes and failures.

6. Discuss efforts in the West at land reclamation through irrigation; assess the role played by state and federal governments in these efforts; and explain the debate over water rights that accompanied reclamation efforts.

7. Examine the impact of the expansion of the railroad industry on the American economy, perceptions of time and space, standardization of time, technology, and business organization.

8. Examine and assess the role played by federal, state, and local governments in the expansion of the railroad industry.

9. Explain the responses of Plains' settlers to the living conditions and challenges they encountered, and discuss the impact of their experience on their lives.

10. Discuss the forces responsible for the transformation of American agriculture in the late nineteenth century, and explain the consequences of this agricultural revolution.

THEMATIC GUIDE

Chapter 17 begins a series of four chapters that analyze the transition of American society from an agrarian society to an urban, industrialized society. The expansion westward in the late nineteenth century closed the physical frontier that had been part of American society since its beginnings. As in the past, American expansion was carried out at the expense of Indians. Americans were and are an ethnocentric people. They see their civilization, their society, and their value and belief systems as being better than those of other peoples. This ethnocentrism led Americans to believe that they had a right to expand and to impose their values and beliefs on the peoples and societies they encountered. It is this attitude that formed the basis of the failed Dawes Severalty Act.

As Americans sought opportunity in this vast western region, they discovered and developed the riches of the land, thus conquering the natural-resource frontier—a prerequisite for the subsequent development of an industrialized economy. Exploitation of the land and its resources for profit raised questions in several areas: (1) who owns the resources, private developers or the American people; (2) which takes precedence—the desire for progress and profit or the desire to protect the natural landscape; and (3) who has rights to the precious streams, rivers, and basins of the West, only those along their banks or all those who intend a beneficial use of river water.

The natural-resources frontier, especially the mining and lumbering frontiers, produced personalities who enriched American folklore; but reality was far different from folk tales. Most westerners worked long hours as they attempted to eke out an existence for themselves and their families. Women and nonwhites suffered discrimination, especially with the development of racial categories by the dominant Anglo-Americans and European immigrants. Furthermore, although individual initiative was important in the development of the West, individuals usually gave way to corporate interests, which had the capital necessary to undertake the expensive extraction of minerals, timber, and oil. In addition, the federal government, as owner of the western lands, encouraged the development of the area by actively aiding individuals and corporations through measures such as the Timber and Stone Act and the Newlands Reclamation Act.

As frontiers of opportunity were conquered in the West, the expansion of regional and transcontinental railroad lines—made possible by generous government subsidies—helped create a vast national marketplace. Besides providing nationwide economic opportunities to farmers and industrialists, the railroad altered concepts of time and space, gave rise to new communities, and brought technological reforms as well as organizational reforms that affected modern business practices.

Railroad expansion and Indian removal made possible the successful settlement and development of the farming and ranching frontiers. These frontiers shared the characteristics of the natural-resource frontier: use of public land for private enrichment; the importance of technological innovations to successful development; government promotion of settlement and development; the bowing of the individual to corporate interests; the emergence of a frontier folk culture, especially in relation to the ranching frontier; and contributions to urbanization and to national economic growth and expansion.

BUILDING VOCABULARY

Listed below are important words and terms that you need to know to get the most out of Chapter 17. They are listed in the order in which they occur in the chapter. After carefully looking through the list, (1) underline the words with which you are totally unfamiliar, (2) put a question mark by those words of which you are unsure, and (3) leave the rest alone.

As you begin to read the chapter, when you come to any of the words you've put question marks beside or underlined (1) slow your reading; (2) focus on the word and on its context in the sentence you're reading; (3) if you can understand the meaning of the word from its context in the sentence or passage in which it is used, go on with your reading; (4) if it's a word that you've underlined or a word that you can't understand from its context in the sentence or passage, look it up in a dictionary and write down the definition that best applies to the context in which the word is used.

Definitions

expound _____

egalitarian _____

persevere _____

relegate _____

rogue _____

exploit _____

infinity _____

avenge _____

nomad _____

sinew _____

reciprocity _____

lethal _____

decimate _____

convergence _____

impede _____

preponderance _____

qualms _____

preempt _____

embellish _____

interloper _____

categorize _____

impute _____

commandeer _____

degrade _____

succumb _____

recalcitrance _____

relentless _____

acculturate _____

assimilation _____

diligence _____

servile _____

dissolution _____

messianic _____

forswear _____

induce _____

dupe _____

demoralize _____

eradicate _____

lode _____

crescent _____

mestizo _____

ascribe _____

demeaning _____

tier _____

miscegenation _____

benevolent _____

hedonism _____

notoriety _____

exploits (noun) _____

posterity _____

eccentricity _____

reclamation _____

subsidy _____

salutary _____

exemplify _____

formidable _____

burgeoning _____

harrow _____

drover _____

Difficult-to-Spell Names and Terms from Reading and Lecture

FINDING THE MAIN IDEA

When you begin to read material assigned to you in the textbook, it is important for you to look for (and mark) the main idea and supporting details in each paragraph or paragraph series. To see how to do so, reread "Finding Main Ideas" in the Introduction to this study guide. Then work the following two exercises, and check your answers.

Exercise A

Read the paragraph on pages 460–462 of the textbook that begins with this sentence:

> Cutting fir and spruce trees for lumber to satisfy the demand for construction and heating materials needed vast tracks of forest land to be profitable.

1.   What is the topic of this paragraph?

2.   What is its main idea?

3.   What details support the main idea?

Exercise B

Read the two successive paragraphs on pages 462–463 of the textbook that begin with this sentence:

> To control labor and social relations within this complex population, white settlers made race an important distinguishing social characteristic in the West.

1.   What is the topic of this paragraph series?

2.   What is its main idea?

3.   What details support the main idea?

IDENTIFICATION AND SIGNIFICANCE

After studying Chapter 17 of *A People and a Nation,* you should be able to identify fully *and* explain the historical significance of each item listed below.

- Identify each item in the space provided. Give an explanation or description of the item. Answer the questions *who, what, where,* and *when.*

- Explain the historical significance of each item in the space provided. Establish the historical context in which the item exists. Establish the item as the result of or as the cause of other factors existing in the society under study. Answer this question: *What were the political, social, economic, and/or cultural consequences of this item?*

1. Frederick Jackson Turner's frontier thesis

    a. Identification

    b. Significance

2. Buffalo Bill Cody

    a. Identification

    b. Significance

3. Indian subsistence cultures

    a. Identification

    b. Significance

4. slaughter of the buffalo

    a. Identification

    b. Significance

5. decline of salmon
    a. Identification

    b. Significance

6. United States government's reservation policy
    a. Identification

    b. Significance

7. the Battle of Little Big Horn
    a. Identification

    b. Significance

8. George Manypenny and Helen Hunt Jackson
    a. Identification

    b. Significance

9. Canada's Indian policy
    a. Identification

    b. Significance

10. the Women's National Indian Association and the Indian Rights Association

    a. Identification

    b. Significance

11. the Dawes Severalty Act

    a. Identification

    b. Significance

12. the government's Indian school system

    a. Identification

    b. Significance

13. the Ghost Dance movement

    a. Identification

    b. Significance

14. Wovoka

    a. Identification

    b. Significance

15. the Massacre at Wounded Knee
    a. Identification

    b. Significance

16. the Clapp rider to the Indian appropriations bill
    a. Identification

    b. Significance

17. the mining frontier
    a. Identification

    b. Significance

18. the Timber and Stone Act
    a. Identification

    b. Significance

19. mining and lumber communities
    a. Identification

    b. Significance

20. women and nonwhites in frontier society

    a.   Identification

    b.   Significance

21. the home mission movement

    a.   Identification

    b.   Significance

22. the conservation movement

    a.   Identification

    b.   Significance

23. the omnibus bill of 1889

    a.   Identification

    b.   Significance

24. the Clanton family and Johnny Ringo

    a.   Identification

    b.   Significance

25. the Earp brothers, "Bat" Masterson, and "Doc" Holliday

    a. Identification

    b. Significance

26. the shoot-out at the OK Corral

    a. Identification

    b. Significance

27. riparian rights versus prior appropriation

    a. Identification

    b. Significance

28. California irrigation legislation of 1887

    a. Identification

    b. Significance

29. the Newlands Reclamation Act

    a. Identification

    b. Significance

30. standard time zones

    a. Identification

    b. Significance

31. westward migration, 1870–1890

    a. Identification

    b. Significance

32. life on the Plains

    a. Identification

    b. Significance

33. the Great Blizzard of 1888

    a. Identification

    b. Significance

34. grasshopper plagues

    a. Identification

    b. Significance

35. the Homestead Act of 1862

    a. Identification

    b. Significance

36. mail-order houses and Rural Free Delivery

    a. Identification

    b. Significance

37. mechanization of agriculture

    a. Identification

    b. Significance

38. the Morrill Land Grant Acts of 1862 and 1890

    a. Identification

    b. Significance

39. the Hatch Act of 1887

    a. Identification

    b. Significance

40. dry farming

   a. Identification

   b. Significance

41. Luther Burbank and George Washington Carver

   a. Identification

   b. Significance

42. the ranching frontier

   a. Identification

   b. Significance

43. the long drive

   a. Identification

   b. Significance

44. open range ranching

   a. Identification

   b. Significance

45. barbed wire

    a.   Identification

    b.   Significance

ORGANIZING, REVIEWING, AND USING INFORMATION

Look over the following chart or charts and select the one whose subject best fits in with the learning objectives your instructor is emphasizing in your own class. Then, after you complete each reading assignment and attend each class covering Chapter 17, enter appropriate notes on relevant information you derive from the chapter and what your instructor says about the chart's subject in the blanks in that chart. Of course if this chapter provides more than one chart you may complete more than one. Please note that these instructions apply to every Organizing, Reviewing, and Using Information segment in every chapter in your study guide.

ASSIGNMENT 1 Prepare for your next test by reviewing the information in the rows and columns in your Chapter 17 Organizing Information chart(s) that relate most closely to the learning objectives your instructor has adopted for your class.

ASSIGNMENT 2 Get a topic for an oral presentation from your instructor. Using relevant information that you have entered in rows, columns, or combination of rows or columns in your Chapter 17 Organizing Information chart(s) as a guide, practice giving your presentation.

ASSIGNMENT 3 Once you have completed the Chapter 17 Organizing Information charts, determine whether information you have entered in any of their rows or columns is the information needed to answer questions implied by any of the learning objectives at the beginning of this chapter or essay questions at the end of the chapter.

Write out the questions in interrogative (question) form and choose the one your instructor is most likely to confront you with on a chapter test. Write a mock essay in direct response to that question.

The West: Perspectives in Conflict, 1877–1920					
Areas Illustrating Conflicting Perspectives	**Native Americans**	**Euro-American (predominantly males)**			**White Women and Groups Mislabeled As "Races"**
		Settlers and Others Migrating to the West	**Makers and Interpreters of Policies and Laws**	**Promoters of Religious and Cultural Values**	
Wealth and Economic System					
Resources and Resource Management					
Settlement by Whites					
Promotion of Religious or Spiritual, Cultural, and Class Values					
Gov't Policies and Positions (Reservations, Indian Citizenship, Railroad Expansion)					
Treaty-Making and Treaties					
Social Attitudes, Relations, and Conditions					

IDEAS AND DETAILS

Objective 1

1. To achieve subsistence, the economies of most western Indian tribes
    a. relied solely on the buffalo.
    b. combined capitalistic trading practices with crop growing.
    c. sold clothing, shoes, and blankets to get the money necessary to buy food in the marketplace.
    d. relied on a balance among activities such as crop growing, livestock raising, hunting, and trading.

Objective 1

2. The slaughter of the buffalo by whites
    a. was encouraged by Indians of the Great Plains.
    b. was undertaken to prevent the spread of lethal animal diseases to sheep and goat herds.
    c. was only one of a combination of circumstances that doomed the buffalo.
    d. began the process that led to the bison's virtual extinction.

Objective 1

3. Which of the following undermined the subsistence culture of Northwestern Indians?
    a. Salmon reduction
    b. Slaughter of the buffalo
    c. The lack of irrigation facilities during prolonged periods of drought
    d. Animal diseases

Objective 2

4. Which of the following assumptions was generally made by whites settling the Great Plains?
    a. Fearing competition from African American workers, white settlers assumed that the federal government would bar blacks from the territories.
    b. Well-schooled in egalitarian principles, white settlers assumed that equality of opportunity would be extended to all ethnic groups in the territories.
    c. Disregarding the rights of Plains Indians, white settlers assumed that they could settle wherever they wished.
    d. Out of concern for Indian cultures, white settlers assumed that the land rights of Native Americans would have to be respected.

Objective 2

5. Which of the following was a feature of the federal government's reservation policy?
    a. It did not allow Indians any say over their own affairs.
    b. It helped foster mutually beneficial trade relationships between Indians and whites.
    c. It forced Indians to concentrate on crop production.
    d. It protected Indians against white encroachment.

Objectives 1 and 2

6.   As a result of the Dawes Severalty Act,

    a.   thousands of Indian children educated in white boarding schools rejected Indian culture.

    b.   most western Indians were Christianized.

    c.   community-owned Indian property was dissolved and land allotments were granted to individual Indian families.

    d.   the western Indians were encouraged to actively participate in decisions that would affect their lives and their culture.

Objective 3

7.   The mining, timber, and ranching frontiers had which of the following characteristics in common?

    a.   In the earliest stages of development, these frontiers required large capital outlays.

    b.   Those associated with the development of these frontiers found ways of using the Timber and Stone Act to their advantage.

    c.   Individuals were ultimately replaced by corporations in the development of these frontiers.

    d.   Those involved in the development of these frontiers understood the need for careful and planned use of natural resources.

Objectives 3 and 4

8.   In the frontier communities, ethnic minorities

    a.   were welcomed because of the skills they brought with them.

    b.   usually had to endure white prejudice.

    c.   found that opportunities abounded.

    d.   were usually able to gain economic and political power.

Objective 7

9.   To help solve scheduling problems, the railroads in 1883

    a.   began to coordinate all their schedules through a central clearing-house.

    b.   requested that the government establish daylight-saving time.

    c.   asked that the government create the Interstate Commerce Commission.

    d.   established four standard time zones.

Objectives 3 and 8

10.   Both the cattle-ranching industry and the railroad industry

    a.   profited from free use of public lands.

    b.   developed a mutually beneficial relationship with farmers.

    c.   were respectful of Indian rights and culture.

    d.   welcomed government regulation of industry.

Objective 9

11.   Which of the following is associated with the Great Plains?

    a.   A temperate climate

    b.   An abundance of timber for housing and fuel

    c.   Grasshopper plagues

    d.   Vast stretches of desert

Objective 9

12. Social isolation was a characteristic of life on the Plains because
    a. the competitive frontier spirit did not create an atmosphere conducive to social interaction.
    b. the rugged terrain made traveling difficult.
    c. the absence of farm machinery resulted in no time for socializing.
    d. farmhouses on the 160-acre tracts received by settlers under the Homestead Act were widely separated.

Objective 9

13. Which of the following helped lessen the sense of isolation experienced by farm families in the Plains in the late nineteenth century?
    a. Railroad expansion
    b. The radio
    c. The telegraph
    d. Rural Free Delivery

Objectives 3 and 10

14. The extension of the farming frontier, including the conquering of the Plains, would not have been possible without
    a. the expanded use of farm machinery.
    b. new pesticides.
    c. better fertilizers.
    d. extensive use of migrant labor.

Objectives 3 and 10

15. The federal government encouraged the advancement of farming technology by
    a. subsidizing the research of George Washington Carver.
    b. passing the Hatch Act of 1887.
    c. appointing Luther Burbank to head the research division of the Department of Agriculture.
    d. funding a vast irrigation network in the Plains.

ESSAY QUESTIONS

Objectives 1 and 2

1. Discuss the federal government's reservation policy, and explain its impact on western Indian tribes.

Objective 3

2. Discuss the characteristics of the natural-resource frontier and the methods by which developers gained land and extraction rights. What role did the federal government play in the development of this frontier?

Objective 6

3. Discuss the controversy over water rights in the West and assess the importance of this debate and its outcome.

Objective 7

4.   Discuss the impact of the expansion of the railroad industry on the American economy.

Objective 8

5.   Explain the role of federal, state, and local governments in the expansion of the railroad industry, and discuss the effects of that role.

Objective 9

6.   Describe the life of a farm family of the Plains.

ANSWERS

Finding the Main Idea

Exercise A

The first sentence is a transition sentence from a discussion of the mining frontier to a discussion of the lumbering frontier. It also makes the point that lumbering required vast stretches of land.

1. *Paragraph topic:* Methods by which the lumber industry gained land.

2. *Main idea:* The main idea is developed in the first three sentences.

    a. Lumber production required vast stretches of land.

    b. Due to the depletion of forests in the upper Midwest and South, lumber companies moved into the Northwest.

    c. These lumber corporations exploited an act of Congress (the Timber and Stone Act) for their own purposes rather than adhering to the intent of the act. By doing so they obtained the vast stretches of land required in lumber production.

3. *Supporting details:*

    a. The Timber and Stone Act was passed by Congress in 1878 to stimulate western settlement. Provisions of the act are noted to provide evidence that the intent of the act was to stimulate western settlement and to establish that the act was intended for "private citizens."

        The point about Congress's intent in passing the Timber and Stone Act—to aid the settlement and development of the frontier—is an underlying theme in this chapter's discussions of natural resources, ranching, and farming.

    b. Lumber companies hired seamen to register claims to timberland; these claims were then turned over to the lumber companies. The point provides further evidence of exploitation.

    c. Most of the 3.5 million acres bought by 1900 under the Timber and Stone Act belonged to corporations.

Exercise B

Paragraph 1   The first paragraph establishes the theme for the two-paragraph series and develops the first part of that theme.

1. *Paragraph topic:* The establishment of racial categories by white settlers in the West.

2. *Main idea:* White settlers separated people in the West into racial categories and used those categories to control labor and social relations.

3. *Supporting details:* The details used in this paragraph support the first part of the theme for the two-paragraph series. The first part of the theme is: White settlers separated people in the West into racial categories.

    a. White settlers in the West established four nonwhite racial categories.

    b. All such nonwhites were considered inferior by white settlers using these categories.

Paragraph 2   The second part of the theme established in the first paragraph is developed in the second paragraph of this two-paragraph series. The second part of the theme is: Racial categories were used by white settlers in the West to control labor and social relations.

1.   *Paragraph topic:* The development of a two-tiered labor system in western communities

2.   *Main idea:* Race was used by white western settlers to determine whether a person was in the top tier or the bottom tier of a two-tiered labor system.

3.   *Supporting details:*

    a.   Whites were to be in the top tier as managers and skilled laborers.

    b.   Racial minorities occupied the bottom tier of this labor system.

        (1)   Work done by the Irish, Chinese, and Mexicans

        (2)   Work done by blacks

    c.   All nonwhites plus the Irish experienced prejudice.

        (1)   Experience of the Chinese when they were hired by the Union Pacific Railroad to replace white workers

        (2)   Experience of the Mexicans

Multiple-Choice Questions

1.   d.   Correct. Although western Indian tribes differed culturally, they all depended on a balance among four main economic activities to achieve subsistence—crop growing; livestock raising; hunting, fishing, and gathering; and trading and raiding. This system depended on an ecological balance that was destroyed as whites moved west. See page 453.

    a.   No. Much of the life of Plains Indians centered on the buffalo, but they did not rely solely on the buffalo for subsistence. See page 453.

    b.   No. Although the western Indian tribes traded with whites and with other Indians, they did so mainly to obtain necessities and not for reasons of profit. Furthermore, they did not believe that they could depend only on trade and crop growing to achieve subsistence. See page 453.

    c.   No. The western Indians were not part of a market economy in which they sold items for the purpose of obtaining money to buy food and other necessities. See page 453.

2.   c.   Correct. Slaughter of the buffalo by whites was simply one a many factors that doomed the buffalo to near extinction. Other factors were: increased buffalo kills by Indians, competition with humans for space and water, lethal animal diseases, and competition for grazing land with Indian and white-owned livestock. See pages 454–455.

    a.   No. Indians of the Great Plains depended on the buffalo for food, clothing, and tools. Because of the importance of the buffalo in their lives, they did not encourage whites to slaughter the buffalo. See pages 454–455.

    b.   No. Since animal diseases such as anthrax and brucellosis were brought into the Plains by white-owned livestock, whites did not slaughter the buffalo to prevent the spread of such diseases to sheep and goat herds. Of course, these animal diseases spread to the buffalo and caused many to die. See pages 454–455.

    d.   No. The process that led to the virtual extinction of the buffalo began before whites began to slaughter the buffalo in the late 1800s. See pages 454–455.

3. a.   Correct. The subsistence culture of the Northwestern Indians was centered on salmon. Therefore, the decline of the salmon population, due to the actions of white commercial fishermen and canneries, undermined the subsistence culture of Northwestern Indians. See page 455.

    b.   No. The Northwestern Indians were not affected by the slaughter of the buffalo because the buffalo was not important to their subsistence. See page 455.

    c.   No. Lack of irrigation facilities did not undermine the subsistence culture of Northwestern Indians. See page 455.

    d.   No. Animal diseases were not an important factor in the undermining of the subsistence culture of Northwestern Indians. See page 455.

4. c.   Correct. White settlers to the Great Plains in the 1870s and 1880s held white-racist and white-superiority beliefs and tended to see Indians as "barbarians." As a result, these white settlers generally assumed that they had a right to settle wherever they pleased. See pages 455–456.

    a.   No. White settlers to the Great Plains did not assume that the federal government would bar African American workers from settling in that area. See pages 455–456.

    b.   No. White settlers who moved into the Great Plains in the 1870s and 1880s generally carried with them the ethnocentric frame of reference of the age. Those settlers assumed that there would be equality of opportunity among white males; but, because of their prejudices against nonwhites, they did not apply that concept to other ethnic groups. See pages 455–456.

    d.   No. White settlers to the Great Plain in the 1870s and 1880s had little or no concern for Indian cultures and did not generally believe that they had to respect the land rights of Native Americans. See pages 455–456.

5. a.   Correct. The reservation policy was designed to "civilize" the Indian tribes. Three major problems characterized the policy: (1) the Indians had no say over their own affairs; (2) it was impossible to keep reservations isolated; and (3) the government disregarded variations among tribes. See pages 456–457.

    b.   No. Many Indians, in order to preserve their own culture, resisted involvement in a market economy. Furthermore, the trade relationships that emerged were generally imposed on the Indians, were beneficial to whites, and made Indians more dependent on whites. See pages 456–457.

    c.   No. Under the reservation policy, the government, in an effort to engage the Indians more completely in the market economy, promised to provide natives with food, clothing, and necessities. As Indians concentrated on producing trade items demanded by whites, many were forced to give up crop production. See pages 456–457.

    d.   No. Although the government, through the reservation policy, promised the Indians protection from white encroachment, in the long run it was impossible to keep the reservations isolated. Therefore, since whites continued to seek Indian land for their own purposes, they continued to encroach on that land. See pages 456–457.

6.   c.   Correct. The Dawes Act attempted to "civilize" western Indians by dissolving tribal, or community-owned, lands and dividing this land among individual families. The policy was ineffective, was misused by whites, and was abandoned. See page 458.

a.   No. A boarding-school program was established by the Dawes Severalty Act in an attempt to "civilize" Indian children. However, most Indian children educated in such schools did not reject their culture and returned to their reservations. See page 458.

b.   No. Under the Dawes Act the Indian Bureau did establish religious schools among the Indians in an attempt to Christianize them. However, most Indians continued to practice their native religions. See page 458.

d.   No. Indians had no voice in United States Indian policy as established under the Dawes Act and carried out by the Indian Bureau. The United States government assumed a paternalistic attitude and assumed that it knew what was best for Indians. See page 458.

7.   c.   Correct. Corporate interests had the capital necessary for profitable long-term development of these industries and replaced the individual lumberman, prospector, and cowboy. See pages 460–462 and page 475.

a.   No. In the earliest stages of development one sees the individual prospector in relation to the mining frontier, the individual rancher and cowboy in relation to open-range ranching, and, to some extent, the individual timberman. Such individuals did not need large outlays of capital. See pages 460–462 and page 475.

b.   No. Misuse of this act was important in the development of the lumber industry but not in the development of the mining and ranching industries. See pages 460–462 and page 475.

d.   No. Those involved in the development of these frontiers were usually more interested in profit than in conservation or planned use of natural resources. See pages 460–462 and page 475.

8.   b.   Correct. Although there was an ethnic mixture in many of the frontier communities, ethnic minorities such as blacks, Chinese, Mexicans, and Indians experienced abuse as a result of white prejudice. See pages 462–463.

a.   No. Passage of immigration laws in 1881 and 1882 to exclude Chinese immigrants and additional evidence noted on pages 462–463 do not support the conclusion that ethnic minorities were welcomed into the frontier communities.

c.   No. Undoubtedly some opportunities were available to ethnic minorities in the frontier communities, but the evidence does not support the conclusion that "opportunities abounded." See pages 462–463.

d.   No. Blacks, Indians, Mexicans, and Chinese did not usually gain economic or political power in the frontier communities. See pages 462–463.

9. d. Correct. Because of the difficulties posed by the hodgepodge of times throughout the United States, the railroads established four standard time zones for the whole country in 1883. They did so without consulting anyone in government. See pages 468–469.

    a. No. Although some individual railroad companies turned to central business offices to keep track of equipment, freight, rates, and schedules, the railroads did not collectively coordinate all their schedules through a "central clearing house." See pages 468–469.

    b. No. The idea of daylight-saving time was first suggested by the resourceful and pragmatic Benjamin Franklin in the eighteenth century. The railroads did not request government establishment of this in 1883. See pages 468–469.

    c. No. Railroad companies generally accepted the philosophy of laissez-faire capitalism. Therefore, believing that property owners should be free to make their own economic decisions without government interference, the railroads did not ask for the creation of the ICC. See pages 468–469.

10. a. Correct. The railroads were given some 180 million acres of land by the federal government (page 468). Much of this land was used as security for bonds or sold for cash. Ranchers often bought land bordering streams and allowed their cattle to graze on adjacent public domain (page 474).

    b. No. Although farmers became dependent on the railroad for transportation of goods, they bitterly complained about railroad abuses. Many farmers also complained about ranchers who denied them the use of fenced-in pastureland. See pages 468, 474.

    c. No. There is no indication from the evidence given that either the cattle industry or the railroad industry respected the rights and culture of Indians. See pages 468, 474.

    d. No. Both the railroad industry and the cattle industry objected to government regulation. See pages 468, 474.

11. c. Correct. One of the hardships of farm life on the Great Plains was the periodic grasshopper plagues of the 1870s and 1880s. See page 470.

    a. No. The Great Plains is characterized by climatic extremes. See page 470.

    b. No. Because of the absence of timber in the Great Plains, many farm families had to build their houses of sod and use buffalo and cow chips for fuel. See page 470.

    d. No. Although rainfall in the Plains was unpredictable and often inadequate during the fall and summer, the area was often plagued by flooding during March and April. These characteristics are not descriptive of a desert area. See page 470.

12. d.   Correct. Settlers acquired 160-acre rectangular plots of land under the Homestead Act if they agreed to live on and improve the land. This restriction prevented European-style villages from emerging and led to social isolation. See pages 470–471.

a.   No. Plains settlers were not so much in competition with each other as with their environment. At any rate, a competitive frontier spirit was not the cause of social isolation on the Plains. See pages 470–471.

b.   No. A plain is by definition an area of flat, level land. Therefore, the Great Plains region of the United States is not an area in which travel is difficult because of "rugged terrain." See pages 470–471.

c.   No. The authors of the text state that increased use of farm machinery made conquering the Plains possible. Therefore, farm machinery was widely used in the Great Plains. See pages 470–471.

13. d.   Correct. The availability of RFD after 1896 meant farmers could receive letters, newspapers, advertisements, and catalogues at home on a daily basis. See pages 471–472.

a.   No. Railroad expansion in the late nineteenth century linked farmers of the Great Plains with an international marketplace, but the railroad did not relieve the loneliness of farm life. See pages 471–472.

b.   No. Commercial radio broadcasts did not begin until 1920. In addition, most rural areas did not have electricity until the 1940s. See pages 471–472.

c.   No. Since the majority of farm families did not have electricity until the 1940s, the telegraph did not lessen farm isolation in the late nineteenth century. See pages 471–472.

14. a.   Correct. Machines, increasing productivity and reducing the time and cost of farming various crops, made the extension of the farming frontier possible. See pages 472–473.

b.   No. Truly effective and selective pesticides were not used on a wide scale until the mid-twentieth century. See pages 472–473.

c.   No. Although scientists in the nineteenth century began to identify the nutrients necessary for plant growth, commercial fertilizers did not become widely available until the twentieth century. See pages 472–473.

d.   No. Extensive use of migrant labor did not make the extension of the farming frontier possible. See pages 472–473.

15. b.   Correct. The Hatch Act of 1887 provided for agricultural experiment stations in every state, thus encouraging the advancement of farming technology. See page 473.

a.   No. Carver worked as a botanist and an instructor at Tuskegee Institute from 1896 until his death in 1943. His agricultural research was not subsidized by the federal government. See page 473.

c.   No. Luther Burbank, noted plant breeder and horticulturist, never headed the research division of the Department of Agriculture. See page 473.

d.   No. The federal government did not fund a vast irrigation network in the Great Plains. See page 473.

CHAPTER 18

The Machine Age, 1877–1920

LEARNING OBJECTIVES

After you have studied Chapter 18 in your textbook and worked through this study guide chapter, you should be able to:

1. Cite the technological advances that furthered the process of industrialization in the United States.

2. Discuss the specific innovations and contributions of Thomas Alva Edison, Henry Ford, and the du Ponts to the process of industrialization in the United States; and examine the political, social and economic consequences of those innovations and contributions.

3. Discuss the impact of technology on the development of southern industry.

4. Explain and assess the late-nineteenth-century obsession with time studies and scientific management.

5. Discuss late-nineteenth-century changes in the nature of work, in working conditions, and in the workplace itself, and explain the impact of these changes on American workers.

6. Examine the rise of unionism and the emergence of worker activism in the late nineteenth century, and discuss the reaction of employers, government, and the public to these manifestations of worker discontent.

7. Examine the position of women, children, immigrants, and blacks in the work force and in the union movement in the late nineteenth century.

8. Explain the emergence of the consumer society, and discuss the factors that determined the extent to which working-class Americans were able to participate in this society.

9. Discuss the impact of scientific developments and education on living standards between 1900 and 1920.

10. Discuss the impact of each of the following on American attitudes and lifestyles:

    a. The indoor toilet

    b. Processed and preserved foods

    c. The sewing machine

    d. Department stores and chain stores

11. Explain the characteristics of modern advertising and examine its role in industrial America.

12. Examine the corporate consolidation movement of the late nineteenth century, and discuss the consequences of this movement.

13. Explain and evaluate the ideologies of Social Darwinism, laissez-faire capitalism, and the Gospel of Wealth. Explain the impact of these ideas on workers and on the role of government in society.

14. Discuss and evaluate the ideas and suggested reforms of those who dissented from the ideologies of the Gospel of Wealth, Social Darwinism, and laissez-faire capitalism.

15. Discuss the response of all branches of government at the state and national levels to the corporate consolidation movement on the one hand and to the grievances of workers on the other hand.

THEMATIC GUIDE

The theme of Chapter 18 is industrialization as a major component of American expansion in the late nineteenth century. Three technological developments that fostered the "second" industrial revolution of the late nineteenth and early twentieth centuries are mentioned in the chapter's introduction (the rise of electric-powered machines; the expanded use of engines powered by internal combustion; and new applications in the use of chemicals). The relationship between these three developments and industrialization is obvious in the discussion of Thomas A. Edison and the electric industry, Henry Ford and the automobile industry, the du Ponts and the chemical industry, and the influence of technology on certain industries in the South. Keep these developments in mind as you study the chapter, and try to determine which developments apply to the various topics discussed in the chapter.

Industrialism changed the nature of work and in many respects caused an uneven distribution of power among interest groups in American society. Industrial workers were employees rather than producers, and repeating specialized tasks made them feel like appendages to machines. The emphasis on quantity rather than quality further dehumanized the workplace. These factors, in addition to the increased power of the employer, reduced the independence and self-respect of workers, but worker resistance only led employers to tighten restrictions.

Industrialism also brought more women and children into the labor force. Although job opportunities opened for women, most women went into low-paying clerical jobs, and sex discrimination continued in the workplace. Employers also attempted to cut wage costs by hiring more children. Although a few states passed child-labor laws, such laws were difficult to enforce and employers generally opposed state interference in their hiring practices. Effective child-labor legislation would not come until the twentieth century.

As the nature of work changed, workers began to protest low wages, the attitude of employers, the hazards of the workplace, and the absence of disability insurance and pensions. The effectiveness of legislation designed to redress these grievances was usually limited by conservative Supreme Court rulings. Out of frustration, some workers began to participate in unions and in organized resistance. Unionization efforts took various directions. The Knights of Labor tried to ally all workers by creating producer and consumer cooperatives; the American Federation of Labor strove to organize skilled workers to achieve pragmatic objectives; and the Industrial Workers of the World attempted to overthrow capitalist society. The railroad strikes of 1877, the Haymarket riot, and the Homestead and Pullman strikes were all marked by violence, and they exemplify labor's frustration as well as its active and organized resistance. Government intervention against the strikers convinced many workers of the imbalance of interest groups in American society, whereas the middle class began to connect organized working-class resistance with radicalism. Although this perception was by and large mistaken, middle-class fear of social upheaval became an additional force against organized labor.

Not only did industrialization affect the nature of work, it also produced a myriad of products that affected the everyday lives of Americans. As America became a consumer-oriented society, most of its citizens faced living costs that rose faster than wages. Consequently, many people could not take advantage of the new goods and services being offered. But, as has been seen, more women and children became part of the paid labor force. Although many did so out of necessity, others hoped that the additional income would allow the family to participate in the consumer society.

Increased availability of goods and services to a greater number of people was not the only reason for a general improvement in living standards. The era also witnessed advances in medical care, better diets, and improved living conditions. Furthermore, education, more than ever a means to upward mobility, became more readily available through the spread of public education.

American habits and attitudes were further affected by the democratization of convenience that resulted from the indoor toilet and private bathtub. At the same time, the tin can and the icebox altered lifestyles and diet, the sewing machine created a clothing revolution, and department stores and chain stores emerged that both created and served the new consumerism.

As American society became more consumer oriented, brand names for products were created. Used by advertisers to sell products, these brand names in turn created "consumption communities" made up of individuals loyal to those brands. As producers tried to convince consumers of their need for particular products, advertising became more important than ever. And since the major vehicle for advertising in the late nineteenth century was the newspaper, advertising was transformed into news.

Although the American standard of living generally improved during the late nineteenth century, there were unsettling economic forces at work. Although rapid economic growth is a characteristic of the period, the period is also characterized by the economic instability and uncertainty produced by cycles of boom and bust. In an effort to create a sense of order and stability out of the competitive chaos, industrialists turned to economic concentration in the form of pools, trusts, and holding companies. Therefore, the search for order led to the merger movement and to larger and larger combinations that sought domination of their markets through vertical integration.

Defenders of business justified the merger movement and the pursuit of wealth and profits by advancing the "Gospel of Wealth," which was based on Social Darwinism and on the precepts of laissez-faire capitalism. The business elite also used this philosophy to justify both its paternalistic attitude toward the less fortunate in society and its advocacy of government aid to business. The paradoxes and inconsistencies associated with the Gospel of Wealth gave rise to dissent from sociologists, economists, and reformers. The general public also began to speak against economic concentration in the form of monopolies and trusts. The inability of state governments to resolve the problems associated with economic concentration led to passage of the Sherman Anti-Trust Act by Congress in 1890, but this legislation represented a vaguely worded political compromise, the interpretation of which was left to the courts. Narrow interpretation by a conservative Supreme Court and failure by government officials to fully support the act meant that it was used more successfully against organized labor than against business combinations, again illustrating the uneven distribution of power among interest groups in late-nineteenth-century American society.

BUILDING VOCABULARY

Listed below are important words and terms that you need to know to get the most out of Chapter 18. They are listed in the order in which they occur in the chapter. After carefully looking through the list, (1) underline the words with which you are totally unfamiliar, (2) put a question mark by those words of which you are unsure, and (3) leave the rest alone.

As you begin to read the chapter, when you come to any of the words you've put question marks beside or underlined (1) slow your reading; (2) focus on the word and on its context in the sentence you're reading; (3) if you can understand the meaning of the word from its context in the sentence or passage in which it is used, go on with your reading; (4) if it's a word that you've underlined or a word that you can't understand from its context in the sentence or passage, look it up in a dictionary and write down the definition that best applies to the context in which the word is used.

Definitions

tedious _____

incandescent _____

filament _____

publicist _____

entrepreneur _____

entice _____

squelch _____

facilitate _____

integral _____

temperance _____

debauchery _____

docile _____

menial _____

pervade _____

induce _____

maim _____

acute _____

notorious _____

remonstrate _____

liability _____

rationale _____

carnage _____

portend _____

spontaneous _____

anarchist _____

malicious _____

pragmatic _____

autonomy _____

dictum _____

rout _____

paternalistic _____

catechize _____

charismatic _____

arbitration _____

ostensibly _____

espouse _____

rhetoric _____

myriad _____

scourge _____

amenity _____

inequity _____

vanguard _____

relegate _____

compensate _____

tentative _____

exemplify _____

mammoth _____

wield _____

extol _____

inception _____

emanate _____

ardent _____

eclipse (verb) _____

profiteering _____

consign _____

consumerism _____

Difficult-to-Spell Names and Terms from Reading and Lecture

IDENTIFICATION AND SIGNIFICANCE

After studying Chapter 18 of *A People and a Nation*, you should be able to identify fully *and* explain the historical significance of each item listed below.

- Identify each item in the space provided. Give an explanation or description of the item. Answer the questions *who, what, where,* and *when.*

- Explain the historical significance of each item in the space provided. Establish the historical context in which the item exists. Establish the item as the result of or as the cause of other factors existing in the society under study. Answer this question: *What were the political, social, economic, and/or cultural consequences of this item?*

1. Thomas A. Edison

    a. Identification

    b. Significance

2. Menlo Park

    a. Identification

    b. Significance

3. the patent system

    a. Identification

    b. Significance

4. the Edison Electric Light Company

    a. Identification

    b. Significance

5. George Westinghouse

    a. Identification

    b. Significance

6. Samuel Insull

    a. Identification

    b. Significance

7. the General Electric Company

    a. Identification

    b. Significance

8. Granville T. Woods

    a. Identification

    b. Significance

9. Henry Ford

    a. Identification

    b. Significance

10. mass production and the assembly line

    a. Identification

    b. Significance

11. the Five-Dollar-Day Plan

    a. Identification

    b. Significance

12. the du Pont family

    a. Identification

    b. Significance

13. James B. Duke

    a. Identification

    b. Significance

14. southern textile mills

    a. Identification

    b. Significance

15. economies of scale

    a.   Identification

    b.   Significance

16. Frederick W. Taylor

    a.   Identification

    b.   Significance

17. producer versus employee

    a.   Identification

    b.   Significance

18. the occupational patterns of employed women

    a.   Identification

    b.   Significance

19. child labor

    a.   Identification

    b.   Significance

20. industrial accidents

    a. Identification

    b. Significance

21. New York City's Triangle Shirtwaist Company fire

    a. Identification

    b. Significance

22. the "iron law of wages"

    a. Identification

    b. Significance

23. *Holden v. Hardy*

    a. Identification

    b. Significance

24. *Lockner v. New York*

    a. Identification

    b. Significance

25. *Muller v. Oregon*

    a.   Identification

    b.   Significance

26. the general railway strike of 1877

    a.   Identification

    b.   Significance

27. the National Labor Union

    a.   Identification

    b.   Significance

28. the Knights of Labor

    a.   Identification

    b.   Significance

29. Terence V. Powderly

    a.   Identification

    b.   Significance

30. the Southwestern Railroad System Strike of 1886

    a. Identification

    b. Significance

31. the Haymarket riot

    a. Identification

    b. Significance

32. John P. Altgeld

    a. Identification

    b. Significance

33. the American Federation of Labor

    a. Identification

    b. Significance

34. Samuel Gompers

    a. Identification

    b. Significance

35. the Homestead strike

    a.   Identification

    b.   Significance

36. the Pullman strike

    a.   Identification

    b.   Significance

37. Eugene V. Debs

    a.   Identification

    b.   Significance

38. the Industrial Workers of the World

    a.   Identification

    b.   Significance

39. "Mother" Jones, Elizabeth Gurley Flynn, and William D. (Big Bill) Haywood

    a.   Identification

    b.   Significance

40. the "Uprising of the 20,000"

    a. Identification

    b. Significance

41. the Telephone Operators' Department of the International Brotherhood of Electrical Workers

    a. Identification

    b. Significance

42. the Women's Trade Union League

    a. Identification

    b. Significance

43. fraternal societies

    a. Identification

    b. Significance

44. consumer communities

    a. Identification

    b. Significance

45. public high school enrollment
    a. Identification

    b. Significance

46. the indoor toilet
    a. Identification

    b. Significance

47. the tin can
    a. Identification

    b. Significance

48. railroad refrigerator cars
    a. Identification

    b. Significance

49. the home icebox
    a. Identification

    b. Significance

50. John H. Kellogg, William K. Kellogg, and Charles W. Post
    a. Identification

    b. Significance

51. the sewing machine
    a. Identification

    b. Significance

52. department stores and chain stores
    a. Identification

    b. Significance

53. the Great Atlantic and Pacific Tea Company
    a. Identification

    b. Significance

54. modern advertising
    a. Identification

    b. Significance

55. consumption communities

    a. Identification

    b. Significance

56. brand names

    a. Identification

    b. Significance

57. boom and bust business cycles

    a. Identification

    b. Significance

58. pools

    a. Identification

    b. Significance

59. John D. Rockefeller

    a. Identification

    b. Significance

60. the trust

    a.   Identification

    b.   Significance

61. the holding company

    a.   Identification

    b.   Significance

62. vertical integration

    a.   Identification

    b.   Significance

63. the merger movement

    a.   Identification

    b.   Significance

64. the U.S. Steel Corporation

    a.   Identification

    b.   Significance

65. Social Darwinism

    a.   Identification

    b.   Significance

66. the principles of laissez faire

    a.   Identification

    b.   Significance

67. the Gospel of Wealth

    a.   Identification

    b.   Significance

68. protective tariffs

    a.   Identification

    b.   Significance

69. Lester Ward

    a.   Identification

    b.   Significance

70. Richard Ely, John R. Commons, and Edward Bemis

    a.   Identification

    b.   Significance

71. Henry George

    a.   Identification

    b.   Significance

72. Edward Bellamy

    a.   Identification

    b.   Significance

73. the Sherman Anti-Trust Act

    a.   Identification

    b.   Significance

74. *United States v. E. C. Knight Co.*

    a.   Identification

    b.   Significance

ORGANIZING, REVIEWING, AND USING INFORMATION

Chart A

Worker Activism in the Machine Age, 1877–1920			
	Haymarket Riot 1886	**Railroad Strikes (widespread) 1877**	**Railroad Strike (Southwest) 1886**	**Pullman Strike 1893**
Immediate Cause(s)				
Unions and Union Leaders Involved				
Workers' Demands				
Workers' Tactics				
Employers' Reactions				
Government Involvement (State or Federal)				
Public Reaction and Its Causes				
Outcome				

Chart B

Quality of Life in the Machine Age			
Kind or Indicator of Change	**Change (from 1877 to 1920)**	**Causes of Change, Factors**	**Effects of Change**
Family Income			
Cost of Living			
Access to Consumer Goods and Conveniences			
Class Mobility			
Privacy			

Chart C

The Merger Movement in the Machine Age, 1877–1920			
New or Revamped Forms of Business Organizations	Advantages Sought	Reactions of Governments and Courts and Their Results	Effects on Consumers and the General Population
CORPORATIONS *Definition*			
POOLS *Definition*			
TRUSTS *Definition*			
HOLDING COMPANIES *Definition*			

IDEAS AND DETAILS

Objective 2

1. Which of the following innovations by Henry Ford reduced the cost of his automobiles and made them more affordable?

    a.   Interchangeable parts
    b.   The machine-tool industry
    c.   The assembly line
    d.   Team production

Objective 4

2. The emphasis on efficient production had the effect of

    a.   making skilled labor more valuable.
    b.   lowering the wage scale for most workers.
    c.   increasing the size of the work force.
    d.   making time as important as quality in the measure of acceptable work.

Objectives 5 and 6

3. In relation to the wage system, most wage earners

    a.   appreciated the freedom it gave them to negotiate with the employer for higher wages.
    b.   recognized that job competition among workers caused the base pay of all workers to rise steadily.
    c.   advocated that Congress establish a minimum wage for all workers.
    d.   felt trapped and exploited in a system controlled by employers.

Objectives 6 and 15

4. In cases involving legislation that limited working hours, the Supreme Court

    a.   declared that Congress, not the states, had the power to enact such legislation.
    b.   declared that the Fourteenth Amendment did not apply to state actions.
    c.   reduced the impact of such legislation by narrowly interpreting which jobs were dangerous and which workers needed protection.
    d.   consistently upheld the regulatory powers of the states.

Objectives 6 and 7

5. The Knights of Labor, unlike the American Federation of Labor,

    a.   advocated the use of violence against corporate power.
    b.   pressed for pragmatic objectives that would bring immediate benefits to workers.
    c.   believed in using strikes as the primary weapon against employers.
    d.   welcomed all workers, including women, blacks, and immigrants.

Objective 6

6.   Which of the following was a consequence of the Haymarket riot?

   a.   National legislation was passed mandating an eight-hour workday for industry in the United States.

   b.   The military forces of the United States were put on alert because of fear of revolution.

   c.   Revival of the middle-class fear of radicalism led to the strengthening of police forces and armories in many cities.

   d.   The Knights of Labor was strengthened.

Objectives 6 and 7

7.   Which of the following is true of the Women's Trade Union League?

   a.   Although initially dominated by middle-class women, working-class leaders gained control in the 1910s.

   b.   Although its members opposed the idea, its leaders actively worked for a constitutional amendment guaranteeing equal rights to women.

   c.   Both its leaders and its members worked tirelessly against extension of the vote to women.

   d.   As an anarchist organization, it advocated working-class unity and the waging of war against capitalist society.

Objective 8

8.   Data on wages and living costs in the late nineteenth and early twentieth centuries indicate which of the following?

   a.   Most working-class wage earners suffered because of declining wages and increasing living costs.

   b.   While wages rose for farmers and factory workers, they declined for most members of the middle class.

   c.   While incomes rose for most workers, the cost of living usually rose at a higher rate.

   d.   Professional workers suffered more from the rising cost of living than did industrial workers.

Objective 10

9.   As a result of the indoor bathroom, Americans of the late nineteenth and early twentieth centuries

   a.   became conscious of personal appearance for the first time.

   b.   viewed bodily functions in a more unpleasant light.

   c.   insisted on private facilities in hotels.

   d.   were unconcerned about human pollution.

Objectives 8 and 11

10.   The main task of advertisers in a society of abundance is to

   a.   respond to an individual's particular need by offering a product that uniquely fills that need.

   b.   persuade groups of consumers that they have a need for a particular product.

   c.   display products in an attractive way.

   d.   convince the consumer that a particular product is a quality product offered at a fair price.

Objective 12

11. Businessmen turned to devices like trusts and holding companies because

    a.   they were a means by which to combat the uncertainty of the business cycle.
    b.   such cooperative business arrangements were responsive to consumer needs.
    c.   they allowed business owners to concentrate on quality production while financial specialists handled monetary matters.
    d.   they encouraged an open market in which many people had economic opportunity.

Objective 13

12. Social Darwinists believed that in a free society run in accordance with natural law

    a.   there would be no poverty.
    b.   power would flow into the hands of the most capable people.
    c.   wealth would be distributed equally.
    d.   people would become less aggressive.

Objective 13

13. The philosophy accepted by most businessmen in the late nineteenth century included the idea that

    a.   government could intervene if it were doing so to protect the disadvantaged.
    b.   government power could rightly be used to protect consumers from unfair prices.
    c.   government should extend a helping hand to workers by encouraging the development of labor organizations.
    d.   government should extend a helping hand to business interests through tariff protection.

Objective 14

14. Lester Ward expressed the belief that

    a.   cooperative action and government intervention could be useful in creating a better society.
    b.   business forms, like life forms, evolved from the simple to the complex as part of the natural order of things.
    c.   tampering with natural economic laws would lead to economic disaster.
    d.   the government had no responsibility in society other than national defense.

Objective 15

15. In the case of *United States v. E. C. Knight Co.*, the Supreme Court

    a.   held all trusts to be illegal.
    b.   strengthened the powers of the Interstate Commerce Commission.
    c.   reduced the government's power under the Sherman Anti-Trust Act to combat combinations in restraint of trade.
    d.   held that workers had the right to organize and strike.

ESSAY QUESTIONS

Objectives 5 and 6

1. Discuss the grievances of workers in the late nineteenth century, the means by which they sought redress and the effectiveness of those means.

Objectives 5, 6, and 15

2. Discuss the Haymarket riot, the Homestead strike, and the Pullman strike. Explain the reaction of the government and the public to these instances of labor unrest.

Objective 7

3. Examine the changing position of women in the labor market in the late nineteenth century.

Objectives 9 and 10

4. Indicate the developments that made the indoor bathroom possible, and discuss its impact on American attitudes and life styles.

Objective 11

5. Explain changes that took place in advertising in American society in the late nineteenth and early twentieth centuries, and discuss the impact of these changes on American society.

Objective 13

6. Explain the concept of Social Darwinism and its use by business leaders to justify their position and wealth in society.

Objectives 13 and 15

7. Analyze the relationship between the three branches of the federal government and the business community in the period between 1877 and 1920.

ANSWERS

Multiple-Choice Questions

1.   c.   Correct. When the Ford Motor Company began operation in 1903, it utilized mass production and, through use of the electric conveyor belt, introduced the moving assembly line at its Highland Park plant in 1913. This drastically reduced the time and cost of producing cars. See pages 482–483.

a.   No. The use of precision machinery to make interchangeable parts was first seen as part of the "American system of manufacturing" during the first half of the nineteenth century. Therefore, the manufacture and use of interchangeable parts was well established long before the Ford Motor Company began operation in 1903. See pages 482–483.

b.   No. The machine-tool industry—the mass manufacture of specialized machines for various industries—was born in the 1820s, long before the Ford Motor Company opened for operation in 1903. See pages 482–483.

d.   No. Team production suggests that a team of workers is responsible for making and assembling the entire automobile. The Ford Motor Company was not organized in this way when it began operation in 1903. See pages 482–483.

2.   d.   Correct. Systems of efficiency, such as those espoused by Frederick Taylor, equated time with money. As a result, the time taken to perform specific tasks became as important as the quality of the end product. See page 487.

a.   No. To increase efficiency in the work place, work was divided into specific tasks. A worker could then specialize in the repetitious performance of a given task in as little time as possible. Such a process does not increase the value of skilled labor. See page 487.

b.   No. Efficiency in the production of a product can lead to decreased production costs, higher profits, and higher wages. See page 487.

c.   No. In many cases efficiency in production leads to a reduction in the work force. For example, after studying the shoveling of ore, Frederick Taylor designed fifteen different shovels and outlined the proper motions for using each. As a result, a work force of 600 was reduced to 140. See page 487.

3.   d.   Correct. Many employers of the late nineteenth century believed in the "iron law of wages." In other words, they believed that labor is sold in the marketplace and, like any other commodity, its price (wages in this case) should be dictated by the law of supply and demand. It was further held that if workers are paid unnaturally high wages they will simply be able to support more children. That, in turn, will lead to an increase in the supply of workers and to more unemployment. Therefore, many employers held that they were actually doing workers a favor by keeping wages at a low level, in accordance with the "natural" economic law of supply and demand. In such a system, most wage earners felt trapped and exploited in a system controlled by employers. See pages 490–491.

     a.   No. Many workers of the late nineteenth century were very dissatisfied with the wage system because they believed it was weighted in favor of the employer. Theoretically the wage system was based on the idea that workers were free to negotiate with the employer for the highest wages possible. However, this theory was based on the worker and the employer having equal power in such negotiations. In fact, this was not true and many workers felt at the mercy of employers. See pages 490–491.

     b.   No. Competition for jobs among workers did not cause the base pay of all workers to rise steadily during the late nineteenth century, and most wage earners did not see the wage system in this way. See pages 490–491.

     c.   No. Although some forward-looking thinkers of the late nineteenth century may have believed that Congress should establish a minimum wage, such a concept was beyond the frame of reference of most workers of the era. See pages 490–491.

4.   c.   Correct. The Court's decisions in the Holden, Lochner, and Muller cases demonstrated a narrow interpretation of what constituted a dangerous job and, therefore, of which workers needed protection. See page 491.

     a.   No. This was not a distinction made by the Court in cases involving limitations on working hours. See page 491.

     b.   No. In striking down a maximum-hours law for bakers, the Court in Lochner v. New York held that the law violated the Fourteenth-Amendment guarantee that no state may deprive any person of property (wages) without due process of law. In this way, the Court applied the Fourteenth Amendment to state action. See page 491.

     d.   No. The Lochner v. New York case is evidence that the Court did not always uphold the regulatory powers of the states. See page 491.

5.   d.   Correct. The Knights of Labor welcomed all workers into its ranks, including women, blacks, and immigrants, and including both skilled and unskilled workers. In contrast, the AFL allowed only skilled workers, was openly hostile to women, and often excluded immigrants and blacks. See pages 492–494.

     a.   No. Neither the Knights of Labor nor the American Federation of Labor advocated the use of violence against corporate power. See pages 492–494.

     b.   No. Many of the goals of the Knights of Labor were long range, abstract, and vague. The objectives of the American Federation of Labor, in contrast, were much more specific and pragmatic. See pages 492–494.

     c.   No. The Knights of Labor generally opposed strikes. See pages 492–494.

6.   c.   Correct. As a result of strikes and labor unrest, a sense of crisis existed at the time of the Haymarket riot (May 1886) and increased as a result of the riot. This led to the consequences stated in the choice. See pages 492–493.

a.   No. This answer suggests that Congress was receptive to organized labor and to its demands at the time of the Haymarket riot in 1886. Reread the section on the union movement on pages 492–493.

b.   No. Although the Haymarket riot was falsely identified in the newspapers and in the minds of many people as an "anarchist riot," the government did not respond by putting military forces on alert. See pages 492–493.

d.   No. As a result of its association with the Haymarket riot, the Knights of Labor was weakened rather than strengthened. See pages 492–493.

7.   a.   Correct. Initially, the WTUL was dominated by middle-class as opposed to working-class women. However, this changed in the 1910s. See page 496.

b.   No. The leadership of the WTUL accepted the idea that women needed protection from exploitation. On these grounds it supported protective legislation for women and argued against a constitutional amendment guaranteeing equal rights to women. See page 496.

c.   No. The WTUL worked for women's suffrage. See page 496.

d.   No. The WTUL did join with the Ladies Garment Workers Union in a strike against New York City sweatshops, but it did not advocate a war against capitalist society. Gradually, the union even backed away from active union organization. See page 496.

8.   c.   Correct. Although the income of factory workers, farm laborers and middle-class workers rose in the period from 1890 to 1920, the cost of living rose as well and usually outpaced wage increases. See page 497.

a.   No. The data indicate that the wages of working-class wage earners increased between 1890 and 1920. See page 497.

b.   No. The data indicate that wages increased for farm laborers, factory workers, and middle-class workers. See page 497.

d.   No. We are not given enough data on the income of professionals to determine the rate of increase from 1890 to 1920. We cannot logically infer from the data supplied that inflation caused professionals to suffer more than industrial workers. See page 497.

9.   b.   Correct. Americans began to see bodily functions in a more unpleasant light as a result of two factors: (1) the germ theory of disease, which raised fears about the link between human pollution and water contamination, and (2) the indoor bathroom's association with cleanliness and privacy. See page 498.

a.   No. Most bathrooms have mirrors and mirrors make people conscious of personal appearance, but mirrors were available before indoor bathrooms. See page 498.

c.   No. Although there is a certain amount of truth in this choice, it is important to remember two factors: (1) in the late nineteenth century few Americans could afford to stay in hotels; and (2) there is not sufficient evidence in the text to support this choice. See page 498.

d.   No. The fact that indoor bathrooms became more and more common in American society in the late nineteenth and early twentieth centuries indicates that Americans were concerned about human waste as a source of infection and water contamination. See page 498.

10. b.   Correct. In a society of abundance, supply often outstrips demand. In such a society, it is the task of advertisers to create demand by convincing groups of consumers that they need a particular product. It is in this way that "consumption communities" are created. See pages 500–501.

a.   No. Although that was the task of the traditional salesperson, it is not the task of the advertiser in a society of abundance. See pages 500–501.

c.   No. The task of advertisers goes far beyond simply displaying products in an attractive way. See pages 500–501.

d.   No. Advertisers are not necessarily concerned with the quality of the product with which they are dealing or with the price, except as those factors relate to their primary task. See pages 500–501.

11. a.   Correct. Both centralized management, in the form of trusts, and centralized ownership, in the form of holding companies, were means by which business leaders of the late nineteenth century attempted to deal with the uncertainties of the business cycle. See pages 502–504.

b.   No. Trusts and holding companies were "devices of control" within a particular industry. Businesspeople did not turn to such devices out of a desire to be more responsive to the needs of consumers. See pages 502–504.

c.   No. Trusts and holding companies did not separate the management of production from the management of finances and were not used by businesspeople to achieve that end. See pages 502–504.

d.   No. Trusts, which brought several companies under centralized management, and holding companies, which brought several companies under centralized ownership, did not create a more open market. See pages 502–504.

12. b.   Correct. Social Darwinists believed that human society should be allowed to operate in accordance with natural laws, with "survival of the fittest" being one of those laws. Therefore, they believed, wealth and power would flow into the hands of the "most capable." See page 504.

a.   No. Social Darwinists believed that there would always be people within society who were less "fit" than others. Because of this belief, they argued that poverty would always be present. See page 504.

c.   No. Social Darwinists believed that if natural laws were allowed to operate freely, wealth would continue to be maldistributed. They did not desire, nor did they advocate, an equal distribution of wealth. See page 504.

d.   No. Social Darwinists believed that people are aggressive by nature. Therefore, if natural laws were allowed to operate freely, this aggressiveness would continue to be part of human society. See page 504.

13. d.   Correct. Although business leaders argued against government aid to the disadvantaged, to labor unions, or to consumers, they advocated government aid to business interests in the form of protective tariffs, government loans, and the like. See pages 504–505.

a.   No. Since most businesspeople accepted the ideas of Social Darwinism and laissez-faire conservatism, they believed that extending help to the disadvantaged was beyond the proper sphere of government. See pages 504–505.

b.   No. In accepting the tenets of laissez-faire conservatism, most businesspeople believed that the use of government power to regulate prices would threaten the right of the producer to charge the highest price the market would bear. See pages 504–505.

c.   No. In accepting the tenets of laissez-faire conservatism, most businesspeople stood against organized labor as a threat to the rights of both factory owners and factory workers. See pages 504–505.

14. a.   Correct. Ward challenged the determinism of Social Darwinism by arguing that human beings, unlike other animals, are not at the mercy of natural laws. On the contrary, they can, through cooperative activities, create a better society. See page 505.

b.   No. Lester Ward did not accept the theory, espoused by Social Darwinists, that human institutions and corporate structures are the product of an evolutionary process that follows the dictates of natural law. See page 505.

c.   No. Lester Ward did not accept the idea that a society's economy should be allowed to operate in accordance with natural economic laws, and he rejected the notion that tampering with such laws would have disastrous consequences. See page 505.

d.   No. Lester Ward believed that government, as the agent of the people, could act as a positive force for good in human society. This, he believed, entailed more than merely providing for the national defense. See page 505.

15. c.   Correct. In this case the Court narrowly interpreted Congress's power to regulate interstate commerce by ruling that manufacturing (in this case the refining of sugar) took place within a state and did not fall under congressional control. See page 506.

a.   No. The Court did not declare all trusts to be illegal in this case involving the so-called Sugar Trust. See page 506.

b.   No. The case did not involve the Interstate Commerce Commission, which was established by Congress in 1887 to regulate the rail industry. See page 506.

d.   No. The E. C. Knight Co. case did not deal with organized labor. See page 506.

CHAPTER 19

The Vitality and Turmoil of Urban Life, 1877– 1920

LEARNING OBJECTIVES

After you have studied Chapter 19 in your textbook and worked through this study guide chapter, you should be able to:

1. Examine the factors responsible for the birth of the modern city in late- nineteenth- early-twentieth-century America, and discuss the characteristics associated with the modern city.

2. Examine the factors responsible for urban growth during the late nineteenth century.

3. Discuss the similarities and differences between the immigrants of the period from 1880 to 1920 and previous immigrants.

4. Examine the means by which upward socioeconomic mobility could be achieved in the late nineteenth century, and discuss the extent to which such mobility was possible.

5. Examine the interaction between immigrants of the late nineteenth century and American society, and discuss the changes brought about by this interaction.

6. Discuss the impact of prejudice and discrimination on nonwhite immigrants and nonwhite Americans of the late nineteenth century.

7. Examine the problems associated with American cities of the late nineteenth century, and evaluate the responses to those problems.

8. Examine the impact of engineers on urban America and on home life in the United States from 1877 to 1920.

9. Examine and evaluate the urban political machines and political bosses of the late nineteenth century.

10. Discuss the ideological bases of the urban reform movements of the late nineteenth and early twentieth centuries, and explain the successes and failures of the reformers associated with these movements.

11. Examine household, family, and individual life patterns in American society between 1877 and 1920.

12. Explain the emergence and characteristics of each of the following, and discuss their impact on American society:

    a.   Sports

    b.   Show business

    c.   Motion pictures

    d.   Still pictures and the phonograph

    e.   Popular journalism

13. Define *cultural pluralism*, and discuss its impact on American society.

THEMATIC GUIDE

In Chapter 19, we examine urban growth, the third major theme (along with natural resource development and industrialization) associated with American expansion in the late nineteenth century. Urban industrial development combined with mass transportation and urban growth destroyed the old pedestrian city of the past. The physical expansion of the city attracted industry, capital, and people. By the early 1900s, the modern American city, with its urban sprawl and distinct districts, was clearly taking shape.

Cities grow in three ways: through physical expansion, by natural increase, and through migration and immigration. In the late nineteenth century, immigration from domestic and foreign sources was the most important cause of urban growth, with native whites, foreigners, and African Americans being the three major migrant groups of the period. We consider why these groups moved to the cities, how they differed from and resembled each other, and, in the case of immigrants, how they differed from and resembled earlier immigrants.

American society of the late nineteenth and early twentieth centuries was, even more than today, a transient society. There was constant movement to and from geographic areas and constant movement within urban areas. Migration, in fact, provided one of the two paths to improved opportunity, with occupational change being the second path. Within the context of the discussion of paths to improved opportunity, we dispel certain myths concerning the availability and extent of upward mobility and look at the limiting impact of sexism and racism.

In the late nineteenth and early twentieth centuries, ethnic enclaves or immigrant districts emerged in America's urban areas as migrants and the "new" immigrants poured into the country. Within these districts there was constant cultural interaction between foreign immigrants and American society. Therefore, as is stated in the text: "Rather than yield completely to pressures to assimilate, migrants and immigrants interacted with the urban environment in a complex way that enabled them to retain their identity while also altering both their own outlook and the social structure of cities themselves." At the same time, we find the emergence of multiethnic neighborhoods, called urban borderlands, in such industrial cities as Chicago and Detroit. Some ethnic groups, most notably African Americans, Asian immigrants, and Mexicans met with prejudicial attitudes and discrimination. Overall, however, we find that the city of the late nineteenth century nurtured the cultural diversity that so strongly characterizes modern America.

Rapid urban growth created and then intensified urban problems such as inadequate housing, overcrowding, and intolerable living conditions. This situation led to reforms that strengthened the hand of local government in regulating the construction of housing, but American attitudes toward the profit motive and toward private enterprise placed limits on the reforms enacted.

Although scientific and technological breakthroughs improved urban life, the burden of urban poverty remained. While some reformers began to look to environmental factors to explain poverty, traditional attitudes toward poverty—attitudes that blamed the victim—restricted what most Americans were willing to do to alleviate poverty. Even private agencies insisted on extending aid only to the "worthy poor" and on teaching the moral virtues of thrift and sobriety.

Urban areas also had to contend with crime and violence. Whether crime actually increased or was merely more conspicuous can be debated, but in many cases native whites blamed crime on those they considered to be "outsiders" in American society—foreigners and blacks. The ethnic diversity of the cities, combined with urban overcrowding and uncertain economic conditions, hardened antiforeign and white-racist attitudes and increased the incidence of violence in urban areas. Uneven, sometimes prejudicial, application of laws by law enforcement officials raised questions about the nature of justice, equality, and individual freedom in American society.

As America became a culturally pluralistic society, interest groups often competed for influence and opportunity in the political arena. This competition and the rapidity of change in the urban environment caused confusion. In the midst of this confusion, political machines and political bosses emerged to bring some order out of chaos. Eventually, however, a civic reform movement developed. Most reformers strove for efficiency and focused on structural reform in city government. Some concerned themselves with social reform and with city planning and city design. Whatever the goal, American attitudes limited and undermined these reforms. As noted in the textbook, "urban reform merged idealism with naiveté and insensitivity."

Despite these limiting attitudes, there were technical accomplishments in solving problems such as sanitation, garbage disposal, streetlighting, and bridge and street building. In this respect city engineers, who applied their technical expertise to urban problems, became very important to city governments. Furthermore, engineers also had a tremendous impact on the home life of Americans.

In "Family Life" the focus of the chapter shifts to a discussion of the family in American society and American life. Once distinctions are made between the household and the family, we identify the factors responsible for the high percentage of nuclear families. We also note the varying ways in which households expanded and contracted to meet changing circumstances. Changes in society changed family, as well as individual, lifestyles. Reduction in family size freed adults at an earlier age from the responsibilities of parenthood. Longer life expectancy increased the number of older adults. Childhood and adolescence became more distinct stages of life. As the authors state: "Americans became more conscious of age and peer influence. People's roles in school, in the family, on the job, and in the community came to be determined by age more than by any other characteristic."

The leisure-time revolution brought about by labor-saving devices and by a shortened workweek changed the American way of life. As the average workweek decreased to forty-seven hours by 1910, individuals turned to croquet, bicycling, tennis, and golf as favorite leisure activities. Entertaining the public through spectator sports, the circus, show business, and motion pictures became a profitable business endeavor. Moreover, the mass production of sound and images made possible by the phonograph and the still camera dissolved the uniqueness of experience. Even news was transformed into big business and a mass commodity by the "yellow journalism" tactics of Joseph Pulitzer and William Randolph Hearst.

Mass entertainment and mass culture had a nationalizing effect; however, even though show business provided new opportunities for women, blacks, and immigrants, too often it reinforced prejudicial stereotypes—especially concerning black Americans. Furthermore, in an America that was becoming more culturally diverse, different groups pursued their own form of leisure. This often caused concern on the part of some reformers who tended to label individuals as un-American if their activities did not conform to the Puritan traditions of the nation's past. These reformers wanted to use government to impose their values and lifestyles on immigrant groups. These attempts to create a homogeneous society led to questions concerning the role of government in society and in the life of the individual, questions that are as relevant today as they were in the late nineteenth century.

The cultural pluralism that resulted from the late-nineteenth-century influx of immigrants, African Americans, and native white Americans into expanding cities is one of the dominant characteristics of modern America. This heterogeneity is one of America's greatest strengths and has created the richness and the variety that is modern America. In large measure, this diversity is also a reason for the failure of attempts to enforce homogeneity, because the very presence of a number of competing cultural groups prevented any one group from becoming dominant. This has meant, overall, the continued protection of individual rights and the gradual inclusion of more and more groups under the protective umbrella of the Bill of Rights.

BUILDING VOCABULARY

Listed below are important words and terms that you need to know to get the most out of Chapter 19. They are listed in the order in which they occur in the chapter. After carefully looking through the list, (1) underline the words with which you are totally unfamiliar, (2) put a question mark by those words of which you are unsure, and (3) leave the rest alone.

As you begin to read the chapter, when you come to any of the words you've put question marks beside or underlined (1) slow your reading; (2) focus on the word and on its context in the sentence you're reading; (3) if you can understand the meaning of the word from its context in the sentence or passage in which it is used, go on with your reading; (4) if it's a word that you've underlined or a word that you can't understand from its context in the sentence or passage, look it up in a dictionary and write down the definition that best applies to the context in which the word is used.

Definitions

travail _____

inception _____

disquieting _____

mercantile _____

centrifugal _____

centripetal _____

facilitate _____

prima donna _____

burgeon _____

induce _____

transience _____

demeaning _____

extort _____

intersperse _____

foment _____

covenant _____

amulet _____

repertoire _____

accede _____

minimal _____

epitomize _____

erratic _____

indigence _____

rationalize _____

disparate _____

notoriety _____

desperado _____

unsavory _____

median _____

resilient _____

enmesh _____

pneumatic _____

scruple _____

demure _____

titillate _____

pander _____

foible _____

whet _____

potentate _____

sordid _____

muckraking _____

homogenizing _____

apolitical _____

Difficult-to-Spell Names and Terms from Reading and Lecture

IDENTIFICATION AND SIGNIFICANCE

After studying Chapter 19 of *A People and a Nation,* you should be able to identify fully *and* explain the historical significance of each item listed below.

- Identify each item in the space provided. Give an explanation or description of the item. Answer the questions *who, what, where,* and *when.*

- Explain the historical significance of each item in the space provided. Establish the historical context in which the item exists. Establish the item as the result of or as the cause of other factors existing in the society under study. Answer this question: *What were the political, social, economic, and/or cultural consequences of this item?*

1. product specialization

    a. Identification

    b. Significance

2. the electric trolley

    a. Identification

    b. Significance

3. the electric interurban railway

    a. Identification

    b. Significance

4. urban growth

    a. Identification

    b. Significance

5. African American migration
   a. Identification

   b. Significance

6. the "new" immigration
   a. Identification

   b. Significance

7. residential mobility
   a. Identification

   b. Significance

8. occupational mobility
   a. Identification

   b. Significance

9. acquisition of property
   a. Identification

   b. Significance

10. urban borderlands
    a. Identification

    b. Significance

11. ghettos
    a. Identification

    b. Significance

12. Denis Kearney
    a. Identification

    b. Significance

13. Chinese Exclusion Act
    a. Identification

    b. Significance

14. Geary Act
    a. Identification

    b. Significance

15. *barrios*
    a.   Identification

    b.   Significance

16. Conservative Judaism
    a.   Identification

    b.   Significance

17. New York State tenement legislation
    a.   Identification

    b.   Significance

18. "model tenements"
    a.   Identification

    b.   Significance

19. public health regulations
    a.   Identification

    b.   Significance

20. steel-frame construction

    a.   Identification

    b.   Significance

21. urban poverty

    a.   Identification

    b.   Significance

22. Charity Organization Societies

    a.   Identification

    b.   Significance

23. Rufus Minor

    a.   Identification

    b.   Significance

24. urban crime and violence

    a.   Identification

    b.   Significance

25. the East St. Louis riot of 1917

    a.   Identification

    b.   Significance

26. city engineers

    a.   Identification

    b.   Significance

27. professional law enforcement

    a.   Identification

    b.   Significance

28. political machines

    a.   Identification

    b.   Significance

29. the political boss

    a.   Identification

    b.   Significance

30. the urban reform movement

    a. Identification

    b. Significance

31. Mayors Hazen Pingree, Samuel Jones, and Tom Johnson

    a. Identification

    b. Significance

32. social reformers

    a. Identification

    b. Significance

33. the settlement house

    a. Identification

    b. Significance

34. Jane Hunter and Modjeska Simkins

    a. Identification

    b. Significance

35. the City Beautiful movement

    a. Identification

    b. Significance

36. family and household structures in late-nineteenth- and early-twentieth-century America

    a. Identification

    b. Significance

37. the birthrate decline

    a. Identification

    b. Significance

38. the practice of boarding

    a. Identification

    b. Significance

39. the importance of kinship

    a. Identification

    b. Significance

40. the gay subculture

    a. Identification

    b. Significance

41. the stages of life

    a. Identification

    b. Significance

42. board games

    a. Identification

    b. Significance

43. baseball, croquet, bicycling, tennis, golf, college football, and basketball

    a. Identification

    b. Significance

44. Intercollegiate Athletic Association

    a. Identification

    b. Significance

45. the circus

    a. Identification

    b. Significance

46. popular drama

    a. Identification

    b. Significance

47. musical comedies

    a. Identification

    b. Significance

48. George M. Cohan

    a. Identification

    b. Significance

49. vaudeville

    a. Identification

    b. Significance

50. Eva Tanguay

    a. Identification

    b. Significance

51. the minstrel show

    a. Identification

    b. Significance

52. Burt Williams

    a. Identification

    b. Significance

53. motion pictures

    a. Identification

    b. Significance

54. *Birth of a Nation*

    a. Identification

    b. Significance

55. the still camera

    a.   Identification

    b.   Significance

56. the phonograph

    a.   Identification

    b.   Significance

57. Joseph Pulitzer and William Randolph Hearst

    a.   Identification

    b.   Significance

58. yellow journalism

    a.   Identification

    b.   Significance

59. mass-circulation magazines

    a.   Identification

    b.   Significance

60. the telephone

    a. Identification

    b. Significance

61. cultural pluralism

    a. Identification

    b. Significance

ORGANIZING, REVIEWING, AND USING INFORMATION

Kinds of Help Available for the Urban Poor (and Their Drawbacks), 1877–1920					
Supplier of Help	**Problem Areas Addressed**				
	Employment	**Housing**	**Health, Safety, and Security**	**Social Life and Attitudes**	**Other**
Family					
Community, Ethnic group					
Private Charities					
Political Figures, Political Organizations					
Social Reformers					
Technologists, Technological Advances					
Entertainers and Publications					

IDEAS AND DETAILS

Objective 1

1. Which of the following was the primary agent in making suburban life practical and possible?

    a. Long-term mortgage financing
    b. The automobile
    c. Neighborhood shopping centers
    d. Mechanized mass transit

Objective 2

2. Which of the following was the major contributor to urban population growth in late-nineteenth- and early-twentieth-century America?

    a. Natural increase
    b. Mergers
    c. Migration and immigration
    d. Annexation of outlying areas

Objective 6

3. Black migrants to urban areas differed from other migrants in which of the following ways?

    a. Black migrants were more likely to be males.
    b. Blacks did not have the rural background of most other migrants.
    c. Blacks found it more difficult to get factory employment.
    d. Black migrants did not usually move for economic reasons.

Objective 3

4. "New" immigrants differed from "old" immigrants in that new immigrants were

    a. more likely to be non-Protestants.
    b. less family oriented.
    c. attracted to rural as opposed to urban areas.
    d. escaping from persecution rather than seeking opportunity.

Objective 4

5. Studies of occupational mobility in the late nineteenth and early twentieth centuries indicate that

    a. American society had become a static society in which there was little chance for occupational advancement.
    b. at least 10 percent of the population could expect to travel the rags-to-riches path.
    c. major urban areas had approximately equal upward and downward occupational movement.
    d. advancement resulting from movement to a higher status job was relatively common among white males.

Objective 5

6. Information about immigrant cultures in the United States supports the statement that most immigrants

    a.   quickly shed Old World attitudes and behaviors.
    b.   retained their native languages.
    c.   found that religion was the one area not affected by American society.
    d.   found that their habits and attitudes had to be modified as they interacted with American society.

Objective 7

7. As a result of concern about urban housing conditions in the late nineteenth and early twentieth centuries,

    a.   private investors pooled their resources to build low-income housing.
    b.   some states enacted legislation that imposed light, ventilation, and safety codes on new tenement buildings.
    c.   federal legislation was enacted that established a standard housing code throughout the United States.
    d.   state governments established subsidized housing for the disadvantaged.

Objective 7

8. In the face of urban poverty, most Americans accepted which of the following beliefs?

    a.   One's socioeconomic position within society is based largely on luck.
    b.   Poverty can be cured by improving the conditions in which people live and work.
    c.   Poverty is a sign that a person is unfit, weak, and lazy.
    d.   The government can be a force for good in alleviating the ills of poverty.

Objective 9

9. Urban political machines successfully gained and retained their power because they

    a.   were successful in winning and retaining popular support.
    b.   brought honesty to city government.
    c.   lowered taxes by making city government more efficient.
    d.   distributed favors evenly to all groups and classes.

Objective 10

10. Most civic reform leaders

    a.   were among the biggest supporters of the accomplishments of political bosses.
    b.   concentrated on structural changes rather than on dealing with social problems.
    c.   were interested in making government responsive to the social ills of urban society.
    d.   supported district representation in city government.

Objective 10

11. Which of the following statements best describes the goals of settlement-house founders?

    a. They wanted to establish an agency through which immigrants could find housing and employment.

    b. They wanted to provide for the needs of street people.

    c. They wanted to establish city-run, tax-supported social welfare agencies.

    d. They wanted to offer a variety of activities through which the lives of working-class people could be improved.

Objective 11

12. The practice of boarding was important in which of the following ways?

    a. It provided a means through which people could find employment.

    b. It provided a transitional stage for many young people between living with their parents and setting up their own households.

    c. It provided childcare facilities to working mothers.

    d. It contributed significantly to overcrowding.

Objective 12

13. As a result of the popularity of bicycling,

    a. the activities of men and women became more separated.

    b. groups began to demand lighted suburban streets.

    c. women's fashions began to change toward freer styles.

    d. stop and go lights were installed in most cities.

Objectives 6 and 12

14. Both the moral theme of *Birth of a Nation* and the information concerning Burt Williams's career support which of the following?

    a. Blacks were subjected to prejudicial stereotyping in popular entertainment in the United States.

    b. The ethnic humor in popular entertainment was gentle and sympathetic.

    c. Show business provided economic opportunities to immigrants.

    d. Vaudeville was the most popular form of entertainment in early-twentieth-century America.

Objective 13

15. The "new" American society created by the urbanization of the late nineteenth century was

    a. a pluralistic society in which different groups competed for power, wealth, and status.

    b. a society in which various ethnic groups had blended into one, unified people.

    c. a smoothly functioning society.

    d. a society in which most people accepted government as an agent for moral reform.

ESSAY QUESTIONS

Objective 1

1. Examine the impact of mass transportation on late-nineteenth-century American cities.

Objective 3

2. Discuss the similarities and differences between "old" immigrants and "new" immigrants, and examine the response of Americans to the latter.

Objective 4

3. Discuss occupational mobility as a means to get ahead and improve one's status in American society between 1870 and 1920.

Objective 5

4. Discuss the interaction between Old World culture and New World reality as experienced by immigrants to the United States in the late nineteenth and early twentieth centuries. What changes in immigrant culture resulted from these interactions?

Objective 7

5. Discuss the problem of urban poverty in the United States and the responses of Americans to this problem in the late nineteenth century.

Objective 7

6. Discuss the problem of urban crime and the responses of Americans to this problem in the late nineteenth century.

Objective 9

7. Analyze the emergence and evaluate the effectiveness of the urban political machines.

Objective 11

8. Explain the usefulness of the practice of boarding in American society during the late nineteenth and early twentieth centuries.

Objective 12

9. Discuss the emergence of mass entertainment as a commodity in American society.

Objective 12

10. Discuss the characteristics of popular journalism in late-nineteenth-century America.

ANSWERS

Multiple-Choice Questions

1. d.   Correct. Development of an inexpensive and efficient mass-transit system, such as the electric trolley, made it possible for people of the late nineteenth and early twentieth centuries to commute from a suburban home to an inner-city job. See page 512.

    a.   No. Long-term mortgage financing did not become widely available until the early twentieth century; therefore, it was not the "primary agent" in making suburban life practical and possible. See page 512.

    b.   No. The automobile revolutionized American life and was ultimately a factor in the success of suburban development, but the first suburbs were well established by the time the Model T began to come off the assembly line. Therefore, the automobile was not the "primary agent" in making suburban life practical and possible. See page 512.

    c.   No. Since shopping centers followed successful suburban development, the success of the suburbs did not depend on shopping centers. See page 512.

2. c.   Correct. Of the three ways by which the population of a place may grow, migration and immigration contributed most to urban population growth in the late nineteenth and early twentieth centuries. See pages 512–513.

    a.   No. In the late nineteenth and early twentieth centuries, urban death rates declined, but so did urban birthrates. Therefore, although some urban growth may be attributed to natural increase, it was not the most important factor in such growth. See pages 512–513.

    b.   No. Although an urban area can grow by merging with surrounding areas (e.g., Manhattan's merger with four boroughs in 1898), such mergers were not the most important cause of urban population growth in the late nineteenth and early twentieth centuries. See pages 512–513.

    d.   No. Annexation of outlying areas is one of the ways in which a place may grow, but it was not the most important source of urban population growth in the late nineteenth and early twentieth centuries. See pages 512–513.

3. c.   Correct. Blacks found it more difficult than foreign immigrants to find employment in northern factories. As a result, many went into the lower-paying service sector. See pages 513–515.

    a.   No. Most foreign immigrants were male, but most black migrants were women. Most jobs available to blacks in the cities were in domestic and personal service, and such jobs were traditionally held by women. See pages 513–515.

    b.   No. Blacks, like foreign immigrants, came from a peasant background. In other words, both had been small farmers or farm laborers in the areas from which they moved. See pages 513–515.

    d.   No. One characteristic that black migrants and foreign immigrants had in common was that both generally moved for economic reasons. See pages 513–515.

4. a. Correct. Since most of the new immigrants came from eastern and southern Europe, they were usually non-Protestants. See pages 515–516.

b. No. Family bonds were strong for both old and new immigrants. See pages 515–516.

c. No. Both old and new immigrants settled mainly in the cities. See pages 515–516.

d. No. The new immigrants were no more likely to be escaping from persecution than were the old immigrants, and most immigrants, old and new, sought opportunity in the United States. See pages 515–516.

5. d. Correct. The evidence indicates that movement along the path from "poverty to moderate success" was relatively common among white males. See page 518.

a. No. Statistics showing that the rate of upward mobility among manual laborers in Atlanta, Los Angeles, and Omaha was one in five do not support the conclusion that American society was static and offered little chance for occupational advancement. See page 518.

b. No. Although there were instances of people traveling the rags-to-riches path, this most certainly did not apply to 10 percent of the population of the United States. See page 518.

c. No. The evidence indicates that in general the rates of upward mobility were almost always double those of downward mobility. This would hold true in urban areas because that is where most opportunities for advancement existed. See page 518.

6. d. Correct. Although immigrants kept many Old World customs, the evidence supports the conclusion that as they interacted with the diversity of peoples and ideas in American society, they were forced to change their traditional habits and attitudes. See page 521.

a. No. The description of immigrant communities as "urban borderlands" does not support the idea that most immigrants quickly shed their Old World attitudes and beliefs. See pages 519–521.

b. No. Although many immigrants wanted to retain their native language, the fact that English was taught in the schools and necessary on the job made this virtually impossible. See pages 519–521.

c. No. The statement that immigrants "practiced religion as they always had" is later qualified by the statements that churches ultimately "had to appeal more broadly to the entire nationality in order to survive" and that groups accommodated their faiths to the new environment. This clearly implies change in the area of religion. See pages 519–521.

7. b. Correct. Traditional attitudes about the role of government often restricted what local government could do or was willing to do to solve urban problems, but some states did take action by legislating light, ventilation, and safety codes for new tenement buildings. See page 523.

a. No. Private investors, whether as individuals or collectively, were not willing to build housing for low-income residents because they would have to accept lower profits on such units. See page 523.

c. No. Most Americans did not believe it was either the responsibility of the federal government or within the government's power to legislate a national housing code. See page 523.

d. No. People's beliefs and perceptions concerning the role of government placed restrictions on the response of local, state, and national governments to housing problems. It was believed that government subsidies would undermine private enterprise. See page 523.

8.   c.   Correct. Most Americans believed that the poor were unfit, weak, and lazy. By the same token, they believed that anyone could escape poverty through hard work, thrift, and clean living. See page 524.

     a.   No. Most Americans believed that factors other than luck were responsible for a person's socioeconomic position. See page 524.

     b.   No. Although some reformers, most notably welfare workers, believed that poverty could be eliminated by changing the environment in which people lived, most Americans did not agree with this view of poverty. See page 524.

     d.   No. Most Americans of the late nineteenth and early twentieth centuries did not believe it to be the responsibility of the federal government to assist the poor. See page 524.

9.   a.   Correct. Rapid city growth created governmental chaos from which political machines emerged. Machine politicians gained and retained power by getting to know new urban voters and responding to their needs. See pages 527–528.

     b.   No. Machine politicians often engaged in bribery, thievery, and extortion. They did not gain and retain their power because they brought honesty to city government. See pages 527–528.

     c.   No. Urban political machines were not efficient or cost effective. Bosses solved many urban problems, but they often did so in a way that was costly to taxpayers. See pages 527–528.

     d.   No. Urban political bosses granted "favors" to their supporters. Therefore, favors were not evenly distributed to all groups and classes. See pages 527–528.

10.   b.   Correct. In an effort to remove politics from government, most civic reform leaders concentrated on structural changes. They focused only on the waste and corruption associated with political bosses and failed to recognize that bosses succeeded because they used government to meet people's needs. See page 528.

     a.   No. Civic reform leaders of the late nineteenth and early twentieth centuries saw political bosses as irresponsible leaders and a threat to American society. See page 528.

     c.   No. Most civic reform leaders wanted to make city government more businesslike and efficient. Only a few reformers, such as Thomas L. Johnson, attempted to make government responsive to the social ills of society. See page 528.

     d.   No. Most civic reform leaders supported citywide election of government officials and were opposed to the district representation associated with the ward system. See page 528.

11.   d.   Correct. Settlement-house founders believed that they could improve the lives of working class people by providing education, job training, childcare, and other benefits to the residents of working-class neighborhoods. See page 529.

     a.   No. Although settlement-house founders worked with immigrants, acting as an employment and housing agency for immigrants was not their primary focus. See page 529.

     b.   No. Settlement-house founders were not primarily concerned with "street people." See page 529.

     c.   No. It was not the aim of settlement-house founders to establish city-run, tax-supported social welfare agencies. See page 529.

12.   b.   Correct. Although housing reformers complained that boarding caused overcrowding and lack of privacy, it provided many young people who had left home with the semblance of a family environment. Therefore, it was a transitional stage between dependence and total independence. See page 531.

a.   No. Although boarding sometimes provided extra income to middle- and working-class families, it was not a means by which people found employment. See pages 530–531.

c.   No. Boarding was not important as a provider of childcare for working mothers. See pages 530–531.

d.   No. Housing reformers charged that boarding caused overcrowding and a loss of privacy. This may have been true, but it does not indicate the importance of boarding, which was useful to many people. See pages 530–531.

13.   c.   Correct. Bicycling was an important sport for both men and women. In order to ride, women's garments had to be less restrictive than the traditional Victorian fashions. The freer styles necessary for cycling gradually influenced everyday fashions. See page 534.

a.   No. Since both sexes could participate in bicycling, it was instrumental in bringing men and women together. This was especially true of the bicycle-built-for-two. (The most popular song of 1892 was "Daisybelle.") See page 534.

b.   No. There is no indication that bicycling groups demanded lighted suburban streets. See page 534.

d.   No. Stop and go lights were a response to the advent of the automobile in the 1920s and were not installed because of the popularity of bicycling. See page 534.

14.   a.   Correct. Burt Williams mainly played stereotypical roles. Birth of a Nation depicts blacks in a stereotypical way and as a threat to white moral values. Therefore, information about both supports the inference that blacks were subjected to prejudicial stereotyping in popular entertainment in the United States. See page 537.

b.   No. Ethnic humor was often gentle and sympathetic, allowing people to laugh at the human condition. However, such an inference about ethnic humor cannot be drawn from information about Burt Williams's career or from Birth of a Nation. See page 537.

c.   No. The statement that show business provided economic opportunities to immigrants is a true statement. However, it is not an inference that is logically derived from the information about Burt Williams's career or from Birth of a Nation. See page 537.

d.   No. Although vaudeville was the most popular form of entertainment in early-twentieth-century America, this statement is not supported by the information about Burt Williams's career or by Birth of a Nation. See page 537.

15. a.   Correct. Urbanization in the late nineteenth century created a culturally pluralistic society. In such a society, politics became important as the arena in which different interest groups were competing for power, wealth, and status. See pages 538–539.

     b.   No. The idea of a society in which ethnic groups had blended into one, unified people is an expression of the "melting pot" idea. Such a society was not created by the urbanization in America in the late nineteenth century. See pages 538–539.

     c.   No. The discussion of urban growth in Chapter 19 deals with overcrowding, inadequate housing, urban poverty, urban crime and violence, ethnic prejudice, and governmental confusion. These topics do not suggest the emergence of a "smoothly functioning society." See pages 538–539.

     d.   No. Although some Americans attempted to use government as an agent for moral reform, the evidence does not support the conclusion that urbanization created a society in which most Americans accepted this as the proper role of government. See pages 538–539.

CHAPTER 20

Gilded Age Politics, 1877–1900

LEARNING OBJECTIVES

After you have studied Chapter 20 in your textbook and worked through this study guide chapter, you should be able to:

1. Discuss the characteristics of American politics at the national and state levels during the Gilded Age.

2. Discuss the major political and economic issues of the Gilded Age, and examine governmental action on these issues.

3. Explain the characteristics of American presidents during the Gilded Age, and discuss how each carried out the duties of his office.

4. Explain the social, economic, and political oppression of southern blacks during the late nineteenth century, and discuss the response of the Supreme Court to this oppression.

5. Examine the progress of the women's suffrage movement during the Gilded Age.

6. Discuss the various forces affecting the lives of southern, midwestern, and western farmers during the late nineteenth century, and explain the social, economic, and political impact of these forces.

7. Explain the organizational and ideological development of rural activism from the Grange through the formation of the Populist party and the 1896 presidential election, and discuss the roadblocks encountered by the Populists.

8. Explain the causes and consequences of the depression of the 1890s, and evaluate Grover Cleveland's response to the depression.

9. Discuss the nature and extent of working-class activism during the era of protest, and explain the reaction of government officials and the public to this activism.

10. Analyze the presidential campaign and election of 1896, and explain the political and economic significance of the outcome.

THEMATIC GUIDE

In Chapter 20, we focus on the interaction of the political, economic, and social forces within American society during the Gilded Age. This period is characterized by high public interest in local, state, and national elections, political balance between Democrats and Republicans at the national level, and factional and personal feuds within the two parties. Democrats and Republicans in Congress were split on the major national issues: sectional controversies, civil service reform, railroad regulation, tariff policy, and monetary policy. Though Congress debated these issues, factionalism, interest-group politics, and political equilibrium resulted in the passage of vaguely worded, ineffective legislation such as the Pendleton Civil Service Act, the Interstate Commerce Act, and the Sherman Anti-Trust Act. Combined with a conservative Supreme Court, weak presidential leadership, and political campaigns that focused on issues of personality rather than issues of substance, these factors caused the postponement of decisions on major issues affecting the nation and its citizens.

The political impasse built up frustration within aggrieved groups in the nation. Southern blacks, who lived under the constant threat of violence and who remained economically dependent on whites, had to endure new forms of social oppression in the form of disfranchisement and "Jim Crow" laws. This oppression was, in turn, upheld by the Supreme Court, which interpreted the Fourteenth Amendment narrowly. Women were frustrated in their attempts to gain the right to vote by the sexist attitudes prevalent in the male-dominated power structures of the era. Aggrieved workers turned to organized labor, to strikes, and, at times, to violence (discussed in Chapter 18). Aggrieved farmers also began to organize. In "Agrarian Unrest and Populism," we examine the reasons for agrarian discontent and trace the manifestation of that discontent from the Grange, through the Farmers' Alliances, to the formation of the Populist party and the drafting of the Omaha platform in 1892.

The depression of the 1890s added to the woes of the United States. President Grover Cleveland failed to deal with the crisis effectively, and an air of crisis settled over the nation. Workers' protests multiplied; the Socialist Party of America, under the leadership of Eugene V. Debs, reorganized; Coxey's Army, demanding a federal jobs program, marched on the nation's capital; and fear of social revolution led business owners and government officials to use brute force to control what they perceived to be radical protest.

As the crisis persisted, the Populist party gained ground but was hampered both by the reluctance of voters to abandon their loyalties to the two major parties and by issues of race. At the national level, Populists, convinced that the "money power" and its imposition of the gold standard on the nation was the root cause of farm distress and the nationwide depression, continued to call for a return of government to the people and crusaded for the "free and unlimited coinage of silver."

The frustrations that had built up in the Gilded Age—an age of transition from rural to urban, from agrarian to industrial society—came to a head in the emotionally charged presidential contest of 1896. An analysis of the issues, outcome, and legacy of this election, which ended the political equilibrium of the age, is offered in the last section of the chapter.

BUILDING VOCABULARY

Listed below are important words and terms that you need to know to get the most out of Chapter 20. They are listed in the order in which they occur in the chapter. After carefully looking through the list, (1) underline the words with which you are totally unfamiliar, (2) put a question mark by those words of which you are unsure, and (3) leave the rest alone.

As you begin to read the chapter, when you come to any of the words you've put question marks beside or underlined (1) slow your reading; (2) focus on the word and on its context in the sentence you're reading; (3) if you can understand the meaning of the word from its context in the sentence or passage in which it is used, go on with your reading; (4) if it's a word that you've underlined or a word that you can't understand from its context in the sentence or passage, look it up in a dictionary and write down the definition that best applies to the context in which the word is used.

Definitions

venality _____

obscure _____

partisan _____

avid _____

coalition _____

contentious _____

crassness _____

flamboyant _____

aspirant _____

mesmerize _____

pompous _____

roguish _____

taint _____

parlay _____

harangue _____

cajole _____

potency _____

gingerly _____

conciliator _____

averse _____

temperate _____

retort _____

enfranchise _____

subjugation _____

mandate _____

inequity _____

strident _____

nostalgic _____

egalitarianism _____

collateral _____

formidable _____

reprisal _____

amalgamation _____

canny _____

apocalyptic _____

fervor _____

garner _____

ominous _____

vehemence _____

portend _____

injunction _____

commandeer _____

dregs _____

vestige _____

corral _____

quip _____

repudiate _____

inequity _____

succinct _____

retrograde _____

personable _____

Difficult-to-Spell Names and Terms from Reading and Lecture

IDENTIFICATION AND SIGNIFICANCE

After studying Chapter 20 of *A People and a Nation,* you should be able to identify fully *and* explain the historical significance of each item listed below.

- Identify each item in the space provided. Give an explanation or description of the item. Answer the questions *who, what, where,* and *when.*

- Explain the historical significance of each item in the space provided. Establish the historical context in which the item exists. Establish the item as the result of or as the cause of other factors existing in the society under study. Answer this question: *What were the political, social, economic, and/or cultural consequences of this item?*

1. Mary Elizabeth Lease

   a. Identification

   b. Significance

2. James G. Blaine

   a. Identification

   b. Significance

3. the Stalwarts, the Half Breeds, and the Mugwumps

   a. Identification

   b. Significance

4. "waving the bloody shirt"

   a. Identification

   b. Significance

5. the Grand Army of the Republic

   a. Identification

   b. Significance

6. the Pendleton Civil Service Act

    a. Identification

    b. Significance

7. *Munn v. Illinois*

    a. Identification

    b. Significance

8. the *Wabash* case

    a. Identification

    b. Significance

9. the Interstate Commerce Act

    a. Identification

    b. Significance

10. the *Maximum Freight Rate* case

    a. Identification

    b. Significance

11. the *Alabama Midlands* case

    a.   Identification

    b.   Significance

12. the tariff controversy

    a.   Identification

    b.   Significance

13. the McKinley Tariff of 1890

    a.   Identification

    b.   Significance

14. the Wilson-Gorman Tariff of 1894

    a.   Identification

    b.   Significance

15. the Dingley Tariff of 1897

    a.   Identification

    b.   Significance

16. the currency controversy

    a. Identification

    b. Significance

17. the Bland-Allison Act of 1878

    a. Identification

    b. Significance

18. the Sherman Silver Purchase Act of 1890

    a. Identification

    b. Significance

19. Rutherford B. Hayes

    a. Identification

    b. Significance

20. James A. Garfield

    a. Identification

    b. Significance

21. Chester A. Arthur
    a. Identification

    b. Significance

22. the presidential campaign and election of 1884
    a. Identification

    b. Significance

23. Grover Cleveland
    a. Identification

    b. Significance

24. "rum, Romanism, and rebellion"
    a. Identification

    b. Significance

25. the presidential election and campaign of 1888
    a. Identification

    b. Significance

26. Benjamin Harrison

    a.   Identification

    b.   Significance

27. the Dependents' Pension Act

    a.   Identification

    b.   Significance

28. the "Billion Dollar Congress"

    a.   Identification

    b.   Significance

29. Ida B. Wells

    a.   Identification

    b.   Significance

30. the poll tax

    a.   Identification

    b.   Significance

31. *United States v. Reese*
    a.   Identification

    b.   Significance

32. the Mississippi Plan
    a.   Identification

    b.   Significance

33. the "grandfather clause"
    a.   Identification

    b.   Significance

34. the *Civil Rights cases*
    a.   Identification

    b.   Significance

35. *Plessy v. Ferguson* and *Cummins v. County Board of Education*
    a.   Identification

    b.   Significance

36. Jim Crow laws

    a. Identification

    b. Significance

37. the National Woman Suffrage Association

    a. Identification

    b. Significance

38. the American Woman Suffrage Association

    a. Identification

    b. Significance

39. Susan B. Anthony

    a. Identification

    b. Significance

40. the crop-lien system

    a. Identification

    b. Significance

41. the Grange movement

    a. Identification

    b. Significance

42. the White Hats

    a. Identification

    b. Significance

43. the Farmers' Alliances

    a. Identification

    b. Significance

44. the subtreasury plan

    a. Identification

    b. Significance

45. the Populist (People's) party

    a. Identification

    b. Significance

46. the Omaha platform

    a.   Identification

    b.   Significance

47. James B. Weaver

    a.   Identification

    b.   Significance

48. the depression of the 1890s

    a.   Identification

    b.   Significance

49. the Cleveland-Morgan deal

    a.   Identification

    b.   Significance

50. the Coeur d'Alene strike

    a.   Identification

    b.   Significance

51. Karl Marx

    a. Identification

    b. Significance

52. Daniel DeLeon

    a. Identification

    b. Significance

53. Eugene V. Debs

    a. Identification

    b. Significance

54. Jacob S. Coxey

    a. Identification

    b. Significance

55. free coinage of silver

    a. Identification

    b. Significance

56. the presidential campaign and election of 1896

    a. Identification

    b. Significance

57. William McKinley

    a. Identification

    b. Significance

58. William Jennings Bryan

    a. Identification

    b. Significance

59. the Gold Standard Act

    a. Identification

    b. Significance

ORGANIZING, REVIEWING, AND USING INFORMATION

Chart A

The Likelihood of a Viable Coalition of Populist Groups in the Election of 1896			
Groups or Regions That Might Form an Alliance	**Factors Making These Groups or Regions Likely Allies**	**Factors Working Against These Groups Or Regions Becoming Allies**	**How Far These Groups or Regions Came in Producing an Alliance** (Election of 1896)
Sections of the Country			
Types of Workers			
People Lacking Political Power			
Reformer Elements Of the Two Major Political Parties			
Other Groups			

Chart B

How Populist Causes Fared, 1877–1900			
What Populists Wanted on Key Issues			
Tariffs	Currency	Prices and Rates	Distribution of Political Power
What Populists Got on Key Issues			
Potential Supporters	**Potential Supporters' Actions on Key Populist Issues**		
	Tariffs	Currency	Prices and Rates	Distribution of Political Power
Congress				
Presidents				
Supreme Court				
State Governments				

Chart C

Ways and Means of Governmental Reform, 1877–1900

	Legislation	Court Rulings	Constitutional Amendments	Use of Powers, Special Tools of Office	Citizens' Activism
Spoils System/Bribery					
Size, Makeup of Electorate; Voting Rights					
Method of Election					
State Govmt.-Federal Govmt. Balance of Power					
Federal Govmt's Recognized Responsibilities					
Political Parties/Party Structure					
Power of Special Interests					

IDEAS AND DETAILS

Objective 1

1. Which of the following characterized politics during the Gilded Age?

     a. Party allegiance among the voters was so evenly distributed that no one party gained control for very long.

     b. Americans insisted that the government actively pursue solutions to social problems.

     c. There was little public interest in national elections.

     d. Political contests were very impersonal.

Objective 2

2. In cases arising from the Interstate Commerce Act, the Supreme Court

     a. broadly interpreted the regulatory powers of Congress.

     b. established that government aid to private industry was unconstitutional.

     c. reduced the regulatory powers of the Interstate Commerce Commission.

     d. completely rejected the principle of government regulation of industry.

Objectives 1 and 2

3. Which of the following hastened the move toward civil service reform?

     a. The rejection of Chester Arthur as the Republican party's vice-presidential nominee in the 1880 election

     b. The assassination of President James Garfield

     c. Public disclosure of testimony by former President Ulysses Grant before the National Civil Service Reform League

     d. The suicide of Charles Guiteau, a disgruntled office seeker.

Objective 3

4. Which of the following words best describes the presidents of the Gilded Age?

     a. Inspiring

     b. Lazy

     c. Honest

     d. Forceful

Objective 1

5. Which of the following was an important factor in Grover Cleveland's defeat in the presidential election of 1888?

     a. The Republicans successfully engaged in vote fraud in Indiana and New York.

     b. The British minister in Washington publicly supported Benjamin Harrison.

     c. Cleveland's ethnic jokes offended Irish Catholics.

     d. Cleveland offended consumers by suddenly calling for higher tariffs.

Objectives 1 and 2

6.   The action taken by Congress on the issue of veterans' pensions demonstrates that

    a.   Congress was determined to give equal treatment to Union and Confederate veterans.

    b.   memories of the Civil War no longer had an impact on national politics.

    c.   Congress was opposed to all forms of welfare legislation.

    d.   Congress responded to interest-group pressure.

Objective 5

7.   Which of the following was the most common argument used by senators voting against the Women's Suffrage amendment?

    a.   If women are given the right to vote, they will demand that the nation disarm.

    b.   Giving women the right to vote will interfere with their family responsibilities.

    c.   Women are not well enough educated to vote.

    d.   Women are too emotional to be given the privilege of voting.

Objective 6

8.   As a result of the crop-lien system, many southern farmers

    a.   were able to increase the prices they received for their goods.

    b.   sank deeper and deeper into debt.

    c.   were given the opportunity to become landowners.

    d.   began to diversify their crops.

Objectives 6 and 7

9.   Farmers hoped that implementation of the subtreasury plan would

    a.   lower the cost of farm machinery.

    b.   make second mortgages available to farmers facing bankruptcy.

    c.   provide higher prices for farm products and low-interest loans to farmers.

    d.   lower transportation costs for farm goods.

Objectives 6 and 7

10.   The Omaha platform called for

    a.   the establishment of national agricultural colleges in all states.

    b.   a comprehensive welfare program for destitute farmers.

    c.   a two-year moratorium on all debts.

    d.   government ownership of railroad lines.

Objective 8

11.   The broad-based nature of the 1890s depression was the result of

    a.   an interdependent economy.

    b.   overspeculation in the stock market.

    c.   the Sherman Silver Purchase Act.

    d.   the withdrawal of foreign investments.

Objective 9

12. Which of the following became the leading spokesperson for American socialism in the late 1890s?

    a. Jacob Riis
    b. Eugene V. Debs
    c. Ignatius Donnelly
    d. Leonidas Polk

Objective 9

13. To end the depression, Jacob Coxey advocated

    a. government aid to business.
    b. a return to the gold standard.
    c. tax cuts to encourage spending.
    d. the infusion of money into the economy through a federal jobs program.

Objectives 4, 7, and 10

14. Which of the following was a factor that prevented the Farmers' Alliances from uniting and from gaining political power?

    a. The Socialist Party's endorsement of the policies of the Farmers' Alliances caused confusion in the minds of farmers and voters.
    b. Leaders of the Northern Alliance called for equality under the law for African Americans throughout the United States.
    c. The disfranchisement of southern African Americans prevented the emergence of a biracial coalition.
    d. Their endorsement of Jacob Coxey's demands caused voters to associate the Farmers' Alliances with extremist causes.

Objectives 7 and 10

15. Which of the following best explains Bryan's defeat in the 1896 election?

    a. The silver issue prevented Bryan from building an urban-rural coalition.
    b. Bryan could not match McKinley's spirited campaign style.
    c. The Populists refused to endorse Bryan.
    d. Endorsement of Bryan by the Socialist party caused people to believe that he was a radical.

ESSAY QUESTIONS

Objective 1

1. Discuss the nature of politics, political parties, and political campaigns during the Gilded Age.

Objective 2

2. Discuss the problems that led to passage of the Interstate Commerce Act, and assess the act's effectiveness.

Objective 2

3. Explain the tariff issue, and trace tariff legislation from passage of the McKinley Tariff in 1890 through passage of the Dingley Tariff of 1897. What were the consequences of the tariff policies of the United States during this period?

Objective 4

4. Explain the process that led to the disfranchisement of southern blacks and to the segregation of southern society by law. How did the Supreme Court respond to this process?

Objectives 2, 6, and 7

5. Explain the emergence of the farm protest movement, and examine its development through the 1896 election.

Objective 8

6. Discuss the causes and consequences of the depression of the 1890s.

Objectives 2 and 10

7. Examine the personalities and issues of the 1896 presidential campaign, and explain the election's outcome.

ANSWERS

Multiple-Choice Questions

1. a.   Correct. Since voters were evenly divided between the two political parties, neither party was the "majority party" during the period from 1877–1897. As a result, there were frequent power shifts that prevented the passage of effective, lasting legislation. See page 543.

    b.   No. Americans generally accepted a passive federal government that did not involve itself in economic and social matters. See page 543.

    c.   No. This was an age in which party identification was important; voters were interested in politics, believed their votes were important, and voted in large numbers. See page 543.

    d.   No. Politics was a popular form of mass entertainment and people formed strong loyalties to politicians and political parties. Consequently, political contests were often deeply personal. See page 543.

2. c.   Correct. In the Wabash case the Supreme Court ruled that only Congress could limit railroad rates involving interstate commerce. However, in cases arising under the Interstate Commerce Act, the Court narrowly interpreted those powers. In so doing, the Court reduced the regulatory powers of the Interstate Commerce Commission. See page 546.

    a.   No. Although the Supreme Court placed responsibility for the regulation of interstate commerce in the hands of Congress through the Wabash case, the Court did not broadly interpret those powers in cases arising under the Interstate Commerce Act. See page 546.

    b.   No. The Interstate Commerce Act did not extend government aid to private industry; therefore, the Court did not rule on this issue in cases arising under the Interstate Commerce Act. See page 546.

    d.   No. In the Wabash case the Court accepted the principle of government regulation of industry by holding that only Congress could limit railroad rates involving interstate commerce. This decision was not overturned by the Court in cases arising under the Interstate Commerce Act. See page 546.

3. b.   Correct. After the election of James Garfield to the presidency in 1880, Charles Guiteau, who had actively campaigned for Garfield, requested a patronage position in the diplomatic corps. After having been rebuffed several times, Guiteau shot President Garfield twice in the back as the President was about to board a train in Washington, D. C. This act along with revelations about the spoils system during Guiteau's trial are factors that led Congress to pass the Pendleton Civil Service Act in 1883. See page 548.

    a.   No. Chester Arthur was chosen as the Republican party's vice-presidential nominee in the 1880 presidential election. See page 548.

    c.   No. Former President Grant never testified before the National Civil Service Reform League. See page 548.

    d.   No. Charles Guiteau did not commit suicide. After having been found guilty of the assassination of President James Garfield, Guiteau was executed on June 30, 1882. See page 548.

4.   c.   Correct. The presidents during the Gilded Age did not evoke much of an emotional response from the electorate, but they were honest, honorable, and proper. See page 548.

a.   No. The presidents during the Gilded Age were not "inspiring" figures to most of the electorate. See page 548.

b.   No. The presidents during the Gilded Age were hardworking men and may not accurately be described as lazy. See page 548.

d.   No. Believing that it was their job to execute the laws passed by Congress, the presidents during the Gilded Age may not be described as forceful or active. See page 548.

5.   a.   Correct. Partly as a result of bribery and vote fraud, the Republicans carried Indiana by 2,300 votes and New York by 14,000 votes. See page 549.

b.   No. The British minister, to the delight of the Republicans, said that Democrat Grover Cleveland's election would be good for England. This offended Irish Democrats and weakened Cleveland's campaign. See page 549.

c.   No. Grover Cleveland is not known to have told ethnic jokes offensive to Irish Catholics. See page 549.

d.   No. Grover Cleveland was against high tariffs, and, even though he was convinced to temper his attacks against tariffs for political reasons, he never called for higher tariffs. See page 549.

6.   d.   Correct. Although angered by tactics of lobbyists for the Grand Army of the Republic, congressmen still voted in favor of providing generous pensions for Union veterans and their widows. They did so, in large measure, because of pressure from this politically powerful interest group. See pages 549–550.

a.   No. The question of pensions to Civil War veterans and their widows concerned Union veterans only. Congress never considered pensions for Confederate veterans. See pages 549–550.

b.   No. The events leading to congressional action on pensions for Civil War veterans and their widows make it obvious that the memories of the war were still alive and affected the decisions of Congress. See pages 549–550.

c.   No. By providing generous pensions to Union veterans and their widows, Congress made one of the largest welfare commitments it has ever made. See pages 549–550.

7.   b.   Correct. The most common argument in the Senate against the extension of the right to vote to women was the contention that it would interfere with their family responsibilities and ruin female virtue. See page 553.

a.   No. The contention that women will demand national disarmament was not the most common argument against giving women the right to vote. See page 553.

c.   No. The contention that women were not well enough educated to vote was not the most common argument used by senators opposed to the extension of the vote to women. See page 553.

d.   No. The contention that women were too emotional was not the most common argument used by senators opposed to the extension of the vote to women. See page 553.

8. b. Correct. The operation of the crop-lien system forced many farmers into perpetual debt and into a state of helpless peonage. See page 554.

    a. No. The crop-lien system did not make it possible for southern farmers to increase the prices of their agricultural products. See page 554.

    c. No. The crop-lien system was at the heart of sharecropping and tenant farming and did not create the opportunity for more southern farmers to become landowners. See page 554.

    d. No. The growing of traditional cash crops, especially cotton, was emphasized rather than agricultural diversification. See page 554.

9. c. Correct. The subtreasury system would give farmers a place to store their crops while waiting for higher prices, and it would allow them to borrow subtreasury notes amounting to 80 percent of the value of their crops. Through this system, farmers hoped to solve their cash and credit problems. See page 556.

    a. No. Although farmers complained about the cost of farm machinery, they did not see the subtreasury system as a way to lower those costs. See page 556.

    b. No. The subtreasury system was not proposed as an agency that would make second mortgages available to farmers facing bankruptcy. See page 556.

    d. No. The subtreasury system was not a means by which transportation costs could be lowered. See page 556.

10. d. Correct. Farmers believed that railroads had been built on public land with public funds, and it angered them that railroads were operated for the private enrichment of a few individuals. Therefore, the Omaha platform called for government ownership of the railroad lines. See page 557.

    a. No. Although the Omaha platform called for increased government regulation of trusts, it did not call for the nationalization of the oil and steel industries. See page 557.

    b. No. Although Populists did call for a more active federal government in the Omaha platform, they did not advocate a welfare program for destitute farmers. They believed that an expansive money supply, brought about by the free coinage of silver, would solve farmers' monetary problems. See page 557.

    c. No. The Populists clearly recognized the debt problems of farmers but did not call for a moratorium on debts in the Omaha platform. They believed that a graduated income tax, the creation of a postal savings bank, and the free coinage of silver would solve farmers' monetary problems. See page 557.

11. a. Correct. The national economy had reached the point where business failures in one area had a ripple effect throughout the economic system, causing failures in other areas. See pages 558–559.

    b. No. In some measure, the depression of the 1890s was due to overspeculation in certain industries, but it was not due to overspeculation in the stock market. See pages 558–559.

    c. No. Although the Sherman Silver Purchase Act had a psychological impact that led to the dwindling of the nation's gold reserves, it was not the reason for the broad-based nature of the depression. In addition, repeal of the act did not halt the run on the Treasury. See pages 558–559.

    d. No. The impact of the depression of the 1890s on other countries and the subsequent withdrawal of foreign investments from the United States are indications of the broad-based nature of the depression. However, this withdrawal did not cause the depression to be broad-based. See pages 558–559.

12. b.   Correct. Eugene Debs, president of the American Railway Union, was jailed in 1894 for defying a federal court injunction against the Pullman strike. While in jail, Debs became a socialist and, after his release, became the leading spokesperson for American socialism. See page 560.

   a.   No. Jacob Riis (page 523) was a New York journalist and the author of How the Other Half Lives, published in 1890. The book exposed the horrors of life in the slums of New York. Although Riis was an active reformer, he was not a socialist. See page 560.

   c.   No. Ignatius Donnelly (page 558) was a leading Minnesota Populist during the 1890s and was not the leading spokesperson for American socialism. See page 560.

   d.   No. Leonidas Polk (page 558) was president of the Southern Alliance in 1891 and a leading North Carolina Populist. See page 560.

13. d.   Correct. Jacob Coxey advocated that the government purposefully cause inflation by pumping $500 million of paper money into the economy through a federal jobs program. See page 560.

   a.   No. Although Jacob Coxey was a wealthy businessman from Ohio, his plan for dealing with the depression did not include government aid to business. See page 560.

   b.   No. The United States was already on the gold standard in 1894 when Coxey's "commonweal army" marched on the nation's capital. Coxey believed that the government's insistence on backing currency with gold was prolonging the depression. See page 560.

   c.   No. The nation did not have a federal income tax in 1894, and Jacob Coxey did not advocate tax cuts as a way to end the depression. See page 560.

14. c.   Correct. Out of fear that a biracial Populist coalition would jeopardize their power in the South, southern white Democrats disfranchised southern African Americans. The removal of African Americans from southern politics thus prevented the emergence of a coalition of southern whites and blacks. Furthermore, due to their racist attitudes, poor white farmers rejected attempts to end white-only membership in the Southern Alliance. See pages 550–551 and page 557.

   a.   No. The Socialist Party's ideology was attractive primarily to disaffected workers, not farmers.. See pages 550–551 and page 557.

   b.   No. Although some southern leaders attempted to forge an alliance between poor southern whites and blacks, leaders of the Northern Alliance did not call for equality under the law for African Americans. See pages 550–551 and page 557.

   d.   No. Although some voters may have labeled members of the Farmers' Alliances as extremists, it was not because the Farmers' Alliances endorsed Coxey's demand for a public-works relief program. See pages 550–551 and page 557.

15. a.   Correct. Free silver was attractive to many farmers of the West and South, but its promise of inflation was not attractive to city dwellers and factory workers. As a result, Bryan was never able to build an urban-rural coalition. See pages 563–564.

   b.   No. McKinley conducted a "front-porch" campaign that can hardly be called "spirited." See pages 563–564.

   c.   No. When the Democrats nominated Bryan and endorsed many Populist ideas, the Populists decided to nominate Bryan for the presidency and Tom Watson of Georgia for the vice-presidency. See pages 563–564.

   d.   No. Bryan was not endorsed by the Socialist party. See pages 563–564.

CHAPTER 21

The Progressive Era, 1895–1920

LEARNING OBJECTIVES

After you have studied Chapter 21 in your textbook and worked through this study guide chapter, you should be able to:

1. Explain the emergence of progressivism and discuss the movement's basic themes.

2. Discuss the similarities and differences among the ideologies, goals, and tactics of the various groups that constituted the Progressive movement, and analyze the successes and failures of these groups in achieving political, social, and moral reform.

3. Explain the emergence of the Socialist movement, and indicate how it differed from progressivism in ideology, goals, and tactics.

4. Discuss and evaluate the impact of progressive ideas in education, law, and the social sciences; and examine the ideas associated with the Social Gospel and with eugenics.

5. Explain and evaluate the approaches of African Americans, American Indians, and women to the problems they faced during the Progressive era, and discuss the extent to which they were successful in achieving their goals.

6. Explain the relationship between Theodore Roosevelt's political, social, and economic beliefs and his approach toward the major issues of the day.

7. Indicate the reasons for the break between William Howard Taft and Theodore Roosevelt, and explain the impact of this break on the 1912 election.

8. Examine the similarities and differences between Roosevelt and Woodrow Wilson.

9. Explain and evaluate the reform legislation of the Wilson presidency.

10. Assess the political, social, and economic impact of the Progressive era on American society.

THEMATIC GUIDE

In Chapter 21, we focus on the Progressive era and progressivism: a series of movements that brought together reform-minded individuals and groups with differing solutions to the nation's problems in the years 1895 to 1920. The progressives were members of nationwide organizations that attempted to affect government policy. They were people interested in urban issues and urban political and social reform. Although progressives came from all levels of society, new middle-class professionals formed the vanguard of the movement and found expression for their ideas in muckraking journalism.

Revolted by corruption and injustice, the new urban middle class called for political reform to make government more efficient, less corrupt, and more accountable. Such government, they believed, could be a force for good in American society. Some business executives argued for a society organized along the lines of the corporate model; women of the elite classes formed the YWCA and the Woman's Christian Temperance Union. Working-class reformers pressed for government legislation to aid labor and improve social welfare. Although some reformers turned to the Socialist party, they were a decided minority and cannot be considered progressives. Progressives generally had far too great a stake in the capitalist system to advocate its destruction and, as a result, were political moderates rather than radicals.

The many facets of progressivism can be seen in the section "Governmental and Legislative Reform." Progressives generally agreed that government power should be used to check the abuses associated with the industrial age, but they did not always agree on the nature of the problem. At the city and state levels, progressives were initially interested in attacking the party system and in effecting political reform designed to make government more honest, more professional, and more responsive to the people. These aims can be seen through the accomplishments of Robert M. La Follette, one of the most effective progressive governors, and in the Seventeenth Amendment, one of the major political reforms achieved by progressives at the national level. Some progressives also worked for social reform at the state level, to protect the well-being of citizens from exploitative corporate power. Still other progressives believed in using the power of government to purify society by effecting moral reform. Such efforts were behind the Eighteenth Amendment and the Mann Act (White Slave Traffic Act).

In "New Ideas in Social Institutions" we find that the Progressive era also witnessed an assault on traditional ideas in education, law, and the social sciences. The ideas that constituted this assault and the changes resulting from this assault are examined and evaluated. This section also looks at progressive reforms in public health, the religious foundations of the Social Gospel and of much Progressive reform, and the movement based on the pseudoscience of eugenics.

The Progressive spirit also had an impact on those seeking equal rights for African Americans, American Indians, and women. After looking at the dilemma faced by activists within these groups, we contrast the approaches of Booker T. Washington and W. E. B. Du Bois toward white racism, and we look at attempts by American Indians to advance their interests through the formation of the Society of American Indians. We then turn to the various aspects of "the woman movement," contrasting the aims and goals of women involved in the women's club movement with those involved in the feminist movement and discussing the contrasting viewpoints of elite women and feminists involved in the suffrage movement.

The Progressive era reached the national level of government when Theodore Roosevelt became president in 1901. We examine Roosevelt's political, economic, and social frame of reference and evaluate the progressive legislation passed during his administration. The contrast between the Taft administration that followed and the Roosevelt years spurred progressives to found the Progressive party under Roosevelt's leadership. We also discuss the similarities and differences between Roosevelt's New Nationalism and Woodrow Wilson's New Freedom, and we examine the reasons for Wilson's election in 1912.

In "Woodrow Wilson and the Extension of Reform," we analyze Wilson's frame of reference and evaluate the legislation passed during his two administrations. The chapter ends with a summary and evaluation of the Progressive era.

BUILDING VOCABULARY

Listed below are important words and terms that you need to know to get the most out of Chapter 21. They are listed in the order in which they occur in the chapter. After carefully looking through the list, (1) underline the words with which you are totally unfamiliar, (2) put a question mark by those words of which you are unsure, and (3) leave the rest alone.

As you begin to read the chapter, when you come to any of the words you've put question marks beside or underlined (1) slow your reading; (2) focus on the word and on its context in the sentence you're reading; (3) if you can understand the meaning of the word from its context in the sentence or passage in which it is used, go on with your reading; (4) if it's a word that you've underlined or a word that you can't understand from its context in the sentence or passage, look it up in a dictionary and write down the definition that best applies to the context in which the word is used.

Definitions

guerrilla _____

odyssey _____

ardent _____

cornucopia _____

amenity _____

entrench _____

aura _____

spearhead _____

vexing _____

adulterate _____

pinnacle _____

rebuke _____

unfettered _____

ideological _____

brothel _____

ostensibly _____

vista _____

grapple _____

amenable _____

inviolable _____

invidious _____

perpetuate _____

assimilation _____

articulate (verb) _____

accommodate _____

subtle _____

redress _____

poignant _____

bedevil _____

promulgate _____

condescension _____

exhortation _____

indispensable _____

inherent _____

persevere _____

criterion _____

unscrupulous _____

rebuff _____

cajole _____

exposé _____

adulterate _____

forage _____

malefactors _____

insurgent _____

impetuous _____

Armageddon _____

resolute _____

jurisprudence _____

exude _____

repudiate _____

bellicose _____

exemplify _____

deprivation _____

Difficult-to-Spell Names and Terms from Reading and Lecture

IDENTIFICATION AND SIGNIFICANCE

After studying Chapter 21 of *A People and a Nation,* you should be able to identify fully *and* explain the historical significance of each item listed below.

- Identify each item in the space provided. Give an explanation or description of the item. Answer the questions *who, what, where,* and *when.*

- Explain the historical significance of each item in the space provided. Establish the historical context in which the item exists. Establish the item as the result of or as the cause of other factors existing in the society under study. Answer this question: *What were the political, social, economic, and/or cultural consequences of this item?*

1. Florence Kelley

   a. Identification

   b. Significance

2. interest-group politics

   a. Identification

   b. Significance

3. muckrakers

   a. Identification

   b. Significance

4. direct primaries and nonpartisan elections

   a. Identification

   b. Significance

5. the initiative, the referendum, and the recall

   a. Identification

   b. Significance

6. Alfred E. Smith, Robert F. Wagner, David I. Walsh, and Edward F. Dunne

   a. Identification

   b. Significance

7. Eugene V. Debs

   a. Identification

   b. Significance

8. southern progressivism

   a. Identification

   b. Significance

9. "old guard" Republicans

   a. Identification

   b. Significance

10. Robert M. La Follette

    a.   Identification

    b.   Significance

11. the Seventeenth Amendment

    a.   Identification

    b.   Significance

12. the National Child Labor Committee

    a.   Identification

    b.   Significance

13. the American Association for Old Age Security

    a.   Identification

    b.   Significance

14. the war on alcohol

    a.   Identification

    b.   Significance

15. the Eighteenth Amendment

    a. Identification

    b. Significance

16. white slavery

    a. Identification

    b. Significance

17. *The Social Evil in Chicago*

    a. Identification

    b. Significance

18. the Mann Act

    a. Identification

    b. Significance

19. G. Stanley Hall and John Dewey

    a. Identification

    b. Significance

20. the expansion of colleges and universities

    a.   Identification

    b.   Significance

21. Oliver Wendell Holmes, Jr.

    a.   Identification

    b.   Significance

22. Louis D. Brandeis

    a.   Identification

    b.   Significance

23. *Mueller v. Oregon*, *Lochner v. New York*, and *Holden v. Hardy*

    a.   Identification

    b.   Significance

24. Richard T. Ely

    a.   Identification

    b.   Significance

25. Lester Ward, Albion Small, and Edward Ross

    a.   Identification

    b.   Significance

26. Charles A. Beard

    a.   Identification

    b.   Significance

27. the National Consumers League

    a.   Identification

    b.   Significance

28. the Social Gospel

    a.   Identification

    b.   Significance

29. eugenics

    a.   Identification

    b.   Significance

30. *The Passing of the Great Race*

    a. Identification

    b. Significance

31. Booker T. Washington

    a. Identification

    b. Significance

32. the Atlanta Compromise

    a. Identification

    b. Significance

33. W. E. B. Du Bois

    a. Identification

    b. Significance

34. the Niagara movement

    a. Identification

    b. Significance

35. the National Association for the Advancement of Colored People

    a. Identification

    b. Significance

36. the Society of American Indians

    a. Identification

    b. Significance

37. "the woman movement"

    a. Identification

    b. Significance

38. the women's club movement

    a. Identification

    b. Significance

39. the National Association of Colored Women

    a. Identification

    b. Significance

40. the feminist movement

    a. Identification

    b. Significance

41. Charlotte Perkins Gilman

    a. Identification

    b. Significance

42. Margaret Sanger

    a. Identification

    b. Significance

43. the women's suffrage movement

    a. Identification

    b. Significance

44. Harriott Stanton Blatch

    a. Identification

    b. Significance

45. the Nineteenth Amendment

    a.   Identification

    b.   Significance

46. Theodore Roosevelt

    a.   Identification

    b.   Significance

47. the Northern Securities Company

    a.   Identification

    b.   Significance

48. the Hepburn Act

    a.   Identification

    b.   Significance

49. *The Jungle*

    a.   Identification

    b.   Significance

50. the Meat Inspection Act

    a. Identification

    b. Significance

51. the Pure Food and Drug Act

    a. Identification

    b. Significance

52. the coal strike of 1902

    a. Identification

    b. Significance

53. the Newlands Reclamation Act

    a. Identification

    b. Significance

54. Gifford Pinchot

    a. Identification

    b. Significance

55. the Panic of 1907

    a. Identification

    b. Significance

56. William Howard Taft

    a. Identification

    b. Significance

57. the Payne-Aldrich Tariff

    a. Identification

    b. Significance

58. the revolt against "Cannonism"

    a. Identification

    b. Significance

59. the Mann-Elkins Act of 1910

    a. Identification

    b. Significance

60. the Sixteenth Amendment

    a. Identification

    b. Significance

61. the National Progressive Republican League

    a. Identification

    b. Significance

62. the Progressive party

    a. Identification

    b. Significance

63. Woodrow Wilson

    a. Identification

    b. Significance

64. the presidential election of 1912

    a. Identification

    b. Significance

65. New Nationalism

    a. Identification

    b. Significance

66. New Freedom

    a. Identification

    b. Significance

67. the Clayton Anti-Trust Act

    a. Identification

    b. Significance

68. the Federal Trade Commission

    a. Identification

    b. Significance

69. the Federal Reserve Act of 1913

    a. Identification

    b. Significance

70. the discount rate

    a. Identification

    b. Significance

71. the Underwood Tariff

    a. Identification

    b. Significance

72. the income tax

    a. Identification

    b. Significance

73. the Federal Farm Loan Act of 1916

    a. Identification

    b. Significance

74. the Adamson Act of 1916

    a. Identification

    b. Significance

75. the presidential election of 1916

    a. Identification

    b. Significance

76. the War Industries Board

    a. Identification

    b. Significance

ORGANIZING, REVIEWING AND USING INFORMATION

Chart A

Approaches to Achieving Rights and Protection for Those with Limited Power, 1895–1920					
Vulnerable Groups	**Goals**	**Group Leaders and Advocates**	**Strategies**	**Impact of Non-Leaders' Activities**	**Helpful and Hindering Factors**
WOMEN					
AFRICAN AMERICANS					
INDIANS					
WORKERS					
CONSUMERS					

Chart B

Key Aspects of The "Trust- Buster" Presidencies, 1901–1913: Theodore Roosevelt

POLITICAL CHARACTER

Style and Handling of People	Philosophy and Principles	Position *vis-à-vis* Republican Party
		1901
		1908
		1912

RELATIONSHIP WITH BIG BUSINESS

	Policies, Approach	Appointments, Dismissals	Legislation	Supreme Court Rulings	Effect
Regulation					
Prices/Rates					
Taxation					
Tariffs					
Land/Resource Management					

RELATIONSHIP WITH LABOR

Strikes		
Working Conditions		

Chart C

Key Aspects of The "Trust- Buster" Presidencies, 1901–1913: William Howard Taft

POLITICAL CHARACTER

Style and Handling of People	Philosophy and Principles	Position *vis-à-vis* Republican Party
		1908
		1912

RELATIONSHIP WITH BIG BUSINESS

	Policies, Approach	Appointments, Dismissals	Legislation	Supreme Court Rulings	Effect
Regulation					
Prices/Rates					
Taxation					
Tariffs					
Land/Resource Management					

RELATIONSHIP WITH LABOR

Strikes		
Working Conditions		

IDEAS AND DETAILS

Objective 1

1. Organizations such as the American Bar Association, the National Consumers League, and the National Municipal League

    a.   increased the loyalty of the electorate to political parties.
    b.   introduced charismatic personalities to political campaigns.
    c.   stifled debate on major urban issues.
    d.   made politics more issue oriented than in previous eras.

Objective 2

2. In calling for direct primaries, middle-class progressives demonstrated which of the following beliefs?

    a.   Government should be placed in the hands of professional politicians.
    b.   All citizens should be allowed to participate in the decision-making process.
    c.   Politics can be improved by taking the nomination of candidates for political office out of the hands of party bosses and putting that power in the hands of the electorate.
    d.   Government should respect the rights of the individual.

Objectives 1 and 2

3. With regard to governmental reform, progressives wanted to

    a.   bargain with different interest groups to accomplish needed reforms.
    b.   use scientific principles to achieve political efficiency and to promote social and economic order.
    c.   require literacy tests for voting to ensure that the electorate was educated and responsible.
    d.   require full financial disclosure by all political candidates to ensure their independence from special-interest groups.

Objective 2

4. Unlike middle-class progressives, working-class progressives

    a.   were interested more in political reform than in social reform.
    b.   rejected the idea that the government should regulate the workplace.
    c.   usually supported moral reform movements such as prohibition.
    d.   often realized that urban political bosses could aid their reform efforts.

Objectives 1, 2, and 3

5. Most progressives did not ally with the socialists because progressives

    a.   were offended by the abrasive personality of Eugene Debs.
    b.   had a stake in the capitalist system and did not want to overthrow it.
    c.   rejected the nationalist appeals of the socialists.
    d.   accepted the basic tenets of the laissez-faire philosophy.

Objective 2

6.   Governor Robert M. La Follette believed that

   a.   corporations should be driven out of politics.
   b.   the working classes could never gain social justice in a capitalist society.
   c.   regulatory commissions represented a threat to the free enterprise system.
   d.   the federal government should nationalize the railroads.

Objective 4

7.   John Dewey believed that

   a.   public education should concentrate on the teaching of basic moral principles.
   b.   public school teachers should be accredited by a national accreditation agency.
   c.   mastery by students of a given body of knowledge should be the primary aim of public education.
   d.   public school curricula should be relevant to the lives of students.

Objective 5

8.   Which of the following best expresses the beliefs of Booker T. Washington?

   a.   Blacks should passively accept their inferior position in a white-dominated society.
   b.   Blacks should prove themselves worthy of equal rights by working hard and acquiring property.
   c.   Blacks should demand political and social equality in American society.
   d.   Blacks should challenge discriminatory legislation in the courts.

Objective 5

9.   The most decisive factor in the decision to extend the right to vote to women was

   a.   acceptance of the argument that all Americans are equal and deserve the same rights.
   b.   acceptance of the idea that women would humanize politics.
   c.   the contributions made by women on the home front during the First World War.
   d.   the militant tactics of women like Carrie Chapman Catt.

Objective 6

10.   President Roosevelt's handling of trusts suggests that he accepted which of the following beliefs?

   a.   Businesses must be allowed to operate and organize without government interference.
   b.   Antitrust laws should be used to prosecute unscrupulous corporations that exploit the public and refuse to regulate themselves.
   c.   Bigness is bad in and of itself.
   d.   The tax power of the government should be used to punish irresponsible corporations.

Objective 7

11.   Theodore Roosevelt and William Howard Taft differed in which of the following ways?

   a.   Roosevelt acted assertively to expand presidential power; Taft was cautious in his use of power.
   b.   Roosevelt took care not to offend business leaders; Taft was tactless and abrasive.
   c.   Roosevelt insisted on operating within the letter of the law; Taft was willing to bend the law to his purposes.
   d.   Roosevelt was sympathetic to reform; Taft found reform dangerous and unnecessary.

Objective 8

12. Roosevelt's New Nationalism, unlike Wilson's New Freedom, called for
    a. the destruction of big business.
    b. a restoration of laissez faire.
    c. cooperation between big business and big government through the establishment of regulatory commissions.
    d. equality of economic opportunity.

Objectives 8 and 9

13. By advocating passage of the Clayton Anti-Trust Act and the creation of the Federal Trade Commission, President Wilson
    a. demonstrated his belief that it was possible to legislate open competition.
    b. indicated his determination to challenge rulings of the Supreme Court.
    c. stubbornly challenged the probusiness Democratic leadership in Congress.
    d. acknowledged that government regulatory powers had to be expanded to deal with the reality of economic concentration.

Objective 9

14. The Underwood Tariff
    a. fostered competition by lowering tariff rates.
    b. was rejected by President Wilson because it levied a tax on personal income.
    c. established a 50 percent tax on incomes over $100,000.
    d. led to a trade war among the major trading nations.

Objective 10

15. In the final analysis, the progressives were able to
    a. bring about a redistribution of power in the United States.
    b. remove state and national government from the influence of business and industrial interests.
    c. establish the principle that government should intervene in social and political affairs to ensure fairness, health, and safety.
    d. unite behind a comprehensive reform program for American society.

ESSAY QUESTIONS

Objectives 1 and 2

1. Explain the social, political, and economic ideas of middle-class progressives, and evaluate their accomplishments at the local level of American society.

Objective 5

2. Discuss the similarities and differences between the approaches of Booker T. Washington and W. E. B. Du Bois to the problems faced by black Americans.

Objective 5

3. Discuss and evaluate the varying approaches of women to the problems they faced in early twentieth-century America.

Objective 6

4.   Explain Theodore Roosevelt's approach to big business and the philosophy behind that approach.

Objectives 8 and 9

5.   Defend the following statement: "As president, Wilson had to blend his New Freedom ideals with New Nationalism precepts, and in so doing he set the direction of federal economic policy for much of the twentieth century."

ANSWERS

Multiple-Choice Questions

1.   d.   Correct. Organizations such as those mentioned lobbied for their own interests and, as a result, caused politics to become more fragmented. At the same time, however, their attempts to educate the public stimulated debate and made politics more issue-oriented. See page 570.

   a.   No. Voter loyalty to political parties began to decline during the Progressive era. See page 570.

   b.   No. These organizations were not responsible for introducing charismatic personalities to political campaigns. See page 570.

   c.   No. These organizations often served to stimulate debate on urban issues rather than stifle it. See page 570.

2.   c.   Correct. Most middle-class progressive reformers were opposed to party politics, which they believed had been corrupted by political machines and political bosses. Therefore, the reforms they advocated were intended to improve government by reducing the power of political parties and party bosses. See page 571.

   a.   No. Progressives disliked professional politicians and disliked the fact that such politicians often selected candidates through the party caucus. It was for this reason that Progressives advocated the use of direct primaries to nominate candidates. See page 571.

   b.   No. Although middle-class progressive reformers advocated direct primaries as a way of returning government to "the people," they often meant middle-class people like themselves, excluding the working classes, blacks, and women from their definition of "the people." See page 571.

   d.   No. The direct primary was advocated as a way to nominate political candidates for office and does not demonstrate the belief that government should respect the rights of the individual. See page 571.

3.   b.   Correct. Professionals of the new middle class generally formed the progressive movement's leadership. They believed that practices important in their professions, such as systematic investigation and application of the scientific method, could be used by government to plan, control, and predict, thus achieving the goal of social and political efficiency. See pages 570–571.

   a.   No. Progressives were not necessarily against compromise, but they disliked the bargaining associated with "old style" politics. See pages 570–571.

   c.   No. Although the evidence indicates that progressives wanted political reforms designed to make government more responsive to "the people" by correcting the ills of "boss-ridden" party politics, progressives did not advocate literacy tests as a requirement for voting. See pages 570–571.

   d.   No. Although progressives advocated political reforms designed to make politicians more responsive to "the people," they did not suggest requiring full financial disclosure by all political candidates. See pages 570–571.

4.   d.   Correct. In their belief that government should be responsible for alleviating many of the problems associated with urban-industrial growth, working-class progressives realized that political bosses could be useful and that they were not necessarily enemies of reform. See page 571.

a.   No. Evidence indicates that most middle-class progressives were interested in political reform (the initiative, referendum, and recall), and most working-class progressives were interested in social reform (improvements in housing, safe factories, workers' compensation). See page 571.

b.   No. By advocating reforms that would shorten working hours and ensure safe factories, working-class progressives demonstrated their belief that government should ensure the safety and welfare of the worker by regulating the work place. See page 571.

c.   No. Working-class progressives usually rejected moral reforms such as prohibition and Sunday closing laws. See page 571.

5.   b.   Correct. Most progressives of the middle and working classes accepted the capitalist system, had relatively comfortable economic and social positions within that system, and had too much of a stake in that system to advocate its overthrow. See page 572.

a.   No. Eugene Debs's personality is not the reason that most progressives rejected socialist ideology. See page 572.

c.   No. A nationalist appeal is one that emphasizes devotion to country and nation. Progressives had a strong sense of devotion to the United States and often saw socialism as a radical attack against the nation's fundamental principles. See page 572.

d.   No. Progressives rejected the basic tenets of the laissez-faire philosophy as outdated and obsolete in an age of urban-industrial growth. See page 572.

6.   a.   Correct. La Follette believed that corporate involvement in politics was a source of political corruption and that corporations had amassed power at the expense of the people. Therefore, he advocated that corporations be driven out of politics. See page 574.

b.   No. Although this was a belief held by Eugene Debs (the leader of the Socialist party), La Follette, a progressive, did not share this belief. See page 574.

c.   No. La Follette's program (known as the "Wisconsin Idea") involved the establishment of regulatory commissions staffed with experts. See page 574.

d.   No. Although La Follette advocated regulation of railroad rates, he did not advocate nationalization (government ownership) of the railroads. See page 574.

7.   d.   Correct. Dewey believed that education should be related to the interests of students and that the subjects taught should relate directly to their lives. See page 577.

a.   No. Dewey did not believe that the teaching of moral principles should be the primary concern of public education. Furthermore, when such principles were dealt with, Dewey, who rejected the idea of moral absolutes, believed that they should be subjected to scientific inquiry. See page 577.

b.   No. Dewey did not propose the accreditation of public school teachers by a national accreditation agency. See page 577.

c.   No. Dewey rejected the idea that there was a fixed body of knowledge to be conveyed to students. He favored the "student-centered" as opposed to the "subject-centered" school. See page 577.

8. b.   Correct. Washington argued that while temporarily accepting their inferior position in American society, blacks should prove themselves worthy of equal rights by adopting a strategy of self-help. See pages 580–581.

    a.   No. It is incorrect to say that Washington believed that black Americans should "passively" accept their position in American society. See pages 580–581.

    c.   No. Washington believed that actively demanding and fighting for their political and social rights would prove to be counterproductive for black Americans. See pages 580–581.

    d.   No. Although it is true that Washington secretly contributed money to support legal challenges to discriminatory legislation, he did not believe that black Americans should challenge such legislation in an open, direct, or active manner. See pages 580–581.

9. c.   Correct. The efforts of women during the First World War were probably the most decisive factor in convincing legislators to extend the vote to women. See page 584.

    a.   No. Although the suffrage crusade grew out of the 1830s abolitionist argument in favor of equal rights for all Americans, the idea was rejected by many Americans in the 1910s just as it had been rejected in the 1830s. See page 584.

    b.   No. Since most Americans accepted traditional gender roles and the restrictions such roles placed on women, some suffragists used a traditionalist view (that women have "unique" qualities) to defend female suffrage. However, use of this argument was not "the most decisive factor" in the extension of the vote to women. See page 584.

    d.   No. Although Carrie Chapman Catt organized women at the precinct level so that pressure could be put on male politicians who opposed the extension of the vote to women, she is considered a moderate and did not engage in militant tactics. See page 584.

10. b.   Correct. Roosevelt preferred cooperation between government and business and preferred that business regulate itself. However, he was willing to prosecute trusts that unscrupulously exploited the public and refused to regulate themselves. See page 586.

    a.   No. Roosevelt's policy toward the Northern Securities Company and his support of the Hepburn Act, the Pure Food and Drug Act, and the Meat Inspection Act demonstrate his rejection of the idea that business must be allowed to organize and operate without government interference. See page 586.

    c.   No. Roosevelt, recognizing that business consolidation could bring efficiency, did not see bigness as bad in and of itself. See page 586.

    d.   No. Roosevelt's handling of the trusts does not indicate that he believed in using the tax power of the government (which was minimal since there was no income tax) to punish irresponsible corporations. See page 586.

11. a.   Correct. Roosevelt's handling of the trusts, his labor policy, and his actions on the issue of conservation indicate an assertion of presidential power. On the other hand, Taft's handling of the tariff issue and his inability to publicize issues he supported indicate caution and restraint. See pages 586–588.

    b.   No. Although Roosevelt preferred cooperation between business and government to confrontation, he often offended business leaders by speaking against their unscrupulous abuse of power. In contrast, although Taft supported federal regulation of business, he was quieter and his accomplishments were less publicized. See pages 586–588.

    c.   No. On the contrary, Roosevelt was far more willing to bend the law to his purposes than was Taft, who believed in the strict restraint of the law. See pages 586–588.

    d.   No. Both Roosevelt and Taft were sympathetic to reform. See pages 586–588.

12. c. Correct. Roosevelt called for federal regulatory commissions to establish cooperation between big business and big government, thereby protecting citizens' interests; but Wilson emphasized breaking up monopolies, returning to open competition, and using government to accomplish both. See page 589.

a. No. Neither Roosevelt nor Wilson called for the "destruction" of big business. See page 589.

b. No. Neither Roosevelt nor Wilson called for a restoration of the laissez-faire philosophy. See page 589.

d. No. Both Roosevelt and Wilson supported equality of economic opportunity. See page 589.

13. d. Correct. As president, Wilson realized that economic concentration had gone so far that a return to free competition was impossible. With this realization, Wilson accepted expansion of the government's regulatory powers to deal with the reality of economic concentration in the hands of big business. Wilson's acceptance of this principle is demonstrated by his support of the Clayton Anti-Trust Act and creation of the FTC. See page 590.

a. No. Wilson's support of the Clayton Antitrust Act and creation of the FTC demonstrates his acceptance of the fact that a return to open competition was impossible. See page 590.

b. No. Neither the Clayton Antitrust Act nor the bill creating the FTC was passed as a consequence of Supreme Court rulings. Therefore, they do not indicate a challenge by Wilson to the Court. See page 590.

c. No. The Democratic leadership in Congress favored passage of the Clayton Act and the bill creating the FTC. See page 590.

14. a. Correct. By reducing tariffs and thus encouraging imports, the Underwood Tariff encouraged free competition and free trade. See page 590.

b. No. President Wilson proposed and actively supported passage of the Underwood Tariff, including the income-tax provision. See page 590.

c. No. The Underwood Tariff imposed a graduated income tax on residents of the United States; the maximum rate was 6 percent, and that rate was applied to incomes over $500,000. See page 590.

d. No. Since the Underwood Tariff dramatically reduced tariff rates on imports, it did not lead to a trade war. See page 590.

15. c. Correct. By gaining public support for trust-busting and for legislation such as the Pure Food and Drug Act and the Meat Inspection Act, Progressives established the principle that government power could be used for the common good by ensuring fairness, health, and safety. See pages 591-592.

a. No. The strength of opposition to reform, court rulings against progressive legislation, and shortcomings of regulatory agencies are a few indications that, in many respects, progressives failed to bring about a redistribution of power. In 1920 government remained under the influence of business and industry. See pages 591–592.

b. No. Use of such devices as the initiative, the referendum, and the recall by special interests indicates that business and industrial interests still had influence and power at the state level, and the shortcomings of regulatory agencies indicate the same was true at the national level. See pages 591–592.

d. No. Progressives stressed different themes and different causes and often worked at cross-purposes. See pages 591–592.

CHAPTER 22

The Quest for Empire, 1865–1914

LEARNING OBJECTIVES

After you have studied Chapter 22 in your textbook and worked through this study guide chapter, you should be able to:

1. Examine the late-nineteenth-century sources of American expansionism and imperialism.

2. Discuss the role of ideology and culture in American expansionism and imperialism during the late nineteenth and early twentieth centuries.

3. Describe the expansionist vision of William H. Seward, and indicate the extent to which this vision was realized by the late 1880s.

4. Examine and evaluate relations between the United States and the following nations in the late nineteenth and early twentieth centuries:

    a.   Great Britain

    b.   Canada

5. Discuss the modernization of the United States Navy in the late nineteenth century.

6. Discuss the causes and consequences of the Hawaiian and Venezuelan crises.

7. Examine the causes (both underlying and immediate) and discuss the conduct of the Spanish-American-Cuban-Filipino War, and indicate the provisions of the Treaty of Paris.

8. Outline the arguments presented by both the anti-imperialists and the imperialists in the debate over acquisition of an empire, and explain why the imperialists prevailed.

9. Examine and evaluate late-nineteenth- and early-twentieth-century American policy toward Asia in general and toward the Philippines, China, and Japan, specifically.

10. Examine and evaluate United States policy toward the countries of Latin America in the late nineteenth and early twentieth century.

THEMATIC GUIDE

The expansionist and eventually imperialistic orientation of United States foreign policy after 1865 stemmed from the country's domestic situation. Those who led the internal expansion of the United States after the Civil War were also the architects of the nation's foreign policy. These national leaders, known collectively as the foreign policy elite, believed that extending American influence abroad would foster American prosperity, and they sought to use American foreign policy to open and safeguard foreign markets.

Many Americans harbored fears of the wider world, but the foreign policy elite realized that those fears could be alleviated if the world could be remade in the American image. Therefore, after the Civil War, these leaders advocated a nationalism based on the idea that Americans were a special people favored by God. Race-based arguments, gender-based arguments, and Social Darwinism were used to support the idea of American superiority and further the idea of expansion, and American missionaries went forth to convert the "heathen." Furthermore, a combination of political, economic, and cultural factors in the 1890s prompted the foreign policy elite to move beyond support of mere economic expansion toward advocacy of an imperialistic course for the United States—an imperialism characterized by a belief in the rightness of American society and American solutions.

The analysis of American expansionism serves as a backdrop for scrutiny of the American empire from the end of the Civil War to 1914. William H. Seward, as secretary of state from 1861 to 1869 and as a member of the foreign policy elite, was one of the chief architects of this empire. In examining Seward's expansionist vision and the extent to which it was realized by the late 1880s, we again see the relationship between domestic and foreign policy.

Acquisition of territories and markets abroad led the United States to heed the urgings of Captain Alfred T. Mahan and to embark on the building of the New Navy. The fleet gave the nation the means to protect America's international interests and to become more assertive, as in the Hawaiian, Venezuelan, and Cuban crises of the 1890s. The varied motives that led the United States into the Spanish-American-Cuban-Filipino War offer another striking example of the complex links between domestic and foreign policy. In these crises of the 1890s, the American frame of reference toward peoples of other nations became more noticeable in the shaping of foreign policy. In the Cuban crisis, as in the Venezuelan crisis, Americans insisted that the United States would establish the rules for nations in the Western Hemisphere.

The Treaty of Paris, which ended the Spanish-American-Cuban-Filipino War, sparked a debate between imperialists and anti-imperialists over the course of American foreign policy. We examine the arguments of the two groups and the reasons for the defeat of the anti-imperialists.

In the last two sections of the chapter, we turn to the American empire in Asia and Latin America. The American frame of reference with regard to other ethnic groups, along with American political, economic, and social interests, led to U.S. oppression of the Filipinos and shaped the Open Door policy as well as relations with Japan. The same factors determined American relations with Latin America. But in Latin America the United States used its power to impose its will and, through the Roosevelt Corollary to the Monroe Doctrine, assumed the role of "an international police power."

BUILDING VOCABULARY

Listed below are important words and terms that you need to know to get the most out of Chapter 22. They are listed in the order in which they occur in the chapter. After carefully looking through the list, (1) underline the words with which you are totally unfamiliar, (2) put a question mark by those words of which you are unsure, and (3) leave the rest alone.

As you begin to read the chapter, when you come to any of the words you've put question marks beside or underlined (1) slow your reading; (2) focus on the word and on its context in the sentence you're reading; (3) if you can understand the meaning of the word from its context in the sentence or passage in which it is used, go on with your reading; (4) if it's a word that you've underlined or a word that you can't understand from its context in the sentence or passage, look it up in a dictionary and write down the definition that best applies to the context in which the word is used.

Definitions

proselytize _____

ardent _____

derogatory _____

gape _____

indigenous _____

lucrative _____

usurp _____

unabashed _____

espouse _____

cosmopolitan _____

luminary _____

debase _____

tutelage _____

ethnocentric _____

obviate _____

aggrandizement _____

fruition _____

waft _____

lampoon _____

persevere _____

protectorate _____

postulate _____

oligarchy _____

rectitude _____

collusion _____

fiat _____

sensibility _____

insurgent _____

jettison _____

hegemony _____

inveterate _____

motley _____

rue _____

chafe _____

condescending _____

futile _____

embroilment _____

garner _____

consortium _____

rapprochement _____

augment _____

Difficult-to-Spell Names and Terms from Reading and Lecture

IDENTIFICATION AND SIGNIFICANCE

After studying Chapter 22 of *A People and a Nation,* you should be able to identify fully *and* explain the historical significance of each item listed below.

- Identify each item in the space provided. Give an explanation or description of the item. Answer the questions *who, what, where,* and *when.*

- Explain the historical significance of each item in the space provided. Establish the historical context in which the item exists. Establish the item as the result of or as the cause of other factors existing in the society under study. Answer this question: *What were the political, social, economic, and/or cultural consequences of this item?*

1. Lottie Moon

    a. Identification

    b. Significance

2. expansionism versus imperialism

    a. Identification

    b. Significance

3. the foreign policy elite

   a. Identification

   b. Significance

4. the idea of a racial hierarchy

   a. Identification

   b. Significance

5. male ethos and imperialism

   a. Identification

   b. Significance

6. *Our Country*

   a. Identification

   b. Significance

7. the Burlingame Treaty

   a. Identification

   b. Significance

8. the massacre at Rock Springs, Wyoming

    a. Identification

    b. Significance

9. the San Francisco School Board's segregation order

    a. Identification

    b. Significance

10. Student Volunteers for Foreign Missions

    a. Identification

    b. Significance

11. William H. Seward

    a. Identification

    b. Significance

12. the purchase of Alaska

    a. Identification

    b. Significance

13. the transatlantic cable

    a.   Identification

    b.   Significance

14. Hamilton Fish

    a.   Identification

    b.   Significance

15. the Washington Treaty

    a.   Identification

    b.   Significance

16. the Samoan Islands

    a.   Identification

    b.   Significance

17. navalism

    a.   Identification

    b.   Significance

18. Captain Alfred T. Mahan

    a.   Identification

    b.   Significance

19. the New Navy

    a.   Identification

    b.   Significance

20. Turner's frontier thesis

    a.   Identification

    b.   Significance

21. the Hawaiian-annexation question

    a.   Identification

    b.   Significance

22. Hawai'i's 1887 constitution

    a.   Identification

    b.   Significance

23. the McKinley Tariff of 1890

    a.   Identification

    b.   Significance

24. the 1893 overthrow of the Hawaiian government

    a.   Identification

    b.   Significance

25. the Venezuelan crisis of 1895

    a.   Identification

    b.   Significance

26. the Cuban revolution

    a.   Identification

    b.   Significance

27. José Martí

    a.   Identification

    b.   Significance

28. the Wilson-Gorman Tariff

    a.   Identification

    b.   Significance

29. General Valeriano Weyler

    a.   Identification

    b.   Significance

30. the *Maine*

    a.   Identification

    b.   Significance

31. the de Lôme letter

    a.   Identification

    b.   Significance

32. McKinley's war message

    a.   Identification

    b.   Significance

33. the Teller Amendment

    a.   Identification

    b.   Significance

34. the Spanish-American-Cuban-Filipino War

    a.   Identification

    b.   Significance

35. Commodore George Dewey

    a.   Identification

    b.   Significance

36. the Treaty of Paris

    a.   Identification

    b.   Significance

37. anti-imperialist arguments

    a.   Identification

    b.   Significance

38. imperialist arguments

    a. Identification

    b. Significance

39. Emilio Aguinaldo

    a. Identification

    b. Significance

40. the Philippine Insurrection

    a. Identification

    b. Significance

41. the Moros

    a. Identification

    b. Significance

42. the Jones Act

    a. Identification

    b. Significance

43. the Open Door policy

    a. Identification

    b. Significance

44. the Boxer Rebellion

    a. Identification

    b. Significance

45. the United Fruit Company

    a. Identification

    b. Significance

46. the Platt Amendment

    a. Identification

    b. Significance

47. Walter Reed

    a. Identification

    b. Significance

48. Puerto Rican–United States relations

    a.   Identification

    b.   Significance

49. the Hay-Pauncefote Treaty of 1901

    a.   Identification

    b.   Significance

50. the Panamanian revolution

    a.   Identification

    b.   Significance

51. the Panama Canal

    a.   Identification

    b.   Significance

52. the Roosevelt Corollary to the Monroe Doctrine

    a.   Identification

    b.   Significance

53. American investments in Mexico

    a. Identification

    b. Significance

54. the Portsmouth Conference

    a. Identification

    b. Significance

55. the Taft-Katsura Agreement

    a. Identification

    b. Significance

56. the Root-Takahira Agreement

    a. Identification

    b. Significance

57. the Great White Fleet

    a. Identification

    b. Significance

58. dollar diplomacy

    a.   Identification

    b.   Significance

59. Anglo-American rapprochement

    a.   Identification

    b.   Significance

ORGANIZING, REVIEWING, AND USING INFORMATION

Chart A

American Use of Its Power and Influence Abroad, 1865–1914

Purpose	Diplomatic Activity	Military Activity	Economic Activity	Conspiratorial Activity	Effect
Protection of property of Americans or American companies abroad					
Acquisition of territory or access to assets of military or economic value					

Chart A

American Use of Its Power and Influence Abroad, 1865–1914

Purpose	Diplomatic Activity	Military Activity	Economic Activity	Conspiratorial Activity	Effect
Guarantee of trade and tariff policies favorable to American business interests					
Management of a civil war, insurrection, or potential secession in another country					

Chart A

American Use of Its Power and Influence Abroad, 1865–1914

Purpose	Diplomatic Activity	Military Activity	Economic Activity	Conspiratorial Activity	Effect
Control of the form of government, constitution, legal institutions, trade agreements or treaties of another country/territory					
Influence on another country's cultural development, religious makeup, or value system					

Chart B

America's Quest for Empire
Territorial Expansion, 1865–1914

	How Acquired *(military force or intimidation, agreement with indigenous leaders, plot to overthrow government, etc.)*	Type of Acquisition *(claim, purchase, treaty after war, annexation, etc.)*	Primary Reason for Acquisition *(Advantage to U.S—naval base, resources, protection of trade, etc.)*	Advantages and Disadvantages to Indigenous Population	Indigenous People *(Opposition to American role, local autonomy, etc.)*
NORTH AMERICA (INCL. CENTRAL AMERICA) Alaska (1867)					
Panama Canal Zone (1903)					
CARIBBEAN AND EXTREME W. ATLANTIC Puerto Rico (1898)					
SOUTH PACIFIC American Samoa (1899)					

Chart B

America's Quest for Empire Territorial Expansion, 1865–1914

	How Acquired (military force or intimidation, agreement with indigenous leaders, plot to overthrow government, etc.)	Type of Acquisition (claim, purchase, treaty after war, annexation, etc.)	Primary Reason for Acquisition (Advantage to U.S—naval base, resources, protection of trade, etc.)	Advantages and Disadvantages to Indigenous Population	Relations with Indigenous People (Opposition to American role, local autonomy, etc.)
CENTRAL PACIFIC Hawai'i (1897)					
Midway Islands (1867)					
WEST PACIFIC Wake Island (1898)					
Guam (1898)					
EAST ASIA Philippines (1898)					

IDEAS AND DETAILS

Objective 1

1.   Foreign policy decisions in the late nineteenth century were shaped largely by

     a.   the opinions of the American people.
     b.   the business community.
     c.   the foreign policy elite.
     d.   generals and admirals.

Objective 1

2.   One of the sources of the expansionist sentiment of the late nineteenth century was the

     a.   desire of American farmers to learn new agricultural techniques from foreign agricultural specialists.
     b.   belief that foreign economic expansion would relieve the problem of overproduction at home.
     c.   belief that more immigrants would solve domestic labor problems.
     d.   desire of Latin American countries for the United States to exert political control over them.

Objectives 1 and 2

3.   *Our Country* by Josiah Strong provides evidence that

     a.   most American religious leaders in the late nineteenth century were critical of American foreign policy in general and of American imperialism in particular.
     b.   belief in the superiority of Anglo-Saxons was used in the late nineteenth century to justify American expansion.
     c.   late-nineteenth-century American foreign policy was based on the principle that all nations in the world should be allowed to determine their own form of government and economic system.
     d.   the unprofessional nature of the American diplomatic corps in the late nineteenth century was a constant embarrassment to the United States.

Objective 3

4.   William H. Seward's vision of an American empire

     a.   was confined to the Americas.
     b.   included the building of a Central American canal.
     c.   involved acquisition of territory by military conquest.
     d.   took a giant step forward with the purchase of the Danish West Indies in 1867.

Objective 5

5.   The person largely responsible for popularizing the New Navy was

     a.   Andrew Carnegie.
     b.   Ulysses Grant.
     c.   Hamilton Fish.
     d.   Alfred T. Mahan.

Objective 6

6.   President Grover Cleveland opposed the annexation of Hawai'i because he

    a.   saw no economic advantages to it.

    b.   wanted no close ties with people of another race.

    c.   learned that a majority of Hawaiians opposed annexation.

    d.   was afraid it would lead to war.

Objective 6

7.   In the settlement of the Venezuelan crisis of 1895,

    a.   the United States showed a disregard for the rights of Venezuela.

    b.   the United States insisted that Venezuela adopt a democratic form of government.

    c.   Great Britain was able to bully the United States into submission.

    d.   the United States Navy showed its inability to operate in a crisis.

Objectives 7 and 10

8.   The Teller Amendment

    a.   announced that the United States would annex Cuba.

    b.   led to the declaration of war against Spain.

    c.   expanded the theater of war to the South Pacific.

    d.   renounced any American intentions to annex Cuba.

Objective 7

9.   Which of the following is the best explanation for the United States's declaration of war against Spain in 1898?

    a.   The war was undertaken out of a humanitarian desire to help the Cuban people.

    b.   Many farmers and businesspeople believed that victory would open new markets for America's surplus production.

    c.   Many conservatives believed that the war would act as a national unifier by unleashing a spirit of patriotism.

    d.   All of the above were motives for the war because different groups justified the war in different ways.

Objective 7

10.   Most American casualties in the Spanish-American-Cuban-Filipino War were incurred

    a.   through diseases contracted during the war.

    b.   in the Santiago campaign.

    c.   in Admiral Dewey's battle with the Spanish fleet in Manila Bay.

    d.   by the Rough Riders in the charge up San Juan Hill.

Objective 8

11.   The anti-imperialist campaign against the Treaty of Paris was

    a.   based on purely constitutional arguments.

    b.   hindered by the inconsistency of the anti-imperialist arguments.

    c.   successful because of the influence of people like Mark Twain and Andrew Carnegie.

    d.   successful because of Bryan's decision to support the treaty.

Objective 9

12. In the Philippines, the United States

   a.   fought to suppress an insurrection against American rule.
   b.   quickly lived up to its promise to give the country its independence.
   c.   held a referendum to determine the wishes of the Filipino people.
   d.   established a democratic government that guaranteed the same basic rights enjoyed by Americans.

Objective 9

13. Which of the following best expresses the ideology behind the Open Door policy?

   a.   The self-determination of other nations must be preserved.
   b.   The closing of any area to American trade is a threat to the survival of the United States.
   c.   Freedom of the seas will lead to the economic expansion of the world community of nations.
   d.   All nations of the world should be considered equals.

Objective 10

14. Which of the following best explains the rationale behind the Roosevelt Corollary to the Monroe Doctrine and the imperialistic behavior of the United States in Latin America?

   a.   The United States believed it had the duty to help Latin Americans find the political system best suited to their culture.
   b.   The United States believed prevention of outside intervention in Latin America, and thus the preservation of its own security, required stability in the region.
   c.   The United States believed it should share its wealth and resources with the people of Latin America.
   d.   The United States believed that it had the right to colonize Latin America to exploit the resources of the region.

Objective 9

15. Relations between the United States and Japan were negatively affected by

   a.   the extension of American aid to French colonies in Indochina.
   b.   American refusal to recognize Japanese hegemony in Korea.
   c.   President Roosevelt's extension of military aid to Russia during the Russo-Japanese war.
   d.   the involvement of American bankers in an international consortium to build a Chinese railway.

ESSAY QUESTIONS

Objectives 1, 2, 6, 7, 8 and 10

1.   Defend or refute the following statement in the context of American policy toward Central America and the Caribbean in the late nineteenth and early twentieth centuries: "The persistent American belief that other people cannot solve their own problems and that only the American model of government will work produced what historian William Appleman Williams has called 'the tragedy of American diplomacy.'"

Objective 1

2. Explain the relationship between domestic affairs and foreign affairs. How did domestic affairs during the late nineteenth century lead to an expansionist foreign policy?

Objective 8

3. Discuss the debate between the imperialists and the anti-imperialists, and explain why the former prevailed.

Objective 9

4. Explain American foreign policy toward China in the late nineteenth and early twentieth centuries.

MAP EXERCISE

On the outline map that follows and using the map on page 614 in the textbook as a guide:

1. Label the southernmost states of the United States.

2. Locate and mark the following Latin American countries and cities:

Countries

- Mexico
- Guatemala
- British Honduras (now Belize)
- Honduras
- El Salvador
- Nicaragua
- Costa Rica
- Panama
- Colombia
- Venezuela
- Cuba
- Jamaica
- Haiti
- Dominican Republic
- Puerto Rico

Cities

- Miami
- New Orleans
- Columbus, New Mexico

- Mexico City
- Tampico
- Veracruz

3. Using an atlas, mark the locations of the capitals of the Latin American countries that are shown on the outline map.

4. The United States has long been interested in and involved in Latin American affairs. Why?

ANSWERS

Multiple-Choice Questions

1. c. Correct. The foreign policy elite, made up of "opinion leaders" from many areas of American society (business, politics, the military, labor, agriculture), were instrumental in the late nineteenth century, as they are instrumental today, in shaping American foreign policy. See pages 598–599.

    a. No. The American public has not traditionally paid a great deal of attention to nor been well educated on foreign policy issues. As a result, foreign policy, unlike domestic policy, is not usually "shaped" by the people. See pages 598–599.

    b. No. Although the business community has a hand in the shaping of foreign policy, it is a mistake to say that the business community alone was "largely" responsible for foreign policy decisions. See pages 598–599.

    d. No. Although military leaders have a hand in the shaping of foreign policy, it is a mistake to say that such policy in the late nineteenth century was "shaped largely" by this one group. See pages 598–599.

2. b. Correct. In the final third of the nineteenth century, depressions affected the U.S. economy about once a decade. Many business and farm leaders believed overproduction was a major cause of economic declines and advocated expansion into foreign markets as a preventive measure. See page 599.

    a. No. American farm leaders did not seek an expansionist foreign policy for the purpose of learning new agricultural techniques from foreign agricultural specialists. See page 599.

    c. No. The expansionist sentiment of the late nineteenth century was not fueled by the belief that domestic labor problems could be solved by increasing the number of immigrants. See page 599.

    d. No. Although U.S. economic and political influence increased in Latin America in the late nineteenth century, especially after the Spanish-American War, the states of Latin America did not want the United States to exert political control over them. See page 599.

3. b. Correct. In his book, Reverend Josiah Strong stated the belief that the Anglo-Saxon race was superior to and was destined to lead others. See page 600.

    a. Although some religious leaders doubtless criticized American foreign policy in the late nineteenth century, it is a mistake to say that "most" did so. Certainly, Reverend Josiah Strong was not critical of American imperialism in Our Country. See page 600.

    c. No. Our Country does not provide evidence that late-nineteenth-century American foreign policy was based on the principle of self-determination. See page 600.

    d. No. Although it is true that the American diplomatic corps was one of the worst in the world in the late nineteenth century, this was not a topic that Reverend Josiah Strong dealt with in his book. See page 600.

4.   b.   Correct. Seward advocated a canal through Central America as essential to the unity of the large American empire that he envisioned. See page 602.

a.   No. Seward's vision of an American empire included Iceland, Greenland, Hawai'i, and certain Pacific islands as well as expansion throughout the Americas. See page 602.

c.   No. Seward believed that other peoples would find the republican principles of American society attractive. Therefore, they would naturally gravitate toward the United States, making expansion by military means unnecessary. See page 602.

d.   No. Although in 1867 Seward signed a treaty with Denmark to buy the Danish West Indies, the treaty was not ratified by the Senate. The Danish West Indies did not become part of the American empire until 1917. See page 602.

5.   d.   Correct. Alfred T. Mahan argued that a modern, efficient naval force was essential for any nation that aspired to great-power status. Through his lectures and published works, he had an enormous impact on the successful drive to modernize the United States Navy, popularly known as the "New Navy." See page 604.

a.   No. Andrew Carnegie was founder of the Carnegie Steel Company, which controlled most of the steel production in the United States by 1900. Although he supported the concept of the "New Navy" and signed a lucrative naval contract in 1883, he was not responsible for "popularizing" the New Navy. See page 604.

b.   No. Ulysses Grant was not responsible for popularizing the New Navy. See page 604.

c.   No. Hamilton Fish, secretary of state under President Grant, was not responsible for popularizing the New Navy. See page 604.

6.   c.   Correct. Cleveland supported economic expansion but did not believe it should lead to imperialism. (See page 597 for the distinction between economic expansion and imperialism.) The facts of the Hawaiian revolution, revealed to him through an investigation he ordered, convinced the new president that annexation was being forced on the Hawaiians and was, therefore, imperialistic. See page 605.

a.   No. Grover Cleveland was an expansionist who recognized the economic advantages of annexing the Hawaiian islands. His opposition to annexation was not based on economic questions. See page 605.

b.   No. Cleveland's opposition to the annexation of Hawaii was not based on racial questions. See page 605.

d.   No. Cleveland's opposition to the annexation of Hawaii was not based on fear that it would lead to war. See page 605.

7.   a.   Correct. The boundary dispute between Venezuela and Great Britain was settled by an Anglo-American arbitration board that barely consulted Venezuela in its deliberations. By disregarding Venezuela's rights and sensibilities in this manner, the United States displayed an imperialistic attitude. See pages 605–606.

b.   No. The crisis did not center on the question of the type of government Venezuela had. See pages 605–606.

c.   No. The United States sent a strong protest to the British concerning their actions in Venezuela. The British stalled at first but then, not wanting war, bowed to American pressure. As a result, the Monroe Doctrine was strengthened and the United States and Great Britain began to form closer ties. See pages 605–606.

d.   No. The United States Navy did not become involved in the Venezuelan crisis of 1895. See pages 605–606.

8.   d.   Correct. After passing resolutions declaring Cuba to be free, Congress adopted the Teller Amendment, which disclaimed any intention by the United States to annex Cuba. See page 607.

a.   No. The Teller Amendment did not announce American intentions to annex Cuba. See page 607.

b.   No. The Teller Amendment, passed by the U.S. Congress, was related to the Spanish-American-Cuban-Filipino War, but it was not a reason for the war. See page 607.

c.   No. The Teller Amendment did not have the effect of expanding the Spanish-American-Cuban-Filipino War to the South Pacific. See page 607.

9.   d.   Correct. Those who supported the war came from a variety of groups in the United States, with each group having its own reason for supporting the war. To review the mixed and complex motives for the war, see page 608.

a.   No. Although there was a humanitarian aspect to United States entry into the Spanish-American War, this is not the best answer to this question. See page 608.

b.   No. Although farmers and businesspeople did support the war because they believed victory would open new markets for America's surplus production, this is not the best answer to the question. See page 608.

d.   No. Although many conservatives supported the war because they believed it would act as a national unifier by unleashing a spirit of patriotism, this is not the best answer to the question. See page 608.

10.   a.   Correct. Of the over 5,400 Americans who died in the war, only 379 died in combat. All others died from malaria or yellow fever. See pages 608–609.

b.   No. In the destruction of the Spanish fleet outside Santiago harbor, the Spanish suffered 474 killed and wounded, and the United States suffered one killed and one wounded. This does not constitute "most" of the 5,400 Americans who lost their lives in the Spanish-American War. See pages 608–609.

c.   No. In the Battle of Manila Bay (May 1, 1898) Spanish losses numbered 381 killed, and American casualties consisted of 8 wounded. See pages 608–609.

d.   No. In the charge up San Juan Hill, the Rough Riders lost about 89 men. This does not constitute "most" of the 5,400 Americans who lost their lives in the Spanish-American War. See pages 608–609.

11. b.   Correct. The anti-imperialists came from many different interest groups in American society. Each group looked at domestic issues differently and also found it impossible to speak with one voice on foreign policy issues. Therefore, they were hindered by the inconsistency of their arguments. See page 610.

a.   No. The anti-imperialists used a variety of arguments in their campaign against the Treaty of Paris. See pages 609–610.

c.   No. Although Mark Twain and Andrew Carnegie spoke against the Treaty of Paris, the treaty passed by a 57-to-27 vote in the Senate. See pages 609–610.

d.   No. Believing it best to end the war and then push for Filipino independence, William Jennings Bryan supported the Treaty of Paris. However, his support for the treaty did not aid the anti-imperialist campaign. The treaty passed by a 57-to-27 vote. See pages 609–610.

12. a.   Correct. The Filipinos felt betrayed by the Treaty of Paris and, under the leadership of Emilio Aguinaldo, fought for their independence in the Philippine Insurrection. American forces finally suppressed the insurrection in 1901, leaving 5,000 Americans and 200,000 Filipinos dead. See page 610.

b.   No. The Philippines were not granted independence until 1946. See page 610.

c.   No. The United States assumed that it knew what was best for the Filipino people and held no referendum. See page 610.

d.   No. The United States held sovereignty over the Philippines for forty-eight years. Although it attempted to establish a democratic government over the years, the United States did not guarantee to the Filipino people the same rights enjoyed by American citizens. See page 610.

13. b.   Correct. The ideology expressed in the Open Door was that the United States required exports; therefore, any area closed to American products, citizens, or ideas threatened the survival of the United States. See page 613.

a.   No. As an ideology rather than just a policy, the Open Door was not based on the preservation of the self-determination of other nations. See page 613.

c.   No. As an ideology rather than just a policy, the Open Door was not based on the idea that freedom of the seas would lead to the economic expansion of the world community of nations. See page 613.

d.   No. As an ideology rather than just a policy, the Open Door was not based on the belief that all nations of the world should be considered equals. See page 613.

14. b.   Correct. The United States believed that the debts-default crisis in Latin America invited intervention by European powers acting to protect the financial interests of European banks. President Roosevelt deemed this to be a threat to the security of the United States and its interests in the region, which included not only American commercial and investment interests, but the Panama Canal as well. Therefore, the United States, to preserve its own security, believed that financial and political stability were essential in Latin America. Both the Roosevelt Corollary and U.S. behavior in the region demonstrate that the United States was willing to be the policeman of the region to protect its economic interests, its dominance, and to establish order. See page 616.

a.   No. Both the Roosevelt Corollary and U.S. actions in Latin America support the idea that in the late nineteenth and early twentieth centuries the United States believed in the rightness of its political system for Latin America. See page 616.

c.   No. Although the United States has shared some of its wealth and resources with the people of Latin America, this clearly is not the rationale behind the Roosevelt Corollary. See page 616.

d.   No. The Roosevelt Corollary to the Monroe Doctrine was an attempt to prevent European intervention in Latin America, not encourage it. See page 616.

15. d.   Correct. In an effort to increase American influence in Manchuria, President Taft was able to gain agreement on the inclusion of a group of American bankers in a four-power consortium to build a Chinese railway. In response (and in defiance of the Open Door policy), Japan signed a treaty with Russia by which the two staked out spheres of influence in China for themselves. This strengthened Japan's position in Manchuria and caused more friction between the U.S. and Japan. See page 617.

a.   No. The United States did not extend aid to French colonies in Indochina in the early twentieth century. See page 617.

b.   No. In its efforts to protect American interests in the Pacific (especially in the Philippines), the United States made concessions to Japan—the dominant power in Asia. Therefore, in the Taft-Katsura Agreement of 1905 the United States recognized Japanese hegemony in Korea and, in return, the Japanese pledged not to interfere with American interests in the Philippines. See page 617.

c.   No. The United States did not want either Russia or Japan to become dominant in Asia but wanted each to balance the power of the other. Therefore, the U.S. remained neutral in the conflict and President Roosevelt, at the request of the Japanese, agreed to mediate the crisis. See page 617.

CHAPTER 23

Americans in the Great War, 1914–1920

LEARNING OBJECTIVES

After you have studied Chapter 23 in your textbook and worked through this study guide chapter, you should be able to:

1. Discuss Europe's descent into the First World War.

2. Discuss both President Woodrow Wilson's attempts and the attempts of antiwar activists to keep the United States out of the First World War, and explain the ultimate failure of those efforts.

3. Discuss the response of Americans to the First World War and to American entry into the war, and indicate the extent to which United States participation influenced the outcome of the conflict.

4. Describe the characteristics of draftees and volunteers in the American armed forces during the First World War and discuss their lives as soldiers.

5. Examine the impact of the First World War on the American home front, including its impact on the federal government, business, labor, women, and African Americans.

6. Explain and evaluate the record of government at the local, state, and national levels on civil-liberties questions during and after the war.

7. Explain the differences and similarities between Wilsonianism as stated in Wilson's Fourteen Points and the provisions of the Treaty of Versailles.

8. Examine the debate over ratification of the Treaty of Versailles and American entry into the League of Nations, and explain the Senate's rejection of the treaty.

9. Examine the impact of the First World War on America's role in world affairs

THEMATIC GUIDE

In Chapter 23, we deal with the causes of the First World War, American entry into the war, and the political, social, and economic impact of the war on the United States and its people. The nation's entry into the war is discussed in "Precarious Neutrality" and "The Decision for War." Although President Wilson proclaimed the United States to be a neutral in the European conflict, three realities made neutrality practically impossible. Those realities confirm the interrelation of domestic and foreign policy (a dominant theme in Chapter 22). Furthermore, the discussion of the tenets of Wilsonianism and Wilson's strict interpretation of international law reinforces the concept that a nation's foreign policy is based on its perception of the world community of nations and of its relationship to those nations.

Besides the underlying reasons for American entry into the war, there were obvious and immediate reasons for that decision: the naval warfare between Great Britain and Germany, the use of the submarine by the Germans, and Wilson's interpretation of international law as he attempted to protect the rights of the United States as a neutral nation. The authors' inference that Americans got caught in the crossfire between the Allies and the Central Powers is supported through the tracing of United States policy from the sinking of the *Lusitania* to the adoption of unrestricted submarine warfare by the

Germans. Therefore, the Zimmermann telegram, perceived as a direct threat to American security by American officials, the arming of American commercial ships, and additional sinkings of American ships by German submarines brought a declaration of war by Congress. Finally, America went to war because of a special sense of mission. The country went to war to reform world politics, war being the only means that guaranteed Wilson a seat and an insider's voice at the peace table.

In spite of antiwar sentiment in the United States, the country began to prepare for war before the actual declaration, as can be seen in the passage of the National Defense Act, the Navy Act, and the Revenue Act. Once war was declared, the country turned to the draft (the Selective Service Act) to raise the necessary army. Even though American military and political leaders believed that American virtue could reshape the world, they feared that the world would reshape the virtue of American soldiers. Despite attempts to protect that virtue, venereal disease became a serious problem within the army. Furthermore, American soldiers could not be shielded from the graver threat of influenza and pneumonia, and more soldiers died from disease than on the battlefield. Another serious problem in the American army—one that government and army officials did little to combat—was racism. Not only were African Americans segregated within the army, but they were also subjected to various forms of racial discrimination.

Mobilization of the nation for the war effort altered American life. Government power increased, especially in the economic sphere. Government-business cooperation became part of official government policy. Centralized governmental control and planning of the nation's economy were largely successful, but there were mistakes and problems. Government policy caused inflation; government tax policies meant that only one-third of the war was financed through taxes; and, although organized labor made some gains, it usually took a back seat to the needs of corporations.

The war intensified the divisions within the pluralistic American society. Entry of more women into previously "male" jobs brought negative reactions by male workers. Increased northward migration of African Americans intensified racist fears and animosities in factories and neighborhoods. The government's fear of dissent and of foreigners led to the trampling of civil liberties at the national, state, and local levels. In the immediate aftermath of the war, events both within and outside the country heightened these fears, culminating in the Red Scare and the Palmer Raids. The American effort to "make the world safe for democracy" brought actions on the home front that seemed to indicate a basic distrust of democracy.

Divisions also intensified on the political front, as the debate over the Treaty of Versailles indicates. In "The Defeat of Peace" Wilson's Fourteen Points are contrasted with the actual terms of the treaty. The divergence was an issue used in the arguments of those opposed to the treaty and to American entry into the League of Nations. But the core of the problem lay in Article 10 of the League covenant. Critics charged that the collective-security provisions of this article would allow League members to call out the United States Army without congressional approval. The *belief* of many that this was true was at the heart of the debate against the League. Fear that the United States would be forced to forgo its traditional unilateralism in foreign affairs led the Senate to reject the treaty and American entry into the League of Nations.

The American experience in the First World War influenced every aspect of American life, producing consequences for the future. The war changed America's place in world affairs to one of world prominence, and it continued to shape America's institutions and decisions both at home and abroad long after 1920.

BUILDING VOCABULARY

Listed below are important words and terms that you need to know to get the most out of Chapter 23. They are listed in the order in which they occur in the chapter. After carefully looking through the list,

(1) underline the words with which you are totally unfamiliar, (2) put a question mark by those words of which you are unsure, and (3) leave the rest alone.

As you begin to read the chapter, when you come to any of the words you've put question marks beside or underlined (1) slow your reading; (2) focus on the word and on its context in the sentence you're reading; (3) if you can understand the meaning of the word from its context in the sentence or passage in which it is used, go on with your reading; (4) if it's a word that you've underlined or a word that you can't understand from its context in the sentence or passage, look it up in a dictionary and write down the definition that best applies to the context in which the word is used.

Definitions

distraught _____

lament _____

pacifist _____

portentous _____

chide _____

engorge _____

goad _____

conflagration _____

fervently _____

archetype _____

prophesy _____

confiscation _____

waive _____

flout _____

deftly _____

marauding _____

decadent _____

acquisitive _____

filibuster _____

maelstrom _____

miasmic _____

retort _____

menial _____

carnage _____

circumscribe _____

abdicate _____

stymie _____

virulent _____

pandemic _____

forage _____

sleuth _____

exhort _____

scurrilous _____

throttle _____

extol _____

despotic _____

ominous _____

stalwart _____

belfry _____

ardent _____

formidable _____

reparations _____

indemnity _____

preponderant _____

punitive _____

euphoric _____

rectify _____

peevish _____

placate _____

Difficult-to-Spell Names and Terms from Reading and Lecture

IDENTIFICATION AND SIGNIFICANCE

After studying Chapter 23 of *A People and a Nation,* you should be able to identify fully *and* explain the historical significance of each item listed below.

- Identify each item in the space provided. Give an explanation or description of the item. Answer the questions *who, what, where,* and *when.*

- Explain the historical significance of each item in the space provided. Establish the historical context in which the item exists. Establish the item as the result of or as the cause of other factors existing in the society under study. Answer this question: *What were the political, social, economic, and/or cultural consequences of this item?*

1. the *Luisitania*

    a. Identification

    b. Significance

2. the resignation of Secretary of State William Jennings Bryan

    a. Identification

    b. Significance

3. the assassination of Archduke Franz Ferdinand

    a. Identification

    b. Significance

4. President Wilson's proclamation of neutrality

    a. Identification

    b. Significance

5. Wilsonianism

  a. Identification

  b. Significance

6. British naval policy

  a. Identification

  b. Significance

7. neutral rights

  a. Identification

  b. Significance

8. the submarine and international law

  a. Identification

  b. Significance

9. the *Arabic*

  a. Identification

  b. Significance

10. the *Sussex*

    a.   Identification

    b.   Significance

11. the peace movement

    a.   Identification

    b.   Significance

12. unrestricted submarine warfare

    a.   Identification

    b.   Significance

13. the Zimmermann telegram

    a.   Identification

    b.   Significance

14. the armed-ship bill

    a.   Identification

    b.   Significance

15. Wilson's war message

   a. Identification

   b. Significance

16. Jeannette Rankin

   a. Identification

   b. Significance

17. the National Defense Act of 1916 and the Navy Act of 1916

   a. Identification

   b. Significance

18. the Selective Service Act

   a. Identification

   b. Significance

19. African American enlistees in the military

   a. Identification

   b. Significance

20. "evaders," "deserters," and COs

   a. Identification

   b. Significance

21. General John J. Pershing

   a. Identification

   b. Significance

22. trench warfare and poison gas

   a. Identification

   b. Significance

23. shell shock (war psychosis)

   a. Identification

   b. Significance

24. venereal disease among American soldiers

   a. Identification

   b. Significance

25. the Bolshevik Revolution
    a. Identification

    b. Significance

26. Wilson's Fourteen Points
    a. Identification

    b. Significance

27. the Food Administration, the Railroad Administration, and the Fuel Administration
    a. Identification

    b. Significance

28. the War Industries Board
    a. Identification

    b. Significance

29. the Revenue Act of 1916
    a. Identification

    b. Significance

30. the War Revenue Act of 1917

     a. Identification

     b. Significance

31. women in the work force

     a. Identification

     b. Significance

32. the Women's Committee of the Council of National Defense

     a. Identification

     b. Significance

33. African American migration

     a. Identification

     b. Significance

34. the National War Labor Board

     a. Identification

     b. Significance

35. the civil liberties issue

    a. Identification

    b. Significance

36. the Committee on Public Information

    a. Identification

    b. Significance

37. the Espionage and Sedition Acts

    a. Identification

    b. Significance

38. Eugene V. Debs

    a. Identification

    b. Significance

39. *Schenck v. United States* and *Abrams v. U.S.*

    a. Identification

    b. Significance

40. the Red Scare
    a. Identification

    b. Significance

41. mail bombs of May 1919
    a. Identification

    b. Significance

42. the Boston police strike
    a. Identification

    b. Significance

43. the steel strike of 1919
    a. Identification

    b. Significance

44. William Z. Foster
    a. Identification

    b. Significance

45. the American left

    a. Identification

    b. Significance

46. the American Legion

    a. Identification

    b. Significance

47. Mitchell Palmer

    a. Identification

    b. Significance

48. the Palmer Raids

    a. Identification

    b. Significance

49. the East St. Louis riot of 1917

    a. Identification

    b. Significance

50. the "Red Summer" of 1919
    a. Identification

    b. Significance

51. Wilson's anti-Bolshevik actions
    a. Identification

    b. Significance

52. the Paris Peace Conference
    a. Identification

    b. Significance

53. the principle of self-determination
    a. Identification

    b. Significance

54. the mandate system
    a. Identification

    b. Significance

55.   the Balfour Declaration of 1917

    a.   Identification

    b.   Significance

56.   the League of Nations

    a.   Identification

    b.   Significance

57.   Article 10 of the League Covenant

    a.   Identification

    b.   Significance

58.   the Treaty of Versailles

    a.   Identification

    b.   Significance

59.   the Lodge reservations

    a.   Identification

    b.   Significance

60. the "Irreconcilables"

    a. Identification

    b. Significance

61. collective security versus unilateralism

    a. Identification

    b. Significance

ORGANIZING, REVIEWING, AND USING INFORMATION

Chart A

Causes and Effects of American Entrance into World War I		
	CAUSES	**EFFECTS**
Military (self-defense, acquisition of territory, attitudes about war, etc.)		
Economic (trade and commerce, technology, jobs, working conditions, economic system etc.)		
Social (ethnicity, relations among national and racial groups in the populations involved, etc.)		
Political (political philosophy and ideals, diplomatic failures, alliances, administration in office, treaties and agreements, etc.)		
Psychological (pride, self-image, fears, etc.)		
Philosophical (moral positions, religious beliefs)		

Chart B

The Wilson Government's Fear of the Left, 1917–1920

Issues Stirring Individuals or Groups To Action	Actions Taken by Groups American Government Perceived as Threat				American Government's Response		Aftermath (U.S.-U.S.S.R Relations, etc.)
	American Labor Movement's Radicals	American Pacifists, Reformers	Other Americans Perceived as Threats	Soviet Bolsheviks (communists)	During War	After War	
	Examples:	Examples:	Examples:				
COMMUNISM							
International							
American							
DISSIDENCE							
Strikes							
Criticism of Government							

Chart B

The Wilson Government's Fear of the Left, 1917–1920

Issues Stirring Individuals or Groups To Action	Actions Taken by Groups American Government Perceived as Threat				American Government's Response		Aftermath (U.S.-U.S.S.R Relations, etc.)
	American Labor Movement's Radicals	American Pacifists, Reformers	Other Americans Perceived as Threats	Soviet Bolsheviks (communists)	During War	After War	
CAPITALISM							
BUSINESS-MANAGEMENT RELATIONSHIPS							
FACTIONS IN RUSSIA'S CIVIL WAR							
AMERICAN PARTICIPATION IN WORLD WAR							

IDEAS AND DETAILS

Objective 1

1. Great Britain entered the First World War in response to

    a.   the Austro-Hungarian invasion of Russia.
    b.   acts of Russian terrorism in the Balkans.
    c.   the Serbian invasion of Austria-Hungary.
    d.   the German invasion of Belgium.

Objective 2

2. American neutrality in response to the First World War was never a real possibility because

    a.   Wilson wanted to enter the war and force Germany into submission.
    b.   the American press had built broad-based sympathy for Serbian nationalism.
    c.   the United States had stronger economic ties to the Allies than to the Central Powers.
    d.   Secretary of State Bryan worked secretly to bring the United States into the war.

Objective 7

3. The body of ideas known as Wilsonianism and summarized in the Fourteen Points included the belief that

    a.   secret military alliances were the best means by which to maintain world peace.
    b.   democratic nations should enter into a collective-security agreement to contain and eliminate the communist threat.
    c.   democratic nations should build more arms to demonstrate their resolve against autocracy.
    d.   empires should be dismantled so that nations could be free to determine and control their own destiny.

Objective 2

4. William Jennings Bryan resigned his post as secretary of state because

    a.   he disagreed with President Wilson's refusal to ban American travelers from sailing on belligerent ships.
    b.   the American public responded negatively to his protests concerning Britain's illegal blockade of Germany.
    c.   his pro-German sympathies became a liability to the Wilson administration.
    d.   President Wilson publicly reprimanded him for advocating American entry into the First World War.

Objective 2

5. As a result of the Zimmermann telegram, Wilson

    a.   broke diplomatic relations with Germany.
    b.   decided to rethink his position on international law in relation to the submarine.
    c.   became more convinced that Germany was conspiring against the United States.
    d.   decided that supporting the Mexican Revolution was in the best interest of the United States.

Objective 2

6.   President Wilson responded to the defeat of his armed-ship bill by

   a.   demanding that the antiwar senators responsible for its defeat be censured by the Senate.
   b.   ordering naval escorts for American commercial ships in the Atlantic.
   c.   arming American commercial vessels anyway.
   d.   immediately drafting a declaration of war to present to Congress.

Objectives 4 and 5

7.   While serving as soldiers in France during the First World War, African Americans

   a.   were confined to their barracks due to orders by the French government.
   b.   found that the reception they received from French civilians was better than they were accustomed to in the United States.
   c.   were not allowed to serve alongside French soldiers.
   d.   received certificates of French citizenship from the French government.

Objective 4

8.   General Pershing refused to allow American soldiers to become part of Allied units because he

   a.   disagreed with President Wilson's decision to enter the war.
   b.   was afraid they would be corrupted by European ways.
   c.   did not want them to be commanded by Allied officers who seemed unable to develop a strategy to end the horrors of trench warfare.
   d.   did not believe they were as well trained as their Allied counterparts.

Objective 5

9.   In mobilizing the economy for the war effort, the government

   a.   rigidly enforced antitrust laws.
   b.   protected consumers by instituting a wage and price freeze.
   c.   established a partnership between government and business.
   d.   insisted on annual cost of living wage increases for workers in war-related industries.

Objective 5

10.   During the First World War, women in the work force

   a.   refused to join unions.
   b.   took advantage of new work opportunities, with some moving into jobs previously reserved for men.
   c.   were more valued and received higher wages than men.
   d.   often faced being fired so that their jobs could be given to unemployed men.

Objective 6

11.   In order to achieve its objective, the Committee on Public Information

   a.   encouraged Americans to spy on each other.
   b.   encouraged a free and open debate of the American war effort.
   c.   held daily briefings with reporters to ensure the dissemination of accurate war news.
   d.   sponsored public question-and-answer forums to dispel rumors.

Objective 6

12. In the case of *Schenck v. United States*, the Supreme Court ruled that
    a. members of the Socialist party could be required to register with the government.
    b. freedom of speech could be restricted in time of war.
    c. the Sedition Act was unconstitutional.
    d. the teaching of foreign languages could be banned from public schools.

Objective 6

13. Which of the following statements is accurate in relation to the Palmer Raids?
    a. A well-organized Bolshevik conspiracy against the United States government was crushed.
    b. The attorney general, in dealing with supposed radicals, showed disregard for civil liberties.
    c. Wilson instructed several state legislatures to remove suspected Socialists from their ranks.
    d. Documents confiscated during the raids led the Wilson administration to declare labor unions illegal.

Objective 5

14. Which of the following statements accurately describes the experiences of African Americans during the First World War?
    a. Military leaders attempted to combat racism by integrating their units.
    b. Southern whites welcomed the northward migration of blacks.
    c. The ideology used to justify the war was used to dismantle racial barriers within the United States.
    d. Some northern whites reacted with anger and violence to the northward migration of blacks.

Objectives 7 and 8

15. Opponents of the Treaty of Versailles objected primarily to
    a. the collective-security provision of Article 10.
    b. Wilson's acceptance of the "mandate" system.
    c. the clause that blamed the war on Germany.
    d. Wilson's inability to secure reparations payments from Germany.

ESSAY QUESTIONS

Objective 2

1. Explain Wilson's attempts to keep the United States out of the Great War in Europe. Why was the country eventually drawn into the conflict?

Objective 5

2. Discuss the impact of the First World War on women and African Americans.

Objective 6

3. Discuss the Wilson administration's record in the area of civil liberties during the First World War.

Objective 6

4.   Discuss the fear of communism in American society in the early twentieth century, and explain how that fear manifested itself between 1917 and 1921.

Objective 8

5.   Explain the foreign policy debate over ratification of the Treaty of Versailles and entry into the League of Nations. Why did those opposed to ratification and to League membership carry the day?

ANSWERS

Multiple-Choice Questions

1.   d.   Correct. When Austria-Hungary declared war against Serbia and Germany declared war against Russia and France, Great Britain hesitated. Only when Germany invaded Belgium, whose neutrality was guaranteed by Great Britain, did Britain enter the war. See pages 623–624.

    a.   No. When Russia mobilized its armies to aid Serbia, Germany first declared war against Russia and then against France, Russia's ally. Through all of this, Austria-Hungary did not invade Russia and Britain did not declare war. See pages 623–624.

    b.   No. The act of terrorism that led to war was undertaken by a Serbian nationalist against Archduke Franz Ferdinand, heir to the Austro-Hungarian throne. However, even though that event is seen as the spark that ignited the war, Great Britain did not enter the war in direct response to this act of terrorism. See pages 623–624.

    c.   No. Serbia did not invade Austria-Hungary. See pages 623–624.

2.   c.   Correct. Wilson's appeal for neutrality clashed with three realities: (1) ethnic groups in the United States took sides; (2) economic links with the Allies made neutrality difficult; and (3) administration officials were sympathetic to the Allies. See pages 624–625.

    a.   No. Woodrow Wilson was sincere in his desire to keep the United States out of the war in Europe. See pages 624–625.

    b.   No. The print media had not built broad-based sympathy for Serbian nationalism in the United States. Moreover, Serbian nationalism was not the major issue in the minds of most Americans. See pages 624–625.

    d.   No. Secretary of State William Jennings Bryan insisted on a policy of strict neutrality. See pages 624–625.

3.   d.   Correct. Wilsonianism advocated decolonization (the breaking up of empires) and the principle of self-determination (the right of all people to determine their own future without outside interference). See page 625.

    a.   No. Wilsonianism held that all diplomatic agreements among nations, including all alliance systems, should be openly negotiated. See page 625.

    b.   No. It is true that an army made up of soldiers from fourteen allied nations, including the United States, was sent to Russia and assisted anti-Bolshevik forces. It is also true that Wilson refused to recognize the Soviet government. But, Wilson was instrumental in persuading the Allies to abandon their attempt to overthrow the Bolshevik regime. Furthermore, one of his Fourteen Points stated that Russia should be allowed to determine its own form of government and its own national policy. Therefore, Wilson never explicitly included in the Fourteen Points a provision to form a collective-security agreement for the purpose of containing communism. See page 625.

    c.   No. Wilsonianism advocated reducing world armaments. See page 625.

4.   a.   Correct. Bryan believed that Germany had a right to prevent contraband from going to the Allies and faulted Great Britain for using passenger ships to carry such contraband. When Wilson rejected Bryan's advice that Americans not be allowed to travel on belligerent ships, Bryan resigned. See pages 621–622.

b.   No. Although Bryan protested Great Britain's blockade of Germany, no great public outcry led to his resignation. See pages 621–622.

c.   No. Bryan believed that the United States should remain strictly neutral in its relations with the European belligerents. See pages 621–622.

d.   No. Bryan did not advocate American entry into the war. See pages 621–622.

5.   c.   Correct. Mexican-American relations were strained in 1917, and Wilson saw this proposal of a Mexican-German alliance as proof of a German conspiracy against the United States. Soon after he learned of the telegram, Wilson asked Congress for "armed neutrality." See page 627.

a.   No. Wilson broke diplomatic relations with Germany on February 3, 1917, in response to Germany's resumption of unrestricted submarine warfare on February 1. Thus, relations were severed before the Zimmermann note was given to the United States ambassador to Great Britain on February 24. See page 627.

b.   No. The Zimmermann telegram proposed an alliance between Germany and Mexico and did not cause Wilson to rethink his position on the application of international law to the submarine. See page 627.

d.   No. American troops began to withdraw from Mexico in January 1917 and were fully withdrawn by February 5. Therefore, Wilson decided to change his policy toward Mexico before learning of the Zimmermann telegram on February 24. Furthermore, this change did not constitute "support" for the Mexican Revolution. See page 627.

6.   c.   Correct. After some twelve senators used the filibuster to defeat the armed-ship bill, Secretary of State Robert Lansing advised President Wilson that he had the authority under statute law to arm merchant vessels without congressional approval. Therefore, Wilson proceeded to use that authority. See page 628.

a.   No. Although Wilson referred to the group of senators responsible for filibustering the bill to death as that "little group of willful men," there is no evidence that he ever contemplated asking the Senate to censure them. In fact, such a request from the executive branch would most likely have angered the Senate. See page 628.

b.   No. Wilson did not respond to the defeat of the bill by ordering the navy to escort American commercial ships. See page 628.

d.   No. The armed-ship bill was defeated on March 4, 1917, and Wilson did not deliver his war message to Congress until April 2, 1917. See page 628.

7.   b.   Correct. African American soldiers who served in France were gratified by the reception they received from French civilians and often felt that they were better received and treated that in the United States. Upon their return to the United States, their experience in France and other European countries seems to have been a factor that led African American veterans to become more active and outspoken in the equal rights campaign. See page 630.

a.   No. There was no French law that confined African Americans serving in France to their barracks. See page 630.

c.   No. African American soldiers served alongside French soldiers and often did so with distinction. See page 630.

d.   No. Although the all-black 369th Regiment received the Croix de Guerre, the French government did not extend French citizenship to African American soldiers. See page 630.

8.   c.   Correct. Pershing refused to subject American soldiers to the horrors of trench warfare. For this reason the United States declared itself an Associated power and American soldiers, for the most part, did not become part of Allied units. See pages 630–631.

a.   No. Pershing was a good soldier. If he ever disagreed with America's entry into the war he did not say so publicly and never openly disagreed with the Commander in Chief of the Armed Forces. See pages 630–631.

b.   No. Although General Pershing was concerned about the virtue of American soldiers, it was not for this reason that he refused to allow American soldiers to become part of Allied units. See pages 630–631.

d.   No. General Pershing had tremendous faith in the ability of American soldiers. See pages 630–631.

9.   c.   Correct. Although government tax policies were designed to bring into the Treasury some of the profits reaped by business, the overall relationship between government and business was one of partnership. See pages 635–636.

a.   No. Antitrust laws were virtually suspended during the war. For example, the Webb-Pomerene Act granted immunity from antitrust legislation to companies that combined to operate in the export trade. See pages 635–636.

b.   No. Although the government did not institute a wage and price freeze during the war, it did fix prices on raw materials rather than on finished products. As a result, it lost control of inflation, and workers saw little improvement in their economic standing. See pages 635–636.

d.   No. The government did not demand cost-of-living increases for workers in war-related industries. See pages 635–636.

10. b.   Correct. During the war there was a labor shortage in many key industries because so many men were in the armed forces. As a result, new work opportunities were available to women and many women took advantage of those opportunities. In doing so, some women moved into previously male domains. See pages 637–638.

   a.   No. Except for unions organized by women, organized labor continued to be male dominated and openly hostile toward women. See pages 637–638.

   ac   No. With the labor shortage during the war years, women in the work force were certainly valued. However, men sometimes protested that women were undermining the wage system by working for lower pay than that received by men. See pages 637–638.

   d.   No. One of the advantages of the wartime economy was full-employment, while one of the disadvantages was a labor shortage. As a result, unemployment was rare and women were encouraged by many businesses to fill job vacancies. See pages 637–638.

11. a.   Correct. The CPI was organized to mobilize American opinion behind the war effort. Through its efforts it portrayed antiwar dissenters as being dangerous to national security and encouraged patriotic Americans to spy on their neighbors and report any "suspicious" behavior. See page 639.

   b.   No. The CPI was established by Wilson in 1917 as a propaganda agency. As such, the CPI did not encourage Americans to debate openly the American war effort. See page 639.

   c.   No. The CPI, established in 1917 by President Wilson, was interested in good propaganda. This goal did not always coincide with the dissemination of accurate war news. See page 639.

   d.   No. President Wilson established the CPI in 1917 as a propaganda agency. The committee often found that exaggeration and rumor worked to its advantage. See page 639.

12. b.   Correct. The Court, in a unanimous opinion, upheld the Espionage Act as constitutional. In doing so, the Court applied the "clear and present danger" test to free speech in time of war. See page 641.

   a.   No. There was no law requiring members of the Socialist party to register with the government. See page 641.

   c.   No. The Court upheld the constitutionality of the Sedition Act by a 7 to 2 vote in Abrams v. United States (1919). See page 641.

   d.   No. The Schenck case did not involve the teaching of foreign languages in public schools. See page 641.

13. b.   Correct. In the Palmer Raids, government agents were authorized by Attorney General Palmer to break into meeting halls, poolrooms, and homes without search warrants. Those arrested and jailed were denied legal counsel. These actions demonstrate a disregard for civil liberties. See page 642.

   a.   No. Although political and business leaders believed a conspiracy existed among American radicals, the evidence indicates that the American left was badly divided and not capable of a "well-organized conspiracy" against the United States government. See page 642.

   c.   No. Although the New York State legislature expelled five Socialist legislators, the expulsion was not done on instructions from President Wilson. See page 642.

   d.   No. Although some believed that the Boston police strike and the steel strike indicated radical infiltration of the union movement in the United States, labor organizations were not declared illegal. See page 642.

14. d. Correct. The massive influx of African Americans into the North during the First World War caused anxiety among white northerners. This anxiety found expression in northern race riots in which whites terrorized blacks. See page 642.

a. No. African Americans served in all-black units in the armed forces. Some served in combat units, but most were relegated to menial jobs. Although racism was obvious in the military, military leaders did not suggest integration of units as a solution. See page 642.

b. No. The northward migration of African Americans created problems for southern white landowners and businessmen because it reduced their supply of cheap laborers. The problem was further complicated by the fact that white laborers were also moving away. See page 642.

c. No. African Americans continued to experience racial discrimination at home during and after the First World War. See page 642.

15. a. Correct. The argument at the core of the debate over the treaty concerned the question of collective security versus America's traditional unilateralism. Those who opposed the Treaty of Versailles rejected the idea of collective security contained in Article 10. See pages 646–647.

b. No. Although some of the treaty's opponents charged that Wilson had compromised his stated principles of decolonization and self-determination by accepting the mandate system, opposition to the treaty did not rest on this issue. See pages 646–647.

c. No. Those who opposed the Treaty of Versailles had no problem with the "war guilt clause," which placed most of the blame for the war on Germany and its allies. See pages 646–647.

d. No. The treaty contained a provision that a reparations commission would determine the amount Germany was to pay the Allies. This figure was later set at $33 billion. See pages 646–647.

CHAPTER 24

The New Era, 1920–1929

LEARNING OBJECTIVES

After you have studied Chapter 24 in your textbook and worked through this study guide chapter, you should be able to:

1. Discuss the economic characteristics of the 1920s, and explain the reasons for the economic expansion and recovery that began in 1922.

2. Discuss the relationship between government and business during the 1920s, and indicate the factors responsible for the decline of organized labor.

3. Examine the political, social, and economic characteristics of the Harding and Coolidge administrations.

4. Discuss the nature and extent of reform legislation during the decade of the 1920s.

5. Discuss the federal government's Indian policy during the 1920s, and explain its impact on Native Americans.

6. Examine the social, economic, and political changes in the position and attitudes of women and African Americans in American society during the 1920s.

7. Discuss the expansion of the consumer society in America during the 1920s.

8. Examine the impact of the automobile and modern advertising on American society.

9. Explain both the trend toward urbanization and the growth of the suburbs during the 1920s, and discuss the consequences of both of these factors on American society.

10. Indicate the factors that caused an increase in immigration by Mexicans and Puerto Ricans during the 1920s, and discuss the characteristics of their lives in the United States.

11. Discuss the changes that took place in the way Americans used their time during the 1920s.

12. Discuss the causes and consequences of the 1920s trend toward longer life expectancy, and explain the responses of Americans to the needs of the elderly.

13. Examine the impact of social change during the 1920s on the following:

    a. Americans' values

    b. the American family

    c. women in the American work force

    d. images of femininity

    e. views of human sexuality

14. Examine the emergence of the Ku Klux Klan, nativists, and religious fundamentalists, and discuss their impact on American society in the 1920s.

15. Explain the characteristics of each of the following, and discuss the impact of each on American society during the 1920s:

   a.   Games

   b.   Movies

   c.   Sports

   d.   Prohibition

16. Examine and evaluate the movements in American literature, art, and music during the 1920s.

17. Discuss the issues and personalities in the 1928 presidential campaign, and explain the election's outcome.

18. Discuss the events that led to the 1929 stock market crash, and examine the causes of the crash and the Great Depression that followed.

THEMATIC GUIDE

The decade of the 1920s began with troubling economic signs but soon became an era of economic prosperity for many Americans. Prosperity was accompanied by probusiness attitudes and unparalleled consumerism. The federal government remained active in its support of business interests, and it became more passive in its regulation of those interests. During this period the Supreme Court handed down antiregulatory decisions and organized labor suffered setbacks. Furthermore, probusiness attitudes reminiscent of the Gilded Age marked the Harding, Coolidge, and Hoover administrations. Most reforms took place at the state and local levels. Interest in reform concerning Indian affairs led to the reorganization of the Bureau of Indian Affairs, but Indian policy matters continued to be characterized by paternalism. Furthermore, while newly enfranchised women lobbied and gained passage of some legislation helpful to them, women generally struggled to find their political voice.

The consumerism of the age was fueled by the growing purchasing power of many American families and the accompanying ability to acquire the goods associated with a consumer society. Both the automobile and the sophisticated techniques of modern advertising transformed the American life style.

The urbanization of American society continued in the 1920s. Although movement to cities offered opportunities to many, African American migrants found that white racism was as prevalent in urban areas as it had been in the rural South. However, blacks' urban ghetto experience aroused their class and ethnic consciousness, as seen both in Marcus Garvey's black nationalist movement and in the cultural outpouring known as the Harlem Renaissance. Racism also shaped the lives of Mexicans, Puerto Ricans, and other newcomers to American cities and contributed to "white flight" from the inner city and to suburban growth.

The way in which Americans spent their time changed. For instance, labor-saving devices lightened the tasks of women working in the home. But since women were still expected to clothe and feed the family and since few women produced clothes and preserved food at home, they spent their time shopping for these goods and became the primary consumers in society.

Altered attitudes and values brought about by societal changes found expression in new clothing and hair styles and in a new openness about human sexuality. Increased longevity resulting from improved diets and improved healthcare led to an increase in the number of older Americans and to limited attempts to respond to their needs. At the same time, compulsory-school-attendance laws increased the influence of the peer group in the socialization of children. Furthermore, a combination of consumerism and economic necessity caused more women, including married women, to work outside the home. The work they performed and the wages they earned were largely determined by the sex-segregated characteristics of the labor market and, for nonwhites, by racial bias. In spite of sexism and racism, however, many women placed family needs above individual needs.

Many people felt threatened by change, and some, attempting to protect traditional attitudes and values, reacted defensively, sometimes with attempts to blame change on scapegoats. The emergence of the "new" Klan and the increase in nativism and fear of radicalism (evidenced in the Sacco and Vanzetti case) can be seen in this light. Religious fundamentalism also gained strength, as the Scopes trial revealed.

More leisure time and a search for entertainment meant that spectator sports and the movies became big business. As the conformist aspects of mass culture caused individuality to fade, Americans found heroes in sports figures, movie idols, and media-created personalities. Caught between two value systems, many Americans gave lip service to the old, as evidenced in their professed support of the Prohibition experiment, but chose the new, as the breakdown of Prohibition in the cities shows.

In literature, the 1920s saw the work of the Lost Generation and of the Harlem Renaissance. In music, it was the age of jazz, America's most distinctive art form, and of such talented composers as Aaron Copland and George Gershwin. In architecture, Frank Lloyd Wright predominated. Overall, the period stands as one of the most creative in American history.

In politics, the presidency remained in Republican hands in 1928 as most Americans affirmed their confidence in the building of a New Era of prosperity for all. But with the stock market crash of 1929, the optimism of 1928 gave way to concern and ultimately, with the onset of the Great Depression, to despair. The Jazz Age ended. The American economic system would have to be rebuilt.

BUILDING VOCABULARY

Listed below are important words and terms that you need to know to get the most out of Chapter 24. They are listed in the order in which they occur in the chapter. After carefully looking through the list, (1) underline the words with which you are totally unfamiliar, (2) put a question mark by those words of which you are unsure, and (3) leave the rest alone.

As you begin to read the chapter, when you come to any of the words you've put question marks beside or underlined (1) slow your reading; (2) focus on the word and on its context in the sentence you're reading; (3) if you can understand the meaning of the word from its context in the sentence or passage in which it is used, go on with your reading; (4) if it's a word that you've underlined or a word that you can't understand from its context in the sentence or passage, look it up in a dictionary and write down the definition that best applies to the context in which the word is used.

Definitions

epitomize _____

entice _____

quash _____

languish _____

predatory _____

crony _____

manipulate _____

induce _____

covenant _____

dilapidated _____

agility _____

chaste _____

torrid _____

libertine _____

reactionary _____

mete _____

flout _____

fundamentalist _____

irreverence _____

hedonistic _____

quip _____

Pentecostal _____

poignant _____

satire _____

prodigious _____

pomade _____

deride _____

exuberance _____

aesthetic _____

urbane _____

gregarious _____

precarious _____

edifice _____

lucrative _____

emulate _____

Difficult-to-Spell Names and Terms from Reading and Lecture

IDENTIFICATION AND SIGNIFICANCE

After studying Chapter 24 of *A People and a Nation,* you should be able to identify fully *and* explain the historical significance of each item listed below.

- Identify each item in the space provided. Give an explanation or description of the item. Answer the questions *who, what, where,* and *when.*

- Explain the historical significance of each item in the space provided. Establish the historical context in which the item exists. Establish the item as the result of or as the cause of other factors existing in the society under study. Answer this question: *What were the political, social, economic, and/or cultural consequences of this item?*

1. Charles A. Lindbergh

    a. Identification

    b. Significance

2. the installment plan

    a. Identification

    b. Significance

3. oligopolies

    a. Identification

    b. Significance

4. the "new lobbying"

    a. Identification

    b. Significance

5. *Coronado Coal Company v. United Mine Workers* and *Maple Floor Association v. United States*

    a.   Identification

    b.   Significance

6. *Bailey v. Drexel Furniture Company* and *Adkins v. Children's Hospital*

    a.   Identification

    b.   Significance

7. welfare capitalism

    a.   Identification

    b.   Significance

8. Warren G. Harding

    a.   Identification

    b.   Significance

9. Charles Forbes and Harry Daugherty

    a.   Identification

    b.   Significance

10. the Teapot Dome scandal

    a. Identification

    b. Significance

11. Calvin Coolidge

    a. Identification

    b. Significance

12. the McNary-Haugen bills

    a. Identification

    b. Significance

13. the 1924 presidential election

    a. Identification

    b. Significance

14. the Indian Rights Association, the Indian Defense Association, and the General Federation of Women's Clubs

    a. Identification

    b. Significance

15. American Indians's citizenship status

   a.   Identification

   b.   Significance

16. the Bureau of Indian Affairs

   a.   Identification

   b.   Significance

17. the League of Women Voters

   a.   Identification

   b.   Significance

18. the Sheppard-Towner Act

   a.   Identification

   b.   Significance

19. the Cable Act

   a.   Identification

   b.   Significance

20. the National Woman Party

    a.   Identification

    b.   Significance

21. the automobile

    a.   Identification

    b.   Significance

22. the Federal Highway Act

    a.   Identification

    b.   Significance

23. the radio

    a.   Identification

    b.   Significance

24. urbanization

    a.   Identification

    b.   Significance

25. Marcus Garvey

    a.   Identification

    b.   Significance

26. Mexican immigrants

    a.   Identification

    b.   Significance

27. Puerto Rican immigrants

    a.   Identification

    b.   Significance

28. the growth of the suburbs

    a.   Identification

    b.   Significance

29. the American family of the 1920s

    a.   Identification

    b.   Significance

30. home appliances and household management in the 1920s

    a. Identification

    b. Significance

31. Isaac Max Rubinow and Abraham Epstein

    a. Identification

    b. Significance

32. the peer group and the socialization of children

    a. Identification

    b. Significance

33. women in the 1920s labor force

    a. Identification

    b. Significance

34. the flapper

    a. Identification

    b. Significance

35. homosexual culture

    a. Identification

    b. Significance

36. Ku Klux Klan

    a. Identification

    b. Significance

37. the Emergency Quota Act of 1921

    a. Identification

    b. Significance

38. the National Origins Act of 1924 and the National Origins Act of 1927

    a. Identification

    b. Significance

39. Nicola Sacco and Bartolomeo Vanzetti

    a. Identification

    b. Significance

40. the Scopes trial
    a. Identification

    b. Significance

41. Pentecostal religion
    a. Identification

    b. Significance

42. mahjongg, crossword puzzles, miniature golf, and the Charleston
    a. Identification

    b. Significance

43. motion pictures
    a. Identification

    b. Significance

44. baseball
    a. Identification

    b. Significance

45. Jack Dempsey, Harold "Red" Grange, and George Herman "Babe" Ruth

    a.   Identification

    b.   Significance

46. Rudolph Valentino

    a.   Identification

    b.   Significance

47. Prohibition

    a.   Identification

    b.   Significance

48. Al Capone

    a.   Identification

    b.   Significance

49. the Lost Generation

    a.   Identification

    b.   Significance

50. the Harlem Renaissance

    a.   Identification

    b.   Significance

51. the Jazz Age

    a.   Identification

    b.   Significance

52. the 1928 presidential election

    a.   Identification

    b.   Significance

53. Herbert Hoover

    a.   Identification

    b.   Significance

54. Al Smith

    a.   Identification

    b.   Significance

55. Black Thursday

    a.   Identification

    b.   Significance

56. Black Tuesday

    a.   Identification

    b.   Significance

57. the stock market crash

    a.   Identification

    b.   Significance

ORGANIZING, REVIEWING, AND USING INFORMATION

Chart A

The Federal Government and The Business Climate of the 1920s		
Aspect of Federal Government	**Explanation of the Aspect's Relation to the Decade's Business Climate**	**Central Person(s) or Examples**
President's Beliefs and Attitudes		
Willingness To Intervene in the Marketplace		
Susceptibility of Officials to Improper/Illegal Influences		
Attitudes and Roles in Business-Labor Relationships		
Taxation Policies		
Role of Lobbyists		
Regulation of Business, Upholding of Laws		
Tariff Policies		
Funding of Infrastructure, Communication Outlets		

Chart B

The Welfare of Women and Key Minorities in the 1920s

	Women		African Americans	Mexican, Mexican-Americans	Puerto Ricans	Homosexuals
	Euro-Amer.	Afri-Amer.				
GOVERNMENT ACTIONS						
Supreme Court Rulings						
Legislation						
CHANGE IN CIVIC STATUS						
Citizenship						
Rights as Citizen						
INTER- AND INTRA-CULTURAL RELATIONSHIPS						
Roles in Family Life						
Group Aspirations/Pride, Identity						
Targeting for Intimidation and Violence						
Discrimination in Housing						

Chart B

The Welfare of Women and Key Minorities in the 1920s

	Women		African Americans	Mexican, Mexican-Americans	Puerto Ricans	Homosexuals
	Euro-Amer.	Afri-Amer.				
ECONOMIC STATUS						
Reason for Employment						
Job Opportunities						
Wages/Hours						
SELF-EXPRESSION						
Music						
Literature						
Plastic, Visual Arts						

Chart C

Emotional Currents in the Cultural Transformation of the 1920s			
Emotion	**Groups Affected**	**Specific Expressions or Ramifications**	**Explanation**
YEARNINGS			
Acceptance and Connection To Those Respected within the Culture			
Ability To Keep Up with Social and Technological Change			
Clarity of and Satisfaction with One's Identity			
Economic Security, Economic Advancement			
Social and Political Equality, Independence			
Health and Physical Well-being			
Freedom from Constraints, Self-Expression			
Drama, Escape			

Emotional Currents in the Cultural Transformation of the 1920s			
Emotion	Groups Affected	Specific Expressions or Ramifications	Explanation
FEARS			
Undermining of Traditional Values and Customs			
Spread of Religious Skepticism and Irreverence			
Rise in Licentiousness, Hedonism, Social Chaos			
Loss of Social and Economic Status and Influence			
DISILLUSIONMENT			
Materialism			
Group Aspirations to Belong and Find Acceptance and Respect			

IDEAS AND DETAILS

Objective 2

1. In *Bailey v. Drexel Furniture Company*, the Supreme Court
    a. demonstrated a probusiness stance by striking down restrictions on child labor.
    b. demonstrated that it was moving in a liberal direction in the field of consumer protection.
    c. declared federal aid to a particular industry unconstitutional.
    d. upheld the right to strike by union members.

Objective 2

2. During the 1920s, organized labor
    a. received support from many large corporations.
    b. was encouraged by the rulings of a sympathetic Supreme Court.
    c. continued to attract members in spite of the hostility of the federal government.
    d. was hurt by the policy of welfare capitalism adopted by some large corporations.

Objective 3

3. One area of disagreement between President Coolidge and Congress was
    a. federally funded internal improvements.
    b. farm policy.
    c. foreign policy.
    d. military spending.

Objective 5

4. Reformers were critical of Indian women for which of the following reasons?
    a. They refused to seek gainful employment.
    b. They were reluctant to send their children to boarding schools.
    c. They encouraged their children to abandon their tribes and land and move to urban areas.
    d. They abandoned their cultural traditions by adopting lifestyles and homemaking methods associated with white middle-class women.

Objective 6

5. Urban blacks were drawn to Marcus Garvey because he
    a. emphasized racial pride.
    b. promoted education as the route to assimilation.
    c. preached against the evils of the free enterprise system.
    d. was willing to use military means to achieve his objectives.

Objectives 6, 7, and 11

6. New technology changed the role of housewives in which of the following ways?
    a. Management of the household became a shared family responsibility.
    b. The housewife became the family's chief consumer rather than its chief producer.
    c. Fewer child-raising responsibilities were placed on the housewife.
    d. Housewives began to be seen as specialists in certain tasks.

Objective 13

7.   As a consequence of child-labor laws and compulsory-school-attendance laws,

    a.   daily newspaper circulation increased dramatically in the 1920s.
    b.   consumption of consumer products began to decline in the 1920s.
    c.   the role of the family in socializing children declined while that of the peer group increased.
    d.   many industries faced a severe labor shortage.

Objectives 6 and 13

8.   Which of the following statements concerning women in the work force during the 1920s is correct?

    a.   The number of women in factories increased dramatically.
    b.   Sex segregation in the workplace became less noticeable.
    c.   The number of women in the work force declined.
    d.   Married women joined the work force in increasing numbers.

Objective 14

9.   During the early 1920s, the Ku Klux Klan

    a.   had little power outside the South.
    b.   lost most of its power in the South because of the new mood of militancy among blacks.
    c.   gained power nationally as an antiblack, anti-immigrant, anti-Catholic movement.
    d.   was outlawed by Congress as a terrorist organization.

Objective 14

10.   Which of the following conclusions may be drawn from the Sacco and Vanzetti case?

    a.   The fear of radicalism, which caused the Red Scare, had disappeared.
    b.   In the future, immigration laws would be applied equally to all ethnic groups.
    c.   Blacks could not be guaranteed a fair trial in the South.
    d.   Justice was not necessarily blind to a person's political beliefs or ethnic background.

Objective 15

11.   Jack Dempsey, "Babe" Ruth, and Rudolph Valentino demonstrate that the decade of the 1920s was an

    a.   age of heroes.
    b.   era of great actors.
    c.   era of great baseball players.
    d.   age of lawlessness.

Objective 15

12.   Prohibition failed because

    a.   Americans completely rejected the value system out of which it was born.
    b.   illegal liquor was foisted on the public by organized crime.
    c.   it hurt the nation economically.
    d.   many people were willing to break the law in their quest for pleasure and their desire for personal freedom.

Objective 16

13. Many writers of the Harlem Renaissance
    a. rejected the African past of black Americans.
    b. advocated that black Americans return to Africa.
    c. rejected white culture.
    d. were mainly interested in economic issues.

Objective 17

14. The election of 1928 indicated that
    a. the Democrats were gaining strength in urban areas.
    b. the Democrats were losing their stronghold in the South.
    c. the Republicans were making gains in all sections of the country.
    d. the Republicans had become the minority party.

Objective 18

15. The government contributed to the stock market crash of 1929 and to the depression that followed in which of the following ways?
    a. Government regulations imposed on businesses reduced profits and investments.
    b. Tax policies before the crash took large sums of money out of circulation.
    c. The Federal Reserve Board followed an easy credit policy in the years prior to the crash.
    d. Government policies toward organized labor encouraged large wage increases and inflation.

ESSAY QUESTIONS

Objective 1

1. Discuss the factors responsible for the economic recovery that began in 1922. How long did this economic recovery last? Why is it said that this recovery was "uneven"?

Objective 2

2. Examine the relationship between government and business during the Republican era of the 1920s. What was the philosophy behind this relationship?

Objective 4

3. Examine the attitude toward reform during the 1920s, and discuss and assess the reforms that were achieved during the decade.

Objective 8

4. Discuss the impact of the automobile on American society, American values, and the American family.

Objective 6

5. Explain the emergence and the rise to power of Marcus Garvey.

Objectives 13 and 14

6.   Defend the following statement, and explain how it applies not only to the 1920s but to the twenty-first century as well: "The emotional responses that Americans made to events during the 1920s were part of a larger attempt to sustain old-fashioned values in a fast-moving, materialistic world."

Objective 18

7.   Explain why the 1929 stock market crash led to the Great Depression.

ANSWERS

Multiple-Choice Questions

1. a.   Correct. The judicial branch of the government, along with the legislative and executive branches, took a probusiness, antireform, and antiregulatory stance in the 1920s. The Bailey case serves as an example of this stance. See page 653.

    b.   No. The Bailey case did not deal with the issue of consumer protection, and the Court's stand did not indicate that its views were more liberal. See page 653.

    c.   No. The Bailey case did not deal with the issue of government aid to industry. See page 653.

    d.   No. The Bailey case did not deal with organized labor's right to strike. See page 653.

2. d.   Correct. Large corporations continued their hostility toward organized labor, but they attempted to neutralize the appeal of unions by offering pension plans and other amenities. This policy is known as welfare capitalism. See pages 653–654.

    a.   No. Corporations, large and small, continued to see organized labor as a threat to property rights. See pages 653–654.

    b.   No. The Court continued to demonstrate hostility toward organized labor. In cases such as Coronado Coal Company v. United Mine Workers (1922), the Court ruled that a striking union, like a trust, could be prosecuted for illegal restraint of trade. See pages 653–654.

    c.   No. Union membership fell from 5.1 million in 1920 to 3.6 million in 1929. See pages 653–654.

3. b.   Correct. Coolidge and Congress disagreed over how to respond to the plight of farmers. Coolidge, devoted to the concept of laissez faire, twice vetoed bills that would have established government-backed price supports for staple crops. See page 655.

    a.   No. President Coolidge supported allocation of funds by Congress for construction of a national highway system. See page 655.

    c.   No. Coolidge and Congress agreed in the area of foreign policy. See page 655.

    d.   No. Military spending was not a major issue during the Coolidge administration, and Coolidge and Congress did not disagree on this issue. See page 655.

4. b.   Correct. Many Indian women balked at sending their children to boarding schools and were criticized by reformers for that stance. See page 656.

    a.   No. During the 1920s women were criticized when they sought gainful employment. Indian women were not criticized for refusing to enter the labor force. See page 656.

    c.   No. Most Indian women attempted to protect and preserve Indian culture. Therefore, they did not encourage their children to abandon their tribes and land and move to urban areas. See page 656.

    d.   No. Most Indian women refused to abandon their cultural traditions and, as a result, were criticized for refusing to adopt lifestyles and homemaking methods associated with white middle-class women. See page 656.

5.   a.   Correct. Marcus Garvey preached the idea that blacks have an African heritage of which they should be proud, and he asserted that blackness symbolizes strength and beauty. He taught racial pride in an era in which white racism found expression in race riots and lynchings. See pages 659–661.

b.   No. Marcus Garvey was opposed to the assimilation of blacks into white American society. See pages 659–661.

c.   No. Marcus Garvey encouraged blacks to take advantage of the free enterprise system by sharpening their management skills and opening businesses. See pages 659–661.

d.   No. Although Marcus Garvey preached that blacks could gain respect by lifting their native Africa to world power status, he did not advocate the use of violence to obtain his objectives. See pages 659–661.

6.   b.   Correct. The urban housewife of the 1920s was no longer the producer of food and clothing that her female ancestors had been. However, it was still her responsibility to feed and clothe the family. Therefore, she became the family's chief consumer. See page 663.

a.   No. The new technology did not cause a new sense of responsibility toward household management on the part of husbands and children. In fact, by decreasing the need for servants, the new technology placed the burden of household management more squarely on the shoulders of the wife herself. See page 663.

c.   No. The new technology eliminated the need for servants in many cases. This placed more of the responsibility for childcare on the wife herself. See page 663.

d.   No. The new technology did not relieve most housewives of a wide variety of responsibilities, and in many cases the "labor-saving" machines added new responsibilities. See page 663.

7.   c.   Correct. Children were kept in school longer as a result of child-labor laws and compulsory-school-attendance laws. As a consequence, the influence of the peer group in socializing children increased and the role of the family decreased. See pages 664–665.

a.   No. Newspaper circulation did not increase in the 1920s as a result of children being kept in school longer. See pages 664–665.

b.   No. Consumption of consumer goods increased in the 1920s. See pages 664–665.

d.   No. Child-labor laws and compulsory-school-attendance laws did not cause a severe labor shortage. See pages 664–665.

8.   d.   Correct. Largely because of "need," as defined in the new consumer age, married women joined the work force in increasing numbers during the 1920s. The number of married women who were gainfully employed rose from 1.9 million in 1920 to 3.1 million in 1930. See page 665.

a.   No. The number of women working in factories showed very little increase during the decade of the 1920s. See page 665.

b.   No. Sex segregation in the workplace showed no signs of decline during the 1920s. See page 665.

c.   No. In 1920 there were some 10.4 million women in the work force, and by 1930 there were 10.8 million gainfully employed women. This meant that women constituted 22 percent of the total labor force in 1930, a 1.6 percent increase over 1920. See page 665.

9. c.   Correct. The "new" Klan of the early 1920s was more broadly based than the first Klan, and it also directed its brand of hatred toward groups other than blacks. See page 667.

    a.   No. Although the "new" Klan of the 1920s was founded by William J. Simmons of Atlanta, its power spread into all regions of the country and by 1923 the organization claimed some 5 million members. See page 667.

    b.   No. The new mood of nationalism and militancy among African Americans in the 1920s was more pronounced in the North than in the South. Furthermore, the "new" Klan of the 1920s gained power in the South. See page 667.

    d.   No. Although the Klan operated through terrorism and fear, it was not outlawed by Congress as a terrorist organization. See page 667.

10. d.   Correct. Modern ballistics studies suggest that Sacco was probably guilty, Vanzetti probably innocent. However, the evidence used in the 1920 trial was questionable, and the conviction and sentencing of the two men was based largely on their immigrant background and anarchist beliefs. See page 668.

    a.   No. The case demonstrates that the fear of radicalism, which was an important aspect of the Red Scare, was still very much alive. See page 668.

    b.   No. The Sacco and Vanzetti case is an indication of anti-immigrant sentiment in the United States during the early 1920s. See page 668.

    c.   No. The case did not involve blacks being tried in the South. See page 668.

11. a.   Correct. The age of mass consumerism robbed experiences and objects of their uniqueness, and as individuals became more anonymous and less significant in the fast-moving, materialistic world, they turned to "heroes" as a way of identifying with the unique. See pages 670–672.

    b.   No. In the first place, how one defines a "great" actor is a matter of judgment. In addition, Rudolph Valentino is the only actor among the three people listed. See pages 670–672.

    c.   No. Although "Babe" Ruth may be considered a "great" baseball player, this is not true of Jack Dempsey (boxer) or Rudolph Valentino (actor). See pages 670–672.

    d.   No. The three people listed were not engaged in "lawless" acts. See pages 670–672.

12. d.   Correct. Although most Americans continued to accept the Puritan value system on which prohibition was based, more and more Americans found the new diversions of "the age of play" attractive. Therefore, many willingly broke the law in favor of fun and personal freedom. See page 672.

    a.   No. Prohibition was born out of the Puritan value system, which emphasized hard work and sobriety. Americans did not "completely" reject this value system. See page 672.

    b.   No. Rather than "foisting" illegal liquor on the public, organized crime provided it to a public that wanted to buy it. See page 672.

    c.   No. Although prohibition caused people in the legal liquor industry to lose their jobs, its negative economic impact was not the reason for its failure. See page 672.

13.   c.   Correct. In addressing identity issues, black writers of the Harlem Renaissance rejected white culture and took pride in their African heritage. Instead of advocating assimilation into white society, they urged blacks to find their identity in the richness and uniqueness of black culture. See page 673.

a.   No. Many of the writers of the Harlem Renaissance spoke with pride of the African past of black Americans. See page 673.

b.   No. Most of the writers associated with the Harlem Renaissance were not advocates of black nationalism and did not advocate the return of black Americans to Africa. See page 673.

d.   No. The black writers of the Harlem Renaissance were concerned with issues relating to the reality of the black experience in white American society. They were not concerned primarily with economic issues. See page 673.

14.   a.   Correct. By carrying the nation's twelve largest cities, the Democratic party demonstrated that it was gaining power in the urban areas of the country. See page 675.

b.   No. Al Smith, the Democratic presidential nominee in 1928, carried eight states to Herbert Hoover's forty. Six of these were southern states from which he gained 69 of his 87 electoral votes. See page 675.

c.   No. The election indicated that Republicans had actually lost support in areas that were becoming more important in presidential elections. See page 675.

d.   No. The Republican party was still the majority party—that is, a majority of the people who were registered to vote were registered as Republicans. See page 675.

15.   c.   Correct. The Board's easy-credit policy before 1931 fueled speculation in the stock market, and its shift to a tight-money policy after 1931 denied the economy of funds needed for economic recovery. See page 676.

a.   No. The Hoover administration, like the Harding and Coolidge administrations, adhered to the laissez-faire philosophy and did not "impose" regulations on businesses. See page 676.

b.   No. The government followed a policy of lowering income-tax rates, especially on the wealthy. Therefore, the tax policies of the government did not take large sums of money out of circulation. Furthermore, between 1920 and 1929, the after-tax income of the wealthiest 1 percent rose 75 percent as opposed to the average per-capita increase of 9 percent. This extra disposable income in the hands of the wealthy tended to fuel speculation in the stock market. See page 676.

d.   No. The government did not give aid to organized labor. Furthermore, economic distress among farmers, factory layoffs, technological unemployment, and low wages caused production to outstrip demand. See page 676.

CHAPTER 25

The Great Depression and the New Deal, 1929–1941

LEARNING OBJECTIVES

After you have studied Chapter 25 in your textbook and worked through this study guide chapter, you should be able to:

1. Discuss the impact of the Great Depression on the American economic system and on farmers, industrial workers, marginal workers, and middle class workers and their families.

2. Explain and evaluate the Hoover administration's attempts to deal with the economic and human crises posed by the Great Depression.

3. Examine how and why Americans responded to the Great Depression as they did.

4. Examine the issues and personalities and explain the outcome of the 1932 presidential and congressional elections.

5. Discuss the impact of Franklin D. Roosevelt's personal and professional experiences prior to 1932 on his political, social, and economic views, and examine the relationship between his political, social, and economic views and his handling of the Great Depression.

6. Explain the practical and theoretical basis for the legislative enactments of the First New Deal (l933–1934), and evaluate the effectiveness of the First New Deal in solving the problems of the depression.

7. Examine the variety of criticisms leveled against the New Deal, and discuss the alternatives proposed.

8. Explain the practical and theoretical basis for the legislative enactments of the Second New Deal (1935–1939), and evaluate the effectiveness of the Second New Deal in solving the problems of the depression.

9. Identify the components of the New Deal coalition, and examine the impact of this coalition on the 1936 presidential election.

10. Examine the power struggle between craft unions and industrial unions during the New Deal era; discuss the victories and defeats of organized labor during this period; and assess the overall impact of the New Deal era on organized labor in the United States.

11. Discuss the extent to which the New Deal changed the relationship between the federal government and American citizens.

12. Examine the impact of the New Deal on the West, Native Americans, and the South.

13. Discuss the role played by radio and Hollywood movies in the emergence of a shared national popular culture.

14. Examine the problems encountered by President Roosevelt during his second term.

15. Contrast the Supreme Court's reaction to New Deal legislation before and after 1937, and explain the reasons for the shift.

16. Discuss the issues and personalities and explain the outcome of the 1940 presidential election.

17. Examine the impact of the New Deal on African Americans and Mexican Americans, and explain the responses of these groups to the obstacles they faced.

18. Discuss the legacy of the New Deal.

THEMATIC GUIDE

Chapter 25 opens with a discussion of the Great Depression's impact on people's lives. The human story includes the increase in malnutrition and starvation, altered marital patterns, the sufferings of drought- and debt-ridden farmers, the plight of industrial workers, the desperation of "marginal" workers, and changes to family life.

Hoover's response to appeals from the people that the government extend aid was at first defensive. Hoover was convinced that the nation's economic problems could be solved by business organizations and professional groups voluntarily working together to find solutions, with the government coordinating their efforts. As the depression deepened, Hoover reluctantly began to energize the government. At the same time, however, he pursued policies that caused further deterioration of the economic situation.

In the midst of the depression, few Americans thought in radical, revolutionary terms. However, some did begin to strike out at what they believed to be the cause of their distress. The Farmers' Holiday Association attempted to drive prices up by withholding agricultural products from the marketplace. Unemployed Councils engaged in protest that sometimes became violent. Racial violence also increased, as some attempted to find scapegoats on whom to blame their problems. The most spectacular public confrontation occurred when the Bonus Army converged on Washington, D.C., in the summer of 1932. However, in the case of the Bonus March, it was the government, not the people, that overreacted.

An understanding of Franklin Roosevelt's background, his perception of himself, his society, and American government is important to an understanding of his approach to the Great Depression. That background and Roosevelt's frame of reference are outlined as part of the discussion of the presidential election of 1932. In this discussion, we also see that in spite of a deepening crisis Americans did not adopt radical solutions. Instead, they continued to follow tradition by peacefully exchanging one government for another.

With the aid of the "Brain Trust," Roosevelt adopted a theoretical basis for the New Deal he promised to the American people. Roosevelt believed that government could act as a positive force in American society. In deciding how it should act, he was a pragmatist and thus willing to experiment. At first he accepted the idea that government could and should effectively regulate big business. He accepted the idea that centralized economic planning by the federal government could solve some of the problems associated with the depression, and he was willing to have government engage in direct relief to alleviate the distress of the nation's citizens. Furthermore, the first New Deal was based on the assumption that overproduction was the underlying problem.

Roosevelt's initial actions, outlined in "Franklin D. Roosevelt and the Launching the New Deal," demonstrate both the conservative nature of his approach and his realization that the psychology of pessimism within the country was as great an enemy as the depression itself. The legislation that was passed, as well as the fireside chats, provided a sense of movement that helped break the mood of pessimism.

An attempt to solve the problem of overproduction through centralized planning provided the theoretical framework for passage of the AAA and the NIRA. Belief in giving direct relief to states and to individuals may be seen in acts such as the Federal Emergency Relief Act and the CCC. As these and other measures passed during the Hundred Days were implemented, unemployment began to fall. However, as the immediacy of the crisis began to abate, groups and individuals became more outspoken in their criticism of and opposition to the New Deal. The range of criticism indicates that Roosevelt was a political moderate in the route that he chose. Furthermore, opposition from popular critics like Huey Long, the influence of Eleanor Roosevelt and other advocates of social reform, and the political realities of having to maintain the allegiance of interest groups that were part of the emerging New Deal coalition, help explain the launching of the Second New Deal.

The Second New Deal stemmed from the view that underconsumption was the nation's basic problem, that business and banking interests had to be regulated more closely, and that the government had a responsibility to the aged and the needy in American society. These assumptions were behind the Emergency Relief Appropriation Act, the Social Security Act, and the Wealth Tax Act. The Second New Deal and the forging of the New Deal coalition carried Roosevelt to victory in the 1936 election.

Having discussed the reforms of the New Deal, the authors consider the impact of the New Deal era on organized labor, which benefited from both Section 7(a) of the NIRA and the Wagner Act. Therefore, despite determined resistance by management and a division within the labor movement that led to the creation of the Congress of Industrial Organizations (CIO), the union movement made impressive gains during the 1930s.

In "Federal Power and the Nationalization of Culture," we turn to a discussion of the profound change that the New Deal caused in the relationship between Americans and their government. Examples are offered to support the authors' contention that the federal government, by gaining more control over water, hydroelectric power, and land in the West, gained more control over the region's future. Furthermore, passage of the Indian Reorganization Act not only indicates a more enlightened governmental approach to American Indians, but also demonstrates that federal activism extended to people in the West, not just to the region's natural resources. We also see, through discussion of the Tennessee Valley Authority, the Roosevelt administration's successes and failures in its attempts to transform the South and integrate the region into the nation's culture and economy.

After examining the impact of the radio and movies on the breaking down of regional boundaries and the emergence of a national culture, we look at the limits of the New Deal. Mistakes and political reality meant that Roosevelt did not enjoy successes during his second term like those experienced in his first. He made a political and tactical mistake in his request for a restructuring of the Supreme Court. His dislike of deficit spending and desire for a balanced budget led to drastic cuts in federal spending, which in turn led to a new recession in 1937 and to a renewal of deficit spending. Such mistakes undercut some of Roosevelt's charisma; therefore, even though the New Deal coalition held together in the 1940 presidential election, Roosevelt did not achieve the landslide victory he had enjoyed in 1936.

The experience of African Americans and Mexican Americans demonstrates that racism continued as a force detrimental to the lives of nonwhites and was clearly a reason that all Americans did not benefit equally from the New Deal. The Scottsboro case serves as a symbol of the ugliness of race relations in the depression era. Furthermore, despite the presence of the Black Cabinet, President Roosevelt was never fully committed to civil rights for blacks, and some New Deal measures functioned in a discriminatory way. However, there were some indications that change was on the horizon.

First, in relation to cases arising out of the Scottsboro trial, the Supreme Court ruled that the due process clause of the Fourteenth Amendment made the criminal protection procedures (the right to adequate defense counsel and the right to an impartial jury) of the Sixth Amendment applicable to the states. Second, Roosevelt created the Black Cabinet and had within his administration people committed to racial equality. In addition, Eleanor Roosevelt, the conscience of the New Deal, demonstrated her commitment to racial equality through her vocal and public support of Marian Anderson. Furthermore, African Americans continued, as they had throughout their history, to work in their own behalf to overcome the injustices and abuses associated with white racism.

The chapter ends with a discussion of the way in which historians view the legacy of the New Deal.

BUILDING VOCABULARY

Listed below are important words and terms that you need to know to get the most out of Chapter 25. They are listed in the order in which they occur in the chapter. After carefully looking through the list, (1) underline the words with which you are totally unfamiliar, (2) put a question mark by those words of which you are unsure, and (3) leave the rest alone.

As you begin to read the chapter, when you come to any of the words you've put question marks beside or underlined (1) slow your reading; (2) focus on the word and on its context in the sentence you're reading; (3) if you can understand the meaning of the word from its context in the sentence or passage in which it is used, go on with your reading; (4) if it's a word that you've underlined or a word that you can't understand from its context in the sentence or passage, look it up in a dictionary and write down the definition that best applies to the context in which the word is used.

Definitions

arid _____

squalid _____

exacerbate _____

destitute _____

relegate _____

exhortation _____

moratorium _____

specter _____

maim _____

interregnum _____

mandate _____

dole _____

incendiary _____

demagogue _____

tenuous _____

innocuous _____

vicarious _____

paradox _____

pragmatist _____

ameliorate _____

Difficult-to-Spell Names and Terms from Reading and Lecture

IDENTIFICATION AND SIGNIFICANCE

After studying Chapter 25 of _A People and a Nation,_ you should be able to identify fully _and_ explain the historical significance of each item listed below.

- Identify each item in the space provided. Give an explanation or description of the item. Answer the questions _who, what, where,_ and _when._

- Explain the historical significance of each item in the space provided. Establish the historical context in which the item exists. Establish the item as the result of or as the cause of other factors existing in the society under study. Answer this question: _What were the political, social, economic, and/or cultural consequences of this item?_

1. the Dust Bowl

     a.   Identification

     b.   Significance

2.   Marvin Montgomery

    a.   Identification

    b.   Significance

3.   "Hoovervilles"

    a.   Identification

    b.   Significance

4.   marginal workers

    a.   Identification

    b.   Significance

5.   Herbert Hoover

    a.   Identification

    b.   Significance

6.   "associationalism"

    a.   Identification

    b.   Significance

7. the President's Organization on Unemployment Relief (POUR)

    a. Identification

    b. Significance

8. the Federal Farm Board

    a. Identification

    b. Significance

9. the Hawley-Smoot Tariff

    a. Identification

    b. Significance

10. the Reconstruction Finance Corporation

    a. Identification

    b. Significance

11. Farmers' Holiday Association

    a. Identification

    b. Significance

12. Unemployed Councils

    a. Identification

    b. Significance

13. the Bonus Expeditionary Force

    a. Identification

    b. Significance

14. *Gabriel Over the White House*

    a. Identification

    b. Significance

15. Franklin D. Roosevelt

    a. Identification

    b. Significance

16. the 1932 presidential campaign and election

    a. Identification

    b. Significance

17.   the Twentieth Amendment to the Constitution
  a.   Identification

  b.   Significance

18.   the banking crisis
  a.   Identification

  b.   Significance

19.   Roosevelt's first inaugural address
  a.   Identification

  b.   Significance

20.   national bank holiday
  a.   Identification

  b.   Significance

21.   the Emergency Banking Relief Bill (March 9, 1933)
  a.   Identification

  b.   Significance

22. Roosevelt's fireside chats

    a. Identification

    b. Significance

23. the First Hundred Days

    a. Identification

    b. Significance

24. the Brain Trust

    a. Identification

    b. Significance

25. the National Industrial Recovery Act (June 16, 1933)

    a. Identification

    b. Significance

26. the National Recovery Administration

    a. Identification

    b. Significance

27. the Agricultural Adjustment Act (May 12, 1933)

    a. Identification

    b. Significance

28. the Civilian Conservation Corps (March 31, 1933)

    a. Identification

    b. Significance

29. the Public Works Administration

    a. Identification

    b. Significance

30. the American Liberty League

    a. Identification

    b. Significance

31. Father Charles Coughlin

    a. Identification

    b. Significance

32. Dr. Francis E. Townsend

    a. Identification

    b. Significance

33. Huey Long

    a. Identification

    b. Significance

34. the "Black Cabinet"

    a. Identification

    b. Significance

35. the Second New Deal

    a. Identification

    b. Significance

36. the Emergency Relief Appropriation Act (April 8, 1935)

    a. Identification

    b. Significance

37. the Works Progress Administration

    a. Identification

    b. Significance

38. the Federal Theater, Federal Arts, Federal Music, and Federal Writers Projects

    a. Identification

    b. Significance

39. the Social Security Act (August 15, 1935)

    a. Identification

    b. Significance

40. the Wealth Tax Act (August 30, 1935)

    a. Identification

    b. Significance

41. the 1936 presidential election

    a. Identification

    b. Significance

42. the New Deal coalition

a. Identification

b. Significance

43. the National Labor Relations (Wagner) Act (July 5, 1935)

a. Identification

b. Significance

44. craft unions versus industrial unions

a. Identification

b. Significance

45. John L. Lewis

a. Identification

b. Significance

46. the Congress of Industrial Organizations

a. Identification

b. Significance

47. the United Auto Workers' strike of 1936

    a. Identification

    b. Significance

48. the Memorial Day Massacre

    a. Identification

    b. Significance

49. the Bureau of Reclamation

    a. Identification

    b. Significance

50. the Taylor Grazing Act (June 28, 1934)

    a. Identification

    b. Significance

51. John Collier

    a. Identification

    b. Significance

52. the Indian Reorganization Act (June 18, 1934)

    a. Identification

    b. Significance

53. the Tennessee Valley Authority (May 18, 1933)

    a. Identification

    b. Significance

54. the radio and Hollywood movies

    a. Identification

    b. Significance

55. Roosevelt's court-packing plan

    a. Identification

    b. Significance

56. *NLRB v. Jones and Laughlin Steel Corp.*

    a. Identification

    b. Significance

57.   the recession of 1937–1939

    a.   Identification

    b.   Significance

58.   the 1940 presidential election

    a.   Identification

    b.   Significance

59.   the Scottsboro Boys

    a.   Identification

    b.   Significance

60.   Marian Anderson

    a.   Identification

    b.   Significance

61.   the Southern Tenant Farmers' Union and the Harlem Tenants League

    a.   Identification

    b.   Significance

62.   A. Philip Randolph

   a.   Identification

   b.   Significance

ORGANIZING, REVIEWING AND USING INFORMATION

Chart A

Presidential Responses to the Great Depression, 1929–1939		
	Herbert Hoover	**Franklin D. Roosevelt**
Beliefs about the Proper Role of Government		
Recognition of the Severity of Economic Conditions		
Reliance on Efforts to Stimulate Business at Home and Abroad to Save and Recoup Jobs		
Reliance on Private Charities to Ease the Depression's Impact on Citizens		
Use of Direct Intervention To Ease the Depression's Impact		
Reliance on the Public's Good Will and Cooperation in Confronting the Nation's Economic Problems		
Reliance on Extreme, Controversial Measures To Combat Economic Crises		
Handling of Critics of the Government's Handling of the Economy and of Unrest (Mass Protests)		
Change in Unemployment and Other Economic Indicators During this Presidency's Depression Years		

Chart B

Important Achievements of the First New Deal, 1933–1934					
	Type Act, Program, Governmental Body, Agency, etc.	**Goal & Strategy**	**Authorization** What it authorized or was authorized/ funded by	**Reaction** Court, Critics, Public	**Evaluation** Benefits, Drawbacks, or Legacy
LABOR					
National Industrial Recovery Act (1933)					
National Labor Relations Board (1934)					
AGRICULTURE					
Agricultural Adjustment Act 1933					
Taylor Grazing Act (1934)					
BUSINESS/INDUSTRIAL RECOVERY					
Emergency Banking Act 1933					
National Industrial Recovery Act 1933					

Important Achievements of the First New Deal, 1933–1934					
	Type Act, Program, Governmental Body, Agency, etc.	**Goal & Strategy**	**Authorization** What it authorized or was authorized/ funded by	**Reaction** Court, Critics, Public	**Evaluation** Benefits, Drawbacks, or Legacy
RELIEF					
Civilian Conservation Corps (1933)					
Federal Emergency Relief Act (1933)					
Public Works Administration (1933)					
Civil Works Administration (1933)					
REFORM					
Tennessee Valley Authority (TVA) 1933					
Federal Securities Act (1933)					
Securities Exchange Act (1934)					
Indian Reorganization Act (1934)					

Chart C

Important Achievements of the Second New Deal, 1935–1938					
	Type	Goal	Authorized or Funded by	Reaction	Evaluation
	Act, Program, Governmental Body, Agency, etc.			Court, Critics, Public	Benefits, Drawbacks
LABOR					
National Labor Relations Act (1935)					
Fair Labor Standards Act (1938)					
AGRICULTURE					
Rural Electrification Administration (1935)					
Agricultural Adjustment Act (1938)					
BUSINESS/INDUSTRIAL RECOVERY					

Important Achievements of the Second New Deal, 1935–1938					
	Type	**Goal**	**Authorized or Funded by**	**Reaction**	**Evaluation**
	Act, Program, Governmental Body, Agency, etc.			Court, Critics, Public	Benefits, Drawbacks
RELIEF					
Works Progress Administration (1935)					
National Youth Administration (1935)					
Resettlement Administration (1935)					
REFORM					
Social Security Act (1935)					

Chart D

Roles the Federal Government Assumed or Expanded in the 1930s: The Beginning of the Federal Government's Transformation into "The Government"	
Roles	**Examples**
BOOSTER OF MORALE AND MORAILTY	
Racism/Sexism	
REGULATOR OF PRODUCTION AND THE MARKETPLACE	
Money Supply and Credit	
Business Competition	
Farm Production, Prices	
Imports/Exports	
PROVIDER OF ECONOMIC SAFETY NET FOR INDIVIDUALS	
Dependent Children	
Elderly	
Disabled	
Unemployed	
GUARDIAN OF NATIONAL ECONOMIC/FINANCIAL STABILITY	
Regulator, Protector of Financial Institutions	
Federal Spending and Budgeting	
REDISTRIBUTOR OF WEALTH	

Roles the Federal Government Assumed or Expanded in the 1930s: The Beginning of the Federal Government's Transformation into "The Government"	
Roles	**Examples**
PROTECTOR OF MINORITIES	
African Americans	
Native Americans	
Mexican Americans	
Women	

IDEAS AND DETAILS

Objective 1

1. During the depression, many argued that women workers deprived male breadwinners of jobs. Was this argument valid? Why?

   a. Yes, because women were willing to work for lower wages than men.

   b. Yes, because in the 1920s women had moved into many previously male-dominated jobs.

   c. No, because the sex segregation of the job market made it very unlikely that men would be hired for "women's" jobs.

   d. No, because most women lost their jobs as the depression intensified.

Objective 2

2. Hoover's recommendation that Congress create the Reconstruction Finance Corporation indicated which of the following?

   a. Hoover believed it was more important to extend aid to farmers than to industrial workers.

   b. Hoover believed that by increasing the supply of goods there would be a corresponding increase in demand.

   c. Hoover had compromised his ideological principles by supporting direct aid to private industries.

   d. Hoover placed blame for the depression on large economic entities.

Objective 2

3. Hoover responded to the Bonus March by

   a. calling out troops to disperse the marchers.

   b. establishing a comprehensive pension plan for future army veterans.

   c. encouraging Congress to authorize the immediate payment of veterans' benefits.

   d. meeting with the marchers and negotiating a settlement.

Objective 6

4. Both the Agricultural Adjustment Act and the National Industrial Recovery Act were based, in part, on the belief that

   a. limits should be placed on the production of both agricultural and industrial goods to deal with the problems of the depression.

   b. prices of industrial and agricultural goods had to be lowered.

   c. deficit spending would result in an economic rebound.

   d. the depression could best be dealt with by state and local authorities.

Objectives 8 and 15

5. In 1935, the Supreme Court ruled part of the NIRA unconstitutional because it

   a. violated the First Amendment.

   b. extended federal power beyond its constitutional bounds.

   c. discriminated against small businesses.

   d. violated the due process clause of the Fourteenth Amendment.

Objective 7

6.   In their criticisms of the New Deal, many wealthy business leaders charged that it

   a.   cooperated too closely with environmentalists.
   b.   extended too little aid to the lower classes.
   c.   exercised too little control over national economic forces.
   d.   relied on too much taxation and too much government regulation.

Objective 7

7.   Through the Share Our Wealth program, Huey Long advocated that the government should

   a.   nationalize all major industry in the United States.
   b.   distribute free land to all families requesting it.
   c.   provide a guaranteed annual income to all American families.
   d.   create a national health insurance program.

Objective 8

8.   Which of the following is true of the Social Security Act?

   a.   It established an old-age insurance plan for all workers in the United States.
   b.   Through its enactment, the government acknowledged some responsibility toward the aged, the dependent, and the disabled.
   c.   It established a national health insurance program for all Americans.
   d.   All benefits were paid by employers and the government.

Objectives 6 and 8

9.   The Second New Deal differed from the First in that it

   a.   adopted a more aggressive, less cooperative approach toward big business.
   b.   returned to the concept of laissez faire.
   c.   rejected the concept of deficit spending.
   d.   emphasized the importance of state action.

Objective 10

10.   During the 1930s the growth of organized labor was most impressive among

   a.   skilled workers.
   b.   industrial workers.
   c.   farm workers.
   d.   white-collar workers.

Objective 12

11.   Which of the following is true of the Indian Reorganization Act of 1934?

   a.   It virtually ended the forced assimilation of Indians.
   b.   Tribal governments were no longer recognized by the federal government.
   c.   It gave direct aid to impoverished Indians.
   d.   It promoted individual land ownership among Indians.

Objective 14

12. Roosevelt's 1937 decision to cut federal spending resulted in
    a. a balanced budget.
    b. a lowering of interest rates.
    c. renewed spending by business on capital improvements.
    d. a new recession.

Objective 17

13. Analysis of the AAA and the WPA indicates which of the following?
    a. These measures were quite effective in bringing about a redistribution of wealth in the United States.
    b. Money spent on such programs went mainly to the wealthy.
    c. All of these programs extended benefits to people in the city but not to the people in rural areas.
    d. Some New Deal measures functioned in ways that were discriminatory toward African Americans.

Objectives 9 and 17

14. African Americans supported Franklin Roosevelt for which of the following reasons?
    a. Roosevelt's New Deal relief programs helped many African Americans in their struggle for economic survival.
    b. Roosevelt endorsed congressional enactment of a federal antilynching law.
    c. Congress enacted legislation abolishing the poll tax at Roosevelt's insistence.
    d. Roosevelt's Justice Department supported the NAACP in its legal challenges against Jim Crow laws in the southern states.

Objective 18

15. While some scholars debate Roosevelt's performance, all agree that
    a. the New Deal fundamentally changed the nation's power structure.
    b. Roosevelt transformed the presidency.
    c. the New Deal solved the fundamental question of unemployment.
    d. Roosevelt was essentially a conservative.

ESSAY QUESTIONS

Objective 2

1. Explain President Hoover's response to the depression.

Objective 3

2. Discuss the impact of the Great Depression on the lives of Americans. What was the response of the American people to the Depression? Why did they respond as they did?

Objectives 2 and 5

3. Discuss the similarities and differences between Herbert Hoover and Franklin Roosevelt in terms of personality, governing style, and view of the role of government.

Objectives 6 and 8

4.   Discuss the similarities and differences between the theoretical basis of the First New Deal and that of the Second New Deal, and explain in both cases how the legislation enacted reflected this theory.

Objective 10

5.   Discuss the impact of the New Deal on organized labor.

Objectives 1 and 17

6.   Examine the impact of the depression and New Deal on African Americans.

ANSWERS

Multiple-Choice Questions

1.   c.   Correct. Women were concentrated in jobs such as teaching, clerical and secretarial work, and switchboard operators. These were considered "women's jobs," and it was very unlikely that unemployed men would be hired for such jobs. See pages 682–683.

    a.   No. Despite the fact that women were usually paid less than men, this does not mean that women workers deprived unemployed men of jobs that were open to them. See pages 682–683.

    b.   No. The job market remained sex segregated. See pages 682–683.

    d.   No. At first women did lose their jobs more quickly than men, but as the depression intensified "women's jobs" were not as hard hit as "men's jobs." Furthermore, the fact that the number of women who were gainfully employed increased during the 1930s does not indicate that most women lost their jobs as the depression intensified. See pages 682–683.

2.   c.   Correct. When the depression began, President Hoover believed that it could be dealt with successfully through "associationalism." Therefore, he did not believe that the federal government should directly intervene to solve the nation's economic problems. However, as the depression deepened, Hoover reluctantly supported the chartering of the Reconstruction Finance Corporation (RFC). Through the RFC Hoover supported direct assistance in the form of loans to large entities at the top of the economy. He did so in the belief that such economic assistance would trickle down to the masses. By moving toward the idea of a more active federal role in dealing with the economic crisis, Hoover compromised his ideological principles by accepting limited federal "interference." See page 685.

    a.   No. The RFC did not extend direct aid to either farmers or to industrial workers. See page 685.

    b.   No. The RFC was not based on the basic assumption of "supply-side" economics. See page 685.

    d.   No. The RFC provided federal loans to large economic entities such as banks, insurance companies, and railroads. Hoover's support for the creation of the RFC does not indicate that he blamed large economic entities for the depression. See page 685.

3.   a.   Correct. Hoover saw the Bonus marchers as extremists, refused to meet with them after Congress defeated the Bonus Bill, and finally called out the army to attack and disperse the Bonus Expeditionary Force encamped in Washington. See page 686.

    b.   No. Hoover remained steadfast in his belief in limited government, in individual initiative, and in self-help. He never suggested establishing a comprehensive pension plan for future veterans. See page 686.

    c.   No. President Hoover urged Congress to defeat the Bonus Bill. See page 686.

    d.   No. Hoover refused to meet with leaders of the Bonus Expeditionary Force. See page 686.

4.   a.   Correct. An assumption on which the AAA and the NIRA were based was that overproduction was the major factor preventing economic recovery. Therefore, through centralized national planning, farmers and industries would be encouraged to produce less. See pages 689–690.

b.   No. The AAA sought to raise the prices of farm goods, and the NIRA attempted to do the same for manufactured goods. See pages 689–690.

c.   No. Neither the AAA nor the NIRA called for deficit spending. See pages 689–690.

d.   No. Both the AAA and the NIRA demonstrated Roosevelt's willingness to deal with problems from the national level. See pages 689–690.

5.   b.   Correct. The Court held part of the NIRA to be unconstitutional because it regulated businesses that were wholly involved in intrastate commerce, which, the Court contended, was an extension of federal power beyond its constitutional bounds. Furthermore, the Court held that the NIRA delegated excessive legislative power to the executive branch of the government. See page 689.

a.   No. The First Amendment deals with freedom of religion, speech, and the press and the right to assemble peacefully and petition the government for redress of grievances. The Court did not find that the NIRA abridged these rights. See page 689.

c.   No. The Court held part of the NIRA to be unconstitutional because it regulated businesses that were wholly involved in intrastate commerce, but it did not hold that the act discriminated against small businesses. See page 689.

d.   No. The Court did not rule that the NIRA was in violation of the Fourteenth Amendment. See page 689.

6.   d.   Correct. Wealthy business leaders believed that the New Deal demonstrated excessive government regulation of business and that it relied on too much taxation. See page 692.

a.   No. The Roosevelt administration did not demonstrate a great deal of concern for the environment in drafting New Deal legislation, and wealthy business leaders did not charge that the administration cooperated too closely with environmentalists. See page 692.

b.   No. Wealthy business leaders and conservatives were critical of relief programs such as the CCC and the FERA and claimed that such programs were based on socialist ideology. See page 692.

c.   No. Wealthy business leaders and conservatives, who believed that the economy should be allowed to operate in accordance with natural economic laws, criticized the Roosevelt administration for centralized economic planning. See page 692.

7.   c.   Correct. Long proposed that the government provide a guaranteed annual income of $2,000 to every American family. See page 693.

a.   No. Although Long believed that the New Deal was too closely allied with business interests, he did not advocate nationalizing all major industry in the United States. See page 693.

b.   No. Long proposed a homestead allowance of $5,000, but did not propose actually giving land. See page 693.

d.   No. Although Long proposed a free college education for every American, he did not propose a national health insurance program. See page 693.

8.   b.   Correct. Although the law was a relatively conservative measure and did not apply to all workers, it established the idea of government responsibility toward the aged, dependent, and disabled. See page 697.

a.   No. Although the Social Security Act established an old-age insurance program, the law did not apply to all workers. See page 697.

c.   No. The Social Security Act authorized money grants to the states for public health work, but it did not establish a national health insurance program. See page 697.

d.   No. The measure is considered relatively conservative because benefits were to be paid by workers and employers, not by the government. See page 697.

9.   a.   Correct. Roosevelt believed that business leaders had placed their own interests above those of the nation. Therefore, during the Second New Deal, Roosevelt abandoned business-government cooperation and, to "cut the giants down to size," moved to enforce antitrust laws. See page 697.

b.   No. Both the First and the Second New Deals reflect Roosevelt's belief that the government could act as a positive force in American society. Therefore, he did not return to the idea of passive government embodied in the laissez-faire philosophy. See page 697.

c.   No. Although Roosevelt remained a fiscal conservative and was committed to a balanced budget, deficit spending characterized both the First and the Second New Deals. See page 697.

d.   No. Both the First and the Second New Deals strengthened the role of the federal government. However, state and local governments were given the task of implementing much of the legislation passed under both New Deals. See page 697.

10.   b.   Correct. Workers in many major industries began to organize in industrial unions, such as the UMW and the UAW. See page 698.

a.   No. Skilled workers were already heavily involved in the labor movement through the American Federation of Labor. See page 698.

c.   No. Organized labor did not consist of farm workers. See page 698.

d.   No. White-collar workers were not organizing in the 1930s. See page 698.

11.   a.   Correct. John Collier as Director of the Bureau of Indian Affairs during the Roosevelt administration wanted to reverse the course of America's Indian policy. Instead of forced assimilation, Collier wanted to perpetuate Native American religions and cultures. The Indian Reorganization Act of 1934 was very instrumental in ending forced assimilation of American Indians and in restoring Indian lands to tribal ownership. See page 700.

b. No. The Indian Reorganization Act of 1934 extended federal recognition to tribal government. See page 700.

c.   No. The Indian Reorganization Act of 1934 was not a relief measure and did not extend direct aid to impoverished Indians. See page 700.

d.   No. The Indian Reorganization Act of 1934 restored Indian lands to tribal ownership and did not promote individual land ownership among Indians. See page 700.

12. d.   Correct. The massive spending cuts ordered by Roosevelt in 1937, along with the tightening of credit by the Federal Reserve Board, caused a recession. As a result, Roosevelt returned to deficit spending, which brought some economic recovery by 1939. See page 705.

a.   No. Although Roosevelt's intention in cutting federal spending was to achieve a balanced budget, this was not the end result. See page 705.

b.   No. At the same time that Roosevelt cut spending, the Federal Reserve Board tightened credit, causing interest rates to rise. See page 705.

c.   No. At the same time that Roosevelt cut federal spending, the Federal Reserve Board tightened credit. This, in turn, caused business to cut back on spending for capital improvements. See page 705.

13. d.   Correct. In operation, these acts indicate an antiblack bias and demonstrate that although African Americans benefited from the New Deal, they did not get their fair share. See pages 690 and 706.

a.   No. These measures did not bring about a redistribution of wealth. See pages 690 and 706.

b.   No. Money spent on these programs tended to benefit middle- and lower-income groups, not the wealthy. See pages 690 and 706.

c.   No. The AAA helped people in rural areas more than people in urban areas, and the WPA benefited people in both areas. See pages 690 and 706.

14. a.   Correct. Although African Americans did not receive their fair share from New Deal relief programs and public-works programs, the New Deal helped many African Americans in their struggle for economic survival. Furthermore, African Americans were well aware of the Black Cabinet and of Eleanor Roosevelt's commitment to social justice, especially after the First Lady arranged for Marian Anderson to sing at the Lincoln Memorial on Easter Sunday after the singer was barred from performing in Washington's Constitution Hall. For all of these reasons, African Americans supported Franklin Roosevelt, and most changed their political affiliation from the Republican Party to the Democratic Party. See page 706.

b.   No. Roosevelt needed the support of Southern Democrats to secure passage of his legislative program. As a result, the President did not intervene to break a southern filibuster and secure passage of an antilynching bill in 1938. Despite that, African Americans supported Roosevelt. See page 706.

c.   No. Congress did not act to abolish the poll tax in the southern states. This was not accomplished until the Twenty-fourth Amendment to the Constitution was ratified in 1964. This amendment outlawed the poll tax as a prerequisite for voting in federal elections. See page 706.

d.   No. President Roosevelt was never totally committed to the cause of civil rights. Therefore, the Justice Department did not support the NAACP in its legal challenges against Jim Crow laws in the southern states during the Roosevelt administration. See page 706.

15. b.   Correct. Political scientists and historians agree that Roosevelt transformed the presidency. See pages 707–708.

a.   No. The nation's power structure was not fundamentally changed by the New Deal. In fact, that was never one of President Roosevelt's goals. See pages 707–708.

c.   No. One of the failures of the New Deal was that it did not solve the problem of unemployment. In 1939 the unemployment rate stood at 19 percent. Ultimately, it was massive government spending during the Second World War that solved the problem of unemployment and brought full economic recovery. See pages 707–708.

d.   No. Some scholars believe that Roosevelt was too conservative in his approach to the problems of the depression. However, that does not mean that those who view him in that way label him as a conservative. Furthermore, most scholars agree that Roosevelt was not a radical and that he wanted to save the capitalist system, not destroy it. Therefore, most scholars would label Roosevelt as either a progressive or a liberal. See pages 707–708.

CHAPTER 26

Peaceseekers and Warmakers: Americans in the World, 1920–1941

LEARNING OBJECTIVES

After you have studied Chapter 26 in your textbook and worked through this study guide chapter, you should be able to:

1. Explain the ideas of independent internationalism and isolationism, and discuss how these ideas were manifested in the various attempts by American citizens and the American government to create a stable international order during the interwar years.

2. Examine and discuss the objectives and consequences of United States policies toward world economic issues from 1918 to 1941.

3. Examine the economic and cultural expansion of the United States from 1918 to 1941.

4. Discuss the impact of the Great Depression on international relations, and explain Secretary of State Cordell Hull's response to intensified economic nationalism.

5. Examine and evaluate the interests, methods, and results of United States policy toward Latin America during the 1920s and 1930s.

6. Explain Europe's descent into the Second World War.

7. Explain the nature and growth of isolationist sentiment in the United States, and discuss the Neutrality Acts as an expression of such sentiment.

8. Discuss the foreign-policy ideas and diplomatic leadership of President Franklin Roosevelt from 1933 to United States entry into the Second World War.

9. Examine the erosion of American neutrality toward the war in Europe between September 1939 and December 7, 1941.

10. Examine the deterioration of Japanese-American relations from the 1920s to the Japanese attack against Pearl Harbor, and discuss American entry into the Pacific theater of the Second World War.

THEMATIC GUIDE

In this chapter, the authors seek to explain the instability of the world order in the 1920s and the coming of world war in the 1930s. Involvement in disarmament talks and arms limitation treaties, acceptance of the Kellogg-Briand Pact outlawing war, and international economic expansion by the United States serve as examples of the independent internationalist approach to foreign policy undertaken by the United States during the 1920s. These examples also illustrate the drawbacks of such an approach. United States acceptance of arms limitations treaties that did not include some of the most dangerous weapons of the age—submarines, destroyers, and cruisers—meant the continuation of rearmament. Acceptance of a treaty that outlawed war but had no enforcement provisions served a useful educational purpose but did not prevent war. International economic expansion, high United States tariff rates,

United States policies concerning war debts and reparations, and the onset of the Great Depression caused an upsurge of economic nationalism and destabilized the international economy. Although Secretary of State Cordell Hull's attempts to move in the direction of economic internationalism were positive, they did not have a dramatic short-term impact.

In the 1920s, the United States altered its policy toward Latin America. Blatant military intervention no longer seemed to preserve American interests and maintain the order and stability so important to those interests. A new approach favored support for strong native leaders, training of the national guard in Latin American countries, continued economic expansion, Export-Import Bank loans, and political subversion. Evidence for this change in approach may be found through an examination of American policy toward the Dominican Republic, Nicaragua, Haiti, Cuba, and Puerto Rico during the 1920s and early 1930s. The Good Neighbor policy enhanced American power throughout the region but did not bring to Latin America the stable, democratic governments that the United States professed to desire. Mexico was a special case. In response to the expropriation controversy, President Roosevelt decided compromise was the best course of action.

As the depression, economic nationalism, and aggressive fascist states began slowly to carry Europe into the abyss of war, the United States continued to follow the policy of independent internationalism, as evidenced in American economic ties with the Soviet Union and diplomatic recognition of that country in 1933. At the same time, isolationist sentiment (the desire to remain aloof from European power struggles and war) increased. Such sentiment found expression in the investigations of the Nye Committee, which attempted to prove that business interests had selfishly pulled the United States into the First World War. Although it failed to prove this assertion, the Nye Committee did find evidence of discreditable business practices during the 1920s and 1930s designed to increase arms sales. Furthermore, the chapter includes evidence of American business ties to Nazi Germany and fascist Italy. The publicity generated by the Nye Committee was in part responsible for passage of the Neutrality Acts of 1935, 1936, and 1937. Although Roosevelt supported these acts, events in Europe gradually convinced him that they should be revised and finally repealed.

In "Japan, China, and a New Order in Asia," the authors discuss American interests in Asia and trace the deterioration of United States–Japanese relations during the 1920s and 1930s. This discussion leads to the final section, "U.S. Entry into World War II," where the authors focus on events in Europe and explain President Roosevelt's policies, which carried the United States from neutrality to undeclared war. In addition, we look at the deterioration of relations between the United States and Japan in the early 1940s. Ultimately, Japanese leaders decided that the United States stood in the way of its goal of creating the Greater East Asia Co-Prosperity Sphere. As a result, Japan launched a surprise attack on Pearl Harbor. This attack led Congress to pass a formal declaration of war against Japan on December 8, 1941. Great Britain then declared war on Japan; and, three days later, Germany and Italy declared war on the United States.

BUILDING VOCABULARY

Listed below are important words and terms that you need to know to get the most out of Chapter 26. They are listed in the order in which they occur in the chapter. After carefully looking through the list, (1) underline the words with which you are totally unfamiliar, (2) put a question mark by those words of which you are unsure, and (3) leave the rest alone.

As you begin to read the chapter, when you come to any of the words you've put question marks beside or underlined (1) slow your reading; (2) focus on the word and on its context in the sentence you're reading; (3) if you can understand the meaning of the word from its context in the sentence or passage in which it is used, go on with your reading; (4) if it's a word that you've underlined or a word that you can't understand from its context in the sentence or passage, look it up in a dictionary and write down the definition that best applies to the context in which the word is used.

Definitions

eradicate _____

infrastructure _____

virulent _____

fervent _____

unilateralism _____

elusive _____

pinnacle _____

aversion _____

carnage _____

opportune _____

ape (verb) _____

disseminate _____

magnanimous _____

cataclysm _____

blatant _____

exploitative _____

abrogate _____

tutelage _____

expropriate _____

authoritarianism _____

disparage _____

apex _____

satiate _____

abhorrence _____

discretionary _____

chastise _____

covet _____

protocol _____

abyss _____

deviant _____

affront _____

vestige _____

ignoble _____

abrogate _____

pummel _____

ardent _____

dissipate _____

aggrandizement _____

panacea _____

Difficult-to-Spell Names and Terms from Reading and Lecture

IDENTIFICATION AND SIGNIFICANCE

After studying Chapter 26 of *A People and a Nation,* you should be able to identify fully *and* explain the historical significance of each item listed below.

- Identify each item in the space provided. Give an explanation or description of the item. Answer the questions *who, what, where,* and *when*.

- Explain the historical significance of each item in the space provided. Establish the historical context in which the item exists. Establish the item as the result of or as the cause of other factors existing in the society under study. Answer this question: *What were the political, social, economic, and/or cultural consequences of this item?*

1. the Rockefeller Foundation's anti-mosquito campaign

    a. Identification

    b. Significance

2. independent internationalism

    a. Identification

    b. Significance

3. the American peace movement

    a. Identification

    b. Significance

4. the Washington Naval Conference

    a. Identification

    b. Significance

5. the Five-Power Treaty, the Nine-Power Treaty, and the Four-Power Treaty

    a. Identification

    b. Significance

6. the Kellogg-Briand Pact of 1928

    a. Identification

    b. Significance

7. American economic and cultural expansion

    a. Identification

    b. Significance

8. the Webb-Pomerene Act and the Edge Act

    a. Identification

    b. Significance

9. the war debts and reparations issue
    a. Identification

    b. Significance

10. the Dawes Plan of 1924
    a. Identification

    b. Significance

11. the Young Plan of 1929
    a. Identification

    b. Significance

12. the Johnson Act of 1934
    a. Identification

    b. Significance

13. economic nationalism
    a. Identification

    b. Significance

14.   the London Conference of 1933

    a.   Identification

    b.   Significance

15.   Secretary of State Cordell Hull

    a.   Identification

    b.   Significance

16.   the Reciprocal Trade Agreements Act

    a.   Identification

    b.   Significance

17.   the most-favored-nation principle

    a.   Identification

    b.   Significance

18.   the Export-Import Bank

    a.   Identification

    b.   Significance

19.   diplomatic recognition of the Soviet Union

    a.   Identification

    b.   Significance

20.   the Good Neighbor policy

    a.   Identification

    b.   Significance

21.   Fulgencio Batista

    a.   Identification

    b.   Significance

22.   Lázaro Cárdenas

    a.   Identification

    b.   Significance

23.   the Mexican expropriation controversy

    a.   Identification

    b.   Significance

24. fascism

    a.   Identification

    b.   Significance

25. the Rome-Berlin Axis and the Anti-Comintern Pact

    a.   Identification

    b.   Significance

26. the policy of appeasement

    a.   Identification

    b.   Significance

27. the Abraham Lincoln Battalion

    a.   Identification

    b.   Significance

28. the Munich Conference

    a.   Identification

    b.   Significance

29. American isolationist sentiment

    a. Identification

    b. Significance

30. the Nye Committee

    a. Identification

    b. Significance

31. the Neutrality Acts of 1935, 1936, and 1937

    a. Identification

    b. Significance

32. Roosevelt's Chautauqua speech

    a. Identification

    b. Significance

33. the voyage of the *St. Louis*

    a. Identification

    b. Significance

34. the Nazi-Soviet Pact

    a.   Identification

    b.   Significance

35. the German invasion of Poland

    a.   Identification

    b.   Significance

36. repeal of the arms embargo (the Neutrality Act of 1939)

    a.   Identification

    b.   Significance

37. *The Good Earth*

    a.   Identification

    b.   Significance

38. Jiang Jieshi

    a.   Identification

    b.   Significance

39. Japanese seizure of Manchuria

    a. Identification

    b. Significance

40. the Stimson Doctrine

    a. Identification

    b. Significance

41. the Sino-Japanese War

    a. Identification

    b. Significance

42. Roosevelt's quarantine speech

    a. Identification

    b. Significance

43. the *Panay* incident

    a. Identification

    b. Significance

44. Japan's "New Order"

    a. Identification

    b. Significance

45. the fall of France

    a. Identification

    b. Significance

46. the destroyers-for-bases agreement

    a. Identification

    b. Significance

47. the Selective Training and Service Act

    a. Identification

    b. Significance

48. the Lend-Lease Act

    a. Identification

    b. Significance

49. the Atlantic Charter

    a. Identification

    b. Significance

50. the *Greer*, the *Kearny*, and the *Reuben James*

    a. Identification

    b. Significance

51. the Tripartite Pact

    a. Identification

    b. Significance

52. Japanese occupation of French Indochina

    a. Identification

    b. Significance

53. Operation MAGIC

    a. Identification

    b. Significance

54. the Japanese attack on Pearl Harbor

    a. Identification

    b. Significance

ORGANIZING, REVIEWING, AND USING INFORMATION

Chart A

America's Road to Participation in World War II, DECEMBER 1920–DECEMBER 1941					
	Activity Pursued, Steps Taken by Americans	**How Related To American Entrance into the War**	**Triggering Action or Situation**	**Initial Response of Germany, Japan, and/or Italy**	**Outcome, Aftermath**
Peace Activism within United States					
International Peace Pacts, Accords, or Declarations Proposed and/or Signed					
Plans, Agreements, or Legislation Concerning World War I Debts Owed to U.S.					
American Perception of Threats to its Possessions Interests, or Policies					

America's Road to Participation in World War II, DECEMBER 1920–DECEMBER 1941					
	Activity Pursued, Steps Taken by Americans	How Related To American Entrance into the War	Triggering Action or Situation	Initial Response of Germany, Japan, and/or Italy	Outcome, Aftermath
Arms Limitation Agreements Proposed and/or Signed by U.S.					
U.S. Trade Practices, Restrictions, Tariffs					
American Provision of Military Aid to Belligerents before Entering the War					
American Involvement in Shipping to or by Belligerents (Including Participation in Naval Confrontations)					

America's Road to Participation in World War II, DECEMBER 1920–DECEMBER 1941					
	Activity Pursued, Steps Taken by Americans	**How Related To American Entrance into the War**	**Triggering Action or Situation**	**Initial Response of Germany, Japan, and/or Italy**	**Outcome, Aftermath**
President's Means of Winning Public's Willingness To Go to War					
Other Nations' Attacks on American Property, Ships, or Possessions					

Chart B

U.S. Relations with Latin Americans and the Caribbean in the Roosevelt Years				
	Policies and Practices of the 1920s	Policies and Practices Under Roosevelt	Challenges to American Policies and Practices under Roosevelt	Outcome of Challenges to American Policies and Practices under Roosevelt
Military				
Trade and Finance				
Criticism (from Latin America, Caribbean)				
Criticism (from within United States)				
Latin American and Caribbean Dictators and Dictatorships				

IDEAS AND DETAILS

Objectives 2 and 3

1.   Secretary of State Charles Evans Hughes encouraged United States economic expansion abroad because he believed such expansion

   a.   would promote world stability.
   b.   would foster healthy competition and rivalry.
   c.   would bring power and glory to the United States at the expense of the less-virtuous European nations.
   d.   would promote economic nationalism.

Objective 1

2.   As a result of the Five-Power Treaty,

   a.   Britain, the United States, Japan, France, and Italy agreed to limits on the number of submarines that each nation could build.
   b.   Britain, the United States, and Japan dismantled some major ships to meet the tonnage ratio agreed to.
   c.   provisions for the enforcement of the Open Door policy were accepted by Britain, the United States, Japan, France, and Italy.
   d.   Britain, the United States, France, Italy, and the Soviet Union agreed to impose economic sanctions against Nazi Germany.

Objective 1

3.   The Kellogg-Briand Pact

   a.   placed limits on the number of submarines and destroyers to be built by the world's five major powers.
   b.   called for an end to international arms sales.
   c.   made the United States an official observer at the League of Nations.
   d.   renounced war as an instrument of national policy.

Objectives 2 and 3

4.   Which of the following conclusions may be drawn from an examination of the war debts and reparations issue?

   a.   The United States handled the issue in a selfless manner.
   b.   The triangular arrangement that emerged was economically destabilizing in the long run.
   c.   The European nations demonstrated a willingness to forgive Germany in the aftermath of the First World War.
   d.   The German government used the issue to create tensions between the United States and Great Britain.

Objectives 2, 3 and 4

5.   In response to the Hawley-Smoot Tariff,

   a.   European states raised tariffs against American imports, causing economic nationalism to gain momentum.
   b.   European nations exported inexpensive goods to the United States in record numbers.
   c.   European states pledged to support the Open Door policy.
   d.   Japan imposed an embargo against all American-made goods.

Objectives 2, 3 and 4

6. The central feature of the Reciprocal Trade Agreements Act of 1934 was

    a. the adoption of free trade by the United States.
    b. low-interest loans to foreign countries agreeing to buy American goods.
    c. the most-favored-nation principle.
    d. the establishment of a free trade zone in the Western Hemisphere.

Objective 5

7. The Good Neighbor policy meant that

    a. the United States would strictly adhere to the doctrine of nonintervention in Latin America.
    b. the United States would be less blatant in dominating Latin America.
    c. American businesses in Latin America would invest their profits there rather than in the United States.
    d. the United States would practice isolationism in Latin America.

Objective 5

8. With regard to Latin America, the Roosevelt administration

    a. sought to stimulate economic diversification and industrial development throughout the region.
    b. believed that military intervention by the United States was the best way to deal with political and economic instability in countries throughout the region.
    c. was willing to support dictatorial regimes in the hope they would promote stability in the region.
    d. fostered democracy by sending impartial observers to oversee free elections in the region.

Objective 6

9. As a result of the Munich Conference,

    a. Britain and France accepted Hitler's seizure of the Sudeten region of Czechoslovakia.
    b. Britain agreed to extend financial and military aid to France in the event of German aggression.
    c. Britain, France, and the Soviet Union entered into a defensive alliance against Nazi Germany.
    d. Germany and France agreed to withdraw their troops from Austria and the Rhineland, respectively.

Objectives 2, 3 and 7

10. Records from the 1930s concerning American business practices abroad indicate that

    a. all major American corporations strongly supported arms control in the belief that fewer armaments would generate peace and prosperity.
    b. American petroleum exports to Italy increased after that country's attack on Ethiopia.
    c. all major American corporations severed their business ties with Germany when the Nazis gained power.
    d. all American firms severed economic ties with Germany after learning about the persecution of Jews.

Objective 7

11. The Neutrality Acts of 1935 and 1936

  a. were attempts to provide aid to the Allies while avoiding war with Hitler.
  b. imposed a unilateral freeze on further deployment of destroyer-class vessels.
  c. allowed the president to intervene in the Spanish Civil War.
  d. prohibited arms shipments and loans to nations declared by the president to be in a state of war.

Objective 9

12. As a result of the outbreak of war in Europe in September 1939,

  a. Roosevelt promised that the United States would involve itself in the conflict if British defeat seemed imminent.
  b. Congress, at Roosevelt's urging, approved arms exports on a cash-and-carry basis.
  c. the United States broke diplomatic relations with the Soviet Union.
  d. Roosevelt asked Congress for a declaration of war against Germany.

Objective 10

13. In response to the Japanese invasion of Manchuria, the United States

  a. issued the Stimson Doctrine by which it refused to recognize any impairment of Chinese sovereignty.
  b. froze Japanese assets in this country.
  c. called for economic sanctions against Japan through the League of Nations.
  d. signed a defensive treaty of alliance with China.

Objective 9

14. By the Lend-Lease Act,

  a. the United States traded fifty old destroyers to the British for leases to four British bases.
  b. the provisions of the Neutrality Acts were revoked.
  c. Roosevelt was authorized to ship war materiel to the British.
  d. the United States canceled Allied debts from the First World War.

Objective 10

15. The Roosevelt administration

  a. plotted to start a war with Japan.
  b. was completely surprised by the Japanese decision in favor of war.
  c. was aware of Japanese war plans but did not conspire to leave Pearl Harbor vulnerable.
  d. expected a Japanese attack against the American mainland.

ESSAY QUESTIONS

Objective 1

1. Discuss the Washington Naval Conference's treaty agreements and the Kellogg-Briand Pact as examples of the United States independent-internationalist approach to foreign policy during the 1920s, and explain the strengths and weaknesses of that approach.

Objectives 1, 2 and 3

2. Explain and evaluate American handling of the war debts and reparations issue.

Objective 5

3. Discuss the Good Neighbor Policy and its impact on relations between the United States and Latin America.

Objective 7

4. Explain the sources of isolationist thought in the United States in the 1920s and 1930s, and discuss the actions taken by Congress to prevent United States involvement in European power struggles.

Objective 9

5. Explain the process by which the United States moved from neutrality in 1939 to undeclared war with Germany in 1941.

Objective 10

6. Trace relations between the United States and Japan during the 1920s and 1930s, and explain the Japanese decision to bomb Pearl Harbor.

ANSWERS

Multiple-Choice Questions

1. a.   Correct. Secretary of State Hughes accepted the philosophy that economic expansion was necessary for world peace. As a result, he supported passage of legislation intended to foster international trade. See page 713.

    b.   No. Secretary of State Hughes did not focus on the competition and rivalry that would accompany economic expansion. See page 713.

    c.   No. Secretary of State Hughes did not encourage economic expansion abroad out of a desire to increase the power of the United States at the expense of "less virtuous" European nations. See page 713.

    d.   No. Secretary of State Hughes did not encourage economic expansion abroad as a means by which the United States could promote economic nationalism. See page 713.

2. b.   Correct. As one of a total of three treaties that came out of the Washington Naval Conference, the Five-Power Treaty provided for a ten-year moratorium on the construction of capital ships and established a ratio of capital ships. Britain, the United States, and Japan had to dismantle some ships to meet the ratio. See pages 714–715.

    a.   No. None of the treaties negotiated at the Washington Naval Conference placed limits on the construction of submarines, destroyers, or cruisers—the most destructive weapons of the age. See pages 714–715.

    c.   No. In the Nine-Power Treaty, all the nations represented at the Washington Naval Conference agreed to respect Chinese sovereignty and to accept the Open Door principle. See pages 714–715.

    d.   No. The Five-Power Treaty was drafted at the Washington Naval Conference of 1921–1922. The Nazis were not in power in Germany at that time. See pages 714–715.

3. d.   Correct. The Kellogg-Briand Pact, signed by sixty-two nations in 1928, condemned war as a way of solving international problems and renounced war as an instrument of national policy. See page 715.

    a.   No. No treaty signed during the 1920s placed limits on the number of submarines and destroyers to be built by the five major powers. See page 715.

    b.   No. No limits were placed on international arms sales during the 1920s. See page 715.

    c.   No. Although it is true that the United States began to send observers to League conferences, this was not accomplished by the Kellogg-Briand Pact. See page 715.

4.   b.   Correct. American loans to Germany, German reparations payments to the Allies, and Allied war-debt payments to the United States created a triangular arrangement that depended on German borrowing in the United States and was economically destabilizing. See pages 718–719.

a.   No. Even though it worked a hardship on the debtor nations, the United States insisted that they pay their debts in full. This does not indicate a selfless handling of the war-debt issue. See pages 718–719.

c.   No. The Allies forced Germany to accept guilt for the First World War and insisted that Germany pay the $33 billion reparations bill levied by the Allies. See pages 718–719.

d.   No. The idea that the German government used the war-debt and reparations issue to create tensions between the United States and Great Britain is not a logical inference that can be drawn from the evidence presented. See pages 718–719.

5.   a.   Correct. This tariff measure raised rates an average of 8 percent. As a result, many European nations were priced out of the United States market. In response, the European nations retaliated by raising tariff rates against American imports. See page 719.

b.   No. European imports to the United States declined as a result of the Hawley-Smoot Tariff. See page 719.

c.   No. The Hawley-Smoot Tariff was a general tariff measure and did not deal specifically with the Open Door policy, which applied to China. See page 719.

d.   No. Since most American imports came from Europe, the Hawley-Smoot Tariff primarily affected trade relations with that area. Therefore, this tariff did not give Japan a reason to impose an embargo against American products. See page 719.

6.   c.   Correct. Any nation entering into regular trade agreements with the United States would be given tariff rates matching those given to the "most-favored nation." This principle was important because it brought an overall lowering of tariff rates and fostered economic internationalism. See page 719.

a.   No. Although this act authorized the president to lower American tariffs by as much as 50 percent through special agreements with foreign countries, the United States did not adopt a free trade position. Such a position would have meant repealing all tariffs. See page 719.

b.   No. This act did not offer low-interest loans to countries agreeing to buy American goods. See page 719.

d.   No. This act moved toward freer trade but did not establish a free trade zone within the Western Hemisphere. See page 719.

7.   b.   Correct. Some methods used by the United States to maintain its influence in Latin America had become counterproductive. Therefore, the Good Neighbor Policy was an attempt to use less controversial and less blatant means to accomplish the same end. See page 722.

a.   No. In spite of the Good Neighbor Policy, the United States saw order in Latin American as vital to its national interests. As a result, it was not willing to "strictly adhere" to the doctrine of nonintervention. See page 722.

c.   No. In spite of the Good Neighbor Policy, American businesses in Latin America continued to take their profits out of the region and invest them elsewhere (a process known as decapitalization). See page 722.

d.   No. The Good Neighbor Policy certainly did not mean that the United States would practice isolationism in Latin America. Rather, it included ways for the United States to stay involved in more subtle ways. See page 722.

8.   c.   Correct. Rafael Leonidas Trujillo, president of the Dominican Republic from 1930 to 1961, Anastasio Somoza, ruler of Nicaragua from 1936 to 1979, and Fulgencio Batista, ruler of Cuba from 1934 to 1959, had dictatorial powers in their respective countries. Roosevelt supported each of these regimes during his years as President because he believed that they not only protected American economic interests, but that they also brought stability and order to their respective countries and, therefore, to Latin America. See page 722.

a.   No. The Roosevelt administration did not seek to stimulate economic diversification and industrial development throughout Latin America. See page 722.

b.   No. Roosevelt wanted to maintain U.S. influence throughout Latin America, but through the Good Neighbor Policy, he wanted to use means that were less blatant than military intervention. See page 722.

d.   No. The United States did not send impartial observers to oversee free elections in Latin American states during the Roosevelt administration. See page 722.

9.   a.   Correct. Britain and France, following the policy of appeasement, accepted Hitler's seizure of the Sudetenland in September 1938. Hitler proceeded to take the rest of Czechoslovakia in March 1939. Then, in September 1939, when German forces attacked Poland, Britain and France declared war on Germany. See page 724.

b.   No. The British made no such pledge to France in the years leading up to the Second World War. See page 724.

c.   No. The Munich Conference did not result in a defensive alliance among Britain, France, and the Soviet Union against Nazi Germany. See page 724.

d.   No. At the time of the Munich Conference, Germany had seized the Rhineland (March 1936) and Austria (March 1938). Germany did not withdraw its troops from either area as a result of the conference. See page 724.

10. b.   Correct. After Italy's invasion of Ethiopia, Roosevelt invoked an arms embargo against Italy as required by the Neutrality Act of 1935. The act did not require a ban on petroleum, copper, and iron and steel scrap exports; and, despite Roosevelt's call for a moral embargo on these products, exports of these items to Italy increased. See page 725.

a.   No. Hearings by the Nye Committee indicate that some United States corporations lobbied against arms control and attempted to increase arms sales to foreign nations during the 1920s and 1930s. See page 725.

c.   No. Records indicate that twenty-six of the top one hundred United States firms still had contractual agreements with Germany in 1937, four years after Hitler and the Nazis came to power. See page 725.

d.   No. Many United States firms continued to maintain lucrative economic ties with Germany after learning about the persecution of Jews. One exception was the Wall Street firm of Sullivan and Cromwell, which severed economic ties with Germany to protest Hitler's anti-Semitic practices. See page 725.

11. d.   Correct. Congress believed that bankers and munitions-makers had dragged the United States into the First World War. To prevent this from recurring, Congress passed the Neutrality Acts, which required a mandatory arms embargo against and forbade loans to all belligerents. See page 725.

a.   No. The intent of the Neutrality Acts was to prevent the United States from being drawn into war, not to provide aid to the Allies. See page 725.

b.   No. The Neutrality Acts contained no arms-control provisions. See page 725.

c.   No. In 1937, the United States declared itself neutral in the Spanish Civil War and Roosevelt embargoed arms shipments to both sides. See page 725.

12. b.   Correct. In spite of strong lobbying efforts by isolationists and the presence of strong opposition in Congress, the arms embargo, at Roosevelt's urging, was repealed in November 1939 and the sale of arms was placed on a cash-and-carry basis. See page 727.

a.   No. Although Roosevelt was sympathetic toward the British and saw Germany, Italy, and Japan as "bandit nations," he did not respond to the outbreak of war by promising American involvement if British defeat seemed imminent. See page 727.

c.   No. Although the United States condemned Russia's nonaggression pact with Hitler and the subsequent Russo-German conquest and partition of Poland, Washington did not break diplomatic relations with the Soviet Union. See page 727.

d.   No. In response to the outbreak of war in Europe, President Roosevelt declared the United States to be a neutral nation. See page 727.

13. a.   Correct. President Hoover, who was grappling with the problems of the Great Depression and who realized that the United States did not have the naval power to risk a Pacific war, refused to authorize anything stronger than the Stimson Doctrine, which was a moral condemnation of the Japanese. See pages 727–728.

 b.   No. The United States did not take definitive economic action against Japan in response to that nation's 1931 invasion of Manchuria, and Japanese assets were not frozen until after the Japanese occupation of southern Indochina in July 1941. See pages 727–728.

 c.   No. President Hoover refused to cooperate with the League in imposing economic sanctions on Japan. See pages 727–728.

 d.   No. The United States continued to follow a foreign policy characterized by nonalignment with foreign nations. See pages 727–728.

14. c.   Correct. Designed primarily to aid the British, who were running out of money, the Lend-Lease Act (March 1941) authorized the president to transfer, sell, exchange, lend, or lease war materiel to any country whose defense was considered vital to the United States. See page 732.

 a.   No. In September 1940, in the midst of the Battle of Britain, Roosevelt concluded the Destroyer-Bases Agreement with Great Britain. By this agreement, the United States traded fifty old destroyers to the British for ninety-nine-year leases to eight British bases in Newfoundland and the Caribbean. See page 732.

 b.   No. The Neutrality Acts of 1935, 1936, and 1937 were slightly modified in 1939; and, although the Lend-Lease Act may be considered a further modification, it did not "revoke" the provisions of the Neutrality Acts. See page 732.

 d.   No. In 1931–1932, President Hoover and Congress refused to cancel Allied debts incurred during the First World War. As a result, European nations were forced to default, but that happened some ten years before the Lend-Lease Act. See page 732.

15. c.   Correct. The United States government knew of Japan's war plans but did not know where or when Japan would strike. When the location was learned, the telegram informing the base commanders at Pearl Harbor was delayed. See page 734.

 a.   No. After the Japanese occupation of Indochina, Roosevelt's advisers, acting on the president's advice, tried to prolong talks with the Japanese so that the Philippines could be fortified and the fascists checked in Europe. See page 734.

 b.   No. The United States had broken the Japanese code and knew by December 1 that Japan had decided on war with the United States if the oil embargo was not lifted. See page 734.

 d.   No. The United States government and the base commanders at Pearl Harbor expected an attack at British Malaya, Thailand, or the Philippines. See page 734.

CHAPTER 27

The Second World War at Home and Abroad, 1941–1945

LEARNING OBJECTIVES

After you have studied Chapter 27 in your textbook and worked through this study guide chapter, you should be able to:

1.   Discuss United States military strategy and the major military operations in the Pacific theater that brought America to the verge of victory by 1945.

2.   Describe the military strategy and the major military operations undertaken by the Allies in the European theater; discuss the disagreements that arose concerning strategy; and explain the resolution of these disagreements.

3.   Examine the impact of the Second World War on American businesses, institutions of higher learning, organized labor, and the federal government, and discuss and assess the role played by the federal government in the war effort.

4.   Discuss the impact of the Second World War on American civilians in general and on African Americans, Mexican Americans, women, and American families specifically.

5.   Examine the tensions between America's democratic ideals and its wartime practices, and discuss specifically the civil liberties record of the United States government during the Second World War with regard to Japanese Americans, African Americans, and the plight of Jewish refugees.

6.   Discuss the impact of military life and wartime experiences on the men and women in the United States armed forces during the Second World War.

7.   Examine the relations, the issues debated, and the agreements reached among the Allies from the second-front controversy through the Yalta and Potsdam conferences, and discuss the issues left unresolved after Yalta and Potsdam.

8.   Explain and evaluate President Truman's decision to use the atomic bomb.

9.   Assess the impact of the Second World War on the world community of nations and on the world balance of power.

THEMATIC GUIDE

In Chapter 27, as in Chapters 23 through 25, we look at the changes begot by war. Having dealt with changes fostered by the First World War, Americans entered into an era of "normalcy" during the 1920s. Yet even in the midst of the peace and prosperity of the 1920s, Americans often seemed to be fighting a cultural war that pitted those who adhered to older "traditional" values and beliefs against those who accepted the new values of the era. It was during the Jazz Age that America continued its transition from an agricultural to an industrial nation, women made strides in breaking out of their constraints, and African Americans became more outspoken in their demand for equality. Furthermore, the new openness about sex and the challenges of science to fundamentalist religious beliefs during the 1920s caused anxiety in many quarters. Then came the economic disasters of the Great Depression.

The collapse of the nation's economic system led to the election of Franklin Roosevelt and to the mobilization of the federal government in a war against joblessness, poverty, and homelessness. The Roosevelt revolution forever changed the relationship between the American people and their government. Then, after the Japanese attack on Pearl Harbor on December 7, 1941, Americans had to face the anxiety of change within a nation whose very survival depended on successful mobilization for war. Since this was total war, not only did troops have to be mobilized, but the homefront had to be mobilized as well to produce the materiel necessary to defeat Japan and the Axis Powers.

In the first section of Chapter 27, "The United States at War," we look at the earliest stage of the Second World War in both the Pacific and European theaters. In the Pacific, America was largely on its own to fight the Japanese; and, after initial losses, successfully broke the momentum of Japan's offensive at the Battle of Midway. In turning to the European theater we look at America's "Europe First" strategy and at the undercurrent of suspicion among the Allies, obvious in the second-front controversy. In November 1942 American and British forces landed in North Africa and were eventually successful in defeating General Erwin Rommel and his Afrika Korps. Back in Europe, the Soviet army's successful defense of Stalingrad proved to be a turning point in the European war.

The focus of the chapter then shifts to a discussion of the nation's mobilization for war on the production front. This mobilization brought (1) renewed government-business cooperation and an acceleration of corporate growth, (2) the growth of scientific research facilities through government incentives, (3) new economic opportunities for African Americans, Mexicans, and women, (4) the growth of labor unions, and (5) the successful conversion of American factories from civilian production to military production.

The Second World War, to an even greater extent than the First World War, was a total war, requiring not only military mobilization but mobilization of the civilian population as well. As civilian workers poured into the nation's defense plants, the primary responsibility for coordinating total mobilization of the home front fell on the federal government. Therefore, the federal bureaucracy mushroomed in size as one can see in the coordinating efforts of the War Production Board, the Office of Price Administration, and the Office of War Information. Furthermore, the government relied primarily on deficit spending to finance the war. This massive influx of money into the economic system brought full employment and prosperity. As more Americans than ever before moved to take advantage of the opportunities afforded by wartime prosperity, communities changed and conflict emerged between war workers and native citizens. Although the war provided opportunities for African Americans, the Detroit riot of 1943 made clear that racism remained a shaping force in blacks' lives. The zoot-suit riot in Los Angeles in 1943 demonstrated that the same was true for Mexican Americans.

For women, the war became a turning point. More women, including more married women and mothers, entered the labor force than ever before. As some of the negative attitudes toward women working in heavy industry began to change, women experienced more geographic and occupational mobility. Although they continued to receive lower pay than men and were still concentrated in sex-segregated occupations, more women than ever were deciding to remain in the labor market. But even with those changes, home and family responsibilities continued to fall on their shoulders. In many cases, the wartime absence of husbands and fathers made women fully responsible for the family. The combination of these factors and experiences meant that many women gained a new sense of independence.

In "The Limits of American Ideals" we discuss three significant examples of America's failure to live up to its ideals. While the authors state that, "for the most part, America handled the issue of civil liberties well," it is obvious that the treatment of Japanese Americans was an enormous exception to the nation's generally creditable wartime civil liberties record. Forcibly removed from the West Coast,

Japanese Americans were transported to relocation centers and interned chiefly because of their ethnic origin. As a result, many felt betrayed by their government. There was also the paradox of African American soldiers fighting in a segregated American military against racist Nazi ideology. Furthermore, African Americans on the home front continued to face political, social, and economic discrimination. As in the First World War, African Americans saw the war as an opportunity to achieve their goal of equality in American society. Through the NAACP's "Double V" campaign and through the founding of the Congress of Racial Equality, African Americans became more outspoken in their attempt to realize that goal. We then turn to "America's most tragic failure to live up to its democratic ideas"—America's refusal to help European Jews and others attempting to escape Hitler's Germany. As we saw in Chapter 26, Roosevelt and Congress knew as early as 1938 of Hitler's anti-Semitic policies and actions, and by 1943 FDR was aware of the existence of the Nazi death camps. Although the administration established the War Refugee Board in early 1944, it was a case of too little too late.

Life in the military, life away from family, and the experience of war profoundly affected the men and women who served in the armed forces during the course of the Second World War. The frame of reference of many GIs was broadened by associations with fellow soldiers from backgrounds and cultures different from their own. Many who saw combat endured horrors they could never erase from their memories. As GIs returned to civilian life, they quickly realized that life at home had continued without them; thus, many felt a sense of loss and alienation.

In the last section of the chapter, "Winning the War," the authors turn to the decision to open the second front and to the wars final years. After a brief discussion of D-Day and the Battle of the Bulge, we look at decisions made at the Yalta and Potsdam conferences. The Yalta Conference is often described as "the high point of the Grand Alliance." The agreements reached there are explained in the context of the suspicions among the Allies, the goals of each of the Allies, and the positions of each of the Allied armies. Upon Roosevelt's death in April 1945, Harry S Truman ascended to the presidency, and less than a month later Germany surrendered. As the war continued in the Pacific, allied leaders met once again at the Potsdam Conference. Unlike the Yalta Conference, the Potsdam Conference revealed a crumbling alliance in which any sense of cooperation had given way to suspicions among competitive nation states. These suspicions, so obvious at Potsdam, were a portent concerning the post-war world. Within this context, the authors discuss the final battles in the Pacific theater, the Potsdam Declaration, and President Truman's decision to use atomic bombs on Hiroshima and Nagasaki. Truman's rejection of alternatives to the atomic bomb and the strategic, emotional, psychological, and diplomatic reasons for his decision to use it are explained at chapter's end.

BUILDING VOCABULARY

Listed below are important words and terms that you need to know to get the most out of Chapter 31. They are listed in the order in which they occur in the chapter. After carefully looking through the list, (1) underline the words with which you are totally unfamiliar, (2) put a question mark by those words of which you are unsure, and (3) leave the rest alone.

As you begin to read the chapter, when you come to any of the words you've put question marks beside or underlined (1) slow your reading; (2) focus on the word and on its context in the sentence you're reading; (3) if you can understand the meaning of the word from its context in the sentence or passage in which it is used, go on with your reading; (4) if it's a word that you've underlined or a word that you can't understand from its context in the sentence or passage, look it up in a dictionary and write down the definition that best applies to the context in which the word is used.

Definitions

capitulate _____

decipher _____

vehement _____

precedence _____

din _____

paradox _____

conflagration _____

exhort _____

perpetuate _____

lament _____

putrid _____

consign _____

mollify _____

peripheral _____

novice _____

titular _____

Difficult-to-Spell Names and Terms from Reading and Lecture

IDENTIFICATION AND SIGNIFICANCE

After studying Chapter 27 of *A People and a Nation,* you should be able to identify fully *and* explain the historical significance of each item listed below.

- Identify each item in the space provided. Give an explanation or description of the item. Answer the questions *who, what, where,* and *when.*

- Explain the historical significance of each item in the space provided. Establish the historical context in which the item exists. Establish the item as the result of or as the cause of other factors existing in the society under study. Answer this question: *What were the political, social, economic, and/or cultural consequences of this item?*

1.   the Navajo Code Talkers

　　a.   Identification

　　b.   Significance

2.   the Bataan Death March

　　a.   Identification

　　b.   Significance

3.   the Doolittle raid

　　a.   Identification

　　b.   Significance

4. the Battle of Midway

    a.   Identification

    b.   Significance

5. the "Europe first" strategy

    a.   Identification

    b.   Significance

6. Winston Churchill

    a.   Identification

    b.   Significance

7. Josef Stalin

    a.   Identification

    b.   Significance

8. the second-front controversy

    a.   Identification

    b.   Significance

9.   the battle for Stalingrad

    a.   Identification

    b.   Significance

10. the War Production Board

    a.   Identification

    b.   Significance

11. wartime government-business interdependence

    a.   Identification

    b.   Significance

12. American universities and war research

    a.   Identification

    b.   Significance

13. the Manhattan Project

    a.   Identification

    b.   Significance

14. the March on Washington Movement

    a.   Identification

    b.   Significance

15. Executive Order No. 8802

    a.   Identification

    b.   Significance

16. the bracero program and wartime Mexican workers

    a.   Identification

    b.   Significance

17. women's wartime work

    a.   Identification

    b.   Significance

18. Rosie the Riveter

    a.   Identification

    b.   Significance

19. the no strike–no lockout pledge

    a.   Identification

    b.   Significance

20. the National War Labor Board

    a.   Identification

    b.   Significance

21. the War Labor Disputes (Smith-Connally) Act

    a.   Identification

    b.   Significance

22. the Office of Price Administration

    a.   Identification

    b.   Significance

23. the Office of War Information

    a.   Identification

    b.   Significance

24. the Detroit race riots of 1943

    a.   Identification

    b.   Significance

25. the zoot-suit riots

    a.   Identification

    b.   Significance

26. the Alien Registration Act

    a.   Identification

    b.   Significance

27. the internment of Japanese Americans

    a.   Identification

    b.   Significance

28. *Korematsu v. United States*

    a.   Identification

    b.   Significance

29. the 442nd Regimental Combat Team
    a.   Identification

    b.   Significance

30. the "Double V" campaign
    a.   Identification

    b.   Significance

31. the Congress of Racial Equality
    a.   Identification

    b.   Significance

32. the "Tuskegee Airmen"
    a.   Identification

    b.   Significance

33. the War Refugee Board
    a.   Identification

    b.   Significance

34. the Teheran Conference

    a.   Identification

    b.   Significance

35. Operation Overlord

    a.   Identification

    b.   Significance

36. D-Day

    a.   Identification

    b.   Significance

37. the Battle of the Bulge

    a.   Identification

    b.   Significance

38. the Yalta Conference

    a.   Identification

    b.   Significance

39. the Dumbarton Oaks Conference

    a.   Identification

    b.   Significance

40. Harry S Truman

    a.   Identification

    b.   Significance

41. the Potsdam Conference

    a.   Identification

    b.   Significance

42. the "island-hop" strategy

    a.   Identification

    b.   Significance

43. the Battles of Iwo Jima and Okinawa

    a.   Identification

    b.   Significance

44. the firebombing of Tokyo
    a.   Identification

    b.   Significance

45. the Potsdam Declaration
    a.   Identification

    b.   Significance

46. Hiroshima and Nagasaki
    a.   Identification

    b.   Significance

ORGANIZING, REVIEWING, AND USING INFORMATION

Chart A

American Treatment of Minorities During World War II					
	Women	African Americans	Mexicans, Mexican Americans	Japanese Americans	German Americans
Acceptance in Armed Forces					
Isolation from Community					
Job Opportunities, Job-Related Social Services					
Victimization in Riots or Other Violence					
Support by Government and Court					

Chart B

Military Operations Most Significant to the Outcome of World War II					
Military Operation	**Theater of Operations**	**Type (air, sea, land)**	**Part in Allies' Overall Strategy**	**Relationship to Allies' Strategy Disagreements**	**Outcome and Impact**

IDEAS AND DETAILS

Objective 2

1.   As a result of the Battle of Midway,

    a.   the United States destroyed Japan's merchant marine.

    b.   Japanese momentum in the Pacific was broken.

    c.   American naval losses made Hawai'i more vulnerable to attack.

    d.   President Roosevelt began to harbor private fears of Japanese victory in the Pacific.

Objective 3

2.   The task of the War Production Board was to

    a.   vigorously enforce the nation's antitrust laws.

    b.   minimize the cost of the war by ensuring competitive bidding on government contracts.

    c.   allocate resources and coordinate production among U. S. factories in the conversion of industry from civilian to military production.

    d.   analyze the military situation in order to determine what weapons needed to be produced and in what quantity.

Objective 3

3.   The Second World War affected American industry in which of the following ways?

    a.   To increase competition, the government broke up large manufacturing units.

    b.   The trend toward the consolidation of manufacturing into the hands of a few corporate giants continued.

    c.   The withdrawal of government money from the economy brought a restructuring of industry.

    d.   Heavy industry was virtually nationalized to ensure the availability of war materiel.

Objective 4

4.   During the Second World War, African Americans

    a.   continued to move to northern industrial cities.

    b.   experienced equal opportunity in housing and employment.

    c.   experienced a deterioration of their economic position.

    d.   steadfastly refused to participate in the war effort.

Objective 3

5.   The Smith-Connally Act

    a.   reduced the powers of the National War Labor Board.

    b.   prohibited strikes and lockouts.

    c.   guaranteed cost of living increases to workers in defense-related industries.

    d.   authorized the president to seize and operate any strike-bound plant deemed necessary to the national security.

Objective 4

6. Did Rosie the Riveter accurately portray women in the American work force during the Second World War? Why?

    a. No, because women were not allowed to work in defense plants during the Second World War.

    b. No, because only a small percentage of working women held jobs in defense plants and an even smaller percentage held jobs classified as "skilled."

    c. Yes, because women in the work force filled almost all of the skilled jobs in heavy industry previously held by men.

    d. Yes, because women monopolized jobs in the shipbuilding industry during the war.

Objective 4

7. What impact did the Second World War have on American families?

    a. There was a significant decline in the number of babies born out of wedlock.

    b. There was a significant decline in the number of marriages.

    c. There was a more restrictive sexual-morality code throughout the nation.

    d. There was a significant increase in the divorce rate.

Objective 5

8. Which of the following is the major reason for the internment of Japanese Americans during the Second World War?

    a. Criminal behavior

    b. Evidence of disloyalty to the government of the United States

    c. Their ethnic origin

    d. Their economic challenge to white businesses

Objective 5

9. In response to Nazi persecution of the Jews, the United States

    a. did not act in a decisive manner until the creation of the War Refugee Board in 1944.

    b. relaxed immigration requirements in the mid-1930s in order to allow Jewish refugees free entry into the United States.

    c. cooperated closely with the British in opening Palestine to Jewish refugees.

    d. bombed the gas chambers at Nordhausen toward the end of the war.

Objective 6

10. Those who served in the United States armed forces during the Second World War

    a. often became less prejudiced and less provincial because of associations with people of differing backgrounds.

    b. found that the technical training they received in the military was useless in civilian life.

    c. usually received no training before being sent into combat.

    d. were given no background information on the history and culture of the places to which they were sent.

Objectives 2 and 7

11. As a result of the Teheran Conference, the Allies

    a. reached agreement on launching Operation Overlord.
    b. agreed to launch an attack against North Africa.
    c. reluctantly decided to recognize the pro-Nazi Vichy French regime in North Africa.
    d. made plans for the battle for Stalingrad.

Objective 7

12. A major factor that influenced the agreements at Yalta was

    a. Roosevelt's ill health.
    b. dissension between Roosevelt and Churchill over German reparations.
    c. the military positions of the Allies.
    d. Stalin's insistence that China be recognized as a major power.

Objective 9

13. Which of the following countries suffered the most casualties as a result of the Second World War?

    a. Great Britain
    b. the United States
    c. Japan
    d. the Soviet Union

Objective 9

14. Which of the following countries emerged from the Second World War more powerful than it had been when it entered the war?

    a. Great Britain
    b. the United States
    c. Japan
    d. Russia

Objective 8

15. Which of the following is true concerning President Truman's decision to use the atomic bomb against Japan?

    a. Truman believed it was the only way the United States could win the war in the Pacific.
    b. Truman believed that a quick American victory against Japan would allow the United States to concentrate on defeating Hitler.
    c. In the meeting of the Allies at the Potsdam Conference, Truman convinced Churchill and Stalin that use of the atomic bomb was the quickest and most humane way to defeat Japan.
    d. Truman's decision fit into the U.S. strategy of using machines rather than men to wage the war.

ESSAY QUESTIONS

Objective 3

1.   Discuss the various responsibilities assumed by the federal government as coordinator and overseer of America's war effort, and evaluate its performance.

Objective 3

2.   Discuss the trend toward bigness in American industry during the course of the Second World War.

Objective 4

3.   Discuss the impact of the Second World War on women in American society.

Objectives 4 and 5

4.   Discuss the impact of the Second World War on nonwhite Americans.

Objective 5

5.   Discuss the nature and purpose of the internment of Japanese Americans during the Second World War. How did the Supreme Court respond to the policy?

Objective 5

6.   Explain the response of the United States to the persecution of European Jews during the Second World War.

Objective 6

7.   Explain the impact of military life and wartime experiences on American service people.

Objective 8

8.   Examine and assess President Truman's decision to use the atomic bomb.

ANSWERS

Multiple-Choice Questions

1.   b.   Correct. As a result of Operation Magic, American experts deciphered the secret Japanese code. With prior knowledge of Japanese plans, American forces sank four of Japan's aircraft carriers in the Battle of Midway and broke the enemy's momentum in the Pacific. See pages 742–743.

   a.   No. The United States did not destroy Japan's merchant marine as a result of the Battle of Midway. See pages 742–743.

   c.   No. The Battle of Midway did not make Hawai'i more vulnerable to attack. See pages 742–743.

   d.   No. The Battle of Midway did not cause Roosevelt to harbor fears of Japanese victory. See pages 742–743.

2.   c.   Correct. Factories had to be converted from production of consumer goods to production of war materiel. The War Production Board successfully oversaw this task and in doing so was responsible for allocating resources and coordinating production among U.S. factories. See pages 744–745.

   a.   No. Cooperation between government and business was essential for successful execution of the war effort. As a result, the government guaranteed that companies would be exempt from antitrust prosecution during the war. See pages 744–745.

   b.   No. Since the government had to produce war materiel in the shortest time possible, competitive bidding was usually not possible. Although some attempts were made to award contracts to small businesses, most government contracts were awarded to big businesses. See pages 744–745.

   d.   No. The WPB was not responsible for analyzing the military situation. The WPB concentrated its efforts on the home front rather than on the military front. See pages 744–745.

3.   b.   Correct. Since most government contracts were awarded to big corporations, the dominance of those corporations increased. Furthermore, the trend toward consolidation in agriculture also accelerated during the war because the expense of farm machinery led to a decline in the number of family farms. See page 745.

   a.   No. The U.S. government had to produce war materiel as quickly as possible and, in doing so, did not attempt to increase competition among American industries. Furthermore, the government exempted companies from antitrust prosecution during the war; and, therefore, the government did not break up large manufacturing units. See page 745.

   c.   No. During the Second World War the government poured massive sums of money into the economy. This may be seen in the increase of the national debt from $49 billion in 1941 to $259 billion in 1945. See page 745.

   d.   No. Heavy industry remained in private hands. See page 745.

4.   a.   Correct. Some 1.5 million African Americans moved to industrial cities in the North and West during the war. Having moved into areas where they could exercise the right to vote, the political power of blacks in national, state, and local elections increased. See pages 745–746.

b.   No. Blacks continued to experience political, economic, and social discrimination during World War II. See pages 745–746.

c.   No. Overall, the economic position of African Americans improved during World War II. See pages 745–746.

d.   No. African Americans eagerly participated in and supported the American war effort. See pages 745–746.

5.   d.   Correct. This act, passed over President Roosevelt's veto, broadened the power of the president in handling labor disputes in war-related industries. See page 747.

a.   No. Under the Smith-Connally Act, the NWLB's powers were broadened to include the legal authority to settle labor disputes until the end of the war. See page 747.

b.   No. Although the act established a mandatory thirty-day cooling-off period before a strike could be called in a war-related industry, it did not prohibit strikes and made no reference to lockouts (the shutdown of a plant to bring workers to terms). See page 747.

c.   No. The Smith-Connally Act did not guarantee cost-of-living increases to workers in defense-related industries. See page 747.

6.   b.   Correct. "We Can Do It!" read the caption on the most famous Rosie the Riveter poster distributed during the Second World War. Therefore, women were encouraged to help the war effort by taking jobs that men in the service left behind. In fact, many women did take advantage of new employment opportunities during the war. However, the Rosie the Riveter image does not accurately portray women in the work force because only 16 percent of working women held jobs in defense plants, and they held only 4.4 percent of jobs classified as "skilled." See pages 746–747.

a.   No. Women were allowed to work in defense plants during the Second World War. See pages 746–747.

c.   No. Women in the workforce held only 4.4 percent of jobs classified as "skilled" during the war years. See pages 746–747.

d.   No. Women did not monopolize jobs in the shipbuilding industry during the war. See pages 746–747.

7.   d.   Correct. The divorce rate increased from 16 divorces per 1000 marriages in 1940 to 27 divorces per 1000 marriages in 1944. See pages 750–751.

a.   No. During the war the number of babies born out of wedlock increased from .7 percent of all births to 1 percent of all births. See pages 750–751.

b.   No. The number of marriages increased during the war from 73 per 1000 unmarried women in 1939 to 93 per 1000 unmarried women in 1944. See pages 750–751.

c.   No. If anything, there seemed to be a relaxation of sexual morality on the homefront during the war. As the text says, "Many young men and women, caught up in the emotional intensity of war, behaved in ways they never would have in peacetime." See pages 750–751.

8. c. Correct. Japanese Americans, most of whom were native-born citizens, were interned in "relocation centers" because of their Japanese descent. See pages 753–754.

    a. No. The evidence does not support the conclusion that Japanese Americans were interned because of criminal behavior. Charges of criminal behavior were never brought against any Japanese Americans; none was ever indicted or tried for espionage, treason, or sedition. See pages 753–754.

    b. No. Japanese Americans were not engaged in treasonable activities and did not display disloyalty toward the United States government. See pages 753–754.

    d. No. Although many of those who were engaged in economic competition with Japanese Americans spoke in favor of internment, this competition was not the major reason for that action. See pages 753–754.

9. a. Correct. Both United States immigration policy and the voyage of the St. Louis (see Chapter 26) indicate reluctance by the United States to deal decisively with the Jewish refugee problem. Decisive action was not taken until 1944, when Roosevelt created the War Refugee Board. See pages 755–756.

    b. No. The United States refused to relax its immigration rules and restrictions. As a result many Jewish refugees were turned away because they did not have the legal documents required. See pages 755–756.

    c. No. The British refused to open Palestine to Jewish refugees. See pages 755–756.

    d. No. The death camp at Nordhausen was not bombed by U.S. forces. See pages 755–756.

10. a. Correct. Many soldiers who had never seen the world beyond their own cities, farms, and neighborhoods came into contact with other Americans and with peoples from other cultures. As a result of these new associations, many became less prejudiced and less provincial. See page 757.

    b. No. In many instances, the technical training that soldiers received in the military served to foster their ambitions and to give them skills that made them more employable in the postwar years. See page 757.

    c. No. Soldiers went through basic training in which they learned skills basic to combat. In addition, many received advanced training in specialty areas through the military's technical schools. See page 757.

    d. No. Many soldiers were given orientation lectures and booklets that introduced them to the historical backgrounds and social customs of the foreign nations in which they served. See page 757.

11. a. Correct. Meeting at Teheran in December 1943, the Allies agreed, at the insistence of Roosevelt and Stalin, to open the long-delayed second front. In return, Stalin agreed that Russia would enter the war in the Pacific once Germany was defeated. See pages 758–759.

    b. No. The North Africa campaign began in November 1942 and ended in Allied victory in May 1943. The Teheran Conference was held in December 1943. See pages 758–759.

    c. No. Although it is true that General Eisenhower recognized the pro-Nazi Vichy regime in French North Africa, he did so at the time of the Allied invasion of North Africa, which was some thirteen months prior to the Teheran Conference. See pages 758–759.

    d. No. The battle for Stalingrad ended in Russian victory in January 1943, eleven months before the Teheran Conference. See pages 758–759.

12.   c.   Correct. Because of the military positions of the Allied armies, the United States and Great Britain still needed the Soviet Union to win the war. This, and the fact that Russia occupied Eastern Europe, greatly affected decisions at Yalta. See pages 760–761.

a.   No. Although Roosevelt was physically ill while attending the Yalta Conference, the evidence indicates that he was mentally alert and that his health was not a factor in the decisions reached. See pages 760–761.

b.   No. Stalin, rather than Churchill, argued in favor of setting a precise figure for German reparations. Roosevelt and Churchill wanted to determine Germany's ability to pay before agreeing on a figure. Ultimately, the United States and Russia, without British acceptance, agreed to a rough figure of $20 billion as a basis for discussion in the future. See pages 760–761.

d.   No. Recognition of China as a major power was an American demand, not a Russian demand. See pages 760–761.

13.   d.   Correct. The Soviet Union lost some 21 million people in the Second World War. As a result, security was Russia's primary interest in the postwar era. See page 764.

a.   No. About 357,000 Britons died as a result of the Second World War, but the British did not suffer the highest number of casualties in the war. See page 764.

b.   No. About 405,000 Americans died as a result of the Second World War, but this figure was far lower than the number of war dead in other countries. See page 764.

c.   No. Although the Japanese lost some 2 million people in the war, this loss was ten times less than the casualties experienced by the country with the highest number of war dead. See page 764.

14.   b.   Correct. The United States was the only power to emerge from the Second World War more powerful than when it entered. See page 764.

a.   No. Great Britain came out of the Second World War with far less power than when it entered the war. As a result, the British empire was quite vulnerable. See page 764.

c.   No. Japan lay in ruins at the end of World War II. See page 764.

d.   No. The Soviet Union suffered enormously as a result of the war and emerged less powerful than when it entered. See page 764.

15.   d.   Correct. The United States preferred to use machinery to wage the war because doing so usually kept American casualties to a minimum. Beyond the fact that the use of machines was part of U.S. war strategy, Truman decided to drop the bomb for several reasons: (1) it would save American lives by ending the war quickly; (2) it might deter future aggression; (3) it might prevent Soviet entry into the war in the Pacific, thus preventing the Soviet Union from having a role in the reconstruction of postwar Asia; and (4) in the face of United States power, it might cause the Soviet Union to make concessions in Eastern Europe. See page 762.

a.   No. Truman knew that victory over Japan was virtually assured and did not totally depend on use of the atomic bomb. See page 762.

b.   No. Germany surrendered on May 8, 1945, three months before the first atomic bomb was dropped on Hiroshima on August 6. See page 762.

c.   No. The decision to use the atomic bomb was made unilaterally by the United States. Not only did the United States not consult the Allies, but at Potsdam Truman chose not to tell the Soviet Union of the successful atomic test in the New Mexico desert. See page 762.

CHAPTER 28

The Cold War and American Globalism, 1945–1961

LEARNING OBJECTIVES

After you have studied Chapter 28 in your textbook and worked through this study guide chapter, you should be able to:

1. Examine and explain the sources of the Cold War.

2. Examine the reasons for the activist, expansionist, globalist diplomacy undertaken by the United States in the aftermath of the Second World War.

3. Discuss the similarities and differences between American and Soviet perceptions of major international problems and events from 1945 to 1961.

4. Explain the rationale behind the containment doctrine; examine the evolution of the doctrine from its inception in 1947 to the end of the Eisenhower administration in 1961; discuss the history, extent, and nature of criticisms of the doctrine; and evaluate the doctrine as the cornerstone of American foreign policy from 1947 to 1961.

5. Examine the nature and extent of the arms race between the United States and the Soviet Union from 1945 to 1961.

6. Examine, evaluate, and discuss the consequences of the defense and foreign policy views, goals, and actions of the Truman administration.

7. Discuss the reconstruction of Japan after that country's defeat in the Second World War, and discuss relations between the United States and Japan from 1945 to 1961.

8. Discuss the nature and outcome of the Chinese Civil War, and examine United States policy toward the People's Republic of China from 1949 to 1961.

9. Examine and evaluate the events and decisions that led to deepening United States involvement in Vietnam from 1945 to 1961, and discuss the course of the war from 1950 to 1961.

10. Discuss the origins of the Korean War; explain its outcome; and examine its impact on domestic politics and United States foreign policy.

11. Examine, evaluate, and discuss the consequences of the defense and foreign policy views, goals, and actions of the Eisenhower administration.

12. Discuss the rise of the Third World and explain the challenge the Third World posed to the United States from 1945 to 1961.

13. Explain the U.S. view of the Third World and the obstacles to United States influence in the Third World.

14. Discuss the various ways in which the United States attempted to counter nationalism, radical doctrines, and neutralism in the Third World.

15. Examine the role of the CIA as an instrument of United States policy in the Third World during the 1950s.

THEMATIC GUIDE

Chapter 28 surveys the history of the bipolar contest for international power between the United States and the Soviet Union, a contest known as the Cold War, from 1945 to 1961.

We first examine the Cold War as the outgrowth of a complex set of factors. At the end of the Second World War, international relations remained unstable because of (1) world economic problems; (2) power vacuums caused by the defeat of Germany and Japan; (3) civil wars within nations; (4) the birth of nations resulting from the disintegration of empires; and (5) air power, which made all nations more vulnerable to attack. This unsettled environment encouraged competition between the United States and the Soviet Union, the two most powerful nations at the war's end.

Furthermore, both the United States and the Soviet Union believed in the rightness of their own political, economic, and social systems, and each feared the other's system. Their decisions and actions, based on the way each perceived the world, confirmed rather than alleviated these fears. For example, the American resolution to avoid appeasement and hold the line against communism, the American feeling of vulnerability in the air age, and American determination to prevent an economic depression led to an activist foreign policy characterized by the containment doctrine, economic expansionism, and globalist diplomacy. These factors, along with Truman's anti-Soviet views and his brash personality, intensified Soviet fears of a hostile West. When the Soviets acted on the basis of this feeling, American worries that the Soviet Union was bent on world domination intensified.

Despite the fact that the Soviet Union had emerged from the Second World War as a regional power rather than a global menace, United States officials were distrustful of the Soviet Union and reacted to counter what they perceived to be a Soviet threat. They did so because of (1) their belief in a monolithic communist enemy bent on world revolution; (2) fear that unstable world conditions made United States interests vulnerable to Soviet subversion; and (3) the desire of the United States to use its postwar position of strength to its advantage. When the actions of the United States brought criticism, the United States perceived this as further proof that the Soviets were determined to dominate the world.

The interplay of these factors provides the thread running through the examination of American-Soviet relations from 1945 to 1961. The action-reaction theme is evident throughout the chapter, and the events discussed serve as evidence to support the authors' interpretation of the sources of the Cold War. For example, in the discussion of the origins of the Korean War, we find that Truman acted out of the belief that the Soviets were the masterminds behind North Korea's attack against South Korea. However, closer analysis of the situation shows the strong likelihood that North Korea started the war for its own nationalistic purposes and secured the support of a reluctant Joseph Stalin only after receiving the support of Mao Zedong. We examine the conduct of the war, Truman's problems with General Douglas MacArthur, America's use of atomic diplomacy, and the war's domestic political impact. In the war's aftermath, the globalist foreign policy used to justify it became entrenched in U.S. policy. This, in turn, led to an increase in foreign commitments and military appropriations and solidified the idea of a worldwide Soviet threat.

President Dwight D. Eisenhower and his secretary of state, John Foster Dulles, accepted this view of a worldwide communist threat. During Eisenhower's administration, this belief and the fear of domestic subversives that accompanied it led to the removal of talented Asian specialists from the Foreign Service, an action that would have dire consequences later on. Meanwhile, a new jargon invigorated the containment doctrine and the U.S. undertook propaganda efforts to foster discontent in the Communist regimes of Eastern Europe. Despite Eisenhower's doubts about the arms race, the president continued the activist foreign policy furthered during the Truman years and oversaw the acceleration of the nuclear arms race. Therefore, during the Eisenhower-Dulles years, the action-reaction relationship between the superpowers continued. Each action by one side caused a corresponding defensive reaction by the other in a seemingly endless spiral of fear and distrust. As a result, problems continued in Eastern Europe, Berlin, and Asia.

The process of decolonization begun during the First World War accelerated in the aftermath of the Second World War. As scores of new nations were born, the Cold-War rivalry between the United States and the Soviet Union began. Both superpowers began to compete for friends among the newly emerging nations of the Third World; however, both the United States and the Soviet Union encountered obstacles in finding allies among these nations. The factors that created obstacles for the United States in its search for Third World friends included:

1.   America's negative view toward the neutralist movement among Third World nations;

2.   the way in which the United States characterized Third-World peoples;

3.   embarrassing incidents in the United States in which official representatives of the Third World were subjected to racist practices and prejudices;

4.   America's intolerance of the disorder caused by revolutionary nationalism; and

5.   America's great wealth.

To counter nationalism, radical doctrines, and neutralism in the Third World, the United States undertook development projects and, through the United States Information Agency, engaged in propaganda campaigns. In addition, during the Eisenhower administration the United States began increasingly to rely on the covert actions of the Central Intelligence Agency, as demonstrated in the Guatemalan and Iranian examples. Moreover, the attitude of the United States toward neutralism and toward the disruptions caused by revolutionary nationalism may be seen in the discussion of America's deepening involvement in Vietnam and in the Eisenhower administration's reaction to the events surrounding the 1956 Suez Crisis. In the aftermath of that crisis, fear of a weakened position in the Middle East led to the issuance of the Eisenhower Doctrine, which in turn was used to justify American military intervention in Lebanon in 1958, thus expanding the nation's "global watch" approach to the containment of Communism.

BUILDING VOCABULARY

Listed below are important words and terms that you need to know to get the most out of Chapter 28. They are listed in the order in which they occur in the chapter. After carefully looking through the list, (1) underline the words with which you are totally unfamiliar, (2) put a question mark by those words of which you are unsure, and (3) leave the rest alone.

As you begin to read the chapter, when you come to any of the words you've put question marks beside or underlined (1) slow your reading; (2) focus on the word and on its context in the sentence you're reading; (3) if you can understand the meaning of the word from its context in the sentence or passage in which it is used, go on with your reading; (4) if it's a word that you've underlined or a word that you can't understand from its context in the sentence or passage, look it up in a dictionary and write down the definition that best applies to the context in which the word is used.

Definitions

wisp _____

protracted _____

adept _____

indigenous _____

ferment _____

volatile _____

hegemony _____

xenophobia _____

nuance _____

ambiguity _____

ostentatious _____

retort _____

repudiate _____

subjugation _____

lexicon _____

manifesto _____

peripheral _____

permeate _____

cataclysm _____

specter _____

intractable _____

polarize _____

schism _____

tenacious _____

renege _____

amphibious _____

rampant _____

contentious _____

procurement _____

vigilance _____

hector _____

obliteration _____

strident _____

extol _____

monolithic _____

stymie _____

rife _____

garner _____

tutelage _____

ascribe _____

rebuff _____

servile _____

benefactor _____

expropriate _____

blithely _____

cajole _____

tout _____

Difficult-to-Spell Names and Terms from Reading and Lecture

IDENTIFICATION AND SIGNIFICANCE

After studying Chapter 28 of *A People and a Nation,* you should be able to identify fully *and* explain the historical significance of each item listed below.

- Identify each item in the space provided. Give an explanation or description of the item. Answer the questions *who, what, where,* and *when.*

- Explain the historical significance of each item in the space provided. Establish the historical context in which the item exists. Establish the item as the result of or as the cause of other factors existing in the society under study. Answer this question: *What were the political, social, economic, and/or cultural consequences of this item?*

1. Ho Chi Minh

    a. Identification

    b. Significance

2.   the Cold War

    a.   Identification

    b.   Significance

3.   the Third World

    a.   Identification

    b.   Significance

4.   the World Bank and the International Monetary Fund

    a.   Identification

    b.   Significance

5.   the Truman-Molotov encounter

    a.   Identification

    b.   Significance

6.   Soviet actions in Poland, Romania, Hungary, and Czechoslovakia

    a.   Identification

    b.   Significance

7.   atomic diplomacy

    a.   Identification

    b.   Significance

8.   the Baruch Plan

    a.   Identification

    b.   Significance

9.   the "long telegram"

    a.   Identification

    b.   Significance

10.   Churchill's "Iron Curtain" speech

    a.   Identification

    b.   Significance

11.   Henry A. Wallace

    a.   Identification

    b.   Significance

12.   the Truman Doctrine

    a.   Identification

    b.   Significance

13.   the Greek civil war

    a.   Identification

    b.   Significance

14.   the "Mr. X" article

    a.   Identification

    b.   Significance

15.   the containment doctrine

    a.   Identification

    b.   Significance

16.   Walter Lippmann

    a.   Identification

    b.   Significance

17. the Marshall Plan

    a. Identification

    b. Significance

18. the National Security Act of 1947

    a. Identification

    b. Significance

19. the Berlin blockade and airlift

    a. Identification

    b. Significance

20. the North Atlantic Treaty Organization

    a. Identification

    b. Significance

21. the hydrogen bomb

    a. Identification

    b. Significance

22.   NSC-68
      a.   Identification

      b.   Significance

23.   Japanese reconstruction
      a.   Identification

      b.   Significance

24.   the Chinese civil war
      a.   Identification

      b.   Significance

25.   Jiang Jieshi
      a.   Identification

      b.   Significance

26.   Mao Zedong
      a.   Identification

      b.   Significance

27.   the People's Republic of China

    a.   Identification

    b.   Significance

28.   the China lobby

    a.   Identification

    b.   Significance

29.   Vietnam's quest for independence

    a.   Identification

    b.   Significance

30.   the Korean War

    a.   Identification

    b.   Significance

31.   General Douglas MacArthur

    a.   Identification

    b.   Significance

32. the Inchon landing
    a. Identification

    b. Significance

33. Chinese entry into the Korean War
    a. Identification

    b. Significance

34. the POW question
    a. Identification

    b. Significance

35. the Korean armistice
    a. Identification

    b. Significance

36. John Foster Dulles
    a. Identification

    b. Significance

37. liberation, massive retaliation, and deterrence

     a. Identification

     b. Significance

38. the "New Look" military

     a. Identification

     b. Significance

39. brinkmanship

     a. Identification

     b. Significance

40. the domino theory

     a. Identification

     b. Significance

41. Eisenhower's use of the CIA

     a. Identification

     b. Significance

42.   the principle of "plausible deniability"

    a.   Identification

    b.   Significance

43.   the "kitchen debate"

    a.   Identification

    b.   Significance

44.   *Sputnik* and the missile race

    a.   Identification

    b.   Significance

45.   People to People Campaign

    a.   Identification

    b.   Significance

46.   the Hungarian uprising

    a.   Identification

    b.   Significance

47. the Berlin crisis of 1958

    a. Identification

    b. Significance

48. the U-2 incident

    a. Identification

    b. Significance

49. the Jinmen (Quemoy)-Mazu (Matsu) crisis

    a. Identification

    b. Significance

50. the Formosa Resolution

    a. Identification

    b. Significance

51. the process of decolonization

    a. Identification

    b. Significance

52. neutralism among Third World nations

    a. Identification

    b. Significance

53. the G. L. Mehta incident

    a. Identification

    b. Significance

54. United States "development" projects in the Third World

    a. Identification

    b. Significance

55. USIA propaganda campaigns

    a. Identification

    b. Significance

56. *The Ugly American*

    a. Identification

    b. Significance

57. Jacobo Arbenz Guzmán

    a. Identification

    b. Significance

58. Fidel Castro

    a. Identification

    b. Significance

59. recognition of Israel

    a. Identification

    b. Significance

60. Mohammed Mossadegh

    a. Identification

    b. Significance

61. Gamal Abdul Nasser

    a. Identification

    b. Significance

62. the Suez crisis

  a. Identification

  b. Significance

63. the Eisenhower Doctrine

  a. Identification

  b. Significance

64. Dienbienphu

  a. Identification

  b. Significance

65. the 1954 Geneva accords

  a. Identification

  b. Significance

66. Ngo Dinh Diem

  a. Identification

  b. Significance

67. the National Liberation Front (the Vietcong)

    a. Identification

    b. Significance

ORGANIZING, REVIEWING, AND USING INFORMATION

Chart A

The United States and the Cold War		
Evidence of American Fears of the USSR, 1945–1961		
Reflections of Fear	**Truman Years**	**Eisenhower Years**
Pronouncements (Doctrines, Reports, Articles, etc.)		
Expansion of Government (new cabinet-level departments, new agencies, etc.)		
Arms Development and Buildup and Saber Rattling		
Military Action/War		
Defense Alliances		
Attempts To Interfere in USSR's Sphere of Influence		

The United States and the Cold War		
Evidence of American Fears of the USSR, 1945–1961		
Reflections of Fear	**Truman Years**	**Eisenhower Years**
Use of Trade Policy and Dollar Diplomacy To Maintain and Expand American Sphere of Influence		
Use of Covert Operations (Assassination Attempts, Spying, Dissemination of Misinformation and Propaganda, etc.)		
Decisions To Recognize or Not To Recognize New Governments		
Attempts To Undermine, Overthrow or Install Foreign Regimes		
Behavior of Congress (legislation, resolutions, hearings, protection/ceding of constitutional power)		

Chart B

Foreign Relations Focal Points of the '50s (Besides the Soviet Union)					
Arena	**Reason for Special Interest**	**Key Event or Situation**	**Foreign Leader(s)**	**U.S. Action or Reaction**	**U.S. President in Office**

Europe
 	
    Germany
 	
    France
 	
    Britain
 	
    Hungary
 	
       etc.					

Mideast
 	
    Egypt
 	
  Saudi Arabia
 	
Palestine/Israel
 	
    Iran
 	
      etc.					

Far East
 	
    China
 	
   Vietnam
 	
    Japan
 	
    Korea
 	
      etc.					

Latin America, Caribbean
 	
  Guatemala
 	
    Cuba					

United Nations					

IDEAS AND DETAILS

Objective 1

1.   In the aftermath of the Second World War, which of the following destabilized the international system and caused friction between the Soviet Union and the United States?

   a.   The power vacuums created by the collapse of Germany and Japan

   b.   Great Britain's refusal to grant independence to its former colonies

   c.   France's immediate withdrawal from Vietnam, Laos, and Cambodia

   d.   The refusal by the Eastern European states of Yugoslavia, Czechoslovakia, and Hungary to ally with either the United States or the Soviet Union.

Objectives 1 and 3

2.   Which of the following was a major Soviet objective in the aftermath of the Second World War?

   a.   To oversee the rebuilding of a unified German nation

   b.   To prevent another invasion of the Russian homeland

   c.   To share power with the United States in the reconstruction of Japan

   d.   To create a strong, independent China

Objective 2

3.   In the immediate aftermath of the Second World War, the United States

   a.   gave substantial monetary aid to the Soviet government for the rebuilding of its economic system.

   b.   agreed to assume control over the colonies that had been part of the pre-war British empire.

   c.   believed that a world economy based on free trade was essential to its economic well being.

   d.   wanted to prevent economic competition from Germany and Japan by going slowly on rebuilding those war-torn countries.

Objective 4

4.   The containment policy, expressed in the Truman Doctrine and George Kennan's "Mr. X" article, committed the United States to

   a.   extend economic and medical aid to impoverished people throughout the world.

   b.   help only those countries that showed a determination to help themselves.

   c.   assist peoples throughout the world in resisting Communist expansion.

   d.   create a more stable world through the use of diplomatic rather than military means.

Objectives 3, 6, and 8

5.   Which of the following is true of United States policy toward China during the Chinese civil war?

   a.   The United States attempted to open diplomatic relations with Mao's forces but was rebuffed.

   b.   United States officials recognized the nationalist origins of the struggle.

   c.   The United States decided not to take sides in the struggle.

   d.   Most United States officials supported Jiang Jieshi (Chiang Kai-shek) because of their belief that Mao was part of an international communist movement.

Objectives 4, 6, and 9

6.   For which of the following reasons did the United States refuse to recognize Vietnamese independence in 1945?

   a.   The United States feared that such recognition would jeopardize negotiations with China.
   b.   Ho Chi Minh had worked with the Japanese against the United States during World War II.
   c.   FDR had guaranteed the return of French colonies at the end of the Second World War.
   d.   Since Ho Chi Minh was a communist, the United States chose to support the imperialist stance of its Cold War ally, France.

Objectives 3, 4, 6, and 10

7.   Truman's claim that the Soviet Union was the mastermind behind North Korea's invasion of South Korea is questionable because available evidence now indicates that

   a.   the Soviet Union gave no aid to North Korea during the course of the war.
   b.   President Kim Il Sung undertook the war for his own nationalist objectives and drew a reluctant Stalin into the crisis.
   c.   the Soviet Union was sending military aid to South Korea at the time of the invasion.
   d.   North Korea was fiercely independent and had broken its ties with the Soviet Union.

Objective 10

8.   President Truman fired General Douglas MacArthur because

   a.   the general denounced the concept of limited war supported by President Truman and the Joint Chiefs of Staff.
   b.   MacArthur refused to obey Truman's order to attack China with massive bombing raids.
   c.   the United Nations Security Council demanded MacArthur's removal.
   d.   the failure of the Inchon operation destroyed MacArthur's credibility.

Objective 11

9.   The "New Look" military of the Eisenhower-Dulles years emphasized

   a.   nuclear weapons and airpower.
   b.   a United Nations police force.
   c.   conventional military forces.
   d.   Soviet-American cooperation in space.

Objectives 4 and 11

10.   As a result of the 1954 crisis concerning Jinmen (Quemoy) and Mazu (Matsu),

   a.   the United States severed relations with Jiang Jieshi.
   b.   the United States recognized the People's Republic of China.
   c.   Congress formally gave up its constitutional authority to declare war by authorizing the president to use force if necessary to defend Formosa.
   d.   Khrushchev called for "peaceful coexistence" with the United States.

Objectives 1, 2, and 12

11. Because of its strategic and economic interests in the Third World, the United States
    a. tried to thwart challenges to U.S. influence in the region by directing more foreign aid toward the Third World.
    b. suffered more than Western Europe from the worldwide post-war economic depression.
    c. enjoyed improved relations with developing nations during the 1950s.
    d. increased its commitment to and support for the United Nations.

Objective 13

12. The United States found it difficult to make friends in the Third World because
    a. the United States usually supported the propertied, antirevolutionary elements in the Third World.
    b. diplomats from Third World countries disliked America's pluralistic society.
    c. American business interests refused to invest in Third World countries.
    d. the Soviets were more adept at doing so.

Objectives 4, 11, 12, 13, 14, and 15

13. Upon learning that Cuba had signed a trade treaty with the Soviet Union in 1960, the Eisenhower administration responded by
    a. immediately cutting off all trade with Cuba.
    b. establishing a blockade of Cuba.
    c. ordering the CIA to plot Castro's overthrow.
    d. negotiating new trade agreements with Cuba designed to increase Cuban imports into the U.S.

Objectives 4, 11, 12, 14, and 15

14. What do Jacobo Arbenz Guzmán of Guatemala and Mohammed Mossadegh of Iran have in common?
    a. Both agreed to the deployment of Russian intermediate-range missiles in their respective countries.
    b. Both strongly supported United States interests in the Third World.
    c. Both were killed while observing the 1954 test of a 15-megaton H-bomb.
    d. Both threatened American investments in their respective countries and were overthrown in CIA-supported coups.

Objective 9

15. Why did Ngo Dinh Diem and President Eisenhower refuse to allow national elections in Vietnam as called for in the Geneva Accords?
    a. They believed the elections would have been virtually impossible to administer.
    b. They held that the 1955 South Vietnamese election had given Diem a mandate to govern.
    c. They feared that communist leader Ho Chi Minh would win.
    d. They realized that the communists would never allow a genuinely free election.

ESSAY QUESTIONS

Objectives 1, 2, 3, 4, and 5

1. Defend or refute the following statement: "Both the United States and the Soviet Union must share responsibility for the Cold War."

Objectives 3, 4, 7, 8, 9, and 10

2. Explain and evaluate the American perception of events in Asia between the end of the Second World War and North Korea's invasion of South Korea. What bearing did these perceptions have on the Truman administration's response to North Korean aggression?

Objective 10

3. Explain the impact of the Korean War on United States foreign policy.

Objective 5

4. Examine and evaluate the nuclear arms race and attempts at arms control between the United States and the Soviet Union from 1945 to 1961.

Objective 4

5. Examine the containment doctrine as the cornerstone of American foreign policy from 1945 to 1961.

Objective 9

6. Examine the deepening involvement of the United States in Vietnam from 1945 to 1961.

Objectives 12, 13, 14, and 15

7. Explain and evaluate the Eisenhower administration's perception of and response to nationalist movements in the Third World. Illustrate with examples from the Middle East and Latin America. Pay particular attention to the administration's response to Jacobo Arbenz Guzmán and Gamal Abdul Nasser.

MAP EXERCISE

As part of the containment doctrine, the United States in 1949 formed the North Atlantic Treaty Organization (NATO), consisting of the United States, Great Britain, Canada, France, Belgium, the Netherlands, Luxembourg, Italy, Denmark, Norway, Iceland, and Portugal. Greece and Turkey joined NATO in 1952, and West Germany joined in 1954.

To counter NATO, in May 1955 the Soviet Union formed the Warsaw Pact, consisting of the Soviet Union, Albania,[1] Bulgaria, Czechoslovakia, East Germany, Hungary, Poland, and Romania. China did not sign but did pledge support.

In addition, the United States (1) entered into a military alliance with Latin American countries, the Rio Pact, in 1947; (2) sent military advisory missions to Latin America, Greece, Turkey, Iran, China, and Saudi Arabia; (3) activated an air base in Libya in 1948; (4) recognized the new state of Israel in May 1948; (5) entered into a mutual defense agreement, the ANZUS Treaty, with Australia and New Zealand in 1951; and (6) entered into a similar defense agreement in 1954, the Southeast Asia Treaty Organization (SEATO), that first included Britain, France, Australia, New Zealand, Pakistan, Thailand, and the Philippines, and was extended to include South Vietnam, Cambodia, and Laos.

Consider all such alliances, air bases, and military advisory missions in your answers to the following questions:

1. Using two markers of different colors, on the outline map of the world that follows mark the nations allied with or friendly toward the United States in or around 1973 with one color, and those allied with or friendly toward the Soviet Union with the other color. (Refer to Chapters 28, 30, and 31 in the text, to the map in the text entitled "Divided Europe," and to an historical atlas.)

2. How successful was the alliance aspect of the containment doctrine as of 1973?

3. The Soviet Union complained of encirclement in the early 1950s and after. Was there reason to complain?

4. As of 1973, would you feel more secure as a citizen of the Soviet Union or as a citizen of the United States? Why?

---

[1] Albania withdrew from the Warsaw Pact in 1968.

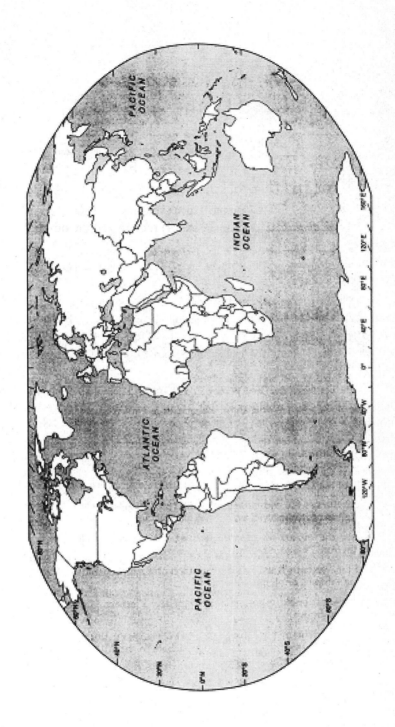

ANSWERS

Multiple-Choice Questions

1.   a.   Correct. The collapse of the former enemies of the United States left a power vacuum in both Asia and Europe. Since both the United States and the Soviet Union sought influence in these regions, these power vacuums caused friction between the two former allies. See page 770.

     b.   No. Great Britain, having been economically devastated by the Second World War, faced severe financial constraints in the war's aftermath. In addition, the Second World War unleashed nationalist movements in some of Great Britain's former colonies. Because of these two factors, Great Britain granted its colonies independence in the aftermath of the Second World War. See page 770.

     c.   No. Indochina (Vietnam, Laos, and Cambodia) was occupied by Japan during the Second World War. After the surrender of Japan in 1945, France attempted to restore its colonial authority over Indochina and fought in vain to do so from 1946 to 1954. See page 770.

     d.   No. In the aftermath of the Second World War, the Soviet Union established buffer states between itself and Western Europe in an effort to secure its borders against another invasion from Western Europe. Although Yugoslavia established a communist government independent of Moscow, the Soviet Union supported communist coups in Hungary in 1947 and in Czechoslovakia in 1948. Both Hungary and Czechoslovakia remained under Soviet domination until the collapse of the Soviet Union in 1990. See page 770.

2.   b.   Correct. Russia was invaded from the West by Napoleon in 1812 and again by Hitler in 1941. Furthermore, after the Bolshevik Revolution brought Lenin to power in 1917, the United States, Great Britain, and France sent troops to Russia to help the anti-Bolshevik forces overthrow Lenin's government. Although the Soviet Union was allied with Great Britain and the United States during World War II, it remained suspicious that the West wanted to destroy its communist government and prevent its expansion. Therefore, in 1945 Stalin was intent on securing the western border of the Soviet Union against another invasion from the West. See page 770.

     a.   No. The Soviet Union saw a unified Germany as a threat to its security. See page 770.

     c.   No. Had the Soviet Union played a substantial role in the Pacific War, it could have claimed a right to share in the reconstruction of Japan. However, the use of the atomic bomb against Japan prevented the Soviets from playing such a role, and the United States monopolized Japan's reconstruction. See page 770.

     d.   No. A strong independent China was seen as a security risk to the Soviet Union. See page 770.

3.   c.   Correct. In 1947 exports constituted about 10 percent of the gross national product of the United States. Therefore, U.S. officials believed that the economic well-being of the country depended on maintaining the flow of American goods into foreign markets. This could best be achieved through a world economy based on free trade. See page 771.

a.   No. Although the United States offered aid to the Soviet Union in 1947 under the Marshall Plan, the Soviets refused to participate. See page 771.

b.   No. In 1947 Great Britain informed the United States that it could no longer financially afford to give aid to Turkey or to the British-supported government of Greece. In response, Truman asked Congress to appropriate $400 million for aid to Turkey and Greece. Even though Congress did vote in favor of this appropriation, the United States did not "assume control" over any pre-war British colonies. See page 771.

d.   No. The United States believed that it was essential to its security to rebuild Germany and Japan as quickly as possible. See page 771.

4.   c.   Correct. The containment policy, as expressed by Truman and Kennan, pledged unconditional aid to peoples resisting Communist expansion. See pages 773–774.

a.   No. The containment policy did not include a specific commitment to extend aid to the impoverished. See pages 773–774.

b.   No. The containment policy did not make American aid conditional on a country's demonstration of its determination to help itself. See pages 773–774.

d.   No. The containment doctrine did not emphasize the use of diplomacy in international relations. See pages 773–774.

5.   d.   Correct. Most American officials believed Mao was part of an international communist conspiracy and failed to see him as an independent communist fighting for a China free from outside interference, and, therefore, free to control its own future. See page 779.

a.   No. Many American officials became convinced that Mao was a Soviet puppet. Therefore, when Mao made secret overtures to the United States to begin diplomatic talks in 1945 and 1949, he was rebuffed by American officials. See page 779.

b.   No. Most American officials saw the Chinese civil war as part of the East-West conflict and did not recognize the nationalist nature of Mao's struggle against Jiang. See page 779.

c.   No. The United States did take sides in the struggle between Jiang Jieshi and Mao Zedong. See page 779.

6.   d.   Correct. American leaders failed to see Ho Chi Minh as a nationalist seeking independence from foreign domination. They could see him only as a communist. See pages 779–780.

a.   No. Although the United States was attempting to negotiate a cease-fire in the Chinese civil war in 1945, recognition of Vietnamese independence would not have jeopardized those negotiations. See pages 779–780.

b.   No. During the Second World War, Ho Chi Minh, a Vietnamese nationalist, worked with the American Office of Strategic Services against Japanese domination of his country. See pages 779–780.

c.   No. FDR never made such a pledge to France. See pages 779–780.

7.   b.   Correct. The collapse of the Soviet Union in the early 1990s led to the opening of previously classified Soviet documents. These documents reveal that North Korean President Kim Il Sung initiated the North Korean attack against South Korea in an attempt to achieve his own nationalist objectives. Stalin, in fact, only reluctantly approved the attack, and his support for North Korea remained lukewarm throughout the war. See page 780.

      a.   No. The Soviet Union did give aid to North Korea during the course of the Korean War. See page 780.

      c.   No. The Soviet Union was not sending military aid to South Korea. See page 780.

      d.   No. Although Kim Il Sung, the Communist leader of North Korea, probably decided to invade South Korea for nationalistic reasons and Joseph Stalin only reluctantly approved the attack, North Korea had not broken its ties with the Soviet Union. See page 780.

8.   a.   Correct. After MacArthur began publicly to question President Truman's war policies, Truman, with the backing of the Joint Chiefs of Staff, fired him for insubordination. See page 781.

      b.   No. MacArthur demanded that Truman allow an attack on China, but Truman never agreed to the policy because he was sure it would widen the war. See page 781.

      c.   No. MacArthur was not removed at the insistence of the U.N. Security Council. See page 781.

      d.   No. The Inchon landing (September 1950) was successful for the United Nations forces under MacArthur's command and led to the liberation of Seoul, the South Korean capital. See page 781.

9.   a.   Correct. Eisenhower's desire to trim federal spending led to the New Look military. Based on the policies of "massive retaliation" and "deterrence," the New Look emphasized nuclear weaponry and airpower over conventional forces. See page 784.

      b.   No. Eisenhower's New Look military did not involve a United Nations police force. See page 784.

      c.   No. Eisenhower's New Look military de-emphasized conventional military force. See page 784.

      d.   No. The New Look military did not involve Soviet-American cooperation in space. In 1957, the Soviets launched Sputnik, to the shock and surprise of many Americans. In response, the United States created the National Aeronautics and Space Agency in 1958. See page 784.

10.   c.   Correct. In reaction to the crisis, the United States signed a mutual defense treaty with Formosa (December 2, 1954) and Congress passed the Formosa Resolution (January 1955) in which it authorized the president to use force if necessary to defend Formosa. Since the resolution did not require the president to obtain Congress' approval for the use of force, Congress formally gave up its constitutional authority to declare war. See page 787.

      a.   No. The islands were bombarded by the People's Republic of China, and this led to the signing of a mutual defense treaty between the United States and Nationalist China (Formosa) on December 2, 1954. The treaty was ratified by the Senate in February 1955. See page 787.

      b.   No. The United States continued to refuse to recognize the People's Republic of China as the legitimate Chinese government. See page 787.

      d.   No. In response to Cold War pressures that increased the likelihood of a nuclear confrontation, Khrushchev called for "peaceful coexistence" between the United States and the Soviet Union. However, this was not in direct response to the Formosa crisis. See page 787.

11. a.   Correct. The United States economy was dependent on exports of finished products, imports of strategic raw materials, and foreign investments. Therefore, disorder caused by nationalist revolutions in the Third World were seen as a threat to the American standard of living and partially explain why America was hostile toward such revolutions. Furthermore, the United States hoped that by directing more foreign aid to the Third World it could help undermine nationalist revolutions in the region and thwart challenges to U.S. influence. See page 787.

   b.   No. Western Europe was economically devastated by the Second World War, while the United States was not. In fact, in order to prevent economic discontent in Western Europe from leading to the emergence of extremists, the United States financed a massive European recovery program known as the Marshall Plan. See page 787.

   c.   No. Extensive American investments abroad did not cause improved relations with developing nations. See page 787.

   d.   No. The United States did not increase its commitment to the United Nations because of extensive American investments abroad. See page 787.

12. a.   Correct. The United States stood against Third World revolutions that threatened the interests of America's allies and threatened American investments and markets. As a major world power interested in its own security, the United States desired order and stability. See page 789.

   b.   No. Racism in American society, rather than a negative reaction by diplomats to America's pluralistic society, made it difficult for the United States to make friends in the Third World. See page 789.

   c.   No. American business interests engaged in economic expansion and invested heavily in Third World countries. In 1959 over one-third of America's private foreign investments were in Third World countries. See page 789.

   d.   No. The Soviet Union enjoyed only a slight edge, if any, in the race to win friends in the Third World. See page 789.

13. c.   Correct. After learning in February 1960 of the trade treaty that Cuba entered into with the Soviet Union, President Eisenhower ordered the CIA to organize an invasion force made up of Cuban exiles for the purpose of overthrowing the Castro government. In addition, President Eisenhower drastically cut U.S. purchases of Cuban sugar. See page 791.

   a.   No. In response to the trade treaty between Cuba and the Soviet Union, the United States cut off all economic aid to Cuba and drastically cut U.S. purchases of Cuban sugar. However, President Eisenhower did not cut off all trade with Cuba. See page 791.

   b.   No. The United States imposed an embargo on all exports to Cuba except food and medicine in the fall of 1960, but the United States did not establish a blockade of Cuba. See page 791.

   d.   No. The Eisenhower administration did not negotiate new trade agreements with Cuba after learning of the trade treaty between Cuba and the Soviet Union in February 1960. See page 791.

14. d.   Correct. Both Arbenz of Guatemala and Mossadegh of Iran threatened the interests of American-owned companies operating in their countries. As a result, the CIA, through covert actions, aided in the overthrow of these men. See pages 790–791.

a.   No. Neither Arbenz of Guatemala nor Mossadegh of Iran agreed to the deployment of Russian missiles in their countries. See pages 790–791.

b.   No. Both Arbenz of Guatemala and Mossadegh of Iran were strongly nationalist in their views. As nationalists, they tended to view American interests in the Third World as exploitative. See pages 790–791.

c.   No. You may be thinking of the 1954 hydrogen-bomb test that destroyed the island of Bikini and caused the death of a crew member aboard the Lucky Dragon, a Japanese fishing boat. See pages 790–791.

15. c.   Correct. Although the United States professed to believe in democracy and in the right of peoples throughout the world to determine for themselves the government they wanted, U.S. policy also called for the containment of communism everywhere. In viewing the situation in Vietnam, both President Eisenhower and Ngo Dinh Diem believed that the national elections to be held in 1956 would result in a communist victory. As a result, with U.S. backing and encouragement, Diem announced in 1956 that South Vietnam would not participate in the national elections. See pages 793–794.

a.   No. President Eisenhower and Diem did not refuse to allow the 1956 national elections because of the belief that those elections would be virtually impossible to administer. See pages 793–794.

b.   No. At the insistence of the Eisenhower administration, Emperor Bao Dai appointed Diem his prime minister in 1954. In 1955, in a referendum rigged and controlled by Diem, South Vietnam was declared a republic. Emperor Bao Dai resigned and Diem declared himself to be the first President of the Republic of Vietnam. The Eisenhower administration knew that the 1955 referendum, in which Diem received over 98 percent of the vote, was rigged; therefore, in its refusal to allow national elections in Vietnam in 1956, the United States did not contend that Diem had a mandate to govern. See pages 793–794.

d.   No. The refusal by the Eisenhower administration and President Diem to participate in national elections in Vietnam in 1956 was not based on the belief that the communist leader of North Vietnam, Ho Chi Minh, would not allow free elections. See pages 793–794.

CHAPTER 29

America at Midcentury, 1945–1960

LEARNING OBJECTIVES

After you have studied Chapter 29 in your textbook and worked through this study guide chapter, you should be able to:

1. Examine the domestic issues that faced the United States during the immediate postwar period; explain the federal government's actions concerning those issues; and discuss the consequences of those actions.

2. Discuss the reasons for and explain the consequences of the postwar baby boom.

3. Examine the forces that caused the growth of the suburbs in the period from 1945 to 1960, and discuss the characteristics of life in the suburbs.

4. Examine the issues and personalities and explain the outcome of the 1948 presidential election.

5. Discuss the goals of Truman's Fair Deal and explain Truman's successes and failures in achieving those goals.

6. Discuss the domestic issues facing the Eisenhower administration; explain and evaluate the administration's handling of those issues; and discuss the consequences of those actions.

7. Discuss the 1950s as an age of consensus and conformity, and explain the beliefs associated with this consensus mood.

8. Discuss the combination of forces and incidents that caused the postwar wave of anti-Communist hysteria, and examine the various ways in which this hysteria manifested itself.

9. Explain Senator Joseph McCarthy's rise to power and his ultimate decline, and discuss the impact of the postwar wave of anti-Communist hysteria on American society.

10. Discuss the gains of African Americans during the late 1940s and early 1950s, and examine the factors responsible for those gains.

11. Examine the reinvigoration of the civil rights movement during the 1950s; discuss the response of white southerners and of the federal government to the demands and actions of African Americans; and explain the extent to which African Americans were successful in achieving their goals.

12. Examine the factors that contributed to the postwar economic boom experienced in American society during the 1950s.

13. Discuss the characteristics of and trends within the labor movement from 1945 to 1960.

14. Discuss the forces that contributed to the growth of the Sunbelt during the 1950s and examine the consequences of that growth.

15. Examine the factors that contributed to the emergence of a national, middle-class culture during the 1950s and discuss the characteristics of that culture.

16. Discuss the growth of organized religion in American society during the 1950s.

17. Discuss characteristics of the American family during the 1950s, and examine the factors that affected the life choices of men and women.

18. Discuss American concepts about sex during the 1950s and explain the challenges that arose to those concepts.

19. Examine the factors that caused the emergence of a distinctive youth culture in America during the 1950s and discuss the characteristics of that culture.

20. Discuss and assess the criticisms leveled against the middle-class culture of the 1950s.

21. Discuss the impact of the postwar economic boom on the environment.

22. Examine the reasons for, extent of, and effects of poverty in America during the postwar era, and discuss the characteristics of the poor.

THEMATIC GUIDE

After the Second World War, the United States experienced an uneasy and troubled transition to peace. Although the unemployment and higher education benefits of the GI Bill were intended, in part, to ease this transition by allowing veterans to be eased into civilian employment, those benefits did not affect the skyrocketing inflation rate and did not prevent a rash of strikes. Despite the fact that the Truman administration's handling of those problems led to widespread public discontent and to Republican victory in the 1946 congressional elections, to the surprise of most analysts, Truman won the presidential election of 1948. Furthermore, even though the transition to a peacetime economy was rocky at first, the economy quickly recovered and, as a result of consumer spending, increased agricultural productivity, and government programs, the United States entered an era of sustained economic growth and prosperity. One of the consequences of this prosperity was the "baby boom," which fueled more economic growth.

During the 1950s, white Americans increasingly fled from the cities to the suburbs. Drawn to the suburbs by many factors, life in suburbia was often made possible by government policies that extended economic aid to families making such a move. Unfortunately, these federal policies did not benefit all Americans equally. As a result, nonwhites were often denied the opportunities offered to white Americans. Federal, state, and local expenditures on highway construction also spurred the growth of suburbia by allowing workers to live farther from their jobs in central cities. Although suburbia had its critics, most Americans seemed to prefer the lifestyle it offered.

During Truman's first elected term (1949–1953), he and the American people had to contend with the domestic consequences of the Korean War. Although the war brought prosperity, it also brought inflation and increased defense spending at the expense of the domestic programs of Truman's Fair Deal. Furthermore, both the nature and length of the Korean War led to disillusionment and discontent on the part of many Americans. These factors, coupled with reports of influence peddling in the Truman administration, caused the President's approval rating to plummet and led to a Republican triumph in the presidential and congressional elections of 1952.

Upon coming to the presidency in 1953, Dwight D. Eisenhower, a moderate Republican, decided against attempting to dismantle New Deal and Fair Deal programs and adopted the philosophy of "dynamic conservatism." Eisenhower meant by this that he was "conservative when it comes to money and liberal when it comes to human beings." While Eisenhower's expansion of the Social Security System was on the liberal side of this philosophy, the increased government funding for education during his administration was, as pointed out by the authors of the text, more a reaction to Cold War pressures than from a liberal frame of reference. The pro-business nature of the Eisenhower administration and Eisenhower's belief that government should actively promote economic development may be seen in the president's tax reform program and the Atomic Energy Act. Despite Eisenhower's fiscal conservatism, the administration's activist foreign policy and three domestic economic recessions caused increased federal expenditures, decreased tax revenues, and deficit spending. As a result, Eisenhower oversaw only three balanced budgets during his eight years in office.

During this "age of consensus"—a period in which Americans agreed on their stance against communism and their faith in economic progress—many people, believing in the rightness of the American system, viewed reform and reformers in a negative light and saw conflict as the product of psychologically disturbed individuals, not as the product of societal ills. It is within this "consensus" context that, during the late 1940s and early 1950s, the United States witnessed a wave of anti-Communist hysteria. The tracing of events from the "Verona project" to Truman's loyalty probe to the "Hollywood Ten" supports the view that fear of communism, long present in American society, intensified during the postwar years. Within this climate of fear and suspicion, Joseph McCarthy began his demagogic anticommunist crusade and, in the process, lent his name to a state of mind that existed before he entered the scene. McCarthyism was further sustained by events, and as Americans pointed accusing fingers at each other, public figures found it difficult to stand against McCarthy's tactics. As a result, liberals and conservatives shared in consensus on anticommunism, as can be seen in the passage of the Internal Security Act and the Communist Control Act. Moreover, since respected public figures such as President Eisenhower chose to avoid direct confrontation with Senator McCarthy, McCarthy continued to add more victims to his list of alleged subversives and continued to jeopardize freedom of speech and expression. Ultimately, McCarthyism declined, with McCarthy himself being largely responsible for his own demise.

One group that challenged the consensus mood of the age was African Americans. Under Truman, the federal government, for the first time since Reconstruction, accepted responsibility for guaranteeing equality under the law—civil rights—to African Americans. Furthermore, work by the NAACP and decisions by the Supreme Court resulted in a slow erosion of the separate-but-equal doctrine and of black disfranchisement in the South. Then the Supreme Court's historic decision in *Brown v. Board of Education of Topeka* gave African Americans reason to believe that their long struggle against racism was beginning to pay off. However, white southerners reacted with hostility to that decision and actively resisted Court-ordered desegregation. This resistance led to the crisis in Little Rock, Arkansas, a crisis in which Eisenhower felt compelled to use federal troops to prevent violence in the desegregation of the city's public schools. But the Little Rock crisis was merely the tip of an emerging civil rights movement, as can be seen through the discussion of the Montgomery bus boycott, the formation of the Southern Christian Leadership Conference, and criticism concerning the ineffectiveness of the Civil Rights Act of 1957.

As many white middle-class Americans made more money, bought more goods, and created more waste, they also continued a mass migration to the Sunbelt that had begun during the war. In addition, a national, middle-class culture began to emerge, and many who were part of this culture were instructed in what behaviors were proper and expected of them through the national mass media, especially television. As Americans sought pleasure through the materialistic values of the era, they were also, paradoxically, drawn to organized religion in unprecedented numbers.

The postwar economic boom also affected the family. The changes it brought included the influence of Dr. Benjamin Spock on the parent-child relationship and the conflicting and changing roles of women as more entered the labor market. While society continued to stress the importance of "proper" female roles, attention was also directed to the "crisis of masculinity," and, therefore, to the plight of the American male.

After a discussion of the influence of the pioneering work of Dr. Alfred Kinsey in the late 1940s and early 1950s on American attitudes toward sexual behavior, we look at the emergence of a distinctive youth culture, the birth of rock 'n' roll, the fads of the era, and the critiques of American society offered by those who criticized the conformity of the age.

Economic growth inspired by government defense spending and by the growth of a more affluent population demanding more consumer goods and larger quantities of agricultural products had a negative impact on the environment. Automobiles and factories polluted the air. Human and industrial waste polluted rivers, lakes, and streams. Pesticides endangered wildlife and humans alike, as did the waste from nuclear processing plants. Disposable products marketed as conveniences made America a "throw-away society."

Prosperity did not bring about a meaningful redistribution of income in American society during the period under study. Therefore, many Americans (about 25 percent in 1962) lived in poverty. As before, the poor congregated in urban areas. African Americans, poor whites, Puerto Ricans, Mexican Americans, and Native Americans continued their movement to low-income inner-city housing, while the more affluent city residents—mostly whites—continued their exodus to the suburbs. Although low-interest government housing loans made life in suburbia possible for many middle-class whites, government programs such as "urban renewal" often hurt the urban poor. Furthermore, the trend toward bigness in American agriculture continued and presented more of a threat than ever to the family farm. The growth of agribusiness pushed many small farmers and tenant farmers off the land, which in turn swelled the ranks of the urban poor. Unfortunately, the burgeoning middle class often turned a blind eye to the poverty around them.

BUILDING VOCABULARY

Listed below are important words and terms that you need to know to get the most out of Chapter 29. They are listed in the order in which they occur in the chapter. After carefully looking through the list, (1) underline the words with which you are totally unfamiliar, (2) put a question mark by those words of which you are unsure, and (3) leave the rest alone.

As you begin to read the chapter, when you come to any of the words you've put question marks beside or underlined (1) slow your reading; (2) focus on the word and on its context in the sentence you're reading; (3) if you can understand the meaning of the word from its context in the sentence or passage in which it is used, go on with your reading; (4) if it's a word that you've underlined or a word that you can't understand from its context in the sentence or passage, look it up in a dictionary and write down the definition that best applies to the context in which the word is used.

Definitions

homogeneity _____

circumscribe _____

stymie _____

flout _____

conglomerate _____

cohort _____

impasse _____

burgeoning _____

fruition _____

filibuster _____

syntax _____

unabashed _____

prudent _____

nadir _____

malign _____

sully _____

virulent _____

resurgence _____

tacitly _____

exuberance _____

utilitarian _____

ostracize _____

bland _____

scrutiny _____

elitist _____

marginalize _____

decrepit _____

entice _____

Difficult-to-Spell Names and Terms from Reading and Lecture

IDENTIFICATION AND SIGNIFICANCE

After studying Chapter 29 of *A People and a Nation,* you should be able to identify fully *and* explain the historical significance of each item listed below.

- Identify each item in the space provided. Give an explanation or description of the item. Answer the questions *who, what, where,* and *when.*

- Explain the historical significance of each item in the space provided. Establish the historical context in which the item exists. Establish the item as the result of or as the cause of other factors existing in the society under study. Answer this question: *What were the political, social, economic, and/or cultural consequences of this item?*

1. G.I. Bill of Rights

    a.   Identification

    b.   Significance

2. Full Employment Act

    a.   Identification

    b.   Significance

3. Council of Economic Advisors

    a.   Identification

    b.   Significance

4. postwar inflation

    a.   Identification

    b.   Significance

5.   the threatened railroad strike of 1946

    a.   Identification

    b.   Significance

6.   the Taft-Hartley Act

    a.   Identification

    b.   Significance

7.   the baby boom

    a.   Identification

    b.   Significance

8.   post-World War II suburbanization

    a.   Identification

    b.   Significance

9.   William Levitt

    a.   Identification

    b.   Significance

10. the Highway Act of 1956

   a.   Identification

   b.   Significance

11. the practice of redlining

   a.   Identification

   b.   Significance

12. Harry S Truman

   a.   Identification

   b.   Significance

13. Roosevelt's "Second Bill of Rights"

   a.   Identification

   b.   Significance

14. the Progressive party

   a.   Identification

   b.   Significance

15. the Dixiecrats

    a. Identification

    b. Significance

16. the presidential campaign and election of 1948

    a. Identification

    b. Significance

17. the Fair Deal

    a. Identification

    b. Significance

18. Dwight D. Eisenhower

    a. Identification

    b. Significance

19. dynamic conservatism

    a. Identification

    b. Significance

20. Sputnik

    a.   Identification

    b.   Significance

21. the National Defense Education Act of 1957

    a.   Identification

    b.   Significance

22. the Atomic Energy Act of 1954

    a.   Identification

    b.   Significance

23. the military-industrial complex

    a.   Identification

    b.   Significance

24. the vital center

    a.   Identification

    b.   Significance

25. the era of consensus
    a.   Identification

    b.   Significance

26. the Verona project
    a.   Identification

    b.   Significance

27. the atomic civil defense program
    a.   Identification

    b.   Significance

28. redbaiting
    a.   Identification

    b.   Significance

29. Truman's loyalty program (Employee Loyalty Program)
    a.   Identification

    b.   Significance

30. the House Committee on Un-American Activities (HUAC)

    a.   Identification

    b.   Significance

31. the Hollywood Ten

    a.   Identification

    b.   Significance

32. Senator Joseph McCarthy

    a.   Identification

    b.   Significance

33. the Internal Security Act of 1950 (McCarran Act)

    a.   Identification

    b.   Significance

34. the Communist Control Act of 1954

    a.   Identification

    b.   Significance

35.   the Alger Hiss case

    a.   Identification

    b.   Significance

36.   Ethel and Julius Rosenberg

    a.   Identification

    b.   Significance

37.   the Army-McCarthy hearings

    a.   Identification

    b.   Significance

38.   *To Secure These Rights*

    a.   Identification

    b.   Significance

39.   Treatment and Opportunity in the Armed Services

    a.   Identification

    b.   Significance

40. the NAACP's Legal Defense and Education Fund
    a. Identification

    b. Significance

41. *Smith v. Allwright and Morgan v. Virginia*
    a. Identification

    b. Significance

42. *Shelly v. Kramer*
    a. Identification

    b. Significance

43. *An American Dilemma, Native Son,* and *Black Boy*
    a. Identification

    b. Significance

44. Jackie Robinson
    a. Identification

    b. Significance

45. *Brown v. Board of Education of Topeka*
    a.　Identification

    b.　Significance

46. Emmett Till
    a.　Identification

    b.　Significance

47. White Citizens Councils
    a.　Identification

    b.　Significance

48. the Little Rock crisis
    a.　Identification

    b.　Significance

49. Rosa Parks
    a.　Identification

    b.　Significance

50. Martin Luther King, Jr.

    a.   Identification

    b.   Significance

51. the Montgomery Bus Boycott

    a.   Identification

    b.   Significance

52. the Southern Christian Leadership Conference

    a.   Identification

    b.   Significance

53. the Civil Rights Act of 1957

    a.   Identification

    b.   Significance

54. "The Treaty of Detroit"

    a.   Identification

    b.   Significance

55. the growth of the Sunbelt

   a.   Identification

   b.   Significance

56. the transistor

   a.   Identification

   b.   Significance

57. the emergence of a national middle class culture

   a.   Identification

   b.   Significance

58. television

   a.   Identification

   b.   Significance

59. the "middle-classness" of television programming

   a.   Identification

   b.   Significance

60. the consumer culture

     a.   Identification

     b.   Significance

61. the post-World War II religious revival

     a.   Identification

     b.   Significance

62. gender roles in families of the 1950s

     a.   Identification

     b.   Significance

63. Dr. Spock

     a.   Identification

     b.   Significance

64. *Modern Woman: The Lost Sex*

     a.   Identification

     b.   Significance

65. the "crisis of masculinity"
    a. Identification

    b. Significance

66. William H. Whyte
    a. Identification

    b. Significance

67. Dr. Alfred Kinsey
    a. Identification

    b. Significance

68. Hugh Hefner
    a. Identification

    b. Significance

69. the "youth culture"
    a. Identification

    b. Significance

70. Slinky, Mr. Potato Head, and Davy Crockett
    a.   Identification

    b.   Significance

71. rock 'n' roll
    a.   Identification

    b.   Significance

72. Elvis Presley
    a.   Identification

    b.   Significance

73. the 1950s upsurge in juvenile delinquency
    a.   Identification

    b.   Significance

74. the critics of 1950s conformity
    a.   Identification

    b.   Significance

75. the environmental costs associated with economic growth
    a.   Identification

    b.   Significance

76. planned obsolescence
    a.   Identification

    b.   Significance

77. *Silent Spring*
    a.   Identification

    b.   Significance

78. urban and rural poverty of the 1950s
    a.   Identification

    b.   Significance

79. the National Housing Act of 1949
    a.   Identification

    b.   Significance

80.   1950s growth of agribusiness

    a.   Identification

    b.   Significance

81.   Eisenhower's termination policy

    a.   Identification

    b.   Significance

ORGANIZING, REVIEWING, AND USING INFORMATION

Chart A

Mid-Century Presidencies		
	Truman **1945–1953**	**Eisenhower** **1953–1961**
Means of Assuming Office/Character of Election (campaign styles, closeness, etc.)		
President's Political Philosophy and Goals		
Actions Reflecting President's Own Position in His Party (left, center, right)		
Impact of President's Actions on His Party's Traditional Power Base, Coalitions		
Major Features of Economy During President's Time in Office		
Efforts Made to Protect or Improve the Domestic Economy (actions, outcomes)		
War / Military Involvement or Intervention Abroad		

Mid-Century Presidencies		
	Truman **1945–1953**	**Eisenhower** **1953–1961**
Taxes, Spending, Deficits		
Relations with Big Business		
Relations with Labor and Unions		
Civil Rights Movement (president's attitude and actions)		
Supreme Court (appointments, rulings)		
Response to or Exploitation of Cold War (fears of USSR and nuclear war, anti-communism activities)		
Doctrines/ Pronouncements/Warn-ings Issued by President		

Chart B

Civil Rights Movement of the 1950s

	Landmark Events or Activities	Key Figures (initiators, supporters, opponents, responders)	Strategy Involved	Goal, Outcome	Involvement of State Governm't, Leaders	Involvement of Courts and Lawyers	Involvement of Public	Impact
Truman Years								
Eisenhower Years								

Chart C

Cultural Portrait of the 1950s			
	Character/Change	**Cause**	**Effect**
Housing			
Sex and Family			
Roles of Youth and Peers			
Inequities in World of Work			
Media Practices and Influence			
Consumer Behavior			

Cultural Portrait of the 1950s			
	Character/Change	**Cause**	**Effect**
Regional Economies			
Education			
Racial Attitudes			
Class Structure/ Perceptions of Class			

IDEAS AND DETAILS

Objective 1

1.   Which of the following was a consequence of the GI Bill?

     a.   Those who took advantage of its educational benefits tended to become more elitist and more provincial in their outlook.

     b.   Due to the rapid influx of thousands of veterans into the nation's colleges and universities, many institutions of higher learning experienced severe economic problems.

     c.   By making higher education available to more people, it created social mobility and fostered the emergence of a national, middle-class culture.

     d.   It caused the federal debt to mushroom, which in turn led to high interest rates on mortgages and consumer loans.

Objective 2

2.   Which of the following is true of the postwar baby boom?

     a.   The boom had little impact on the American economy.

     b.   The boom was largely due to an increase in the birthrate among immigrants and poor Americans.

     c.   Ignorance concerning birth control and family planning was probably the most important reason for the boom.

     d.   As the baby-boom generation grew older, it would have an impact over the decades on such things as housing, education, the job market, and retirement funds.

Objectives 1, 5, and 6

3.   Which of the following is true of many federal programs during the late 1940s and 1950s?

     a.   They led to a significant increase in the number of women receiving college degrees.

     b.   They made it much easier for African Americans to obtain loans for mortgages.

     c.   They caused resentment among middle-class Americans because they primarily benefited those with incomes below the poverty level.

     d.   They were often biased in favor of white males.

Objective 5

4.   Why did President Truman score very few successes in the enactment of his legislative agenda?

     a.   The conservative nature of Truman's legislative agenda was out of step with the electorate.

     b.   Truman's proposals to expand social welfare programs were unrealistic in light of declining tax revenues during the late 1940s and early 1950s.

     c.   A coalition of Republicans and southern Democrats in Congress prevented passage of many legislative measures put forward by the president.

     d.   When Truman refused to support the creation of a national healthcare program, liberal Democratic congressmen sought revenge by defeating his legislative proposals.

Objective 4

5.   Truman won the presidency in 1948, in part, because

   a.   the Dixiecrat and Progressive parties threw their support to Truman in the final weeks of the campaign.
   b.   the Republican party was seriously divided over domestic issues and could not conduct a unified campaign.
   c.   African American voters gave him the edge necessary to carry key northern states.
   d.   the electorate believed that the Republican party platform was too liberal.

Objective 7

6.   Which of the following was a characteristic of American thought in the 1950s?

   a.   A belief that the faults of American society should be publicly debated
   b.   A belief that criticism of American society was unpatriotic
   c.   An often-expressed fear that Americans could not withstand the pressures of the Cold War world
   d.   A belief that people in positions of authority were to be questioned and forced to justify their decisions

Objectives 8 and 9

7.   Which of the following contributed to the emergence of McCarthyism?

   a.   The use of redbaiting by politicians
   b.   News of a treaty of alliance between Mexico and the Soviet Union
   c.   The rapid increase in Communist party membership
   d.   Discovery of a well-formed Communist conspiracy under the leadership of Henry Wallace

Objectives 6, 8, and 9

8.   Which of the following is true of the Communist Control Act of 1954?

   a.   It provided for the internment of known communists during a national emergency.
   b.   It denied employment to communists in defense-related industries.
   c.   The act effectively made membership in the Communist Party illegal.
   d.   It put all labor unions suspected of communist domination under surveillance.

Objective 10

9.   During the post-World War II period, African Americans made gains in their struggle for civil rights because

   a.   Congress passed a strong voting rights bill.
   b.   racist practices at home made it more difficult to compete with the Soviet Union for the support of nonaligned nations.
   c.   Truman persuaded southern congressmen to support federal laws against lynching and against the poll tax.
   d.   Congress took a decisive stand against racist organizations by outlawing the Ku Klux Klan.

Objectives 10 and 11

10. In the *Brown* decision, the Supreme Court held that

     a. the poll tax was unconstitutional.

     b. segregation in public educational facilities was unconstitutional.

     c. African Americans had benefited from segregated public educational institutions.

     d. racial discrimination in public accommodations was unconstitutional.

Objective 12

11. Which of the following was a reason for the sustained economic growth America experienced during the 1950s?

     a. The rising value of stocks and bonds

     b. The rise in GNP

     c. Consumer spending

     d. The computer

Objective 15

12. Which of the following is true of suburban life during the 1950s?

     a. The suburbs brought together people of diverse backgrounds and helped forge a national, middle class culture.

     b. The child-centered nature of suburban life was the major factor in the decline of juvenile delinquency during the 1950s.

     c. Since most residents of the suburbs were white, these communities were far less diverse than the neighborhoods from which most suburbanites had come.

     d. The satisfying nature of suburban life was one reason for the decrease in the number of married women in the work force during the 1950s.

Objective 19

13. Which of the following was the most important factor in defining youth culture during the 1950s?

     a. Music

     b. Television

     c. Movies

     d. Advertising

Objective 20

14. During the 1950s, books such as *The Crack in the Picture Window* and *The Lonely Crowd*

     a. praised rock 'n' roll as the music of a revolutionary generation.

     b. repudiated middle class culture and the rise of conformity in American life.

     c. were shallow, juvenile writings that had virtually no long-term significance.

     d. chastised American teenagers for their political complacency and hedonistic lifestyle.

Objectives 6 and 22

15. As a result of the termination policy supported by the Eisenhower administration,

     a. Indian reservations were expanded and Indian culture further protected.

     b. Indians were successfully relocated to urban areas and assimilated into American society.

     c. the impoverished condition of many Indians was made worse.

     d. the federal government agreed to aid Indian reservations in the extraction of natural resources from tribal lands.

ESSAY QUESTIONS

Objectives 2, 12, and 19

1. Discuss the baby boom, and explain its social and economic impact on American society.

Objectives 1, 5, and 10

2. Discuss the Truman administration's record on civil rights.

Objectives 8 and 9

3. Defend the following statement: "The Cold War heightened anti-Communist fears at home, and by 1950 they reached hysterical proportions. McCarthy did not create this hysteria; he manipulated it to his own advantage."

Objectives 7, 8, and 9

4. Defend or refute the following statement: "During the 1950s, Americans were confident to the verge of complacency about the perfectibility of American society, anxious to the point of paranoia about the threat of communism."

Objectives 6, 10, and 11

5. Discuss the reaction of the southern states and the Eisenhower administration to the *Brown* decision.

Objective 11

6. Discuss the emergence of Dr. Martin Luther King, Jr., as the leader of the civil rights movement that emerged in the aftermath of the *Brown* decision and explain Dr. King's philosophy.

Objectives 10 and 11

7. Discuss the successes and failures of the civil rights movement from the Montgomery bus boycott to the late 1950s.

Objectives 3 and 17

8. Discuss the concept of the American family and American attitudes concerning gender roles during the 1950s and early 1960s.

Objective 17

9. Discuss the following statement: "A reason for woman's dilemma was the conflicting roles she was expected to fulfill."

Objective 22

10. Examine the reasons for and the extent of poverty in American society during the 1950s and early 1960s.

ANSWERS

Multiple-Choice Questions

1. c.   Correct. Veterans who took advantage of the educational benefits of the GI Bill poured into American colleges and universities during the postwar years. As a result of the education and technical training they received, they experienced increased social mobility because their career choices were broadened. Furthermore, while in college, beneficiaries of the GI Bill were exposed to new ideas, new experiences, and a diversity of peoples from different backgrounds. As a result, they tended to be more open-minded and less provincial which, in turn, contributed to the emergence of a national, middle-class culture. See page 801.

    a.   No. Those who took advantage of the educational benefits of the GI Bill were exposed to new ideas, new experiences, and new people from diverse backgrounds. As a result, they tended to become more open-minded and less provincial. See page 801.

    b.   No. Despite the fears of some educators, the influx of thousands of veterans into America's colleges and universities created "a golden age for higher education." See page 801.

    d.   No. The GI Bill was one factor that increased the federal debt during the late 1940s and during the 1950s. However, due to postwar economic growth and prosperity, federal borrowing did not lead to high interest rates on mortgages and consumer loans. See page 801.

2. d.   Correct. As is indicated in Sylvia Porter's quote in the text, the baby-boom generation over the years created a demand for more food, clothing, gadgets, housing, and services. In this sense, the baby-boom generation was a reason for the postwar economic boom. Furthermore, when the baby-boom generation began to reach retirement age, it put a strain on healthcare systems and on retirement funds. See page 801.

    a.   No. The number of births exceeded 4 million per year through the 1950s and into the 1960s. All these extra people had a ripple effect throughout the economy. See page 801.

    b.   No. The urban middle class, consisting of professionals, white-collar workers, and college graduates, contributed disproportionately to the baby boom. See page 801.

    c.   No. Many people having second, third, and fourth children had demonstrated in the past that they knew how to practice birth control, but during the 1950s they chose not to do so. See page 801.

3. d.   Correct. The policies associated with many postwar federal programs usually benefited white men more than women or nonwhites. For example, as a result of the Selective Service Act's guarantee that veterans would receive priority in postwar employment over war workers, many of the women who had kept the factories running during the war years lost their jobs. Other examples supporting the idea that benefits were distributed unevenly in the postwar years may be found in the text. See pages 802–803.

    a.   No. Postwar federal programs that extended educational benefits, such as the GI Bill, were available to veterans, most of whom were males. As a result, these programs did not benefit women wanting to attend college and did not cause an increase in the number of women receiving college degrees. See pages 802–803.

    b.   No. Just the opposite happened. Federal loan officers and bankers often saw African Americans as a higher credit risk than whites. As a result, African Americans usually found it more difficult to receive loans for mortgages. See pages 802–803.

    c.   No. Federal programs were far more beneficial to middle-class Americans than to low-income Americans. See pages 802–803.

4. c.   Correct. The Republicans who dominated the Eightieth Congress (1947–1949) were joined by conservative southern Democrats in rejecting most of Truman's legislative proposals. Even after Truman was elected to the presidency in his own right in 1948, a coalition of Republicans and conservative southern Democrats stood against and were able to defeat most of Truman's proposals. See page 803.

    a.   No. Truman's legislative agenda, which included the Full Employment Act, civil rights legislation, and national health insurance, is considered liberal. See page 803.

    b.   No. Federal tax revenues remained fairly constant at around $40 billion per year from 1946 to 1950. Furthermore, in light of the continued growth in the economy during those years Truman's proposals were rather modest and failure to enact them was due more to the political environment than to lack of funds. See page 803.

    d.   No. Truman was not against the creation of a national healthcare program. In fact, he proposed a national health insurance program on two separate occasions. However, largely due to criticisms from the American Medical Association that the program was "socialized medicine" and criticisms from Republicans and conservative southern Democrats that the program was a "communist plot," the program never passed Congress. See page 803.

5. c.   Correct. Truman acted to secure equal rights for African Americans by establishing the President's Committee on Civil Rights and by ending racial discrimination in the federal government. As a result, Truman won the African American vote in key northern states. As a result, Truman carried those states, received the electoral votes from those states, and was elected to the presidency in 1948. See pages 804 and 809.

    a.   No. Both the Progressive party candidate (Henry Wallace) and the Dixiecrat candidate (Strom Thurmond) continued their independent campaigns for the presidency through election day. See page 804.

    b.   No. The Democratic party, not the Republican party, was divided in 1948. See page 804.

    d.   No. The Republican party had taken a conservative stance on most issues and was perceived by the electorate as more conservative than the Democratic party. See page 804.

6. b.   Correct. During the 1950s, most Americans unquestioningly accepted American society and believed that America was the most powerful and most righteous nation on earth. This belief led most Americans to believe that reform was unnecessary. Furthermore, Americans believed that the United States was engaged in a moral crusade against communism. This belief led many to believe that those who criticized America were aiding the enemy and were unpatriotic. See page 805.

    a.   No. During the 1950s, most Americans paid little attention to the "faults" of American society, shunned idealistic causes, and saw society's critics as maladjusted. See page 805.

    c.   No. During the 1950s, most Americans were convinced of their ability to stand against any foe. See page 805.

    d.   No. During the 1950s, most Americans trusted and respected those in positions of authority and seldom questioned their decisions. See page 805.

7. a.   Correct. Although McCarthy was probably the most successful redbaiter in the country, conservative and liberal politicians, labor leaders, religious leaders, and others used the public's fear of communism against their opponents. They all contributed to the anti-Communist hysteria known as McCarthyism. See pages 806–807.

    b.   No. There was no such treaty. See pages 806–807.

    c.   No. Communist party membership declined from 83,000 in 1947 to 25,000 in 1954. See pages 806–807.

    d.   No. Henry Wallace was a liberal Democrat, not a Communist, and no such conspiracy existed. See pages 806–807.

8. c.   Correct. This act did, in effect, make membership in the Communist party illegal. The act passed with no dissenting votes in the Senate and with only two dissenting votes in the House. This indicates that liberals and conservatives, Democrats and Republicans shared in the anticommunist consensus of the 1950s. See pages 807–808.

    a.   No. The act was anticommunist in its intent; however, it did not provide for the internment of communists during a national emergency. See pages 807–808.

    b.   No. The Communist Control Act did not deal with the employment of communists in defense-related industries. See pages 807–808.

    d.   No. The Communist Control Act did not deal with labor unions. See pages 807–808.

9. b.   Correct. The gap between American ideals and the realities of American society made it difficult to compete with the Soviet Union among the Third World nonaligned nations. To win the support of these nations, the United States had to begin to live up to its ideals. See page 808.

    a.   No. Congress did not pass effective voting rights legislation until 1965. See page 808.

    c.   No. Although Truman sent a special message to Congress in February 1948 calling for federal antilynching and anti-poll tax laws, southern congressmen were openly opposed to such legislation and Congress never formally responded to the message. See page 808.

    d.   No. Congress did not outlaw the Klan. See page 808.

10. b.   Correct. The NAACP's legal campaign against desegregation scored a major victory when the Court ruled separate educational facilities to be "inherently unequal." See page 810.

a.   No. The Brown decision did not declare the poll tax to be unconstitutional. Use of the poll tax to abridge a citizen's right to vote was not made illegal nationally until ratification of the Twenty-fourth Amendment in 1964. See page 810.

c.   No. In the Brown decision, the Supreme Court found that African Americans had suffered from segregated public educational institutions. See page 810.

d.   No. It was not until 1964 that the Civil Rights Act of that year made discrimination in public accommodations illegal. This was upheld by the Court in the same year. See page 810.

11. c.   Correct. During the postwar years the income of most Americans increased. Per capital real income (based on actual purchasing power) rose 6 percent between 1945 and 1950. It then rose another 15 percent during the 1950s. As a result, not only were many Americans able to purchase more, they did purchase more. In addition, many Americans took advantage of the ready availability of credit. If they did not have cash to buy what they wanted, they borrowed. This resulted in consumer the growth of consumer credit from $5.7 billion in 1945 to $58 billion in 1961. See pages 812–813.

a.   No. Although stocks and bonds rose in value, most Americans did not invest heavily in the stock market. Furthermore, rising stock values do not automatically translate into real money or increased purchasing power. See pages 812–813.

b.   No. Although the nation's GNP rose from $286.5 billion in 1950 to $506.5 billion in 1960, this rise was a consequence of sustained economic growth rather than the basis of that growth. See pages 812–813.

d.   No. The computer, although an important technological achievement of the age, did not put money into the hands of consumers, allowing them to purchase consumer goods. Therefore, the computer was not the economic basis of the sustained economic growth during the 1950s. See pages 812–813.

12. a.   Correct. The truth of this answer is made clear in the opening vignette of this chapter. The people who lived on Nancy Circle consisted of (1) a divorced mother who worked as a secretary, dyed her hair blond, drove a convertible, and had a sister born with dwarfism; (2) a Japanese war bride and a German war bride; (3) people from Appalachia and from the small farms in south Georgia; and (4) people who had grown up in inner-city tenements. In all likelihood, that represents far more diversity than any one of those people would have experienced in the neighborhoods in which they grew up. See pages 797–798 and page 815.

b.   No. Although life in the suburbs did tend to be child centered, juvenile delinquency increased during the 1950 rather than declining. See pages 797–798 and page 815.

c.   No. It is true that most suburban residents were white. However, race is not the only determinant of diversity. See pages 797–798 and page 815.

d.   No. Although many women found suburban life satisfying, the number of married women in the work force increased rather than decreased during the 1950s. See pages 797–798 and page 815.

13.   a.   Correct. Although many factors such as fads and movies helped define youth culture during the 1950s, music was the most important factor. See page 819.

     b.   No. While it is true that television was important in youth culture during the 1950s and even helped shape certain fads, television was not the most important factor in defining youth culture. See page 819.

     c.   No. Although movies were important to young people during the 1950s and often helped shape fads and fashions, movies were not the most important factor in defining youth culture. See page 819.

     d.   No. Many times advertising was directed at America's youth during the 1950s; however, advertising was not the most important factor in defining youth culture. See page 819.

14.   b.   Correct. The Crack in the Picture Window by John Keats and The Lonely Crowd by David Resiman were both critical of the conformity that was a component of middle-class culture during the 1950s. See page 821.

     a.   No. Neither The Crack in the Picture Window nor The Lonely Crowd dealt with the music of the 1950s. See page 821.

     c.   No. The Crack in the Picture Window by John Keats and The Lonely Crowd by David Resiman were not juvenile writings. See page 821.

     d.   No. The Crack in the Picture Window by John Keats and The Lonely Crowd by David Resiman did not deal with the political complacency or the "hedonistic" lifestyle of teenagers during the 1950s. See page 821.

15.   c.   Correct. In this attempt to dissolve reservations and end federal services to Native Americans, many Indians were displaced and many joined the ranks of the urban poor. See page 824.

     a.   No. The intent of the termination policy was to dissolve Indian reservations, not expand them. See page 824.

     b.   No. Although one in eight Indians left the reservations between 1954 and 1960, it cannot be said that they were either "successfully relocated" or "successfully assimilated." See page 824.

     d.   No. This was not a program designed to aid Indians in the extraction of natural resources from tribal lands. See page 824.

CHAPTER 30

The Tumultuous Sixties, 1960–1968

LEARNING OBJECTIVES

After you have studied Chapter 30 in your textbook and worked through this study guide chapter, you should be able to:

1. Discuss John F. Kennedy's personal and political background; examine the domestic goals and accomplishments of the Kennedy administration, and evaluate the legacy of the Kennedy presidency.

2. Examine, evaluate, and discuss the consequences of the defense and foreign policy views, goals, and actions of the Kennedy administration.

3. Discuss Cuban-American relations from 1959 to October 1962; explain the causes, outcome, and consequences of the Cuban missile crisis, and evaluate President John Kennedy's handling of the crisis.

4. Discuss the accomplishments and failures of the African American search for equality during the 1960s; explain the transformation of the civil rights movement into the black power movement; and discuss the impact of black activism on American society.

5. Discuss Lyndon B. Johnson's personal and political background; examine the domestic goals and accomplishments of the Johnson administration, and evaluate the legacy of the Johnson presidency.

6. Discuss the issues and personalities and explain the outcome of the 1964 congressional and presidential elections.

7. Examine, evaluate, and discuss the consequences of the defense and foreign policy views, goals, and actions of the Johnson administration.

8. Examine and evaluate the events and decisions that led to deepening United States involvement in Vietnam from 1961 to 1969.

9. Discuss the nature of the Vietnam War, the characteristics of American soldiers who served in the war, and the war's impact on those soldiers.

10. Explain the factors that contributed to the emergence of anti-Vietnam War sentiment and protests within the United States.

11. Discuss the forces that gave rise to the New Left and the counterculture; examine the philosophy, goals, and actions of these two groups; and discuss their impact on American society.

12. Examine the crises that sent shock waves through American society in 1968.

13. Discuss the issues and personalities and explain the outcome of the 1968 presidential election.

THEMATIC GUIDE

In Chapter 30, we examine the impact of the tumultuous 1960s on American society. As can be seen in the discussion of U.S. foreign policy during this period, the containment doctrine, formulated during the Truman administration, continued to be the guiding force behind American foreign policy during the presidencies of John F. Kennedy and Lyndon B. Johnson. Furthermore, the action-reaction relationship between the United States and the Soviet Union that was so much a part of the early Cold War persisted into the 1960s.

Kennedy's policies and actions in the field of foreign policy were shaped by his acceptance of the containment doctrine and his preference for a bold, interventionist foreign policy. In its quest for friends in the Third World and ultimate victory in the Cold War, the Kennedy administration adopted the goal of nation building, to be accomplished, for example, through the Alliance for Progress and the Peace Corps as well as through the concept of counterinsurgency. Such methods perpetuated an idea that had long been part of American foreign policy: that other people cannot solve their own problems and that the American economic and governmental model can be transferred intact to other societies. Historian William Appleman Williams believed that such thinking led to "the tragedy of American diplomacy," and historian Arthur M. Schlesinger, Jr., refers to it as "a ghastly illusion."

Although Kennedy's activist approach to foreign policy helped bring the world to the brink of nuclear disaster in the Cuban missile crisis, in the aftermath of that crisis steps were taken by both superpowers that served to lessen tension and hostility between them. However, the arms race accelerated during both the Kennedy and Johnson years, and the United States and the Soviet Union continued to vie for friends in the Third World.

On the domestic scene, young African Americans, through the sit-in movement begun in Greensboro, North Carolina, in early 1960, reinvigorated the civil rights movement. Although African American civil rights leaders were committed to the philosophy of non-violence, violence began to have an impact on developments, as we see in the discussion of the Freedom Rides, the Freedom Summer of 1964, and the Birmingham Children's Crusade. At first, President Kennedy failed to press forward on civil rights issues. However, in the face of violent challenges from southern segregationists to an expanding black civil rights movement, the Kennedy administration gradually committed itself to a decisive stand in favor of black equality. However, only because of the March on Washington, continuing racial violence, and Kennedy's assassination did Congress finally pass civil rights legislation.

The section "Liberalism and the Great Society" covers the legislative accomplishments of the Johnson administration—the most sweeping reform legislation since 1935. This legislation comprised the Civil Rights Act of 1964, establishment of the Equal Employment Opportunity Commission, the Voting Rights Act of 1965, and legislation associated with Johnson's War on Poverty. The authors look closely at the legislation that constituted the War on Poverty and discuss the problems and successes of this program.

The authors then turn to a discussion of the course of American involvement in Vietnam from deepening U.S. involvement during the Kennedy administration to the escalation of and Americanization of the war during the Johnson administration. This discussion is based on the thesis that disaster befell the United States in Vietnam because of fear in the Johnson administration that America's credibility would suffer in the eyes of friends and foes around the world if the nation failed to achieve its stated goals in Southeast Asia.

As the three branches of the federal government slowly began to deal with such long-standing American problems as poverty and minority rights, frustrations that had built up over generations of inaction manifested themselves. Events convinced civil-rights activists in the South that the "power structure" in American society was not to be trusted. Northern blacks began to reach the same conclusions. Both the civil-rights movement and Johnson's antipoverty programs had offered African Americans hope for a better day in American society. However, as discussion of the social, economic, and political plight of urban blacks reveals, that hope had not been fulfilled. Among other factors, unfulfilled expectations and the continued display of wealth and possessions in the consumer-oriented American society led to the urban riots of the 1960s. Militant black leaders gained prominence and questioned Martin Luther King's philosophy of nonviolence as well as his goal of integration. Malcolm X, Stokely Carmichael, and the Black Panther party called for "black power" within the context of black nationalism.

Along with this revolution of rising expectations among blacks, some whites involved in the civil rights movement began to become disillusioned with American society. Although their disillusionment stemmed from different sources than that of blacks, it led to the political and social activism associated with the New Left and the counterculture. The authors discuss the emergence, characteristics, and goals of both of these groups as well as the reaction of the middle class to their attacks on traditional values. The forces of frustration, rage, and anger born of racism, sexism, poverty, disillusionment, materialism, and the revolution of rising expectations practically ripped America apart in the tumult of 1968. As the Vietnam War escalated and the New Left and the counterculture found common cause in their antiwar stance, the middle class became more and more convinced that traditional society was under siege.

The chapter ends with a discussion of the divisive presidential election of 1968.

BUILDING VOCABULARY

Listed below are important words and terms that you need to know to get the most out of Chapter 30. They are listed in the order in which they occur in the chapter. After carefully looking through the list, (1) underline the words with which you are totally unfamiliar, (2) put a question mark by those words of which you are unsure, and (3) leave the rest alone.

As you begin to read the chapter, when you come to any of the words you've put question marks beside or underlined (1) slow your reading; (2) focus on the word and on its context in the sentence you're reading; (3) if you can understand the meaning of the word from its context in the sentence or passage in which it is used, go on with your reading; (4) if it's a word that you've underlined or a word that you can't understand from its context in the sentence or passage, look it up in a dictionary and write down the definition that best applies to the context in which the word is used.

Definitions

intransigence _____

ruse _____

liaison _____

surly _____

tepid _____

staid _____

verve _____

exude _____

pragmatic _____

broach (verb) _____

benevolent _____

insidious _____

quell _____

exacerbate _____

ratchet _____

rankle _____

bequeath _____

watershed _____

prudence _____

peripheral _____

caste _____

founder (verb) _____

languish _____

rhetoric _____

intractable _____

quip _____

countenance _____

metaphor _____

perseverance _____

attrition _____

volatile _____

implacable _____

fissure _____

espouse _____

infuse _____

transcendent _____

homogeneous _____

revel _____

mantra _____

nascent _____

promiscuous _____

polarize _____

Difficult-to-Spell Names and Terms from Reading and Lecture

IDENTIFICATION AND SIGNIFICANCE

After studying Chapter 30 of A *People and a Nation*, you should be able to identify fully *and* explain the historical significance of each item listed below.

- Identify each item in the space provided. Give an explanation or description of the item. Answer the questions who, what, where, and when.

- Explain the historical significance of each item in the space provided. Establish the historical context in which the item exists. Establish the item as the result of or as the cause of other factors existing in the society under study. Answer this question: What were the political, social, economic, and/or cultural consequences of this item?

1. the Greensboro sit-in

    a. Identification

    b. Significance

2. John F. Kennedy

    a. Identification

    b. Significance

3.   the presidential election of 1960

    a.   Identification

    b.   Significance

4.   "the best and the brightest"

    a.   Identification

    b.   Significance

5.   the concept of nation building

    a.   Identification

    b.   Significance

6.   the Alliance for Progress

    a.   Identification

    b.   Significance

7.   the Peace Corps

    a.   Identification

    b.   Significance

8.   the doctrine of counterinsurgency

   a.   Identification

   b.   Significance

9.   the 1961 Berlin crisis

   a.   Identification

   b.   Significance

10.   the Bay of Pigs invasion

   a.   Identification

   b.   Significance

11.   Operation Mongoose

   a.   Identification

   b.   Significance

12.   the Cuban missile crisis

   a.   Identification

   b.   Significance

13. the nuclear test ban treaty of 1963

    a.   Identification

    b.   Significance

14. the Student Nonviolent Coordinating Committee

    a.   Identification

    b.   Significance

15. the Freedom Rides

    a.   Identification

    b.   Significance

16. the Freedom Summer of 1964

    a.   Identification

    b.   Significance

17. the Mississippi Freedom Democratic Party

    a.   Identification

    b.   Significance

18. the Children's Crusade
    a.   Identification

    b.   Significance

19. James Meredith
    a.   Identification

    b.   Significance

20. George Wallace's stand in the schoolhouse door
    a.   Identification

    b.   Significance

21. Medgar Evers
    a.   Identification

    b.   Significance

22. the March on Washington
    a.   Identification

    b.   Significance

23. Sixteenth Street Baptist Church bombing

    a.   Identification

    b.   Significance

24. the New Frontier

    a.   Identification

    b.   Significance

25. the space program

    a.   Identification

    b.   Significance

26. the assassination of John Kennedy

    a.   Identification

    b.   Significance

27. Lee Harvey Oswald

    a.   Identification

    b.   Significance

28. Jack Ruby
    a.   Identification

    b.   Significance

29. Lyndon Johnson
    a.   Identification

    b.   Significance

30. the Great Society
    a.   Identification

    b.   Significance

31. the Civil Rights Act of 1964
    a.   Identification

    b.   Significance

32. the Equal Employment Opportunity Commission
    a.   Identification

    b.   Significance

33. the presidential and congressional elections of 1964

    a.   Identification

    b.   Significance

34. Barry Goldwater

    a.   Identification

    b.   Significance

35. Fannie Lou Hamer

    a.   Identification

    b.   Significance

36. the Voting Rights Act of 1965

    a.   Identification

    b.   Significance

37. the Immigration Act of 1965

    a.   Identification

    b.   Significance

38.   the War on Poverty

    a.   Identification

    b.   Significance

39.   Medicare and Medicaid

    a.   Identification

    b.   Significance

40.   the Tonkin Gulf incident and the Tonkin Gulf Resolution

    a.   Identification

    b.   Significance

41.   Operation Rolling Thunder

    a.   Identification

    b.   Significance

42.   the "body count" issue

    a.   Identification

    b.   Significance

43. the Fulbright hearings

    a. Identification

    b. Significance

44. the Harlem race riot of 1964

    a. Identification

    b. Significance

45. the Watts race riot of 1965

    a. Identification

    b. Significance

46. the Kerner Commission Report

    a. Identification

    b. Significance

47. Malcolm X

    a. Identification

    b. Significance

48. the Black Muslims
    a.   Identification

    b.   Significance

49. Stokely Carmichael
    a.   Identification

    b.   Significance

50. Black Power
    a.   Identification

    b.   Significance

51. the Black Panthers
    a.   Identification

    b.   Significance

52. Young Americans for Freedom
    a.   Identification

    b.   Significance

53. the New Left

    a.   Identification

    b.   Significance

54. the Port Huron Statement

    a.   Identification

    b.   Significance

55. the Free Speech Movement

    a.   Identification

    b.   Significance

56. the doctrine of *in loco parentis*

    a.   Identification

    b.   Significance

57. Students for a Democratic Society

    a.   Identification

    b.   Significance

58. the youth culture of the 1960s
    a.   Identification

    b.   Significance

59. the Beatles
    a.   Identification

    b.   Significance

60. Bob Dylan
    a.   Identification

    b.   Significance

61. Janis Joplin, James Brown, and Aretha Franklin
    a.   Identification

    b.   Significance

62. Jefferson Airplane and the Grateful Dead
    a.   Identification

    b.   Significance

63. Woodstock

    a.   Identification

    b.   Significance

64. the counterculture

    a.   Identification

    b.   Significance

65. the Summer of Love

    a.   Identification

    b.   Significance

66. the birth control pill

    a.   Identification

    b.   Significance

67. the Tet offensive

    a.   Identification

    b.   Significance

68. the assassination of Martin Luther King
    a. Identification

    b. Significance

69. the assassination of Robert Kennedy
    a. Identification

    b. Significance

70. the 1964 Democratic National Convention
    a. Identification

    b. Significance

71. the globalization of youth protests
    a. Identification

    b. Significance

72. the presidential election of 1968
    a. Identification

    b. Significance

ORGANIZING, REVIEWING, AND USING INFORMATION

Chart A

The Presidency: Vietnam Escalation and Cold War Crises		
	Kennedy	**Johnson**
Means of Obtaining Office—circumstances, campaign styles, closeness of election, etc.		
Focus and Goals		
Changes in Party's Power Base/Support (nature, cause, effect)		
Changes in Nation's Philosophical Tilt in Domestic Politics		
Key Legislation Enacted		
Taxes, Spending, and Deficits		
Changes in Power of President, Power of Congress (nature, cause)		
Administration's Key Crises (domestic and international)		

The Presidency: Vietnam Escalation and Cold War Crises		
	Kennedy	**Johnson**
Vietnam War (involvement, strategies, efforts to conclude)		
Cold War and Relations with Soviet Union (intensity, strategies, highlights)		
Intervention Abroad— Other than Vietnam War (types, instances)		
Major International Agreements		

Chart B

Political and Social Activism and Rioting of the 1960s				
Object of Protest	**Groups/Leaders**	**Goals**	**Favored Tactics**	**Landmark Events**
Racial Segregation and Discrimination				
Race-Related Socioeconomic Conditions				
Liberalism (philosophy and/or goals)				
College Campus Rules and Decision-making				
Vietnam War				
Middle Class Attitudes and Behaviors				

IDEAS AND DETAILS

Objective 2

1. The concept of nation building was based on the idea that

    a. the industrialized nations of the world should pool their resources to aid Third World nations.

    b. the United States could win the friendship of Third World countries by helping them as they struggled through the infant stages of nationhood.

    c. the European states should demonstrate their acceptance of self-determination by allowing their colonies to become independent nations.

    d. a nation's social, political, and economic system must be based on its own unique historical experience.

Objective 2

2. When President Kennedy refused to consent to Soviet demands in the 1961 Berlin crisis, the Soviet Union

    a. denied the Western powers access to their zones in the city of Berlin.

    b. began installing tactical nuclear weapons in East Germany.

    c. built the Berlin Wall.

    d. cut off all trade with the United States, Great Britain, and France.

Objectives 2 and 3

3. In the aftermath of the Bay of Pigs invasion, President Kennedy

    a. vowed to bring down the government of Fidel Castro.

    b. apologized to the Cuban people for infringing on their national sovereignty.

    c. reestablished trade with the Castro regime.

    d. restored diplomatic relations with Cuba.

Objectives 2 and 3

4. A beneficial effect of the Cuban missile crisis was

    a. major improvements in the American civil-defense system.

    b. public support for improving relations with Cuba.

    c. installation of a Washington-Moscow hot line.

    d. tighter control of the CIA by Congress.

Objective 4

5. When Martin Luther King, Jr., put children in the front lines of protest in Birmingham, Alabama, in 1963, the city's police commissioner

    a. allowed the march to proceed without incident.

    b. called out the Alabama National Guard to prevent the march.

    c. used powerful water guns and attack dogs against the protesters.

    d. lined the route of the march with Birmingham police to protect the children from violence.

Objective 5

6. As a result of the Voting Rights Act of 1965,

    a.   the right to vote was extended to eighteen-year-olds.

    b.   the number of registered African American voters in the South dramatically increased.

    c.   literacy tests were required of all voters in federal elections.

    d.   eligible voters were legally required to register through federal registrars.

Objective 5

7. Which of the following is true of the War on Poverty?

    a.   It provided a guaranteed annual income to all Americans.

    b.   It especially benefited female-headed families.

    c.   It directly attacked the housing, health, and nutritional problems of the poor.

    d.   It alone was responsible for alleviating hunger in the United States.

Objectives 7 and 8

8. In the Gulf of Tonkin Resolution, Congress

    a.   publicly questioned President Johnson's escalation of the Vietnam War.

    b.   gave virtually a free hand to President Johnson in conducting the war in Vietnam.

    c.   condemned the My Lai massacre.

    d.   declared war against North Vietnam.

Objectives 7 and 8

9. During the Johnson administration, the United States continued escalating its commitment to the Vietnam War because

    a.   all of the nation's European allies urged it to do so.

    b.   most members of the Johnson administration strongly believed it was inevitable that the United States would win the war.

    c.   the American public demanded victory.

    d.   the administration feared that a failure in Vietnam would lead to a loss of respect for American power throughout the world.

Objective 9

10. America's reliance on such things as carpet bombing, napalm, and crop defoliants in the Vietnam War

    a.   caused Ho Chi Minh to abandon the Vietcong and concentrate his resources on the North Vietnamese army.

    b.   alienated many South Vietnamese, bringing new recruits to the Vietcong.

    c.   made South Vietnamese villages safer and more secure by destroying the Vietcong's ability to wage war.

    d.   led China to send troops and military materiel to aid the Vietcong.

Objective 4

11. The urban race riots of the 1960s and the emergence of black nationalism in the voices of Malcolm X and Stokely Carmichael were the result of

    a.   the deterioration of the social and economic conditions of many northern African Americans.

    b.   communist infiltration of civil rights groups.

    c.   denial of the right to vote to northern African Americans.

    d.   a shift in the tactics of the SCLC from passive resistance to violent confrontation.

Objective 11

12. Which of the following was a major target of student protesters in the 1960s?

    a.   College fraternities and sororities

    b.   Sex discrimination in college-admission policies

    c.   The practice of granting tenure to college professors

    d.   The doctrine of *in loco parentis*

Objective 11

13. Which of the following is true of American popular culture in the late 1960s?

    a.   It was largely created by advertisers.

    b.   It was based almost exclusively on popular television shows like *Father Knows Best*.

    c.   It was primarily influenced by fears of a nuclear holocaust.

    d.   It was heavily influenced by the music and styles of young people.

Objectives 7, 8, 9, 12, and 13

14. As a result of the Tet offensive,

    a.   the Soviet union sent troops to Vietnam.

    b.   the Joint Chiefs of Staff advised American withdrawal from Vietnam.

    c.   the North Vietnamese were driven to the north of the Demilitarized Zone and requested peace negotiations.

    d.   President Johnson decided to open negotiations with the North.

Objectives 12 and 13

15. The 1968 Democratic presidential candidate killed by an assassin's bullet was

    a.   George Wallace.

    b.   Robert Kennedy.

    c.   Edmund Muskie.

    d.   Eugene McCarthy.

ESSAY QUESTIONS

Objectives 2 and 3

1. Discuss the causes and consequences of the Cuban missile crisis and evaluate President John Kennedy's handling of the crisis.

Objective 5

2. Discuss the successes and failures of the War on Poverty.

Objectives 7, 8, and 9

3. Examine the course of the Vietnam War under President Johnson.

Objective 4

4. Examine the factors and forces that pushed the African American protest movement to more radical action in the mid-1960s. What forms did this action take? What were its results?

Objective 11

5. Discuss the characteristics of the youth culture that emerged during the 1960s.

ANSWERS

Multiple-Choice Questions

1. b.   Correct. Nation building was undertaken with the belief that American capitalism and democracy could be transferred to the Third World. As this was done, it was believed, Third World countries would be brought into the American orbit. Presidential adviser Arthur Schlesinger later called this notion "a ghastly illusion." See pages 830–831.

    a.   No. The concept of nation building did not envision a collective effort by the industrialized nations of the world to aid the Third World. See pages 830–831.

    c.   No. The concept of nation building did not insist on decolonization by European countries. See pages 830–831.

    d.   No. Nation building did not pay much attention to the unique historical experiences of other nations. See pages 830–831.

2. c.   Correct. In 1961 the Soviets demanded an end to the Western occupation of West Berlin and the reunification of East and West Germany. When the Kennedy administration refused to consent to these demands, the Soviets built the Berlin Wall to physically separate East Berlin from West Berlin and stop the flight of East Germans to the more prosperous West. See page 831.

    a.   No. The Soviets denied the Western powers land access to their zones in the divided city of Berlin in the Berlin crisis of 1948. In that crisis, the Soviets ultimately acquiesced after the effectiveness of the Berlin airlift. See page 831.

    b.   No. The Soviets did not install tactical nuclear weapons in East Germany as a result of the 1961 Berlin crisis. See page 831.

    d.   No. The Soviet Union did not cut off all trade with the United States, Great Britain, and France as a result of the 1961 Berlin crisis. See page 831.

3. a.   Correct. After the failure of the Bay of Pigs invasion, Kennedy vowed to bring down the Castro government and authorized Operation Mongoose. Through this project, as well as programs of diplomatic and economic isolation, the United States government continued to work to overthrow the government of Fidel Castro. See pages 831–832.

    b.   No. Kennedy recognized the Bay of Pigs invasion as a mistake because it was a defeat, not because it infringed on Cuban sovereignty. The president never apologized to the Cuban people. See pages 831–832.

    c.   No. The United States continued its attempt to isolate Cuba economically. See pages 831–832.

    d.   No. The United States continued its attempt to isolate Cuba diplomatically and did not restore diplomatic relations. See pages 831–832.

4.   c.   Correct. As a result of the Cuban missile crisis, the two superpowers realized that it was important to make real-time communication possible in order to prevent the use of nuclear weapons as the result of misunderstanding or miscommunication during a crisis. Therefore, the Washington-Moscow hotline was installed. Contrary to popular belief, this was not a phone line, but a telegraph circuit. This telegraph circuit was not replaced with a telephone until the 1970s. See page 833.

a.   No. Although fallout shelters gained popularity in the 1950s and 1960s, the Cuban Missile Crisis did not lead to major improvements in the nation's civil-defense system. In fact, in the aftermath of the crisis relations between the United States and the Soviet Union began to gradually thaw, and the public became less concerned about civil-defense preparedness and fallout shelters. See page 833.

b.   No. The public continued to see Cuba as a potential threat to the United States in the aftermath of the crisis, and the public did not generally support improved relations with the Castro regime. See page 833.

d.   No. There was no move after the Cuban Missile Crisis for Congress to have tighter control over the CIA. See page 833.

5.   c.   Correct. "Bull" Connor, Birmingham's police commissioner, used high-powered fire hoses (water guns), police dogs, and cattle prods against the protesters even though many of them were children. See pages 834–835.

a.   No. The Birmingham police commissioner did not allow the march to take place without incident. See pages 834–835.

b.   No. Birmingham's police commissioner did not have the authority to call out the Alabama National Guard. Therefore, he did not try to prevent the march in that way. See pages 834–835.

d.   No. Birmingham's police commissioner did not try to protect the marchers, including many children, by lining the route of the march with police. See pages 834–835.

6.   b.   Correct. Whereas only 29 percent of the South's black population was registered to vote in 1960, around 66 percent was registered by 1969. See pages 838–839.

a.   No. The right to vote was extended to eighteen-year-olds by the Twenty-sixth Amendment, ratified in 1971. See pages 838–839.

c.   No. Literacy and other voter tests were suspended by the Voting Rights Act of 1965 in those states where such tests had been used to bar qualified people from the voting rolls and where less than half of the voting-age residents were registered. See pages 838–839.

d.   No. The act authorized federal supervision of voter registration in areas where less than half of the voting-age minority residents were registered, but it did not require all eligible voters to register through federal registrars. See pages 838–839.

7.   c.   Correct. The Model Cities program provided federal funds to improve housing and health in certain impoverished urban neighborhoods. Furthermore, the expansion of the Food Stamp program was directed toward the health and nutritional needs of the poor, while the Medicaid program guaranteed healthcare for the poor. Therefore, it can correctly be said that Johnson's War on Poverty directly attacked the housing, health, and nutritional problems of the poor. See page 840.

a.   No. The War on Poverty did not provide a guaranteed annual income to all Americans. See page 840.

b.   No. The War on Poverty did not alleviate poverty in female-headed families. In fact, by the end of the 1960s the number of female-headed households in poverty was the same as it had been in 1963, 11 million. See page 840.

d.   No. The War on Poverty was not the sole reason for the alleviation of hunger in the United States during the 1960s. Although the War on Poverty helped, economic growth during the 1960s was also a factor in the alleviation of hunger. See page 840.

8.   b.   Correct. With only two dissenting votes, Congress authorized the president to "take all necessary measures" to defend American forces and "prevent further aggression." In accepting the resolution, Congress, in effect, surrendered its foreign policy powers and gave President Johnson a free hand in conducting the war in Vietnam. See page 842.

a.   No. Congress did not question Johnson's escalation of the Vietnam War through the Tonkin Gulf Resolution. See page 842.

c.   No. The Gulf of Tonkin resolution was passed in 1964; the My Lai massacre occurred in March 1968 and was not made public until twenty months later. See page 842.

d.   No. The Tonkin Gulf Resolution was not an official declaration of war. See page 842.

9.   d.   Correct. Although some members of the Johnson administration saw little chance for success in Vietnam and warned against escalation, President Johnson and other members of his administration were afraid withdrawal would cause America's allies to doubt the reliability of the United States and embolden America's foes. As a result, the administration continued its escalation of the war. See page 844.

a.   No. Almost all of America's allies warned against escalation of the war. See page 844.

b.   No. Some members of the administration opposed escalation. Among those who supported escalation, there was doubt that it would lead to success against North Vietnam and the Vietcong. See page 844.

c.   No. Public discontent with the war grew as the Johnson administration Americanized the war. Although public opinion polls showed that a majority of Americans supported the war until 1969, it cannot be said that the Johnson administration continued to escalate the war because the public "demanded" victory. See page 844.

10.   b.   Correct. The United States was not only fighting against North Vietnam, but against North Vietnamese supporters (the Vietcong) in the South. Therefore, since carpet bombing, napalm, and crop defoliants such as Agent Orange were used against the Vietcong in the South, their use adversely affected the inhabitants of South Vietnamese villages. As a result, America's reliance on these weapons in its "search-and-destroy" missions alienated South Vietnamese peasants who began to give more and more secret aid to the Vietcong. See page 845.

a.   No. America's use of the stated weapons did not cause Ho Chi Minh to abandon the Vietcong, the North's supporters and guerilla fighters in South Vietnam. See page 845.

c.   No. The United States was never able to destroy the Vietcong's ability to wage war in South Vietnam and its use of the stated weapons did not made South Vietnamese villages more secure. See page 845.

d.   No. China did not send troops to help the Vietcong. See page 845.

11.   a.   Correct. The civil rights movement had been largely southern in focus and did not deal with the deteriorating conditions of blacks in northern inner-city ghettos. Black frustration was expressed through urban riots and in the voices of black nationalism. See pages 846–847.

b.   No. There is no evidence to support the contention that there was "communist infiltration" of civil rights groups and that such infiltration caused the urban race riots of the 1960s and the emergence of black nationalism. See pages 846–847.

c.   No. Northern blacks had long had the right to vote and had long exercised that right. See pages 846–847.

d.   No. The SCLC, under the direction of Martin Luther King, Jr., continued to use the nonviolent tactic of passive resistance. See pages 846–847.

12.   d.   Correct. In the 1960s the doctrine of in loco parentis (in the place of parents) allowed colleges and universities to have a great deal of control over the non-academic lives of students, especially female students. Student protests of the 1960s were often targeted against this doctrine, and many student protesters demanded that full rights and responsibilities be extended to them as citizens in a democratic society. See page 849.

a.   No. College fraternities and sororities were not a major target of student protesters in the 1960s. See page 849.

b.   No. Although sexist practices were present in college-admission practices, this was not a major target of student protesters in the 1960s. See page 849.

c.   No. The practice of granting tenure to college professors was not a major target of student protesters in the 1960s. See page 849.

13.   d.   Correct. As the baby-boom generation came of age and became consumers in the 1960s, its music and its styles began to have a tremendous impact on American popular culture. See pages 850–851.

a.   No. Advertising clearly has an impact on popular culture, but American popular culture of the 1960s was not "created by advertisers." See pages 850–851.

b.   No. American popular culture of the 1960s was not based primarily or exclusively on the television show Father Knows Best, which aired from 1954 to 1962. See pages 850–851.

c.   No. American popular culture of the 1960s was not influenced primarily by fear of a nuclear holocaust. See pages 850–851.

14. d. Correct. The Tet offensive demonstrated that three years of search-and-destroy tactics had not destroyed the power of the Vietcong and North Vietnamese. As a result, Johnson announced an end to the bombing of most of the North and requested that Hanoi open peace negotiations. See page 853.

a. No. The Soviet Union did not send troops to Vietnam as a result of the Tet offensive. See page 853.

b. No. The chairman of the Joint Chiefs of Staff, General Earle Wheeler, reacted to the Tet offensive by persuading General Westmoreland to request an additional 206,000 soldiers. Furthermore, he favored calling the army and marine reserves to active duty. See page 853.

c. No. Although the Vietcong and North Vietnamese suffered heavy losses in the Tet offensive, they still had not been defeated and did not retreat to North Vietnam. See page 853.

15. b. Correct. With polls showing him as the leading presidential candidate among Democrats and having just won the California primary, Robert Kennedy was assassinated on June 5, 1968. See page 854.

a. No. George Wallace ran for president under the banner of the American Independent Party in 1968. In 1972 he was a candidate for the Democratic presidential nomination and was seriously wounded by a would-be assassin. See page 854.

c. No. Edmund Muskie was not a Democratic candidate for the presidency in 1968. See page 854.

d. No. McCarthy challenged President Johnson's war policies in 1968, and his victory in the New Hampshire primary was a factor in Johnson's decision to withdraw as a candidate. But McCarthy was not assassinated. See page 854.

CHAPTER 31

Continuing Divisions and New Limits, 1969–1980

LEARNING OBJECTIVES

After you have studied Chapter 31 in your textbook and worked through this study guide chapter, you should be able to:

1. Discuss the problems that African Americans, Mexican Americans, and Native Americans faced in American society during the 1970s; discuss the emergence of identity politics and cultural nationalism as approaches to those problems; and discuss the extent to which these groups were successful in achieving their goals.

2. Discuss the shift in emphasis during the late 1960s and 1970s from individual opportunity to group outcomes as a remedy for discrimination and inequality; and examine the successes and failures of this concept.

3. Explain the emergence, characteristics, and goals of the feminist movement of the 1960s and 1970s, and discuss the successes and failures of this movement and its impact on American society.

4. Discuss the emergence, characteristics, and goals of the antifeminist and anti-abortion movements, and discuss their impact on American society during the 1970s and 1980s.

5. Explain the emergence of the gay rights movement, and discuss the movement's goals and its impact on American society during the 1970s.

6. Discuss the course of the Vietnam War from 1969 to 1975; explain the war's impact on Southeast Asia, American society, and Vietnam veterans; and discuss the debate in the United States over the meaning of the American experience in Vietnam.

7. Examine, evaluate, and discuss the consequences of the defense and foreign policy views, goals, and actions of the Nixon administration.

8. Discuss the domestic issues that faced the Nixon administration in the late 1960s and early 1970s; explain and evaluate the administration's actions concerning those issues; and discuss the consequences of those actions.

9. Examine the issues and personalities and explain the outcome of the 1972 presidential election.

10. Discuss the illegal activities that constituted the Watergate scandal, and explain the threat these activities posed to constitutional government.

11. Examine the impact of the Watergate scandal on the American people, American society, and American institutions, and discuss and evaluate the reforms enacted in the scandal's aftermath.

12. Examine the issues and personalities and explain the outcome of the 1976 presidential election.

13. Discuss Jimmy Carter's personal and political background; examine the domestic issues and political problems that faced the Carter administration; and explain and evaluate the administration's actions concerning those issues and problems.

14. Discuss the causes, characteristics, and consequences of the economic and energy crises of the 1970s, and explain and evaluate the attempts by the Ford and Carter administrations to deal with these crises.

15. Examine the 1970s as an era of cultural transformation, paying particular attention to:

    a.   the environmental movement;

    b.   technological advances;

    c.   the search for spiritual fulfillment and well-being;

    d.   sexuality and the family; and

    e.   the idea of diversity.

16. Examine, evaluate, and discuss the consequences of the defense and foreign policy views, goals, and actions of the Carter administration.

THEMATIC GUIDE

The turbulence of the 1960s continued into the 1970s as the American people seemed to fragment into separate groups, each more concerned with its own agenda than with a broader national agenda. Minorities that had made gains toward social justice and racial equality began to emphasize their own distinct cultural identity and often favored separatism over assimilation and integration into American culture. The advocates of identity politics among young African American, Mexican American, and Native American activists argued that the government should stop viewing the American public as a collection of individuals and should instead address the needs of specific identity-based groups. Evidence of this emphasis on cultural and historical uniqueness may be seen in the emergence of African American cultural nationalism which gave rise to the "black is beautiful" movement, the creation of "Black Studies" departments at many colleges and universities, and the creation of the new holiday "Kwaanza" in 1966.

Among Mexican Americans, migrant workers under the leadership of Cesar Chávez and Delores Huerta began that group's national movement for social justice. Using Mexican *mutualistas*, or cooperative associations, as their model, the strike of Mexican American migrant workers against the large grape growers of California's San Joaquin Valley successfully fostered a nationwide consumer boycott of table grapes. This in turn led the growers to accede in 1970 to the workers' demands for better wages and working conditions. More radical Mexican American activists, calling themselves "Chicanos," rejected integration and assimilation into American society and argued for the liberation of "la Raza" from the oppressiveness of American culture and society. Not only were these more radical Mexican American activists successful in challenging discrimination, they also laid the groundwork for Chicano political power at the local level.

Young Native Americans, influenced by identity politics and cultural nationalism, also rejected assimilation and began to concentrate on a shared culture among all American Indians (the pan-Indian approach) rather than on distinct tribal concerns and differences.

Not only did activists among America's ethnic and cultural minorities begin to emphasize their uniqueness as a group, American policy makers also began to stress group outcomes over individual outcomes in framing remedies for discrimination and inequality. This as well as practical concerns caused a shift in emphasis on the part of the Equal Employment Opportunity Commission and to the first affirmative action program, the "Philadelphia Plan," instituted by the Nixon administration in

1969. Soon, not only was affirmative action applied to government contracts but it led corporations and educational institutions to adopt such programs as well. Critics of such programs argued that efforts to overcome past discrimination against women and minorities through numerical goals or quotas would only create discrimination against other individuals. As the economic problems of the 1970s continued and deepened, the nation witnessed a backlash against affirmative action on the part of white working-class men.

After discussing the impact of identity politics on America's cultural, societal, and political climate in the late 1960s and early 1970s, the authors turn to a discussion of the women's movement and to the emergence, characteristics, and goals of both moderate and radical feminists. While the diverse groups that constituted the "women's movement" scored some notable successes in their campaign against sexism, the authors note the emergence, characteristics, and aims of the antifeminist forces that coalesced in the 1970s. Arguing in favor of "traditional" American values in the midst of a rapidly changing society, antifeminists successfully stalled ratification of the Equal Rights Amendment and began to campaign actively against legalized abortion.

In addition to the activism of women and of cultural and ethnic minorities, the late 1960s and early 1970s also gave rise to gay activism and to the gay rights movement. Gay activists, inspired by the Stonewall Inn riot in June 1969, worked not only for legal equality but also adopted the identity politics of other groups by promoting Gay Pride and the creation of distinctive gay communities and lifestyles.

In "The End in Vietnam," the authors discuss America's continued involvement in Vietnam during the Nixon administration. Although Nixon had implied in his presidential campaign in 1968 that he would end the Vietnam War, the war continued and even widened. As Nixon implemented the policy of Vietnamization, American troops began to withdraw from Vietnam. However, at the same time Nixon, believing as Johnson had believed that American credibility was at stake, intensified the bombing of North Vietnam and began a secret bombing campaign against North Vietnamese arms depots and army sanctuaries in neutral Cambodia. Revelation of the invasion of Cambodia reinvigorated the antiwar movement and led to the disasters at Kent State University and at Jackson State. Ultimately, the United States and North Vietnam signed a cease-fire agreement in January 1973, and withdrawal of American troops began. In April 1975, however, with both the South Vietnamese and the North Vietnamese having violated the cease-fire agreement, the South Vietnamese government collapsed and Vietnam was reunified under the North's communist government. In the aftermath of the Vietnam War, Americans began to debate its causes and consequences. Just as they had disagreed over the course and conduct of the war, they were now unable to reach any real consensus on its lessons for the nation.

Although a great deal of energy was expended on questions relating to the Vietnam War during Nixon's presidency, Nixon considered other foreign policy matters, especially the relationship between the United States and the Soviet Union, to be more important. In an attempt to create a global balance of power, Nixon and Henry Kissinger (Nixon's national security adviser and later his secretary of state) adopted a "grand strategy." By means of détente with the Soviet Union and the administration's opening to the People's Republic of China, Nixon and Kissinger sought to achieve the same goals as those of the old containment doctrine, but through accommodation rather than confrontation. Despite détente, the United States still had to respond to crises rooted in instability. Nowhere was the fragility of world stability via the grand strategy more apparent than in the Middle East, where war again broke out between the Arab states and Israel in 1973. While the Soviet Union and the United States positioned themselves by putting their armed forces on alert, OPEC imposed an oil embargo against the United States. Kissinger was able to persuade the warring parties to agree to a cease-fire; OPEC ended its embargo; and, through "shuttle diplomacy," Kissinger persuaded Egypt and Israel to agree to a United Nations peacekeeping force in the Sinai. But many problems remained, and the instability of the region continued to be a source of tension between the United States and the Soviet Union.

President Nixon also believed, just as previous presidents had believed, in America's right to influence the internal affairs of Third World countries. It was out of this belief and the concomitant belief that the United States should curb revolution and radicalism in the Third World, that Nixon accepted the Johnson Doctrine in Latin America, as evidenced by the overthrow of the Allende government in Chile and in attempts to prevent the radicalization of Africa.

In "Presidential Politics and the Crisis of Leadership" we look first at Nixon's domestic agenda and discuss the question of whether that agenda was liberal, conservative, or simply pragmatic. We also find a Nixon who, with the continuation of chaos into the 1970s, was convinced that society was on the verge of anarchy and that his perceived enemies were responsible for the ills that plagued the nation. Positioning himself for his reelection campaign in 1972, Nixon followed a "southern strategy" to further attract white southerners to the Republican party. That and other factors led to Nixon's landslide victory in the 1972 presidential election. Unfortunately, that victory did not guarantee an end to the crisis atmosphere that had plagued the nation since the late 1960s. Nixon's obsession that he was surrounded with enemies set the stage for the Watergate scandal. Involving a series of illegal activities approved at the highest level of American government, the scandal caused more disillusionment with government and increased the somber mood of the people. Some of these activities, such as the break-in at Daniel Ellsberg's psychiatrist's office, had been undertaken to discredit political opponents; others, such as the paying of hush money to witnesses, were part of an elaborate cover-up.

Beyond the illegal actions, the Watergate scandal was a constitutional crisis; the "imperial presidency" threatened the balance-of-power concept embodied in the Constitution and the guarantees of individual rights embodied in the Bill of Rights. We see the constitutional nature of the crisis in the clash between the executive and judicial branches of government, the impeachment hearings undertaken by the House Judiciary Committee, and ultimately the resignation of the president. Unlike the scandals of previous administrations, the activities linked to Watergate were aimed not at financial gain but at monopolizing political power. After citing the events associated with Watergate, the authors outline and briefly evaluate congressional attempts to correct the abuses associated with the scandal.

The nation's disillusionment with its government—disillusionment produced by the crises of the 1960s and early 1970s—intensified further when governmental leaders could not deal successfully with the disruptive economic forces of the 1970s. In "Economic Crisis" we examine the nature of the economic crisis and its causes. This section also covers the responses of the Nixon, Ford, and Carter administrations to the economic and energy crises, the continued "deindustrialization" of the American economy, the growth of the Sunbelt, the fiscal crisis experienced by some of America's cities in the North and Midwest, and the beginnings of the tax revolt movement.

In the chapter's penultimate section, "An Era of Cultural Transformation," we discuss the emergence of the current environmental movement, the turn by many Americans to "born again" Christianity and to a therapeutic culture in their search for meaning and belonging in an age of conflict and limits. It was also during the 1970s that American culture witnessed a new openness about sex and a sexual revolution, both of which were factors in the changing nature of the American family. The roots of America's emphasis on diversity may also be seen during this decade.

When Jimmy Carter assumed the presidency in 1977, he and Secretary of State Cyrus Vance at first pledged a new foreign-policy course for the United States. However, this course was challenged by Carter's national security adviser Zbigniew Brzezinski, by Democratic and Republican critics, and by the Soviet Union, which reacted in anger and fear to the human rights aspect of Carter's policies. The Cold War seemed to have its own momentum. Despite the Carter administration's achievements in Latin America and the Middle East, it was overwhelmed by critics at home, the Iranian hostage crisis, and the Soviet invasion of Afghanistan. The grain embargo, the 1980 Olympics boycott, and the Carter Doctrine all seemed more reminiscent of the containment doctrine and the sources of the Cold War than of a new course in American foreign policy. Furthermore, the excesses in which the United States had engaged in the past in its attempts to defeat revolutionary nationalism and create stability in the Third World, protect American economic interests, and contain the Communist threat rained down on the Carter administration in the form of Islamic fundamentalism as expressed in the Iranian hostage crisis. In this crisis America's missiles, submarines, tanks, and bombers ultimately meant nothing if the lives of the hostages were to be saved. In this atmosphere, the United States welcomed the threat to Iran by the secularist, anticommunist Saddam Hussein regime in neighboring Iraq.

Having experienced fear of cultural upheaval, disillusionment with government and with politicians, and frustrations over economic and societal crises since the mid-1960s, by the end of the 1970s America was poised for the resurgence of conservatism.

BUILDING VOCABULARY

Listed below are important words and terms that you need to know to get the most out of Chapter 31. They are listed in the order in which they occur in the chapter. After carefully looking through the list, (1) underline the words with which you are totally unfamiliar, (2) put a question mark by those words of which you are unsure, and (3) leave the rest alone.

As you begin to read the chapter, when you come to any of the words you've put question marks beside or underlined (1) slow your reading; (2) focus on the word and on its context in the sentence you're reading; (3) if you can understand the meaning of the word from its context in the sentence or passage in which it is used, go on with your reading; (4) if it's a word that you've underlined or a word that you can't understand from its context in the sentence or passage, look it up in a dictionary and write down the definition that best applies to the context in which the word is used.

Definitions

incontrovertible _____

surreptitiously _____

schism _____

diffuse _____

squalid _____

pervasive _____

pejorative _____

coherent _____

precipitous _____

quash _____

venerable _____

volatile _____

tenacity _____

eunuch _____

sordid _____

astute _____

abate _____

malaise _____

pinnacle _____

reverberate _____

tenet _____

inordinate _____

tenacious _____

presage _____

languish _____

assuage _____

Difficult-to-Spell Names and Terms from Reading and Lecture

IDENTIFICATION AND SIGNIFICANCE

After studying Chapter 31 of A *People and a Nation*, you should be able to identify fully *and* explain the historical significance of each item listed below.

- Identify each item in the space provided. Give an explanation or description of the item. Answer the questions *who, what, where,* and *when.*

- Explain the historical significance of each item in the space provided. Establish the historical context in which the item exists. Establish the item as the result of or as the cause of other factors existing in the society under study. Answer this question: *What were the political, social, economic, and/or cultural consequences of this item?*

1.   the Pentagon Papers
     a.   Identification

     b.   Significance

2.   identity politics
     a.   Identification

     b.   Significance

3.   African American cultural nationalism
     a.   Identification

     b.   Significance

4.   Cesar Chávez and Dolores Huerta
     a.   Identification

     b.   Significance

5.   Reies Tijerina and Rudolfo "Corky" González
     a.   Identification

     b.   Significance

6. the Chicano movement
    a. Identification

    b. Significance

7. 1969 seizure of Alcatraz Island
    a. Identification

    b. Significance

8. American Indian activism
    a. Identification

    b. Significance

9. Indian Self-Determination and Education Assistance Act
    a. Identification

    b. Significance

10. affirmative action
    a. Identification

    b. Significance

11. the "Philadelphia Plan"

    a. Identification

    b. Significance

12. *The Feminine Mystique*

    a. Identification

    b. Significance

13. the National Organization for Women

    a. Identification

    b. Significance

14. radical feminism

    a. Identification

    b. Significance

15. the Equal Rights Amendment

    a. Identification

    b. Significance

16. Title IX of the Higher Education Act
    a. Identification

    b. Significance

17. *Our Bodies, Ourselves*
    a. Identification

    b. Significance

18. *Roe v. Wade*
    a. Identification

    b. Significance

19. Phyllis Schlafly
    a. Identification

    b. Significance

20. the gay liberation movement
    a. Identification

    b. Significance

21. Vietnamization

    a. Identification

    b. Significance

22. the invasion of Cambodia

    a. Identification

    b. Significance

23. Kent State and Jackson State

    a. Identification

    b. Significance

24. fragging

    a. Identification

    b. Significance

25. the My Lai massacre

    a. Identification

    b. Significance

26.   the Christmas bombing

    a.   Identification

    b.   Significance

27.   the Vietnam cease-fire agreement

    a.   Identification

    b.   Significance

28.   the fall of Saigon

    a.   Identification

    b.   Significance

29.   the "boat people"

    a.   Identification

    b.   Significance

30.   Vietnam syndrome

    a.   Identification

    b.   Significance

31. the War Powers Act of 1973

    a.   Identification

    b.   Significance

32. post-traumatic stress disorder

    a.   Identification

    b.   Significance

33. Henry Kissinger

    a.   Identification

    b.   Significance

34. the Nixon Doctrine

    a.   Identification

    b.   Significance

35. détente

    a.   Identification

    b.   Significance

36. Nixon's China trip

    a. Identification

    b. Significance

37. the Six Day War

    a. Identification

    b. Significance

38. the Palestinian Liberation Organization (PLO)

    a. Identification

    b. Significance

39. the 1973 Middle East war

    a. Identification

    b. Significance

40. the OPEC oil embargo

    a. Identification

    b. Significance

41. Salvador Allende

a. Identification

b. Significance

42. Nixon's Africa policy

a. Identification

b. Significance

43. Nixon's goal of devolution

a. Identification

b. Significance

44. Nixon's southern strategy

a. Identification

b. Significance

45. George McGovern

a. Identification

b. Significance

46. the break-in at the Democratic National Committee's offices

   a. Identification

   b. Significance

47. CREEP

   a. Identification

   b. Significance

48. the Plumbers

   a. Identification

   b. Significance

49. the Watergate cover-up and investigation

   a. Identification

   b. Significance

50. Carl Bernstein and Bob Woodward

   a. Identification

   b. Significance

51. the White House tapes

    a. Identification

    b. Significance

52. Spiro Agnew's resignation

    a. Identification

    b. Significance

53. Gerald R. Ford

    a. Identification

    b. Significance

54. the 1973 impeachment hearings of the House Judiciary Committee

    a. Identification

    b. Significance

55. Nixon's resignation

    a. Identification

    b. Significance

56. the 1974 Budget and Impoundment Control Act

    a. Identification

    b. Significance

57. the pardon of Richard Nixon

    a. Identification

    b. Significance

58. Jimmy Carter

    a. Identification

    b. Significance

59. the environmental "superfund"

    a. Identification

    b. Significance

60. stagflation

    a. Identification

    b. Significance

61. the 1970s decline in productivity

    a. Identification

    b. Significance

62. the energy crisis of the 1970s

    a. Identification

    b. Significance

63. the deindustrialization of the American economy

    a. Identification

    b. Significance

64. population shift to the Sunbelt

    a. Identification

    b. Significance

65. the tax revolt movement

    a. Identification

    b. Significance

66.   California's Proposition 13

    a.   Identification

    b.   Significance

67.   the 1970s rise in consumer debt

    a.   Identification

    b.   Significance

68.   1970s environmentalism

    a.   Identification

    b.   Significance

69.   Earth Day

    a.   Identification

    b.   Significance

70.   Neil Armstrong

    a.   Identification

    b.   Significance

71. the 1970s growth of evangelical and fundamentalist Christianity

    a. Identification

    b. Significance

72. the New Age movement

    a. Identification

    b. Significance

73. the "therapeutic" culture

    a. Identification

    b. Significance

74. the sexual revolution of the 1970s

    a. Identification

    b. Significance

75. the 1970s idea of "diversity"

    a. Identification

    b. Significance

76.   *Bakke v. University of California*

    a.   Identification

    b.   Significance

77.   Zbigniew Brzezinski versus Cyrus Vance

    a.   Identification

    b.   Significance

78.   the Panama Canal Treaties of 1977

    a.   Identification

    b.   Significance

79.   the Camp David Accords

    a.   Identification

    b.   Significance

80.   the Soviet invasion of Afghanistan

    a.   Identification

    b.   Significance

81. the Carter Doctrine
    a. Identification

    b. Significance

82. the Iranian hostage crisis
    a. Identification

    b. Significance

83. the Iranian rescue mission
    a. Identification

    b. Significance

84. Saddam Hussein
    a. Identification

    b. Significance

85. the Iran-Iraq War
    a. Identification

    b. Significance

86.   Carter's human-rights policy

    a.   Identification

    b.   Significance

ORGANIZING, REVIEWING, AND USING INFORMATION

Chart A

Presidents and the Domestic Scene			
	Nixon	**Ford**	**Carter**
Character of Election(s)—campaign styles, closeness, etc.			
Relations with Congress			
Major Features of Economy			
Efforts To Protect or Improve Domestic Economy			
Taxes, Spending, and Deficits			
Relations with Big Business, Labor, and the American Worker			
Supreme Court Appointments and Rulings			
Scandals			

Chart B

Presidents and the International Arena			
	Nixon	**Ford**	**Carter**
Basic View of Foreign Affairs, Doctrines Enunciated			
International Agreements			
View of American Power and How It Should Be Used			
Intervention Abroad (willingness, instances, types)			
Cold War and American Relations with Soviet Union and China			
Relations with Middle Eastern Nations and the Islamic World			
Relations with Nations of Latin America			
Military Spending and Military Readiness			
Other (revolutions, dictators, human rights abroad, etc.)			

Chart C

Cultural Turmoil in the 1970s					
	Changes in Roles and Attitudes	Movements and Activism	Legislative and Judicial Actions	Measurement of Successes	Impact
Religious Groups					
Family					
Sex and Sexuality					
Diversity					
Rights and Opportunities					

IDEAS AND DETAILS

Objective 1

1. Like the younger generation of African Americans, the younger generation of Mexican American and American Indian activists in the late 1960s and early 1970s emphasized

    a. local rather than national issues.
    b. assimilation and cooperation with white society.
    c. reparations for past wrongs rather than funding for current programs.
    d. their own distinct cultures and histories.

Objective 2

2. Rather than the EEOC having to prove an employer's intentional discrimination against an individual, some argued that it was possible to prove discrimination by

    a. relying on expert witnesses.
    b. using competency tests as evidence of a job applicant's suitability for employment or an employee's suitability for promotion.
    c. using statistics on the relative number of minorities hired or promoted by an employer.
    d. enlisting the aid of civil rights organizations.

Objective 3

3. In the late 1960s, radical feminists differed from the members of the National Organization for Women in which of the following ways?

    a. Radical feminists opposed the gay rights movement; the members of NOW strongly supported gay liberation.
    b. Radical feminists practiced direct action and personal politics; NOW was a traditional lobbying group.
    c. Radical feminists were concerned exclusively with political issues; NOW members were concerned only with social and economic issues.
    d. The radical feminist movement repudiated the work of Betty Friedan; NOW agreed fully with Friedan's ideas.

Objective 4

4. Antifeminist forces were able to prevent ratification of the Equal Rights Amendment by

    a. successfully organizing a nationwide strike of working women.
    b. persuading the Senate to rescind its approval of the amendment.
    c. publishing a study that proved gender-based discrimination to be nonexistent in the United States.
    d. frightening people with false claims about what would happen if it were ratified.

Objective 5

5. The Stonewall riot

    a. marked the beginning of the gay rights movement.
    b. occurred in Atlantic City when radical feminists disrupted the 1968 Miss America contest.
    c. was the result of overreaction by the Chicago police to street demonstrations at the Democratic national convention.
    d. was an expression of black rage over the assassination of Martin Luther King.

Objective 6

6.   Under the Nixon-Kissinger policy of "Vietnamization,"

    a.   stability slowly returned to Indochina as the Vietnam War de-escalated.

    b.   withdrawal of American troops was accompanied by increased bombing of the North and the invasion of Cambodia.

    c.   the South Vietnamese army proved that it was an effective fighting force.

    d.   a coalition government was established in Hanoi and the war quickly drew to a close.

Objective 6

7.   In the aftermath of the Vietnam War, Americans

    a.   disagreed over the lessons to be drawn from the experience.

    b.   withdrew from the United Nations.

    c.   vowed to support Third World revolutions.

    d.   agreed to increase the powers of the president in foreign policy.

Objectives 6, 7, and 11

8.   The War Powers Act required the president to

    a.   withdraw troops from any foreign assignment after ten days unless Congress specifically authorized otherwise.

    b.   obtain congressional approval in the commitment of U.S. forces to combat action lasting more than sixty days.

    c.   get approval from Congress before sending American troops to foreign territory.

    d.   get a declaration of war from Congress before sending American soldiers into a foreign war.

Objective 7

9.   Which of the following correctly states a major feature of President Nixon's foreign policy?

    a.   Less military commitment to allies; more—but guarded—cooperation with the Soviet Union

    b.   Greater military commitment to allies; more military pressure on the Soviet Union

    c.   Fewer diplomatic concessions to China; fewer diplomatic concessions to the Soviet Union

    d.   Stronger economic and diplomatic ties in Latin America and Africa; weaker economic and diplomatic ties in Europe and Asia

Objective 7

10.   In 1975 Secretary of State Kissinger persuaded Israel and Egypt to accept which of the following?

    a.   An autonomous Palestinian state under United Nations protection

    b.   An end to hostilities and Egyptian recognition of Israel's existence as a nation

    c.   Egyptian withdrawal from Jerusalem and Israeli withdrawal from the West Bank

    d.   A United Nations peacekeeping force in the Sinai

Objectives 10 and 11

11.   As a result of its impeachment hearings, the House Judiciary Committee

    a.   voted in favor of President Nixon's impeachment on three of five counts.

    b.   declared President Nixon to be guilty of tax fraud.

    c.   chose to make no recommendation concerning the impeachment of the president.

    d.   declared President Nixon to be innocent of all charges of wrongdoing.

Objectives 13 and 14

12. As a result of the dramatic increase in energy prices in the early 1970s,

    a.   the nationwide unemployment rate reached 25 percent.
    b.   the Nixon administration deregulated the airline and trucking industries.
    c.   automobile and related industries suffered a lingering recession.
    d.   President Nixon authorized the release of millions of barrels of oil from the nation's strategic petroleum reserve.

Objectives 13 and 14

13. As a result of the slowing of growth in productivity during the 1970s,

    a.   workers realized they could no longer expect the wage increases they had enjoyed during the 1960s.
    b.   interest rates declined.
    c.   American products became less competitive in the global marketplace.
    d.   business investments increased.

Objective 14

14. Which of the following was a reason for the fiscal problems of northern and midwestern cities such as New York and Cleveland in the 1970s?

    a.   The Nixon and Ford administrations gradually eliminated federal revenue-sharing programs.
    b.   The tax base of such cities shrank because of the population shift to the Sunbelt and the continued flight of the middle class to the suburbs..
    c.   Such cities were financially overburdened by new federal laws that established a minimum salary level for urban sanitation workers.
    d.   The annexation policies of such cities meant they had to bear the expense of expanding city services to newly annexed areas.

Objective 16

15. The Carter Doctrine proclaimed that the United States would intervene against Soviet aggression in

    a.   the Persian Gulf.
    b.   the Mediterranean Basin.
    c.   the Indian subcontinent.
    d.   Africa.

ESSAY QUESTIONS

Objective 1

1. Discuss the use of identity politics and cultural nationalism by African Americans, Mexican Americans, and American Indians in their attempt to deal with the problems they experienced in American society during the 1970s. How successful were these groups in achieving their goals?

Objective 3

2. Examine the feminist movement of the 1960s and 1970s and discuss its accomplishments and failures.

Objective 3

3.   Explain the emergence of radical feminism, and discuss its impact on American society in the late 1960s and early 1970s.

Objective 4

4.   Explain the emergence and evaluate the goals of the antifeminist movement.

Objective 6

5.   Examine the course of the Vietnam War under President Nixon. To what extent did President Nixon live up to his 1968 campaign pledge to end the war?

Objective 6

6.   Discuss the domestic debate over the meaning of the American experience in Vietnam.

Objective 7

7.   Explain how events in the Middle East jeopardized the Nixon-Kissinger strategy of maintaining stability among the great powers, and discuss the administration's handling of the Arab-Israeli conflict.

Objectives 10 and 11

8.   Discuss the Watergate scandal as a constitutional crisis, examine President Richard Nixon's role in the scandal, and explain the House Judiciary Committee's decision concerning the articles of impeachment against the President.

Objective 14

9.   Discuss the causes and consequences of America's economic crisis during the 1970s, and explain and assess the handling of that crisis by America's leaders.

Objective 16

10.   Discuss President Carter's foreign policy objectives, and explain his accomplishments and failures in attempting to achieve those objectives.

MAP EXERCISE

Refer to the map "The Middle East" in Chapter 33 to complete this exercise. You may also find it helpful to refer to a historical atlas. You will need three pens of different colors to complete this exercise. (Highlight pens may be used.)

Label each of the following on the map of the Middle East that follows.

Countries	Bodies of Water	Territories	Capital Cities
Egypt	Gulf of Aqaba	Gaza Strip	Amman
Iran	Gulf of Suez	Golan Heights	Beirut
Iraq	Jordan River	Sinai Peninsula	Baghdad
Israel	Mediterranean Sea	West Bank	Cairo
Jordan	Persian Gulf		Damascus
Lebanon	Red Sea		Jerusalem
Saudi Arabia	Sea of Galilee		Riyadh
Syria	Suez Canal		Tehran

Color the map as follows:

- Use one color to denote the Jewish state after the partition of Palestine, 1947

- Use a second color to denote the territory Israel gained as a result of the War of 1948–1949

- Use a third color to denote the territory controlled by Israel after the Six-Day War, 1967

- Place backward slashes (\\\\\) in the Sinai Peninsula to denote that by the Egyptian-Israeli Agreements of 1975 and 1979 Israel withdrew from the Sinai in 1982.

  Do not put backward slashes in the area known as the Gaza Strip. That area was not returned to Egypt when Israel withdrew from the Sinai.

- Place forward slashes (/////) in the Golan Heights to denote that Israel annexed this area in 1981.

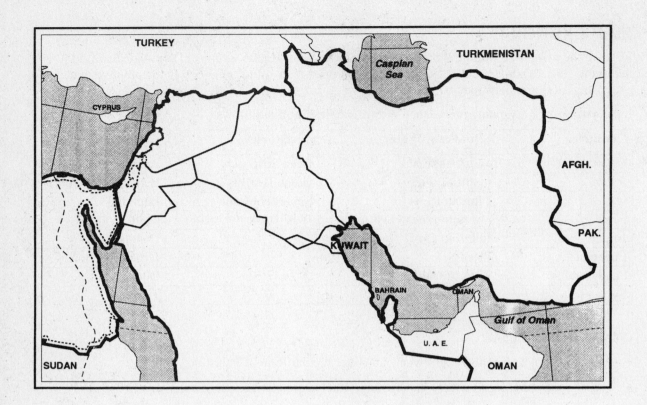

ANSWERS

Multiple-Choice Questions

1. d. Correct. In the late 1960s and early 1970s, the younger generation of Mexican American and American Indian activists, like their African American counterparts, demanded recognition of their distinct cultures and histories. This was part of the "identity politics" of the time and also fostered the concept that the diversity of cultures within the broader American culture was one of the major strengths of American society. See page 861.

    a. No. The younger generation of minority activists in the late 1960s and early 1970s did emphasize the idea that the government should base policy on the needs of identity-based groups rather than the needs of individuals. However, that is not to say that they emphasized local issues rather than national issues. See page 861.

    b. No. The younger generation of minority activists in the late 1960s and early 1970s often emphasized separatism over assimilation. See page 861.

    c. No. The younger generation of minority activists in the late 1960s and early 1970s did not generally emphasize or demand reparations for past wrongs over funding for current programs. See page 861.

2. c. Correct. Within the EEOC there was a shift in emphasis from an individual, case-by-case approach to ending discrimination in employment to an emphasis on group outcomes. Therefore, some people argued that, by looking at an employer's pattern in hiring or promoting minorities, one could establish whether or not there was a discriminatory pattern. See page 864.

    a. No. The argument that expert witnesses could be used to prove the discriminatory practices of an employer's hiring and promotion practices was not put forward. See page 864.

    b. No. The use of competency tests to determine an individual's suitability for employment or promotion and, therefore, to determine whether or not an employer had engaged in intentional discrimination was not an argument that was put forward. See page 864.

    d. No. It was not argued that civil rights organizations could be enlisted to prove whether or not an employer had engaged in discriminatory employment practices. See page 864.

3. b. Correct. Radical feminists became involved in direct action, such as the 1968 protest at the Miss America Pageant, to achieve their goals, while NOW concentrated on lobbying for legislation and testing laws through the courts. See page 865.

    a. No. In the late 1960s radical feminists were more likely to support the gay rights movement than were members of NOW. See page 865.

    c. No. Radical feminists were concerned with the political, social, and economic inequality of women. They also challenged women's legal inequality and sex-role stereotyping. See page 865.

    d. No. Although Friedan inspired the founding of NOW, she was not repudiated by the radical feminists. See page 865.

4.   d.   Correct. Antifeminist forces used scare tactics, for the most part, as part of an emotional campaign against ratification of the Equal Rights Amendment. This had the desired effect, and the ERA fell three states short of ratification. See pages 866–867.

a.   No. A nationwide strike by working women was not a tactic employed by the antifeminist forces in their efforts to prevent ratification of the Equal Rights Amendment. See pages 866–867.

b.   No. The Senate did not rescind its approval of this amendment. See pages 866–867.

c.   No. Antifeminist leaders such as Phyllis Schlafly refused to acknowledge the existence of gender-based discrimination, but no such study was ever conducted and the facts do not support such a conclusion. See pages 866–867.

5.   a.   Correct. The riot that erupted between police and the gay patrons of the Stonewall Inn in New York City is considered to be the beginning of the gay rights movement. See page 867.

b.   No. The Stonewall riot did not occur in Atlantic City and was not undertaken by radical feminists. See page 867.

c.   No. The Stonewall riot occurred in New York City and was not associated with the 1968 Democratic Convention in Chicago. See page 867.

d.   No. The Stonewall riot was not related to King's assassination. See page 867.

6.   b.   Correct. The policy of Vietnamization brought, among other things, a widening of the war into Cambodia, increased bombing of North Vietnam, and the mining of Haiphong harbor. See pages 867–868.

a.   No. Nixon's policy of Vietnamization was accompanied by other policies that further destabilized Indochina. See pages 867–868.

c.   No. The South Vietnamese army proved itself a rather ineffective fighting force, incapable of defending the South. See pages 867–868.

d.   No. Vietnamization did not bring about a coalition government, and the war did not quickly draw to a close. See pages 867–868.

7.   a.   Correct. Some Americans pointed to the war as an example of the softening of American resolve against communism; others questioned, among other things, the containment doctrine. See pages 869–870.

b.   No. The United States did not withdraw from the United Nations in the aftermath of the Vietnam War. See pages 869–870.

c.   No. In fact, many leaders talked of a Vietnam syndrome—a mood that would prevent the United States from becoming involved in any foreign entanglements. See pages 869–870.

d.   No. Some Americans blamed the Vietnam experience on the "imperial presidency" and insisted that Congress retake the foreign policy power it had relinquished to the executive branch. See pages 869–870.

8.   b.   Correct. In an effort to put restrictions on the president's war-making powers, the act required the chief executive to withdraw troops after sixty days (as opposed to ten days) unless Congress authorized otherwise. The act also required the president to consult with Congress "in every possible instance" before sending troops into foreign wars. See page 870.

     a.   No. The act did not put a ten-day limit on the commitment of U.S. troops to a "foreign assignment." See page 870.

     c.   No. The president, as commander-in-chief of the armed forces, still had the authority to respond to threats to national security and send troops to foreign territory. See page 870.

     d.   No. The president, as commander-in-chief of the armed forces, still had the authority to respond to threats to national security and send troops into a foreign war without getting a declaration of war from Congress. See page 870.

9.   a.   Correct. In the Nixon Doctrine, President Nixon stated that America's Asian allies would, in the future, have to provide for their own defense. This was an acknowledgment by the President of the limits of American power. Furthermore, another cornerstone of President Nixon's foreign policy was détente, which called for guarded cooperation with the Soviet Union through negotiations. See page 871.

     b.   No. Nixon did not make a greater military commitment to America's allies and put more military pressure on the Soviet Union, a feature of his foreign policy. See page 871.

     c.   No. President Nixon's foreign policy did not feature the policy of fewer diplomatic concessions to the People's Republic of China and the Soviet Union. See page 871.

     d.   No. Nixon was committed to the status quo in both Latin America and Africa and to a strengthening of economic ties with Europe and Asia. See page 871.

10.   d.   Correct. Kissinger, acting as mediator by shuttling back and forth between Egyptian and Israeli officials, obtained an agreement between the two nations establishing a United Nations peacekeeping force in the Sinai. See page 872.

     a.   No. Kissinger's "shuttle diplomacy" did not lead to the creation of a Palestinian state. See page 872.

     b.   No. In spite of Kissinger's "shuttle diplomacy," Egypt continued to refuse to recognize Israel's right to exist. See page 872.

     c.   No. Egyptian troops were not in Jerusalem and the Israelis did not withdraw from the West Bank. See page 872.

11.   a.   Correct. The committee voted for impeachment on three counts: obstruction of justice, defiance of a congressional subpoena, and abuse of power through the improper use of the CIA, FBI, and IRS. See page 875.

     b.   No. The article of impeachment accusing Nixon of demeaning the office of the presidency by misconduct of his personal financial affairs was voted down by a vote of 26 to 12. Furthermore, one cannot be declared guilty as the result of impeachment hearings. See page 875.

     c.   No. The committee voted on the articles of impeachment brought against Nixon and made a recommendation to the full House. See page 875.

     d.   No. The committee held hearings to determine if there was just cause to refer articles of impeachment to the full House, not to determine Nixon's guilt or innocence. See page 875.

12.   c.   Correct. The 350 percent increase in oil prices from January 1973 to January 1974 brought double-digit inflation, slowed overall economic growth, and led to a lingering recession in the automobile and related industries. See page 878.

a.   No. Although unemployment climbed to 8.5 percent in 1975, it never reached the level of 25 percent. See page 878.

b.   No. The airline and trucking industries were deregulated during the Carter administration, not the Nixon administration. See page 878.

d.   No. The strategic petroleum reserve was not established until 1975 under President Ford. See page 878.

13.   c.   Correct. The slow growth in productivity was one reason that American goods cost more than comparable foreign goods. High prices made American goods less competitive in foreign markets. See page 878.

a.   No. Despite the slow growth in productivity, many workers continued to expect wage increases that would give them more purchasing power each year. See page 878.

b.   No. The slow growth in productivity did not lead to a decline in interest rates. See page 878.

d.   No. The slow growth in productivity did not cause an increase in business investments. See page 878.

14.   b.   Correct. As the population shifted from the north and midwest to the Sunbelt and as middle-class taxpayers continued their flight to the suburbs, cities such as New York and Cleveland suffered severe fiscal problems. See pages 879–880.

a.   No. Nixon promoted revenue-sharing programs, and those programs continued during the Ford administration. See pages 879–880.

c.   No There were no such federal laws. See pages 879–880.

d.   No. The annexation policies of cities such as New York and Cleveland did not cause the fiscal crisis of these cities in the 1970s. See pages 879–880.

15.   a.   Correct. In reaction to the Soviet invasion of Afghanistan, the fall of the Shah's government in Iran to the Khomeini regime, and the Iranian hostage crisis, President Carter announced in January 1980 that the United States would view any attempt by an outside force to gain control of the Persian Gulf region as an assault on the vital interests of the United States, and that such an assault would be repelled by military force if necessary. See page 884.

b.   No. The Carter Doctrine was not directed toward American interests in the Mediterranean Basin. See page 884.

c.   No. The Carter Doctrine was not directed toward the Indian subcontinent. See page 884.

d.   No. The Carter Doctrine was not directed toward Africa. See page 884.

CHAPTER 32

Conservatism Revived, 1980–1992

LEARNING OBJECTIVES

After you have studied Chapter 32 in your textbook and worked through this study guide chapter, you should be able to:

1. Examine the emergence, characteristics, goals, and accomplishments of the new conservative coalition, and discuss the impact of this coalition on the election of 1980.

2. Discuss Ronald Reagan's personal and political background, and explain his political, social, and economic views.

3. Examine the issues and personalities and explain the outcome of the 1980 presidential election.

4. Examine Ronald Reagan's economic policies in relation to federal spending, federal income taxes, organized labor, and federal environmental, health, and safety regulations; explain Congress's reaction to these policies; and assess the impact of these policies on the United States.

5. Discuss the causes and consequences of the 1981–1983 economic recession.

6. Examine the issues and personalities and explain the outcome of the 1984 presidential election.

7. Examine the reasons for, the extent of, and the effects of poverty in America during the 1980s, and discuss the characteristics of the poor.

8. Discuss the expansion of the policy of deregulation during the Reagan administration, and explain the consequences of this expansion.

9. Examine, evaluate, and discuss the consequences of the defense and foreign policy views, goals, and actions of the Reagan administration.

10. Discuss the activities that constituted the Iran-contra scandal, and explain the scandal's impact on the presidency of Ronald Reagan.

11. Examine the forces that caused increased polarization within American society during the 1980s.

12. Discuss the emergence of the religious right as a force in American society and American politics; explain the characteristics and goals of this group; and examine the "culture wars" between the religious right and its opponents.

13. Discuss the problems that nonwhites, immigrants, and women faced in American society during the 1970s and 1980s; explain their approaches to those problems; and discuss the extent to which they were successful in achieving their goals.

14. Discuss the drug epidemic and the AIDS epidemic; explain their impact on the American people and American society; and assess the government's response to the threats posed by these epidemics.

15. Examine the issues and personalities and explain the outcome of the 1988 presidential election.

16. Discuss George Bush's personal and political background; examine the domestic issues and political problems that faced the Bush administration; and explain and evaluate the administration's actions concerning those issues and problems.

17. Examine, evaluate, and discuss the consequences of the defense and foreign policy views, goals, and actions of the George H. W. Bush administration.

18. Discuss the multiplicity of factors that led to the collapse of the Soviet empire in Eastern Europe, the disintegration of the Soviet Union, and the reunification of Germany.

19. Explain the reasons for the end of the Cold War, and discuss the war's legacy for the United States, the former Soviet Union, and the world community of nations.

20. Discuss the causes and consequences of the 1991 Persian Gulf War.

21. Discuss the nomination of Clarence Thomas to the Supreme Court; explain the issues addressed by the Senate Judiciary Committee in its confirmation hearings; and discuss the reaction of the American people to those hearings.

THEMATIC GUIDE

As the American people became more and more deeply troubled and frightened by political, social, and economic changes and forces over which they and their government seemed to have little control, they became more distrustful both of government and of those groups that continued to advocate change within society. This conservative mood was buttressed by the uniting of political and economic conservatives of the "old right" with supporters of the tax-revolt movement and with evangelical Christians of the "new right." The channeling of these forces into a new conservative coalition, plus a distrust of government born of a generation of chaos produced America's "turn to the right" in 1980 and led to Ronald Reagan's victory in the presidential election of that year.

With widespread support from the American people, President Ronald Reagan, the standard-bearer of a new conservative coalition and a strong advocate of supply-side economic theory, persuaded Congress to enact three major aspects of his conservative agenda: (1) deep spending cuts in social and health programs; (2) a five-year, $750 billion tax cut that primarily benefited the wealthy; and (3) a dramatic increase in defense spending. In addition, out of the belief that government regulations reduced business profits and slowed economic growth, the Reagan administration launched an attack against federal environmental, health, and safety regulations. Although the stated intent of "Reaganomics" was the reduction of the federal debt, the federal deficit increased dramatically during the Reagan-Bush years and made the United States the world's largest debtor nation.

Although inflation and interest rates declined during Reagan's first two years in office, these successes resulted from the Federal Reserve Board's policies, a decline in oil prices, which had a ripple effect throughout the economy, and a massive recession lasting from mid-1981 to late 1983. The recession affected both industrial and agricultural workers; and, in spite of an economic recovery that began in 1984, poverty increased to pre-Great Society levels and the gap widened between rich and poor. However, improved economic conditions worked to Reagan's advantage in the 1984 presidential election. Using positive slogans and themes that depicted a renewed, prosperous, and strengthened America, Reagan won a landslide victory over Walter Mondale, his Democratic opponent.

Deregulation, begun during the Carter administration, expanded under President Reagan. With less government oversight of the nation's Savings and Loans institutions, high-risk investments became the order of the day, setting the stage for the industry's collapse. High-risk investments in the "junk-bond" industry were a factor in the merger mania of the decade, characterized by corporate downsizing, debt-burdened corporations, and the further consolidation of sectors of the economy.

After examining the social and economic policies of the Reagan years, the authors, in "Reagan and the World," turn to an examination of foreign policy. Ronald Reagan's election in 1980 marked a return to foreign-policy themes rooted in America's past and reminiscent of the early days of the Cold War. As defense spending increased, the questioning of U.S. intervention in Third World nations, so apparent in the immediate aftermath of the Vietnam disaster, was absent in the Reagan administration. Reagan, simplistically blaming unrest in the world on the Soviets, issued the Reagan Doctrine in which he pledged the support of the American government to anticommunist movements battling the Soviets or Soviet-backed governments. Application of the doctrine in Afghanistan turned the tide against Soviet forces. However, application of the Reagan Doctrine in the Caribbean and Central America led to alliances with antirevolutionary but unrepresentative regimes in El Salvador and Nicaragua. In fact, Reagan's policies toward El Salvador and Nicaragua recall phrases used to describe American policy in previous eras; and Reagan's desire for victory rather than negotiation brings to mind the early years of the Kennedy administration. However, since the Kennedy years the American people had been through the traumas of Vietnam and Watergate, and the power of Congress, relative to that of the president, had increased. Therefore, Congress in the mid-1980s was much more willing to play an active role in foreign policy decisions than it had been in the 1960s. But Congress, reflecting the debate among the American people over the nation's policy toward Nicaragua, vacillated between ending aid to the contras in mid-1984 and again extending aid in 1986. During the period when aid was prohibited, the executive branch of the government, through the National Security Council and the Central Intelligence Agency, acted to circumvent the will of Congress. These actions came to light in 1986 in the Iran-contra scandal, a scandal that deeply wounded Ronald Reagan's ability to lead during his last two years in office.

From this discussion of the Iran-contra scandal, the authors turn their attention to continuing problems in the Middle East, the problem of terrorism against United States citizens and property, America's ill-fated 1983 mission in Lebanon, and to a discussion of Congress's ability to force the Reagan administration to alter its policy of "constructive engagement" toward South Africa.

In 1985 Mikhail Gorbachev entered the world stage as the new leader of the Soviet Union. Perhaps President Reagan was right when he said that he was "dropped into a grand historical moment," because under Gorbachev's leadership the Soviet Union undertook an ambitious domestic reform program and Soviet foreign policy underwent significant changes. These dramatic changes helped reduce international tensions and, in 1987, led to a Soviet-American agreement to eliminate intermediate-range nuclear missiles in Europe.

As tensions between the world's two superpowers subsided, the tensions within American society continued. The crises of the 1960s and 1970s and the social and cultural changes resulting from those crises were factors that led to the resurgence of fundamentalist Christianity during the 1980s. Exemplified in the Moral Majority and the Christian Coalition, the "new right" began a multi-front assault against the secular culture of the American majority. Those opposed to this assault found expression in People for the American Way and warned that the "new right" preached a doctrine of intolerance and threatened basic American freedoms. Thus began the "culture wars" of the 1980s.

The increase in poverty that accompanied the stagnant economy of the 1970s and the recession of the early 1980s occurred most often among nonwhites, children, and female heads of households. While racism continued to play a role in the disproportionate number of nonwhites mired in poverty, the reality of the changing job structure meant that occupational opportunities, especially for unskilled workers, were severely limited. As the gap widened between rich and poor, the crack epidemic, the AIDS epidemic, an increase in violent crime, and urban despair led to even more polarization and tension within pluralistic America. In addition, as waves of new Latin American and Asian immigrants crowded into inner-city ethnic neighborhoods and sought economic opportunities, anti-immigrant sentiment and nativist violence increased.

In 1988 George Herbert Walker Bush rode into the presidency on the back of peace and prosperity. During his first year as president, relations between the United States and the People's Republic of China cooled as a result of the Tiananmen Square massacre. Although repression was the order of the day in China, that was not true elsewhere. Not only did the democratization of South Africa transform that society, but the collapse of communism in Eastern Europe, the reunification of Germany, the disintegration of the Soviet Union, and Mikhail Gorbachev's fall from power signaled the end of the Cold War. After examining the factors responsible for this remarkable event and a look at the costs of the fifty-year contest, the authors turn to a discussion of the Bush administration's attempts to fashion a foreign policy applicable to the post-Cold War world.

Despite the end of the Cold War and an end to civil strife in Nicaragua, El Salvador, and Guatemala, United States relations with the Third World remained turbulent, as can be seen in the discussion of the U.S. invasion of Panama and the Persian Gulf War. A theme that runs through the discussion of the economic and political problems of the Third World is the contribution of the United States to problems that led to turmoil. From the U.S.-financed contra war in Nicaragua to the extension of U.S. aid to the drug-trafficking dictator of Panama, Manuel Noriega, to assistance to Iraq in its war against Iran, the story is much the same. Often in the name of "containment" of Communism and always in the name of national security, United States military aid often engendered the very instability the United States sought to prevent.

Nowhere was this clearer than in Panama and Iraq, two areas in which the United States ultimately used military force to deal with the excesses of dictators it had previously supported. Although Manuel Noriega was removed from power in Panama, the United States had few resources to help rebuild the devastated country. And although Iraq was decisively and humiliatingly defeated in the Persian Gulf War, its dictator Saddam Hussein remained in power and continued to repress the peoples of his war-ravaged nation.

Even though President Bush presented himself as the heir of his conservative predecessor, Ronald Reagan, in deed and action he seemed indecisive and out of touch. Although he most certainly wanted to *be* president, he seldom seemed to know what he wanted to achieve *as* president. Therefore, rather than leading in a decisive and positive direction, he engaged in crisis management as he attempted to maintain the status quo. Wanting an unchanging America over which he could be caretaker, President Bush instead inherited an America in which economic and social problems abounded. Although the American people had been told, and many believed, that government was the problem, a significant number still expected government to respond with meaningful solutions to the real national problems that existed. In this America George Bush's aversion to active government made him seem out of place and out of step.

After the Persian Gulf War, the U.S. economy, already stagnant, drifted into recession. Despite rising unemployment, President Bush remained passive. His ineffectual response to the recession caused Bush's approval rating to fall. As criticism of the administration mounted, the Clarence Thomas–Anita Hill confrontation galvanized many Americans, especially women, and increased opposition to the Republican party as the country entered the election year of 1992.

BUILDING VOCABULARY

Listed below are important words and terms that you need to know to get the most out of Chapter 32. They are listed in the order in which they occur in the chapter. After carefully looking through the list, (1) underline the words with which you are totally unfamiliar, (2) put a question mark by those words of which you are unsure, and (3) leave the rest alone.

As you begin to read the chapter, when you come to any of the words you've put question marks beside or underlined (1) slow your reading; (2) focus on the word and on its context in the sentence you're reading; (3) if you can understand the meaning of the word from its context in the sentence or passage in which it is used, go on with your reading; (4) if it's a word that you've underlined or a word that you can't understand from its context in the sentence or passage, look it up in a dictionary and write down the definition that best applies to the context in which the word is used.

Definitions

ostentation _____

poignant _____

amicable _____

catapult _____

miniscule _____

malevolent _____

dissident _____

clandestine _____

divest _____

penchant _____

condescension _____

resonate _____

gentrify _____

polarize _____

sojourner _____

amnesty _____

scion _____

ascension _____

myriad _____

Difficult-to-Spell Names and Terms from Reading and Lecture

IDENTIFICATION AND SIGNIFICANCE

After studying Chapter 32 of A *People and a Nation*, you should be able to identify fully *and* explain the historical significance of each item listed below.

- Identify each item in the space provided. Give an explanation or description of the item. Answer the questions *who, what, where,* and *when.*

- Explain the historical significance of each item in the space provided. Establish the historical context in which the item exists. Establish the item as the result of or as the cause of other factors existing in the society under study. Answer this question: *What were the political, social, economic, and/or cultural consequences of this item?*

1. Ronald Reagan

    a. Identification

    b. Significance

2. the new conservative coalition of 1980

    a. Identification

    b. Significance

3. Reagan Democrats

    a. Identification

    b. Significance

4. Reagan's policies toward regulatory agencies

    a. Identification

    b. Significance

5. James Watt
   a. Identification

   b. Significance

6. organized labor in the 1980s
   a. Identification

   b. Significance

7. the New Right
   a. Identification

   b. Significance

8. Sandra Day O'Connor
   a. Identification

   b. Significance

9. *Bowers v. Hardwick*
   a. Identification

   b. Significance

10.   *Webster v. Reproductive Health Services*

    a.   Identification

    b.   Significance

11.   Reaganomics

    a.   Identification

    b.   Significance

12.   supply-side economics

    a.   Identification

    b.   Significance

13.   the 1981 tax cuts

    a.   Identification

    b.   Significance

14.   David Stockman

    a.   Identification

    b.   Significance

15. the recession of the early 1980s

   a. Identification

   b. Significance

16. Walter Mondale

   a. Identification

   b. Significance

17. Geraldine Ferraro

   a. Identification

   b. Significance

18. the 1984 presidential election

   a. Identification

   b. Significance

19. deregulation

   a. Identification

   b. Significance

20. the junk bond industry

    a. Identification

    b. Significance

21. insider trading scandals of the late 1980s

    a. Identification

    b. Significance

22. the 1981 tax cuts

    a. Identification

    b. Significance

23. the Reagan defense buildup

    a. Identification

    b. Significance

24. the Strategic Defense Initiative (SDI)

    a. Identification

    b. Significance

25. the Reagan Doctrine

    a. Identification

    b. Significance

26. Grenada and El Salvador

    a. Identification

    b. Significance

27. the contra war in Nicaragua

    a. Identification

    b. Significance

28. the Lebanese crisis of 1982–1983

    a. Identification

    b. Significance

29. intifadah

    a. Identification

    b. Significance

30. the policy of constructive engagement

    a. Identification

    b. Significance

31. Mikhail S. Gorbachev

    a. Identification

    b. Significance

32. perestroika and glasnost

    a. Identification

    b. Significance

33. the 1987 INF treaty

    a. Identification

    b. Significance

34. the religious right

    a. Identification

    b. Significance

35. the Moral Majority

   a. Identification

   b. Significance

36. People for the American Way

   a. Identification

   b. Significance

37. the culture wars

   a. Identification

   b. Significance

38. poverty in the 1980s

   a. Identification

   b. Significance

39. the "crack" epidemic

   a. Identification

   b. Significance

40. homelessness in the 1980s

    a. Identification

    b. Significance

41. the AIDS epidemic

    a. Identification

    b. Significance

42. the Year of the Yuppie

    a. Identification

    b. Significance

43. the "new immigrants" of the 1970s and 1980s

    a. Identification

    b. Significance

44. growth of the Latino population in the 1970s and 1980s

    a. Identification

    b. Significance

45.   the national "sanctuary movement"

    a.   Identification

    b.   Significance

46.   anti-immigrant sentiment of the 1980s

    a.   Identification

    b.   Significance

47.   the Immigration Reform and Control (Simpson-Rodino) Act

    a.   Identification

    b.   Significance

48.   George Herbert Walker Bush

    a.   Identification

    b.   Significance

49.   the 1988 presidential election

    a.   Identification

    b.   Significance

50.   the collapse of communism in Eastern Europe

    a.   Identification

    b.   Significance

51.   the Tiananmen Square Massacre

    a.   Identification

    b.   Significance

52.   F. W. DeKlerk and Nelson Mandela

    a.   Identification

    b.   Significance

53.   the disintegration of the Soviet Union

    a.   Identification

    b.   Significance

54.   General Manuel Antonio Noriega

    a.   Identification

    b.   Significance

55.   Saddam Hussein
   a.   Identification

   b.   Significance

56.   Operation Desert Storm
   a.   Identification

   b.   Significance

57.   Security Council resolutions 687 and 688
   a.   Identification

   b.   Significance

58.   the Americans with Disabilities Act
   a.   Identification

   b.   Significance

59.   the Clean Air Act
   a.   Identification

   b.   Significance

60. recession of 1991

    a. Identification

    b. Significance

61. Clarence Thomas

    a. Identification

    b. Significance

62. Anita Hill

    a. Identification

    b. Significance

ORGANIZING, REVIEWING, AND USING INFORMATION

Key Factors in an Evaluation of Presidents Reagan and Bush (George HW)			
	Reagan (two terms) (1981–1989)	Bush (George H.W.) (1989–1993)	Outcome or Conclusion
Character of Election (campaign styles, closeness, etc.)			
Actions Reflecting President's Own Position in His Party (left, center, right)			
President's Political Philosophy and Goals			
Recognition and Response to Terrorists and Terrorism (Foreign and Domestic)			
Nations to Which President Applies Negative Labels ("rogue," "evil," etc.)			
Legislation and Congressional Resolutions Promoted by President and Passed			
Response to Division of Party Power in Congress			

Key Factors in an Evaluation of Presidents Reagan and Bush (George HW)			
	Reagan (two terms) (1981–1989)	Bush (George H.W.) (1989–1993)	Outcome or Conclusion
Major Features of Economy During Time in Office			
Administration's View of Causes and Solutions to Current (and Future) Economic Problems			
Administration's Position on Taxes, Spending, and Deficits (current and future)			
Efforts Made To Protect or Improve Domestic Economy			
Relations with Big Business, Labor			
Handling of Environmental Issues and Concerns			
Relations with Other Nations, International Community			

Key Factors in an Evaluation of Presidents Reagan and Bush (George HW)			
	Reagan (two terms) (1981–1989)	**Bush (George H.W.) (1989–1993)**	**Outcome or Conclusion**
Military and Diplomatic Intervention Abroad (willingness, instances)			
Actions Concerning International Agreements			
Personal Scandals Threatening Effectiveness			
Other Scandals, Events, or Conditions Threatening Effectiveness			
Supreme Court (appointments, rulings)			

IDEAS AND DETAILS

Objective 1

1.   The political coalition forged by Ronald Reagan in his 1980 bid for the presidency consisted of

   a.   evangelical Christians as well as traditional political and economic conservatives.
   b.   advocates of Keynesian economics as well as environmentalists.
   c.   traditional political conservatives as well as women's rights advocates.
   d.   advocates of supply-side economics as well as abortion rights advocates.

Objective 4

2.   President Reagan's appointees to the National Labor Relations Board

   a.   actively encouraged companies to declare bankruptcy as a way of canceling union contracts.
   b.   questioned the right of union members to strike.
   c.   consistently voted in favor of management.
   d.   campaigned in favor of the closed shop.

Objectives 1 and 12

3.   Which of the following was most likely to vote for Republican presidential candidates in the 1980s?

   a.   An advocate of the Equal Rights Amendment
   b.   An advocate of strict enforcement of the Clean Air Act
   c.   An advocate of abortion
   d.   An advocate of "family values"

Objectives 4 and 16

4.   An issue of growing concern throughout the Reagan and Bush administrations concerned

   a.   the nation's weakening defense posture.
   b.   deep cuts in Social Security and Medicare.
   c.   the growth of the national debt.
   d.   America's lack of influence over Israel.

Objective 4 and 5

5.   A major reason for the dramatic decline in inflation from 1980 to 1982 was

   a.   increasing productivity among American workers.
   b.   the decision by the Federal Reserve Bank to raise interest rates for bank loans to an unprecedented level.
   c.   increased spending by Americans.
   d.   the rise in the Gross National Product due to increased investment spending.

Objective 8

6. Which of the following was a consequence of the expansion of deregulation during the Reagan administration?

    a. Businesses usually became less efficient as the result of downsizing.
    b. The Savings and Loans industry collapsed as the result of billions of dollars of bad investments.
    c. In the telecommunications field, smaller corporations found it impossible to challenge corporate giants.
    d. The wave of mergers lightened the debt burden of most American corporations.

Objective 4

7. Which of the following benefited the most from the 1981 tax reductions?

    a. The poor
    b. The wealthy
    c. The middle class
    d. Married couples

Objective 9

8. What was the Reagan administration's goal in Nicaragua?

    a. To persuade the Sandinista government to hold elections
    b. To remove the Sandinista government from power
    c. To reduce foreign military bases and advisers in that country
    d. To bring about a negotiated settlement between the Sandinista government and the contras

Objective 10

9. As a result of the Iran-contra scandal,

    a. President Reagan apologized for subverting the will of Congress.
    b. the House Judiciary Committee began impeachment hearings against President Reagan.
    c. Defense Secretary Caspar Weinberger was convicted of lying to Congress.
    d. President Reagan's popularity declined.

Objectives 9, 18, and 19

10. The improvement in Soviet-American relations during Reagan's second term may be attributed in large part to

    a. Reagan's apology for his "evil empire" rhetoric.
    b. the Reagan administration's agreement to limit research on the Strategic Defense Initiative.
    c. cooperation between the United States and the Soviet Union to combat international terrorism.
    d. Gorbachev's decision to reduce Soviet military expenditures and decrease foreign aid.

Objective 12

11. Which of the following was the goal of the Moral Majority?

    a. The creation of a "Christian America"
    b. An increase in funding for welfare and job-training programs
    c. A dramatic reduction in the size of the nuclear arsenals of the United States and the Soviet Union
    d. The acceptance and celebration of America as a multicultural society

Objectives 7 and 13

12. As a result of changes in the job market in the 1980s,

    a.   occupational segregation by sex slowly disappeared.

    b.   the number of blue-collar jobs increased dramatically.

    c.   unskilled workers found it increasingly difficult to find well-paid jobs.

    d.   organized labor became more interested in unskilled laborers.

Objective 14

13. Which of the following caused caution to replace the liberated sexual practices associated with the sexual revolution?

    a.   The threat of sexually transmitted diseases

    b.   The health risks associated with the use of birth-control pills

    c.   The graying of America

    d.   The influence of TV evangelists

Objectives 17 and 20

14. What did the United States want to accomplish by sending troops to the Persian Gulf and engaging in the 1991 Persian Gulf War?

    a.   To defend Israel against attack by Syria and Libya

    b.   To defend Saudi Arabian oil exports to the United States and force Iraq to abandon its takeover of Kuwait

    c.   To enforce the cease-fire between Iraq and Iran

    d.   To force the United Arab Emirates to stop preying on American tankers in the Persian Gulf

Objective 21

15. As a result of Anita Hill's testimony before the Senate Judiciary Committee,

    a.   the gender gap in American politics widened.

    b.   the Bush administration withdrew its nomination of Clarence Thomas to the Supreme Court.

    c.   the full Senate failed to confirm Clarence Thomas to the Supreme Court.

    d.   legislation was passed making it easier for women to file sexual harassment charges.

ESSAY QUESTIONS

Objectives 4, 5, and 7

1. Discuss the economic policies of the Reagan administration, and examine the impact of these policies on the United States.

Objectives 4, 5, and 7

2. Examine the reasons for and the extent of poverty in the United States in the 1980s. What groups were most affected? Why?

Objective 9

3. Explain the following statement: "Ronald Reagan's foreign policy was driven by beliefs rooted in America's past."

Objective 9

4.   Discuss and evaluate the Reagan administration's policy toward Third World nations, paying particular attention to its policy toward Central America.

Objectives 9 and 19

5.   Defend or refute the following statement: "The turnaround in Soviet-American relations which began in 1985 stemmed more from changes abroad than from President Reagan's decisions."

Objectives 11 and 12

6.   Discuss the causes and consequences of the "culture wars" that began in American society in the 1980s.

Objective 14

7.   Discuss the extent of the AIDS epidemic, and explain the impact of the epidemic on the sexual behavior and attitudes of Americans.

Objective 13

8.   Discuss the characteristics of the new immigrants of the 1980s and explain the impact of these immigrants on American society.

Objectives 18 and 19

9.   Discuss the factors that brought an end to the Cold War, and discuss the legacy of the war for the United States, the Soviet Union, and the world community of nations.

Objective 17

10.   Discuss the causes and consequences of the 1989 U.S. invasion of Panama.

Objective 20

11.   Discuss the causes and consequences of the 1991 Persian Gulf War.

Objective 21

12.   Examine the controversy surrounding President Bush's nomination of Clarence Thomas to the Supreme Court and discuss the impact of the Senate Judiciary Committee's confirmation hearings on the American electorate.

ANSWERS

Multiple-Choice Questions

1. a.   Correct. Reagan received support from traditional political and economic conservatives who wanted to reduce the size of the federal government, strengthen national defense, and create economic conditions favorable to business and industry. Reagan was also able to obtain support from evangelical Christians by standing against abortion and passage of the Equal Rights Amendment, and by supporting prayer in public schools and "family values." In addition, Reagan attracted middle- and working-class whites who supported the tax revolt movement of the 1970s. In forming an alliance among these groups, Reagan forged a new conservative coalition in his bid for the presidency in 1980. See page 892.

    b.   No. Reagan supported the idea of "supply-side" economics and did not support the concepts of Keynesian economics. In addition, environmentalists found it almost impossible to support a man who stated that "approximately 80 percent of our air pollution stems from hydrocarbons released by vegetation." See page 892.

    c.   No. Traditional political conservatives who wanted to reduce the size of the federal government and increase defense spending supported Reagan. However, since Reagan was against ratification of the Equal Rights Amendment, he did not receive the support of advocates of women's rights. See page 892.

    d.   No. Although advocates of supply-side economics supported Reagan in his 1980 bid for the presidency, that was not true of abortion rights advocates. See page 892.

2. c.   Correct. Reagan's appointees on the NLRB demonstrated their hostility toward organized labor by consistently voting in favor of management. See page 894.

    a.   No. Although this practice was used by companies and was declared constitutional by the Supreme Court, Reagan's appointees to the NLRB did not actively encourage companies to declare bankruptcy as a way of canceling union contracts. See page 894.

    b.   No. The right of union members to strike was not questioned by Reagan's appointees to the NLRB. See page 894.

    d.   No. A closed shop or union shop is a business whose employees are required to be union members. Reagan's appointees to the NLRB did not favor the closed shop. See page 894.

3.   d.   Correct. Cultural conservatives who advocated "family values" were a major element in the Republican coalition that voted for Reagan and for George H. W. Bush. Therefore, an advocate of family values would most likely vote for Republican presidential candidates from the 1980s to today. See pages 892–893.

a.   No. Although some Republicans favored ratification of the Equal Rights Amendment (ERA), the party itself stood against ratification. For that reason, most advocates of the ERA did not support Republican presidential candidates during the 1970s and 1980s. See pages 892–893.

b.   No. The Republican party and Republican presidential candidates tend to take stands against government regulatory agencies and regulatory legislation such as the Clean Air Act. Although President George H. W. Bush signed the 1990 reauthorization of the Clean Air Act, Bush's Council on Competitiveness, headed by Vice President Dan Quayle, gutted enforcement of the act. Therefore, one who advocated strict enforcement of the Clean Air Act would most likely not vote for Republican presidential candidates. See pages 892–893.

c.   No. The Republican party, from the 1980s to the present, has stood against abortion rights. Therefore, an advocate of abortion would most likely not vote for Republican presidential candidates. See pages 892–893.

4.   c.   Correct. Although candidate Reagan promised to balance the federal budget, President Reagan oversaw the accumulation of more new debt than the combined deficits of all previous presidents. When Reagan came into office in 1981, the national debt was about $900 billion. By the end of the Bush presidency in 1993, the national debt had more than tripled to about $3 trillion. See page 895.

a.   No. President Reagan oversaw a multi-trillion-dollar defense-spending program that favored building the B-l bomber, enlarging the navy, increasing the production of poison gas, deploying the MX missile, and deploying an antimissile defense system in space. See page 895.

b.   No. Although Reagan and Bush did oversee cuts in social programs, Congress did not go along with cuts in Social Security and Medicare. See page 895.

d.   No. Although the United States certainly did not dictate to Israel, there was not a "lack of influence" either. See page 895.

5.   b.   Correct. The Federal Reserve Bank raised interest rates for bank loans to 21.5 percent in 1981 to tighten the money supply, slow the economy down, and battle inflation. Although the nation plunged into a recession that brought soaring unemployment, severe economic hardship to many farmers, and an overall increase in the poverty rate, the rate of inflation dropped from 12 percent in 1980 to less than 7 percent in 1982. See pages 895–896.

a.   No. During 1981 and 1982 there was less than a 1 percent increase in the rate of productivity. See pages 895–896.

c.   No. An increase in spending by Americans did not cause prices to decline. See pages 895–896.

d.   No. Both the GNP and investment spending fell during this period. See pages 895–896.

6. b. Correct. Due to the deregulation of the S&L industry in the early 1980s, S&Ls put billions of dollars of depositors' savings into high-risk investments. Ultimately, this led to a collapse of the S&L industry. The bailout of the industry in the Reagan-Bush administrations cost taxpayers around $500 billion. See pages 897 and 898.

a. No. Downsizing (laying off employees to make a corporation more profitable) caused many businesses and industries to become more efficient, not less efficient. See pages 897 and 898.

c. No. In some ways deregulation helped smaller telecommunications corporations challenge the virtual monopolies of giant corporations in the industry. See pages 897 and 898.

d. No. In many cases American corporations became more burdened by debt, not less burdened. See pages 897 and 898.

7. b. Correct. Wealthy people gained the most from the 1981 tax reductions. See pages 898–900.

a. No. Those in the poorest fifth saw their tax rates increase by 16 percent, and by 1984 the after-tax income of those in the second-poorest fifth increased by only 1.4 percent. See pages 898–900.

c. No. Although the after-tax income of those Americans in the middle fifth increased by 2.8 percent by 1984, another group's after-tax income increased by a higher percentage. See pages 898–900.

d. No. Among the groups listed, married couples did not save the most as a result of the 1981 income-tax reductions. See pages 898–900.

8. b. Correct. The Reagan administration believed that the Sandinista government in Nicaragua was becoming a client state of the Soviet Union. Therefore, it initiated an economic embargo against Nicaragua, encouraged covert activities by the CIA, and extended aid to the contras, all in an attempt to topple the Nicaraguan government. See page 902.

a. No. Although the administration criticized the Sandinistas for not holding elections, when elections were held in November 1984, the administration called them a "sham." See page 902.

c. No. Although the Reagan administration criticized the presence of Cuban advisers and Soviet arms in Nicaragua, it wanted more than simply a reduction of foreign military bases and advisers. In fact, it rejected the Contadora peace plan which would have reduced foreign bases and advisers in Nicaragua. See page 902.

d. No. The Reagan administration's actions toward Nicaragua do not indicate a desire for a negotiated settlement. In fact, two peace plans were put forward during the 1980s by representatives of Latin American countries. The administration's out-of-hand rejection of both the Contadora peace plan and the Arias peace plan is further indication that a negotiated settlement was not Reagan's goal in Nicaragua. See page 902.

9.   d.   Correct. Polls from the time indicated a drop in Reagan's approval rating from 67 percent to 46 percent due to the Iran-contra scandal. Polls also indicated that 62 percent of the public believed that Reagan lied about Iran-contra. See page 902.

       a.   No. Reagan never apologized for having subverted the will of Congress by illegally funneling aid to the contras in Nicaragua. See page 902.

       b.   No. The House Judiciary Committee did not hold impeachment hearings against President Reagan. See page 902.

       c.   No. Weinberger was indicted for lying to Congress but was pardoned by President Bush before he left office in 1993. See page 902.

10.   d.   Correct. When Gorbachev assumed power and embarked on a reform program in the Soviet Union in 1985, he reduced military expenditures and expenditures on foreign aid. Therefore, he reduced the Soviet Union's armed forces and withdrew Soviet troops from Afghanistan. Largely because of these policies, Soviet-American relations improved. See pages 904–905.

       a.   No. Reagan never apologized for his statement that the Soviet Union was the source of evil in the world. See pages 904–905.

       b.   No. The Reagan administration did not agree to limit research on the Strategic Defense Initiative. See pages 904–905.

       c.   No. There were no obvious signs of cooperation between the United States and the Soviet Union to combat international terrorism. See pages 904–905.

11.   a.   Correct. The Moral Majority, founded in 1979 by Jerry Falwell, was a political action group composed of fundamentalist Christians. Favoring prayer and the teaching of creationism in public schools, the group was against ratification of the Equal Rights Amendment, gay rights, and abortion rights. Its goal was the creation of a "Christian America." See page 905.

       b.   No. Increased funding for welfare and job-training programs was not the goal of the Moral Majority. See page 905.

       c.   No. The Moral Majority was ardently anticommunist. The group opposed both nuclear disarmament and arms-reduction treaties between the United States and the Soviet Union. See page 905.

       d.   No. By rejecting the idea that different lifestyles and cultures were equally valid, the Moral Majority opposed the concept of multiculturalism. See page 905.

12.   c.   Correct. As the economy shifted from an industrial to a service orientation, well-paid jobs that had traditionally been available to the unskilled decreased. The labor demand was in the area of skilled, white-collar, high-technology jobs. See page 906.

       a.   No. Occupational segregation continued as the shift from an industrialized to a service-oriented economy took place. See page 906.

       b.   No. The shifting occupational structure meant the loss of many blue-collar jobs and an increase in skilled, white-collar, high-technology jobs. See page 906.

       d.   No. The shift from an industrialized to a service-oriented economy, and the resulting shift in labor demand, caused unions to devote more energy to organizing white-collar workers. See page 906.

13. a.   Correct. The threat of AIDS and other sexually transmitted diseases caused many Americans to be more cautious about their sexual practices. See page 908.

b.   No. Although there were some concerns about the possibility that health risks were associated with the use of birth-control pills, these concerns were relatively minor and were not a primary cause for Americans to become more cautious about their sexual practices. See page 908.

c.   No. The fact that Americans were living longer and that the number of elderly Americans was increasing was not a reason for Americans to become more cautious about their sexual practices. See page 908.

d.   No. Although TV evangelists preached against the practices associated with the sexual revolution, their influence was not a major cause for Americans to become "more cautious" about their sexual practices. See page 908.

14. b.   Correct. After Saddam Hussein invaded Kuwait, the United States feared the action might threaten Saudi Arabian oil exports. Therefore, in the 1991 Persian Gulf War the United States acted not only to force Iraq out of Kuwait, but also to defend oil exports from Saudi Arabia to the United States. See pages 912–913.

a.   No. Although the United States feared that unrest in the Middle East might embolden Arab states or even lead to a coalition of Arab states against Israel, the defense of Israel from an attack by Syria and Libya was not the immediate goal of the United States in the 1991 Persian Gulf War. See pages 912–913.

c.   No. The Iran-Iraq war ended in 1988; therefore, the goal of the United States in the 1991 Gulf War was not to enforce a cease-fire between those two nations. See pages 912–913.

d.   No. The United Arab Emirates was not preying on American tankers in the Persian Gulf; therefore, the 1991 Persian Gulf War was not undertaken for the reason stated in this choice. See pages 912-913.

15. a.   Correct. The Senate's disregard of Anita Hill's testimony so angered many women that they vowed to oppose the Republican party in 1992. As a result, the gender gap (the difference in the way in which men and women vote) in American politics widened. See page 914.

b.   No. The Bush administration did not withdraw its nomination of Thomas to the Supreme Court. See page 914.

c.   No. Despite Anita Hill's testimony, the Senate confirmed Thomas's nomination to the Supreme Court. See page 914.

d.   No. The Senate did not pass such legislation. See page 914.

CHAPTER 33

Global Bridges in the New Millennium: America Since 1992

LEARNING OBJECTIVES

After you have studied Chapter 33 in your textbook and worked through this study guide chapter, you should be able to:

1. Discuss both the immediate and underlying causes of the Los Angeles riots of April 1992.

2. Examine the issues and personalities and explain the outcome of the 1992 presidential and congressional elections.

3. Discuss Bill Clinton's personal and political background; examine the domestic issues and political problems that faced the Clinton administration; and explain and evaluate the administration's actions concerning those issues and problems.

4. Examine the issues and personalities and explain the outcome of the 1994 congressional elections.

5. Examine the issues and personalities and explain the outcome of the 1996 presidential and congressional elections.

6. Discuss the roots of the economic boom of the 1990s; explain the impact of this boom on the American people and American society; and examine the response of the Clinton administration to the globalization of business.

7. Examine the debate between proponents and critics of free-trade agreements and globalization, and discuss the actions of anti-globalization activists.

8. Examine, evaluate, and discuss the consequences of the defense and foreign policy views, goals, and actions of the Clinton administration in relation to:

   a. Somalia and Rwanda

   b. Haiti

   c. ethnic wars in the Balkans

   d. the Middle East

   e. global environmental issues

   f. Islamic fundamentalism and the rise of Al Qaeda

9. Discuss the nature, extent, and consequences of the antigovernment sentiment felt by some Americans in the 1990s.

10. Discuss the causes and consequences of the Columbine Massacre and of the hate crimes against James Byrd, Jr., and Matthew Shepherd.

11. Examine Kenneth Starr's investigation of alleged scandals involving President Clinton.

12. Examine relations between President Clinton and Congress; explain the reasons for the President's impeachment; and explain the President's acquittal by the Senate.

13. Examine the issues and personalities and discuss the outcome of the disputed 2000 presidential election.

14. Discuss George W. Bush's personal and political background; examine the domestic issues and political problems that faced the Bush administration; and explain and evaluate the administration's actions concerning those issues and problems.

15. Examine, evaluate, and discuss the consequences of the defense and foreign policy views, goals, and actions of the administration of President George W. Bush in relation to:

    a. a national missile defense system;

    b. global environmental issues;

    c. the terrorist attacks of September 11, 2001;

    d. Afghanistan;

    e. domestic defense against terrorist attacks; and

    f. Saddam Hussein's Iraq.

16. Discuss the causes and consequences of the economic recession that began in 2001.

17. Discuss the causes and consequences of the increasing diversity and of the demographic changes in American society in the late twentieth century and the early twenty-first century.

18. Explain the causes and consequences of the changes in the American family during the 1990s and early twenty-first century.

19. Explain the causes and consequences of global health threats in the early twenty-first century, and discuss the international response to these threats.

THEMATIC GUIDE

Divisions among Americans, obvious in the 1980s and early 1990s, continued into the new millennium. The Los Angeles riots of 1992 were a shocking reminder that racial tensions and anti-immigrant sentiment continued to plague the nation. Moreover, the Bush administration's passivity in dealing with the plight of the urban poor and the problems associated with their plight led many to believe that the President was out-of-touch and unsympathetic. Furthermore, as President George H. W. Bush prepared for a reelection bid in 1992, the country was mired in economic recession. As unemployment mounted and personal income stagnated, the president remained inactive, leading to still more criticism.

As the 1992 election approached, the American people seemed genuinely dissatisfied with "Washington gridlock" and ready for the government to act in solving many long-standing problems. Bill Clinton's election to the presidency in 1992 signaled that the American people wanted a change from the passivity of the Bush years. But the pluralistic America of the 1990s was a fragmented America in which consensus on solutions to long-standing problems was difficult. President Clinton would soon discover in both the gays-in-the-military issue and in the response to his economic proposals just how difficult it was to lead an American people who were deeply divided over their own vision of the nation's future, a division reflected in the lobby groups that vied with each other over control of the national agenda. Although the President and Congress did find consensus in some areas, which produced some legislative successes, the attack of interest-group lobbyists against the President's healthcare reform proposals prevented substantive reform in that area.

Questions about the President's character, which had been part of the 1992 presidential campaign, persisted throughout Clinton's tenure in the Oval Office, and controversy also surrounded the First Lady, Hillary Rodham Clinton. These questions coupled with questions about Clinton's management ability caused American voters in 1994 to show again their disillusionment with government, this time by giving Republicans majorities in both houses of Congress for the first time since 1954. But as the 104th Congress attempted to enact the Republican "Contract with America," political stalemate persisted, leading to government shutdowns and increased anger and disgust among the electorate.

The distrust of government that built up over a thirty-year period led to an American public deeply alienated from politics and deeply cynical. Within this atmosphere, many predicted that voters in 1996 would direct their anger against President Clinton and return a Republican to the White House. But Clinton positioned himself as the protector of certain federal programs that the Republican-dominated 104th Congress attacked. In doing so, he gained the support of women and of those who benefited from such programs. Furthermore, the Republican willingness to allow government shutdowns in their quest for a balanced budget convinced many that Bill Clinton was reasonable and moderate while Congress was "ideologically inflexible." Therefore, despite hints of scandal in the White House and continued Republican attacks against President Clinton on the character issue, Clinton easily defeated his challengers and became the first Democrat to be reelected to the presidency since Franklin D. Roosevelt in 1936.

Clinton was also, undoubtedly, aided in his reelection bid by the economic boom associated with the technology-driven "new economy," which accelerated in the 1990s. Elimination of the federal deficit, which boosted investments by lowering interest rates, further aided the economy. Globalization also gained momentum during the Clinton years. Realizing that U.S. prosperity depended, to a great extent, on foreign trade, the Clinton administration focused on lowering international trade and investment barriers, and, through the creation of the National Economic Council, on promoting trade missions around the world. However, critics of globalization emerged on different fronts, with protests often targeting not only the World Trade Organization but multinational corporations such as McDonald's.

As the United States tried to gain its footing in the post-Cold War world, international issues related to ethnic wars, humanitarian concerns, the Arab-Israeli conflict, global environmental concerns, and the growth of international terrorism caused continuing debate among the American people over the proper role of the United States in the new world of the 1990s. With the United States in the unique position of being the world's only superpower, President Clinton agreed in principle that this power should be used to contain ethnic hatreds, support human rights, and promote democracy; however, President Clinton was cautious in the use of that power. Although he withdrew American troops from Somalia and did not intervene in the brutal civil war in Rwanda, he did intervene in the Haitian crisis by facilitating an agreement negotiated by former president Jimmy Carter. At first reluctant to intervene in the ethnic wars in the Balkans, ultimately U.S. led NATO forces undertook a massive aerial bombardment of Serbia. Having halted the ethnic cleansing of the Milosevic regime, American soldiers joined a U.N. peacekeeping force in the region. Clinton also acted in the Middle East in an attempt to end the escalating violence between Israel and the Palestinian Liberation Organization. Although at times there seemed to be progress, in the end no lasting agreement was reached. Clinton also demonstrated concern over global environmental concerns by signing the 1997 Kyoto protocol. However, due to the increasingly bitter partisan battle between Clinton and the Republican controlled Congress, the treaty was never submitted to the Senate for ratification. Furthermore, the Clinton administration increasingly focused on the threat posed by international terrorists associated with the rise of Islamic fundamentalism and, more specifically, with Al Qaeda, a terrorist organization founded and financed by Osama bin Laden. Although it was known that bin Laden was behind several terrorist bombings aimed at Americans and American interests, the U.S. failed in its attempts to apprehend him.

In this troubled world of the late 1990s, most Americans enjoyed the results of the nation's economic boom. But exuberance associated with prosperity was tempered by Timothy McVeigh's act of domestic terrorism that destroyed the Alfred P. Murrah Federal building in Oklahoma City, the Columbine Massacre, and the hate crimes against African American James Byrd, Jr., and Matthew Shepherd, a gay college student.

In dealing with such "Paradoxes of Prosperity," the authors then turn to a discussion of the Whitewater investigation, the expansion of that investigation, the president's impeachment by the House of Representatives for matters relating to the Monica Lewinsky affair, and his ultimate acquittal by the Senate. The authors also place Clinton's impeachment in the larger context of the partisan political wars and the culture wars of the 1990s and note that 24-hour news networks contributed to the blurring of lines between private conduct and public conduct because of their reliance on sensationalism to lure viewers.

After dealing with the issues, candidates, and outcome of the disputed 2000 presidential election, we turn our attention to the presidency of George W. Bush. While most believed that Bush would govern from the center, in fact his tax plan and his unilateralist approach to foreign policy soon indicated that he would govern from the right. Seemingly adrift at first in both domestic and foreign affairs, the Bush administration was galvanized by the terrorist attacks of September 11, 2001. With counterterrorism as his number one priority, President Bush launched a war against terrorism, striking first against Afghanistan to destroy the Taliban and the Al Qaeda terrorist network it supported. On the domestic front, Congress passed the USA PATRIOT Act, which, some argued, placed American rights and freedoms at risk, and created the new Department of Homeland Security. As domestic economic problems began to mount, the Republican party, nevertheless, gained control over both houses of Congress in the 2002 midterm elections.

In the immediate aftermath of the attacks of September 11, the world community of nations by and large rallied behind the United States. However, the Bush administration's unilateralist approach to foreign policy, apparent in the policy of preemptive action, soon caused a dramatic change in the attitude of foreign governments. Despite the objections of close allies such as France and Germany, the United States and Great Britain decided to act without U.N. approval against the Saddam Hussein regime in Iraq. Although, the Hussein regime was quickly overthrown, continuing instability in Iraq caused some to wonder if the United States would win the war but lose the peace. Furthermore, domestic economic problems, including a mushrooming federal deficit, continued to mount.

The chapter ends with a profile of the American people at the beginning of the twenty-first century. More diverse and more fragmented than ever, niche markets appeared, demographic changes continued, American popular culture became more ethnically diverse, and the shape of the American family continued to change. The nation and its people grappled with legal and ethical questions related to new reproductive and biogenetic technologies. As globalization fostered the interconnectivity of the world's peoples, it also fostered global health threats resulting from the dissemination of diseases and from environmental degradation. However, this interconnectedness also sped the international response to viral threats such as that posed by the cononavirus responsible for SARS. As the war against terrorism continued and as the United States continued to struggle to reconstruct an Iraq based on democratic principles, some wondered if a decisive victory against international terrorism was possible. Furthermore, as budget deficits continued to mount, some questioned if the United States would be able to continue to deal successfully with the nation's far-flung obligations.

BUILDING VOCABULARY

Listed below are important words and terms that you need to know to get the most out of Chapter 33. They are listed in the order in which they occur in the chapter. After carefully looking through the list, (1) underline the words with which you are totally unfamiliar, (2) put a question mark by those words of which you are unsure, and (3) leave the rest alone.

As you begin to read the chapter, when you come to any of the words you've put question marks beside or underlined (1) slow your reading; (2) focus on the word and on its context in the sentence you're reading; (3) if you can understand the meaning of the word from its context in the sentence or passage in which it is used, go on with your reading; (4) if it's a word that you've underlined or a word that you can't understand from its context in the sentence or passage, look it up in a dictionary and write down the definition that best applies to the context in which the word is used.

Definitions

volatile _____

galvanize _____

scourge _____

decimate _____

paradoxical _____

obtuse _____

vehemence _____

rancorous _____

exacerbate _____

incontrovertible _____

glib _____

debacle _____

usurp _____

contrite _____

wonk _____

unilateralist _____

preponderant _____

consternation _____

bellicose _____

castigate _____

conundrum _____

permeable _____

deleterious _____

chagrin _____

vanquish _____

Difficult-to-Spell Names and Terms from Reading and Lecture

IDENTIFICATION AND SIGNIFICANCE

After studying Chapter 33 of *A People and a Nation*, you should be able to identify fully *and* explain the historical significance of each item listed below.

- Identify each item in the space provided. Give an explanation or description of the item. Answer the questions *who, what, where,* and *when.*

- Explain the historical significance of each item in the space provided. Establish the historical context in which the item exists. Establish the item as the result of or as the cause of other factors existing in the society under study. Answer this question: *What were the political, social, economic, and/or cultural consequences of this item?*

1.   September 11, 2001

    a.   Identification

    b.   Significance

2.   globalization

    a.   Identification

    b.   Significance

3.   the Los Angeles riots of 1992

    a.   Identification

    b.   Significance

4.   Proposition 13

    a.   Identification

    b.   Significance

5.   economic recession, 1989–1992

    a.   Identification

    b.   Significance

6.   Bill Clinton

    a.   Identification

    b.   Significance

7.   Ross Perot

    a.   Identification

    b.   Significance

8.   the presidential and congressional elections of 1992

    a.   Identification

    b.   Significance

9.   Hillary Rodham Clinton

   a.   Identification

   b.   Significance

10.   the gays-in-the-military issue

   a.   Identification

   b.   Significance

11.   health-care reform

   a.   Identification

   b.   Significance

12.   the "Contract with America"

   a.   Identification

   b.   Significance

13.   Newt Gingrich

   a.   Identification

   b.   Significance

14. the congressional elections of 1994

    a. Identification

    b. Significance

15. the 104th Congress

    a. Identification

    b. Significance

16. government shutdowns, 1995 and 1996

    a. Identification

    b. Significance

17. the Personal Responsibility and Work Opportunity Act

    a. Identification

    b. Significance

18. the Telecommunications Act of 1996

    a. Identification

    b. Significance

19.   the presidential and congressional elections of 1996

    a.   Identification

    b.   Significance

20.   the gender gap of the 1990s

    a.   Identification

    b.   Significance

21.   information technology

    a.   Identification

    b.   Significance

22.   the microprocessor

    a.   Identification

    b.   Significance

23.   "The New Economy"

    a.   Identification

    b.   Significance

24.   decline in the federal deficit

    a.   Identification

    b.   Significance

25.   the North American Free Trade Agreement, the Uruguay Round of the General Agreement on Tariffs and Trade, and the World Trade Organization

    a.   Identification

    b.   Significance

26.   multinational corporations of the 1990s

    a.   Identification

    b.   Significance

27.   the anti-globalization movement

    a.   Identification

    b.   Significance

28.   Somalia

    a.   Identification

    b.   Significance

29. genocide in Rwanda

    a. Identification

    b. Significance

30. the Haitian crisis

    a. Identification

    b. Significance

31. ethnic wars in the Balkans

    a. Identification

    b. Significance

32. the Middle East peace process, 1993–1997

    a. Identification

    b. Significance

33. Clinton's environmental policies

    a. Identification

    b. Significance

34.   Osama Bin Laden and Al Qaeda

    a.   Identification

    b.   Significance

35.   the stock market boom of the 1990s

    a.   Identification

    b.   Significance

36.   the Oklahoma City bombing

    a.   Identification

    b.   Significance

37.   the Columbine massacre

    a.   Identification

    b.   Significance

38.   James Byrd, Jr.

    a.   Identification

    b.   Significance

39. Matthew Shepherd

    a. Identification

    b. Significance

40. the Whitewater investigation

    a. Identification

    b. Significance

41. the Monica Lewinsky affair

    a. Identification

    b. Significance

42. the impeachment and acquittal of President Clinton

    a. Identification

    b. Significance

43. the congressional elections of 1998

    a. Identification

    b. Significance

44.   24-hour news networks

    a.   Identification

    b.   Significance

45.   partisan political wars of the 1990s

    a.   Identification

    b.   Significance

46.   the Family and Medical Leave Act

    a.   Identification

    b.   Significance

47.   the Health Insurance Portability and Accountability Act

    a.   Identification

    b.   Significance

48.   Al Gore

    a.   Identification

    b.   Significance

49.   George W. Bush

    a.   Identification

    b.   Significance

50.   Ralph Nader

    a.   Identification

    b.   Significance

51.   the contested presidential election of 2000

    a.   Identification

    b.   Significance

52.   the Bush tax plan

    a.   Identification

    b.   Significance

53.   the National Missile Defense system

    a.   Identification

    b.   Significance

54.   Senator James Jeffords

    a.   Identification

    b.   Significance

55.   the Afghanistan war

    a.   Identification

    b.   Significance

56.   the USA PATRIOT Act

    a.   Identification

    b.   Significance

57.   the anthrax scare

    a.   Identification

    b.   Significance

58.   the Department of Homeland Security

    a.   Identification

    b.   Significance

59. the dot-com collapse

    a. Identification

    b. Significance

60. the Enron collapse

    a. Identification

    b. Significance

61. the congressional elections of 2002

    a. Identification

    b. Significance

62. Bush's preemptive-action strategy

    a. Identification

    b. Significance

63. UN Resolution 1441

    a. Identification

    b. Significance

64. the Iraq war and the fall of Baghdad

    a. Identification

    b. Significance

65. the fiscal crisis of the states

    a. Identification

    b. Significance

66. niche markets

    a. Identification

    b. Significance

67. race and ethnicity in the 2000 census

    a. Identification

    b. Significance

68. the American family circa 2000

    a. Identification

    b. Significance

69.   the "Defense of Marriage Act"

   a.   Identification

   b.   Significance

70.   the debate over stem-cell research

   a.   Identification

   b.   Significance

71.   global disease dissemination

   a.   Identification

   b.   Significance

72.   environmental degradation

   a.   Identification

   b.   Significance

73.   the international response to disease

   a.   Identification

   b.   Significance

ORGANIZING, REVIEWING, AND USING INFORMATION

Key Factors in an Evaluation of Presidents Clinton and Bush (GW)			
	Clinton (two terms) (1993–2001)	**Bush (George W.) (2001–)**	**Outcome/Conclusion**
Character of Election (campaign styles, closeness, etc.)			
Actions Reflecting President's Own Position in His Party (left, center, right)			
President's Political Philosophy and Goals			
Recognition and Response to Terrorists and Terrorism (Foreign and Domestic)			
Nations to Which President Applies Negative Labels ("rogue," "evil," etc.)			
Legislation and Congressional Resolutions Promoted by President and Passed			
Response to Division of Party Power in Congress			

Key Factors in an Evaluation of Presidents Clinton and Bush (GW)			
	Clinton (two terms) (1993–2001)	**Bush (George W.) (2001–)**	**Outcome/Conclusion**
Major Features of Economy During Time in Office			
Administration's View of Causes and Solutions to Current (and Future) Economic Problems			
Administration's Position on Taxes, Spending, and Deficits (current and future)			
Efforts Made To Protect or Improve Domestic Economy			
Relations with Big Business, Labor			
Handling of Environment Issues and Concerns			
Relations with Other Nations, International Community			

Key Factors in an Evaluation of Presidents Clinton and Bush (GW)			
	Clinton (two terms) (1993–2001)	**Bush (George W.) (2001–)**	**Outcome/Conclusion**
Military and Diplomatic Intervention Abroad (willingness, instances)			
Actions Concerning International Agreements			
Personal Scandals Threatening Effectiveness			
Other Scandals, Events, or Conditions Threatening Effectiveness			
Supreme Court (appointments, rulings)			

IDEAS AND DETAILS

Objective 1

1.   The immediate cause of the Los Angeles riots of 1992 was the

   a.   enactment of a city ordinance that forbade sleeping on park benches.
   b.   shooting of three unarmed black teenagers by a white police officer.
   c.   closing of a city-operated recreational center in Watts.
   d.   acquittal of four police officers charged with beating a black motorist.

Objective 3

2.   As a result of his handling of the gays-in-the-military issue, President Clinton

   a.   received the support of conservatives.
   b.   was praised by most liberals.
   c.   alienated the gay community.
   d.   won the support of the military.

Objective 3

3.   In the first year of his presidency, President Bill Clinton's major goal, a program to assure affordable healthcare for all Americans, was defeated by

   a.   a close vote in the House of Representatives.
   b.   a betrayal by liberal Democrats who wanted to punish Clinton for being too conservative.
   c.   special interest groups which were too powerful for the health-care task force to defeat.
   d.   the fear of the American public that the health-care plan was the first step toward socialized medicine.

Objective 4

4.   As a result of the 1994 midterm elections,

   a.   Democrats won a majority of the state governorships.
   b.   Republicans gained majorities in both houses of Congress.
   c.   Democrats retained control of the House but lost control of the Senate.
   d.   most Republican incumbents in Congress failed to win reelection.

Objective 5

5.   Which of the following was a reason for Clinton's victory in the 1996 presidential election?

   a.   His liberal agenda
   b.   His stand against gun-control legislation
   c.   The reactionary proposals of his Republican opponent
   d.   The gender gap

Objective 6

6.   The industry most closely associated with the so-called "New Economy" of the 1990s was the

   a.   biogenetics industry.
   b.   computer industry.
   c.   mutual funds industry.
   d.   pharmaceutical industry.

Objective 7

7. Critics of the North American Free Trade Agreement argued that it would
   a. cost jobs in the United States.
   b. increase the federal debt.
   c. make Canadian and Mexican goods less competitive in the world marketplace.
   d. cause a drastic reduction in federal research-and-development funds for United States businesses.

Objective 7

8. Which of the following was a major target of anti-globalization activists in the 1990s?
   a. Hershey's Chocolate Company
   b. McDonald's
   c. the Roman Catholic Church
   d. the United Nations

Objective 8

9. Which of the following is true of U.S. involvement in the United Nations's humanitarian efforts in Somalia in the early 1990s?
   a. Boris Yeltsin responded to the operation by issuing a formal protest with the U.N. Security Council against that body's meddling in African affairs.
   b. The presence of U.N. peacekeepers led rival clans in Somalia to enter into a cease-fire agreement and a democratic regime was installed in the war-ravaged land.
   c. When American soldiers began to die, the United States withdrew its troops.
   d. Libya responded by invading Somalia in an attempt to prevent its "westernization."

Objective 8

10. With regard to international efforts to protect the environment, the Clinton administration
    a. opposed the 1992 Rio de Janeiro Treaty as an attack on American industry.
    b. signed the 1997 Kyoto protocol on carbon dioxide emissions but never submitted it for ratification to the Republican-controlled Senate.
    c. refused to fulfill the previous Bush administration's pledges to support the war against global warming.
    d. showed its disdain for the 1997 Kyoto protocol, which it had signed only to mollify the nation's environmentalists, by secretly lobbying against its ratification in the Senate.

Objective 8

11. Even before the September 11, 2001, terrorist attacks against the World Trade Center and the Pentagon, Osama bin Laden was seen as the mastermind behind a deadly bombing that killed Americans
    a. at embassies in Tokyo and London.
    b. at a World Trade Organization meeting in Seattle.
    c. aboard the *U.S.S. Cole*.
    d. at the Olympics in Atlanta.

Objective 12

12. After the House of Representatives voted to impeach President Clinton, public-opinion polls showed that a majority of Americans

a.   did not believe that partisan politics played a role in the decision by the House.
b.   strongly disapproved of the President's job performance.
c.   did not want the President removed from office.
d.   blamed Monica Lewinsky for the President's problems.

Objective 15

13. President Bush's announcement that the United States would withdraw from the Anti-Ballistic Missile Treaty with Russia and build a national missile defense system was an indication of which of the following?

a.   George W. Bush was more sympathetic to his father's views on foreign affairs than to Ronald Reagan's.
b.   George W. Bush was a sly politician who, by refusing to be swayed by the criticisms of foreign governments, intended to win over the conservative Democrats he needed to push his agenda through Congress.
c.   George W. Bush was an independent thinker who was not going to be controlled by strong-minded members of his administration like Vice President Dick Cheney and Secretary of Defense Donald Rumsfeld.
d.   George W. Bush wanted the United States to plot a unilateralist course in international affairs.

Objectives 14 and 15

14. Among the most controversial federal responses to the terrorist attacks of 9/11 was

a.   the Homeland Security Act.
b.   ordering private planes not to fly over Washington, D.C.
c.   the USA PATRIOT Act.
d.   reducing the amount of time the president and the vice president were present in the same building.

Objective 15

15. Which of the following was the most controversial aspect of the Bush administration's belief that the containment doctrine of the past was outmoded?

a.   The administration adopted the most restrictive immigration policy in the nation's history.
b.   The administration asserted that America would use its military power solely for the physical protection of the United States and U.S. citizens.
c.   President Bush asserted that his administration would not wait for security threats to become real, but would instead employ preemptive action to defend the nation.
d.   President Bush's announcement that he would hold accountable any nation from which an attack on American soil, American facilities, or American citizens was mounted, and that the United States would respond immediately and militarily to any such attack.

ESSAY QUESTIONS

Objective 2

1.   Examine the issues and personalities in the 1992 presidential election, and explain the election's outcome.

Objective 3

2.   Discuss the gays-in-the-military issue and assess how President Clinton handled that issue.

Objectives 3

3.   Explain the healthcare problems in the United States in the 1990s, discuss President Clinton's attempt to address those problems, and explain why that attempt failed.

Objective 4

4.   Examine the 1994 congressional elections and assess the actions of the 104th Congress.

Objective 3

5.   Discuss the domestic accomplishments and failures of the Clinton administration.

Objective 6

6.   Examine the causes of the economic boom of the 1990s and discuss the impact of this boom on the American people and American society.

Objective 6

7.   Discuss the assertion that the post-Cold War world was "the age of globalization."

Objective 7

8.   Examine the emergence of the anti-globalization movement, and discuss the actions of those who were part of this movement.

Objective 8

9.   Discuss the Clinton administration's policy toward the ethnic wars in the Balkans.

Objective 12

10.   Explain the impeachment of President Clinton by the House of Representatives and his subsequent acquittal in the Senate. What implications did Clinton's impeachment have for the future?

Objective 13

11.   Examine the issues and personalities and explain the outcome of the 2000 presidential election.

Objectives 14 and 15

12. Write an essay in which you defend or refute the following statement:

    From the first days of his administration, George W. Bush governed from the right.

Objectives 14, 15, and 16

13. Explain the causes and consequences of the September 11, 2001, terrorist attacks against the towers of the World Trade Center and the Pentagon.

Objective 14 and 15

14. Discuss the rationale behind passage of the USA PATRIOT Act, explain the major provisions of that act, and examine the criticisms leveled against the act.

Objective 15

15. Explain the Bush administration's policy of preemptive action, and discuss the domestic and international debate generated by the adoption of this policy.

Objective 15

16. . Examine the causes and consequences of the 2003 war against Iraq.

Objective 17

17. Discuss the nature, causes, and consequences of the rapid demographic changes within American society during the 1990s and the early twenty-first century.

ANSWERS

Multiple-Choice Questions

1.   d.   Correct. The spark that was the immediate cause of the Los Angeles riots of 1992 was the acquittal by an all-white jury of four Los Angeles police officers in the beating of Rodney King. See page 920.

      a.   No. Although ordinances of this type did cause protest in some American cities, such an ordinance was not the cause of the Los Angeles riots of 1992. See pages 920.

      b.   No. Such an incident did not cause the Los Angeles riots of 1992. See page 920.

      c.   No. The city of Los Angeles did not close a recreational center in Watts and such a closing was not the cause of the Los Angeles riots of 1992. See page 920.

2.   c.   Correct. During the 1992 presidential campaign, candidate Bill Clinton promised that he would end the ban on homosexuals in the military once he was elected. As president, he faced criticism from the military and conservatives when he attempted to fulfill that pledge. Ultimately, he accepted a "Don't ask, don't tell" compromise which alienated both liberals and conservatives, and both the gay community and the military. See page 922.

      a.   No. President Clinton angered conservatives as a result of his handling of the gays-in-the-military issue. See page 922.

      b.   No. President Clinton angered most liberals as a result of his handling of the gays-in-the-military issue. See page 922.

      d.   No. President Clinton angered the military as a result of his handling of the gays-in-the-military issue. See page 922.

3.   c.   Correct. The healthcare reforms recommended by the healthcare task force, co-chaired by First Lady Hillary Rodham Clinton, met with concerted and organized opposition from special interest groups such as the insurance industry, the business community, and the medical community. Ms. Clinton could not forge a coalition strong enough to defeat these interests, which resulted in the defeat of the recommended reforms. See page 922.

      a.   No. The Clinton healthcare plan never came up for a vote in the House. See page 922.

      b.   No. The Clinton healthcare plan was not sabotaged by liberal Democrats. See page 922.

      d.   No. Although the public became concerned over the bureaucratic aspects of the Clinton health-care proposal, the public's fear that it was the first step toward socialized medicine was not the reason for the defeat of the plan. See page 922.

4.   b.   Correct. President Clinton came into office in January 1993 with majorities in both houses of Congress. However, conservative Republicans, under the leadership of Congressman Newt Gingrich, began a concerted effort to change the makeup of Congress. Campaigning on the basis of the "Contract with America" and fueled by money from conservative organizations, Republicans, for the first time since 1954, gained control of both houses of Congress in the 1994 congressional elections. See page 922.

a.   No. Republicans, not Democrats, made gains in the number of states with Republican governors as a result of the 1994 midterm elections. After those elections, thirty of fifty governors were Republicans. See page 922.

c.   No. Democrats did not retain control of the House of Representatives as a result of the 1994 midterm elections. See page 922.

d.   No. In the 1994 midterm elections, all Republican incumbents in Congress won reelection. See page 922.

5.   d.   Correct. One reason for Clinton's victory in the 1996 was a gender gap—the difference in voting patterns between men and women—of 11 percent. While 54 percent of women who voted in the 1996 presidential election voted for Clinton, only 43 percent of men who voted in the election voted for Clinton. See page 923.

a.   No. Clinton ran on a centrist, not a liberal, agenda in the 1996 election. See page 923.

b.   No. Clinton favored gun-control legislation. See page 923.

c.   No. Bob Dole, Clinton's Republican opponent in the 1996 election, did not offer reactionary proposals in his campaign. See page 923.

6.   b.   Correct. The rapid development of computers, fax machines, cellular phones, and the Internet—collectively referred to as "information technology"—are closely associated with the New Economy of the 1990s. See page 924.

a.   No. Although the field of biogenetics, in which the genetic code of an organism is altered to produce particular traits, is associated with scientific and medical breakthroughs in the 1990s, it cannot be said that it is industry "most closely associated" with the New Economy of the 1990s. See page 924.

c.   No. The mutual funds industry, in which professionals manage and invest a pool of money, grew considerably during the 1980s and 1990s. However, this industry is not the industry "most closely associated" with the New Economy of the 1990s. See page 924.

d.   No. The pharmaceutical industry is not the industry "most closely associated" with the New Economy of the 1990s. See page 924.

7. a.   Correct. Critics argued that NAFTA would increase imports to the United States and, as a result, cost jobs. However, when the amount of money flowing out of the U.S. to pay for imports exceeds the amount of money flowing into the country in payment for exports, the larger supply of dollars on world exchange markets causes the value of the dollar to go down. This, in turn, causes U.S. exports to be less expensive and, thus, more competitive, which tends to increase exports, which tends to increase jobs in U.S. export firms and industries. See page 925.

    b.   No. Critics of NAFTA did not argue that the free-trade agreement would increase the federal debt. See page 925.

    c.   No. Critics of NAFTA did not argue that the free-trade agreement would make Canadian and Mexican goods less competitive in the world marketplace. See page 925.

    d.   No. Critics of NAFTA did not argue that it would cause a drastic reduction in federal research-and-development funds for United States businesses. See page 925.

8. b.   Correct. McDonald's, located in over 100 countries, became a major target of anti-globalization activists in the 1990s and early 21st century. From 1996 to 2002, McDonald's had to contend with hundreds of protests and bombings. See page 926.

    a.   No. Hershey's Chocolate Company was not a major target of anti-globalization activists in the 1990s. See page 926.

    c.   No. The Roman Catholic Church was not a major target of anti-globalization activists in the 1990s. See page 926.

    d.   No. The United Nations was not singled out as a major target of anti-globalization activists in the 1990s. See page 926.

9. c.   Correct. In 1992, President George H. W. Bush ordered over 28,000 American troops to Somalia to ensure delivery of humanitarian aid to the people of that beleaguered nation. A U.N. peacekeeping force, which included some 9,000 Americans, took over this effort in 1993. When the mission in Somalia changed from a humanitarian mission to the reform of Somalia, U.S. soldiers were caught in the crossfire as rival clans vied for political power. As a result, U.S. forces were withdrawn by President Clinton in 1994. See page 927.

    a.   No. Boris Yeltsin did not issue a formal protest against the mission of the United Nations in Somalia. See page 927.

    b.   No. Unfortunately, the presence of U.N. peacekeepers did not lead to a cease-fire among the rival clans in Somalia and a democratic government was not installed. See page 927.

    d.   No. Libya did not invade Somalia. See page 927.

10. b.   Correct. Although President Clinton signed the 1997 Kyoto protocol, he realized that the Republican-controlled Senate would not ratify the treaty. As a result, Clinton never submitted the treaty to the Senate for ratification. In 2001 President George W. Bush withdrew the U.S. from the Kyoto protocol. See page 928.

   a.   No. President Clinton indicated his support for the 1992 Rio de Janeiro Treaty by issuing the "Climate Change Action Plan" in October 1993. The plan called on volunteerism on the part of American industry to reduce greenhouse-gas emissions to their 1990 levels. See page 928.

   c.   No. The Bush administration blocked efforts to draft stricter rules to reduce global warming, and the Clinton administration generally supported efforts to support the war on global warming. See page 928.

   d.   No. The Clinton administration did not show disdain for the 1997 Kyoto protocol. See page 928.

11. c.   Correct. Osama bin Laden was the mastermind behind the bombing of the U.S.S. Cole, which claimed the lives of seventeen American sailors. See pages 928–929.

   a.   No. Americans were not killed in bombings of embassies in Tokyo and London. See pages 928–929.

   b.   No. Although there were protests by anti-globalization activists at the meeting of WTO ministers in Seattle in the fall of 1999, Osama bin Laden was not behind these protests and there was not a "deadly bombing" that accompanied these protests. See pages 928–929.

   d.   No. Eric Rudolph is alleged to have been behind the bombing at the 1996 Atlanta Olympics. See pages 928–929.

12. c.   Correct. Although polls showed that most Americans deplored President Clinton's actions in word and deed with relation to the Monica Lewinsky affair, polls also showed that a majority of Americans did not want the president removed from office. See page 931.

   a.   No. Polls showed that many Americans believed that President Clinton's impeachment by the Republican-controlled House of Representatives was politically motivated. See page 931.

   b.   No. Throughout the impeachment process in the House and the trial in the Senate, polls consistently showed that Americans approved of President Clinton's job performance. See page 931.

   d.   No. Most Americans blamed President Clinton for his actions and blamed House Republicans for the political fallout that followed public revelation of the president's sexual relationship with Ms. Lewinsky. See page 931.

13. d.   Correct. Bush's announcement indicated that his administration believed that the United States, as the preeminent power in the world, did not need the help, advice, or acceptance of others in the international system. This was clearly an indication that the country would chart a more unilateralist course in international affairs. See page 934.

   a.   No. Bush's announcement did not indicate that he was closer to his father's views on foreign affairs than to Ronald Reagan's. See page 934.

   b.   No. Bush's announcement did not indicate that the president was shrewdly trying to win the support of conservative Democrats to push his agenda through Congress. See page 934.

   c.   No. Bush's announcement was in line with the thinking and recommendations of Vice president Cheney and Secretary of Defense Rumsfeld. See page 934.

14.   c.   Correct. Many civil libertarians argued that the USA PATRIOT Act compromised the rights of American citizens. See page 935.

   a.   No. The Department of Homeland Security, created by the Homeland Security Act of 2002, did not cause a great deal of controversy. See page 935.

   b.   No. There was widespread agreement over the decision to restrict the air space over the nation's capital. See page 935.

   d.   No. In an age of terrorism, it seemed sensible to most people that the president and vice president should frequently be at separate locations. See page 935.

15.   c.   Correct. The policy of preemptive action—that the United States would strike first without waiting for a security threat to become real—was a major break with U.S. policy and was criticized by some as being overly aggressive and a violation of international law. Some also asked what would happen if other nations, especially those controlled by dictators, assumed the same right of preemption. See page 937.

   a.   No. The Bush administration did not adopt a restrictive immigration policy. See page 937.

   b.   No. The Bush administration did not assert that U.S. military power would be used "solely" to protect the nation and its citizens. See page 937.

   d.   No. Most people believe that a nation has the right to defend itself if attacked. Therefore, it was not controversial for Bush to declare that the United States would hold accountable any nation from which an attack on American soil, American facilities, or American citizens was mounted. See page 937.

NOTES

NOTES